T0367420

JUNIOR

Villains, Hooligans and Scoundrels

*A testament to the social icons in our
lives and the friends I keep.*

JASON ALLDAY

AuthorHouse™ LLC
1663 Liberty Drive
Bloomington, IN 47403
www.authorhouse.com
Phone: 1-800-839-8640

Published by AuthorHouse 07/18/2014

ISBN: 978-1-4969-1365-4 (sc)
ISBN: 978-1-4969-2687-6 (e)

Library of Congress Control Number: 2014912854

Acknowledgements

'Time is promised to no man. Acknowledge today, as you
don't know what fate has in store for you tomorrow'
- J Allday 2010

Firstly for those that have ventured and endured a shared path of pain and sorrow, those I care for and are as much of me as I am them: Our Mum, my wife Nicola, my children Jayline and Alfie, my surviving brother James (I'll always have two brothers). Sisters Jade, Julie and husband Damon, my nieces and nephews. Our family south of the water, cousin Lee and Deb more of a big brother and sister, the Birks girls, all of my family in the four corners of what I once called the greatest city, which is otherwise known as London. Byron Newman @ byronnewman.com, Mike Crawley @photofrentic.com. A best friend from childhood and Cousin Ray Dean-R.I.P, Kloe Dean, Sancho Dean, cousin Kim, Mem' and youngsters. Friends and neighbours that always pop round or stop our mum in the street and ask for her well-being and see she is cared for. Junior's Grandmother Bernice and the whole Whitter family. Junior's Godmother, a lady that is as stern as she is caring Mrs. Hazal Duffy, her son and a shared best friend from childhood Adam-R.I.P. and family, Wayne Watson and Charlie Knott for your dedication to Junior as a youngster in the merits and discipline in sports. Terry Day, shared friends in London, Hillingdon, Uxbridge, Ruislip and Hayes, Mark Gillard, Ben 'YID' Smart, Dave Condron, Mickey Jones, Dave Sims, Matt Robinson, Nigel Tomms, Dean Russell, The Chaffin Family and anyone that has lost someone that you cared for and should've spent more time with as a brother.

Those that simply made all this possible: Steve Guy and Danny Woollard; two men that are top of my tree and are true men amongst men, and at a moment's calling are always there for me. Solid friends and diamond geezers.

West Ham, my family and friends at West Ham: Cass Pennant, Bill Gardner, Carlton Leach, West Ham Steve, Dean Ward, Bunter Marks and Marks Jnr, Lenny Lamb, Colin Burns, Leo Bowers, Paul Read, Phil Dalby, David Rayon, Bill and Baggers Jnr, James Bevan, Paul Foskett, Josey Irons, Bob Straker, Russell 'tea' Knight, Terry Nicholls, Shaun 'ginger' Sheridan, Lee 'pigs' Plaster, Lee Brian, Jim Mawer, Scott Davis, Steve Axford, Hoppo, Alan Stevens, Steve Albert, Danny Brown, John Cooper, Shane Abbott, Lewis Atkinson, Darren Bance, Mickey Bayliss, John Turner, Dave Turner, Djelal 'Jela' Ispanedi, Deane Bennett, Hammers Balkin, Brett Meaks, Andrew M, Tom B, Pete B, James Byrne, Ray C, Steve Muzz, Ricky P, Steve Currie, Sam Davies, Phil Meeke, Alan Merrill, Ray Fielding, Andrew M, Paul Fisher, Kevin F, Terry Hunt, Andy Francis, Billy H, Roger H, Paul H, Gary Smith, Jason Smith, Kevin Taylor, Gavster the 'tiler', Gary Williams, Mark Wyatt, Paul Johnson, Al Diegan, Dave Howell, Stuart S, Sean Mcdermott, Davey Hume, Jeff S, Darren Philcox, Fred Zim, the brotherhood that can't be named, but we'll simply say my brothers from another mother the I.C.F. The Hornchurch chaps, Rainham chaps, the whole claret and blue army and without doubt the best fucking fans in the country, welcome to Upton Park! Bobby Moore lower and Upper, you know where I stand.

In London, Danny Woollard-R.I.P, The Woollard family, The Guy Family, Richie Reynolds, Vic Dark, The Old Guard, Angelo Hayman, Roy Shaw-R.I.P, Tina Shaw, Gary Shaw, Frank Fraser, Joe Pyle Jnr, Jimmy Tippett Snr, Jimmy Tippett Jnr, Jamie O'Keef, Ronnie at Rockstar, Mitch Pyle, Charles Bronson, Dee Morris, Iffty, Julie at Team Bronson, Wayne Anthony, Jason Marriner, Martin 'Chelsea' King, Ricci Harnett, Neil Maskell, Leo Gregory, Danny Dyer, Danny Hansford, Tracey Elvik-Rice, Haley Jane, Mark Crossey, Gary Jordan Smith-R.I.P, Terraces Links, Manny Clark, Paul Knight, Jason Cook, Diamond Dean Kayne, Terry Nichols, Darren Timms, Danny Henry, Tony Barker, Dicky Downes, Nikki Anthony, Harry Holland, Darren 'QPR' Mundee, Terry McGee, Garry Bushell, Gary 'Boatsy' Clarke, Paul Feast, Ashton Seymour, John J Monaghan, Tony Clark, John Shelly, Jeff Maysh, Chris 'Peckings' Price,

Black Tony-Ladbroke Grove, Brixton Paul, Chris Jones-Neasdon, Ray 'Dutch' Peters, Tel Currie-RIP, Michael Nesbit, Dicky Downes

North of The Border: Brother 'Black' Danny Brown Aston Villa, Paddy Conroy, Michael 'the Bull' Bulloch and friends, Frank McAvennie, Matt Legg, Joe Egan, Phil Thorton, Irvine Welsh, Birmingham Bernie, Matt K and the Rochdale lads, Steve Denford-Grimsby lads, Stephen McCluney, Lenni Perkins, Dougie Brimson, Jonathan Keys

Septics: Esher Lutzo; Charlie Kallberg; Natilie Essinger; Michael Gran

Cyprus: Jean Christou

Photo layout: Nuno Barbosa

Proof reading: John J Monaghan CMgr FCMI. FInstLM. MAPM. MIACCM.

Ultra Italias, the whole team at Dogs Bollocks,

Johnny Bresso, Giuseppe Alessandro Gornati, Andrea Longobardi, Andrea Mohr,

I will remember you all, God bless. Your bruva' from another mother, Jase.

A message to the MET, you lost! Fuck you!

Meaning and Purpose

All the experiences I shared with my late brother were pretty much the same for every lad and his peers throughout the U.K. My opinion to this day is that those same 'questionable' parts of our shared lives as young men are what gave each and all of us our memories. It isn't anyone's right to eliminate or take away those memories, just as much as it isn't mine to say what holiday snaps people should take of their own families and friends through their own shared path and experiences. Those photos of the past are the memories we all have of those who are no longer with us. My late brother had a boatload of life experiences, which were typically on the wrong side of the law, but the memories I have are because of us growing up together with the terraces, boxing, social icons with pretty girls at its source and structure. I know that my surviving brother or I would not change them for the world.

Saturdays at football, both home and away. The journey, the banter and the comradery are the very glue that holds our memories together. The laughs, bollocks and bullshit conversations amongst the lads we had as a child, and as an older brother are the ones that we reflect upon. The lifelong friendships we had been typically like most English lads, and that was around the start as a young football fan. Your first fight, cigarette, beer and excessive use of swear words were as common amongst young lads and they were part of the relationship amongst brothers.

The path from childhood to adulthood was a direction for us plotted out by a love for the world's greatest and most watched sport. Those that were never bitten by the 'football bug' will never have and never will have an understanding or appreciation of the dedication from fans traveling the country in the elements whether it is a weekday or weekend. The CEO's and shareholders neither will have a love for the game as much as the true fan; their understanding is an appreciation of your hard-earned money in their tailored Savile Row suit pockets.

One universal truth is men display emotions differently than women. Our over enthusiastic passion, is heavily disguised through our actions by use of fighting, verbal onslaught and as equal as much dedication to defending our teams, friends and the colours they carry. My late brother shared this quality with those he cared for, especially those at his beloved Chelsea football club.

To this day it still makes me laugh that the 'experts' who dubbed football hooligans as mindless, unemployed, uneducated baboons still spin that line each and every time there's a disturbance at a game. That ignorance, really allows anyone that has really been there, to know that men as a species have a genetic imprint that makes us a competitive, defensive, argumentative and rallying species since the dawn of time. We have a pack mentality, which is no different from soldiers, a pride of lions or three brothers. The genetic order is what binds us as human beings. This tied into a competitive team sport is what and why men display the passion they do week in and week out.

The same can be said for boxing. Why do men love to sit and watch two people smash the granny out of each other? It is simple! It is a test of two men competing for that singular display and accomplishment through victory, which is an extension for the spectator to live his childhood dream as a fighter vicariously through another to that all-important king of kings.

All in hand it's part of our natural instinct. We are following our natural path as human beings and delving slightly deeper it helps us identify who we are and gives both meaning and purpose. For those people know that it is a culture that allowed us some of our best memories and without these stories and experiences we would simply be empty shells. Where's the fun in that!

No parent or sibling should outlive a member of his or her family, especially someone as caring and gifted as my brother. I have concluded that the world and life we are handed can ultimately be one of struggle or ease. Some may suggest it is a simple case of ones owns interpretation of life and its obstacles. I accept that the loss of my youngest brother was not a decision of his own and was equally a case of the world was not ready for Junior. Either way, Junior remains one of the best of people anyone could have had the pleasure of knowing and sharing time with him. For me a person I wish I could have spent more hours in the day with.

The older brother

In loving you there was a cost; that is what I used to think with the relationship I had with my youngest brother. We all grew up with either a friend or relative of mixed race. As a child, I had the benefit of not only having a best friend whose parents were of Jamaican decent but also cousins. This education should have allowed grooming for an older brother to help protect a young boy of mixed race into a London upbringing; instead, for the first few years of Junior's life I provided nothing but resentment for Junior and ignored the unwelcome barrage of hate he got from society. In time the harshness that Junior received in his daily life made me become more protective and hate those that claimed to be 'good citizens'. Initially it was easier for me to ignore the racial sarcasm towards my cousins and friends. It never followed me home and it certainly did not affect my feelings. This changed when it was part of my immediate family circle. The first memory of this was when someone of my age group said "there's that kid with a monkey brother." This was one of many examples of the spiteful hatred that existed in everyday life in 1980's London.

The isolation that such spitefulness promotes can lead a person down a solitary path of loneliness. Sometimes the only perceived escape is suicide! Junior chose this path. My thoughts since this event have always concluded that he must have felt alone and no one had the answers to the questions he had. The resolution he needed was in a circle of friends I had and I believe if only had asked these very people, it may well have saved his life. I have accepted that Junior did not know how to ask. His strength and courage in life was also was as strong as his stubbornness.

The following stories of those herein show that even the most feared and respected are affected by the cruel world we live in. If anything, these shared stories will allow you to see that there is resolve, escape and answers that could hopefully save someone else's baby brother.

This book is solely dedicated in memory of Junior Palmer.

R.I.P my baby brother, I will always hold you as a man amongst men.

Your big bruv' Jay

Junior Palmer

Junior or Jun' as we would call him, well where do I start? The 'establishment' will show on record that he was a criminal with a series of events that landed him a few stretches and an equal amount of porridge. What those same establishments will not show you, is the relationship Jun' had with his brothers and those that were part of our lives.

Junior Palmer was born November 3rd 1983, in the London Borough of Hillingdon in Hillingdon Hospital on the out skirts of a great place we all grew up in called London. Jun' had some fantastic mates, and a thousand times as many memories that he would carry with him. Jun' grew up living on a housing estate. A fine example of the government's efforts to supply affordable housing for the minimum waged income families of London. The environment was classic of all housing estates across both London and the country. Full of characters, each with their own story, flavour, a way about them, and more often than not, part of the pantomime we all put on for the people that would come in and out of our lives. Like all those around us, we had sod all, but we were raised by a simple code. All that was needed was food on the table, clothes on your back, and morals. Something, I am proud to say, as a result of our family he presented and stood by his whole life.

There were people that were, and still are a large part of his life. In my days at home, and all of us crammed into that tiny 3-bedroom house. How it worked I will never know, Jun' had some fantastic family, and like all families, we had some good and some not worth mentioning. No one loved Jun' more than mum. She never gave up on him and still carries him daily with her. But let me tell you, if you've ever had an East London family or known East Enders, you will know that they are the salt of the earth, and will give you something to remember. They are quality, characters, real people and your own! Many parts of London and England boast their own flavor of people and way. The East End is something that I am part of and saw in Jun'. He carried more than his fair share, and always with pride and style. On Junior's fathers side, his Nan Bernice. A lovely woman, no matter rain or shine she always smiled and greeted everyone in a way as if she hadn't seen him or her in years. Passion and friendliness was her way. Some uncles and aunts also were good people, cousins, like most families, some mates there also. In later years to come, a way that led me to live in different parts of the world, Jun' had a son. Someone, at time of writing this, I have yet to meet, but if that day comes, and if he is anything like my little brother then brace yourselves. He will be a character and a good man.

Jun' was like the Robin Hood of our family. He took, sometimes shared, and always looked after mum. He always carried a standard of confidence. Something I related to, and often seen in boxers which all too often is confused with arrogance. Each and every day of our lives together as a family was much like a TV sitcom, sometimes good, sometimes bad but typically with a disastrous comical outcome, which resulted in a story that would always be remembered. If a T.V show were to be ever made of the family life of the brothers and sisters in our household, well the cast alone would be a mixture. Me, the big brother, James, Junior; the star of the show, and our sisters Julie and Jade, we all know the roles and characters we'd play, but that's another story, and this is his.

I am lucky, I, like my brother and sisters have many memories. It's a real treat so have a sit with any of his mates and share all the crap that we all pulled growing up together, the difference is, Jun', was never the aggressor always mischievous, the typical London lad.

The life and time we shared with Jun' was a privilege. He gave memories and stories, filled with love and kindness. He never looked for more than just enough for himself and equally for those he cared for. He left behind a family that could never thank him enough. He never held a grudge. He always tried to make his mum proud, and spoke of his family and friends, as those were the best anyone could ever wish.

The relationship that existed between my late brother and I is a tribute to all brothers worldwide. What is not, are the years Junior and I spent apart. One thing that holds is the memory and relationship between my surviving brother, James and Junior. There was only 3 ½ years between the two of them. This paints a picture of closeness and bonding that will be more than I could have. The mold that made Junior and I was different to that of James. My role was to try to pave a way for Junior and that was never going to happen. Not the sort to be coerced and follow instructions, Junior was on a mission, one that would always leave both a trail of humorous destruction and love for all of his family. He embraced life and the hurdles it had for him, the pitfalls and the decisions that would ultimately lead to the taking of his life. James's role was to have a conversation, without judgment or prejudice. They spoke like best friends and mentors. Never a competition between the two, more a sounding board for each other's lessons learned.

Throughout his young life, and as brothers, we were as much apart as we were together. We saw each other's fears and dreams, laughs and tears, and a foundation that would always make us brothers. As both James's life and mine would lead in one direction, Junior's was no different in any other young man's. He too was embarking on a solo trip in the pursuit of manhood, and as fate would dictate, a trip that would be simply one of his own.

The cost of having a brother of mixed race was never more than he was one of my own. Others saw this as a means to practice their bullying.

They created a man, that the mention of his name, would promote never a lone person to make their claim of victory over Jun'. It would take at least two or three to test their minerals. Some of my earliest memories that hold bitterness for me include one spring morning. I was brushing my teeth, outside I could hear the voice of our mum, instructing Jun' to stay seated in the car and she'd be right back, returning inside the house to get whatever it was she'd forgotten, I then heard the voices of a couple of lads. The words 'darkie' and 'gollywog' rang out. I don't remember leaving the bathroom, nor clearing the stairs inside the house, but I remember the look of confusion and innocence on the face of my baby brother, who was no more than 3 or 4 years old, sitting in the front seat of the car. The two brave lads will never forget the fierceness of an older brother and the rain of anger that rained down on them that morning. Another was when Jun' was a little older. I was sitting downstairs at mum's house and mum came into the kitchen with tears in her eyes. With a combination of anger and sorrow she told me that she would found Jun' putting bleach into the bath he was sitting in. When she asked what he was doing, Jun' said he wanted to be like his two big brothers. There are many more stories that will always fuel my anger and bitterness towards those that call themselves 'men'. But when confronted, they were never more than cowards that deserved the beatings they got. I'm not anti-authority. I'm simply a brother that lost one of his own. I have many memories that still make me smile and I'm thankful that those I call friends, aren't of the breed that condone the cowards mentioned here.

There were many iconic people including actors, boxers and celebrities that were a huge part and influence of the culture that my brothers and I grew up with. These stories will highlight the society we came from, and more importantly play tribute to my baby brother.

Football

"It builds legends on and off the pitch."
- Steve Guy 2009

Oh the mighty game! The game instills a level of discipline, something for both inner city youths and adults across the country at all levels to compete in both professional and amateur level competitions and a game accessible for special needs kids. Even while serving under her Majesties care, the great game can be played under strict supervision of course ha, ha! Anything less, simply would not be football. How could you question the world's most watched game? Our nation's pastime, in fact the foundations of our great nation are interwoven into the very game that demands nothing more than our attention for 90 minutes.

I was raised in a house of mixed 'passion'. I was West Ham, which was mum's country. East London, it was in my blood. Then of course James and Jun' being were Chelsea lads, so there was not much room for reserved opinion in our house. It did not worry me that I was raised in deep Chelsea country. Yes, my brothers' are Chelsea, we knew Chelsea had a sizeable following, but I was always the one to be different. I believed in the underdog mentality. It's common to hear the saying 'it's not the size of the dog in the fight, but the size of the fight in the dog', this mixed in with the little toe-rags popping round to see my brothers, and the usual wank comment towards my roots. Well, rarely I would settle for a reserved option. This, again, was all part of the fun involved in teams, their supporters, their rivalry and what makes any competitive sport all the more competitive with 3 brothers and their passion.

Each and every lad, much like us as brothers, had at some time or another kicked a football, even if we never did get to play for our own team. The very game boasts an attraction to the youths of each generation. Every year, it was simply a question of 'where will we end up?' Not like your glory teams, that can boast the biggest bank account to play the table like bloody monopoly money, but now that's all part of the parcel and what once made it any man's game. The passion that is held, can be seen in the eyes of anyone that commits to just a conversation on the game we call football. The players we marveled, for the very mention of their name would allow English lads to mimic the silky smooth skills (or at least in their mind), that chosen player to become more than any super hero he ever could, in the minds of the supporters at least.

It is known to cause divorce for the unappreciated husband that wants to simply commit to his god given right to venture to a game each week. It causes rows with fans from lesser clubs and allows an estimated one billion people worldwide to play the game. That is roughly fifty million refs, balls and pitches and enough fans to invade a neighbouring planet. It is more than the club shirts, the big screen T. V's, and corporate sponsors and over inflated wages of 'star' players. Yes, it is still possible to be a fan and not be exploited. It is a part of our genetic make-up. It is war!

The players, our boys on the field. The very mention of another team coming to our place of worship, how dare they! To think they could even consider trying to win was unthinkable! The sport was made all that it is by our very nation, and it allows a universal language to be spoken it is the reason we come, watch and pray for the all mighty word GOOAAAAAAAAAALLLLLLLLL! This is football!

West Ham United Football Club

The name, the nation and legendary club. Based in the great East End, West Ham's home ground boasts some of the country's most fantastic fucking fans, that will cheer and give support for the claret and blue army. This is a team that has launched the legends that put the title of World Champions of 1966 into the history books.

1895 was a year that can be noted as the birth of the Hammers. Proving at an early age the strength of the club, who gained its colours by way of competition. Originally playing in dark blue kits, as the founding owner was an ex Oxford University fella. Claret and blue was won due to the loss of a sporting bet between three Aston Villa's players, and a member of the coaching team for the mighty Hammers.

The Champions statue commemorating West Ham's three sons who made the 1966 world cup win possible can be seen opposite the academy of English football on Barking Road. Bobby Moore, Geoff Hurst and Martin Peters are still regarded today as the fathers of West Ham and all that is loved about the club.

Having started the youth development system in 1955, promoting, and developing some of the best players in international football and promoting young English talent more than nearly any other club in England and recognising more homegrown talent allows West Ham to earn the title of The Academy of Football.

Frank 'Macca' McAvennie.

When I was given the chance to meet someone that may offer some console in my world of loss and frustration, I could think of a few choices. Football and those that were of a positive influence within the game was something that had crossed my mind. Much like those that had lost something that meant so much to them, many sports figures had watched their careers and success slip away right in front of their own eyes and equally as many had never returned from such a fall.

I needed to speak with someone that would relate to loss, frustration and anguish. Someone that had entered a dark forbidding experience and come out a wiser and stronger person. Not forgetting the pain and emptiness but using it as a lesson in life.

A phone call from a pal up north, gave a suggestion of a person that would tailor fit my needs in terms of a chat. It meant a bit of a journey but I accepted this was just the start I needed. London to Newcastle wasn't a simple bus ride or a few stops on the underground. A few more hours was demanded from a trip up north. But I could use this time to reflect upon the similarities and relevance of my loss and questions with my waiting host and his own past.

The luxury we have in London public transport is everything as an 'on and off' routine. The bus and underground service allowed anyone to get to the four corners of the city and surrounding areas with ease. Typically, the only investment needed was more than a few shiny pennies for the fare and a glance up every now and again to avoid the barrage of daily commuters and the shared tutting as someone came within your shared path.

When the name first hit the players list in 1985, much like myself many said 'who?' Ray Winston said it best. "Frank, Frank the fuck who?" Now if asked the question, the answer would be an easy one. He's a fucking diamond and this is an opinion shared by all those that have either met the man or watched him decimate the field and the competition.

With Frank, he is as a pal as much as a gent. Not one to play up to the high rollers he rubbed shoulders with, but more a case of allowing his loved fans to live vicariously through his evenings out with some of the many beautiful woman, and his much talked about and admired life style on and off the pitch. An action still respected about our beloved Frank, is that he would hold court with a few pals and a bar maid the following night.

Everyone has a story to tell, some have had more than their fair share to say about the blond bombshell that gave grace and style to my beloved West Ham. With the unwelcomed and unfair intrusion of the press into his life, Frank had seen enough personal challenges. I couldn't have wished for a better start in my goal. The strength and determination Frank carried, as a professional football player, was the same strength that allowed him to fight through and over come the pitfalls and perils that faced him in his personal life.

So it was decided that a trek up north would be the start of my journey and an afternoon with a man that could help my understanding of loss in my life. A few hours later and a satisfied amount of time to view over my thoughts and questions, the train pulled up into sunny Newcastle. I say this with sarcasm as the blanket of cloud that was hiding what should have been a sunny day gave as much welcome to me as a visit to an English beach mid December. My host agreed to meet me in a pub not far from the station and his warm greeting over compensated what was missing in terms of a favorable climate.

As soon as we arrived, we made our way to the arranged meeting place. A local pub, which was low key and nothing fancy. Just somewhere we could just have a few jars and mull over the situation in hand.

Frank was waiting for us inside and greeted us with a warm smile and that ever so familiar twinkle in his eye that the press always remarked upon, when Frank was courting a pretty girl. The pub was not too bad. I honestly had not put too much thought into thinking where we should meet. A few locals by assumption casually placed around the bar. It was a clean and tidy little place and not a flat cap or whippet could be seen. I guess I wouldn't have been surprised if I'd had seen Amos, a pipe and his horse tied up outside. But then Newcastle had joined the modern age.

Frank came out in true style by commenting on my girlfriend that had made the journey with me. "Hey, she's a lot better looking than you said she was!" What a charmer! How could anyone fault such humour? After a few laughs and a couple of drinks, Frank asked me how things were going. "Funny you should ask, mate," I replied and smiled producing a list of questions and a camera. We both sat back and prepared ourselves for the start of what would be appreciated by any fan of football.

I asked my first question, "With this in mind the book, the rhyme and reason. Was there a deciding factor, and what was the reason for writing 'Scoring; an experts guide?'"

Frank- "There was really only one reason why I decided to write a book, and that was to put a few wrongs, right. You know a few ex girlfriends, their sob stories and that kind of non-sense and also to put my side of the story across. There's been a few times the papers have made me out to be a bit daft, so there's that reason too. Having a go at me and going into my personal life, and I thought that's just not right, so I thought why not tell me side of the story."

It has been commented in the past, that some of the 'glory teams' had fans and supporters in the media. With this bias in place, it allowed such teams to be 'played-up' by certain commentators. Well with that, who gives a shit! We have Frank. He will do all the talking for us, and wallop! Finishing within arm's reach of the title, and that is without the nobs on their peddle stools and microphones. Frank came to West Ham and scored 26 goals in 41 games allowing West Ham to finish third. He was a king; the fans loved him; and Frank loved life.

Upton Park, the academy of football, was a place of worship for many across the country. Many other clubs, teams and fans will claim rights to the title, but in our eyes, this is not anything more than a myth. I ask Frank boy if there's anything special about Upton Park.

Frank- "Oh yeah! Well at the time, I actually went down to London to sign for Luton, and a meeting with David Pleat. With all the messing about and with one thing leading to another, I was set for a meeting also with West Ham, as it was mentioned they were also interested. That was enough for me. I mean you're talking about fantastic players.

Billy Bonds, Geoff Hurst, Bobby Moore, Trevor Booking, and it was a team that everyone knew, you know! Even with the first day of training, I thought they were taking the piss. They gave me a ball! Well, in fact they gave us all a ball each! I thought someone was going to come around the corner and take the piss. It was the difference in training.

In Scotland, you don't see a ball for about three weeks! I mean, you just run. It was also more than that. I love everything about English football. I scored 26 league goals, and four world cup goals. It was just phenomenal playing for the team. It was also great to be out in the East End and out and about in Essex. It was great to see the looks on the supporter's faces. I'd heard the team seem to fall to the way side after Christmas, and to keep scoring right up until March, the fans kept the feeling we was going to win the league. So it was nice to be part of that feeling, seeing all the fans genuinely happy at the games."

Frank will tell ya', like when I spoke with the fella', a sportsman is just that, loves his chosen 'arena', playing with conviction and passion. Having watched Frank playing with the ball, it was like a cat playing with a mouse whilst at West Ham.

"Did Frank have the same commitment for other clubs he visited down south as he did for the mighty Hammers?"

Frank- "I don't think so. I mean the fans are such a big part of it. I've been all over, and I never saw passion like the fans had at West Ham. Even when

I went away and returned, at one match in particular we was down 5 – 1 down, the fans were doing the 'hokey cokey' up and down the terraces. It's difficult for anyone to comprehend how great the fans are, they were absolutely superb."

The memories made and shared and friend made at the game, was true for Frank and Tony Cottee, unlike the media rabble, and the claims that they never got along. Something not known is the bets Frank and Tony used to make on whose goals were better, but what about any other 'deals' or laughs that maybe are not so well known?

Frank- "Well there was always more of a laugh than anything with everything we did. There was one great bet we had and I never did get the money of him, even though I won. I mean, pre-warm up before a match, didn't make much sense to me.

I mean you'd go out on the pitch, warm up and come back in all sweaty. You would then be told by the manager what you'd be doing then go back out again all wet. It just didn't make much sense. So a few of us decided to go into the gym. Well, me and a few of the boys would run up and down in the gym, get a few balls out, switch the lights out and see who could run into each other. I mean the boss hated us for this, it was hilarious, and this was all pre-match."

Pride and honor are just two of the words that come to mind when we speak of our West Ham. When Frank speaks of West Ham and the fans, you get the impression he has a true love for those that visit the terraces and for those that graced the field at Upton Park.

Frank – "Well they really did take to me, I mean even with all my love for Celtic, I feel more at home when I'm down south, than when I'm at home in Glasgow. Even now, when I'm at Upton Park for the summer programme, there are hundreds of fans that come to see me for the Frank McAvennie day. They're such a great bunch, I'm with 'em all day, and at the end we have a few beers. It's just great fun being with them. What I really think it is that the fans knew when I played for West Ham, I played 110 percent with every tackle. Every time I ran for the ball it was with everything I had. I honestly think the fans simply appreciated that effort I made. I mean it gripes me a bit when I see some of the players playing on teams now, and the money they're earning, and they don't make the effort, but what can you do it's just one of those situations! When I was playing, it certainly wouldn't have happened. I mean Billy Bonds certainly wouldn't have let it happen. There was a great education involved when you played football you know. To see some of the great players, who we could have a laugh with. I mean I'd heard that Tony Cottee and I never got along and that was total nonsense. We are still great friends till this day, but that's the papers for you."

'We're those bastards in claret and blue, Bobby Moore's army'. That's a sense of pride for ya'. It could be said that Frank's one of the best strikers to have graced Upton Park.

"Is there still a sense of pride for the team he once played for?"

Frank- "Well for me it all started at St. Mirren I just love what I do. I get a sense of pride from playing the game. The three teams I identify myself with will always be St. Mirren, Celtic and West Ham. I mean my education went through the roof at West Ham. It was great to go and get trophies and medals at Celtic, but there was great pride in going back and playing for West Ham. Looking back, the day they sacked John Lyall, was the saddest day for me there. It was as if it was the day he'd died. It was just horrendous what they did to that man."

Now the bollocks some of us face of being told to "simmer down and stay seated, son!" Giving an 'Oi, Oi', at the marvels the players give when one hits the back of the net, is now a no, no, but hold tight! It is all seating! It took something away from the fans and the game, no question. If Frank had a vote in the issue, would he change it back?

Frank- "Oh, without a doubt! I honestly believe they're lobbying for it know. I mean they took away the atmosphere. I mean when you sit in the seats, and they're great seats, but you get these stewards and they tell people to sit down when they're simply into the game. Football is all about passion; you're going to get some people that will jump up. You've got to allow the fans some lea-way. I mean, no one likes to sing when they're sitting down. The players on the pitch want to' hear the fans, and that's what I liked about Upton Park. The fans were so close to the pitch. There was only about two yards between the pitch and the terracing and it wasn't the first time a few people were knocked into the chicken run. It was great! It may be true, and I've noticed that some of the stewards aren't even West Ham fans. I mean when I was home to watch Celtic, the stewards weren't even Celtic supporters themselves, and I think that's why they sometimes get joy in telling the supporters to sit down. Stewards should be West Ham supporters at West Ham. Much like they should be Celtic supporters at Celtic. They should support that club."

The '89/ '90 season and return to West Ham, over a choice of Arsenal. Even the road ahead was a more difficult one at West Ham; due to their current situation, Frank still chose the Hammers over the season champions; Arsenal!

Frank- "Yeah, well I'm a loyal person, and John Lyall was a big factor in that. They did tell me that West Ham was going to be relegated and I was thinking if I was going to have anything to do with that! Even more so I couldn't do that to the West Ham fans. I mean it just wasn't in my makeup. For me, when I returned it was going to one of two places, either West Ham or I was going abroad. Those were the only options!"

Share the wealth they say! Why, I say? He is a Hammer! Frank did get a few visits too, by some clubs south of wee bonnie Scotland, but was there the same magic as at West Ham?

Frank- "Well I went on loan to Swindon. I mean it was OK, but they put me in midfield. Then when I had a game against West Ham, I'll be honest, I was fucking terrified! I mean West Ham was my club!

I went out, and I had to play against some of my mates. To see all my mates and play a game against them and then when all the West Ham fans started to sing my name, it was just surreal. I remember the whole place erupting. It was just strange, but that's the West Ham fans and why they made it magic, and even when West Ham management forgot about all the promises they'd made me, that's was fine, but football isn't about the directors and the management, it's about the fans, plain and simple."

Either a tale of a crazed bird on her toes after him for apparently pulling a 'naughty one', or his routine on the club circuits, Frank always seemed to catch the attention of a page 3 stunner along with top faces alike. In the fans eyes, was it Frank's skill on the pitch that made him such a likable character, or were they influenced by his exploits at after hour's events that made him such a cheeky rascal?

Frank – "Oh, I think both. I mean I honestly believe the fans saw a bit of them in me. I really didn't start to play football until I was 19, and was a football fan first and foremost, and the fans identified with me. I was getting headlines away from football. I was playing the game and enjoying myself, and I think the fans appreciated that as they'd probably done the same thing. I think one of the best sayings I've heard recently is from Peter Crouch, when he was asked if he couldn't be a foot baller, what would he be, he replied 'A virgin', and that's what it's all about. Getting out there and enjoying yourself and get the job done. That's what it was for me. I got out there, loved to play the game and enjoyed myself on and off the pitch, and I never allowed it to interfere with my football. It was mainly Monday mornings that I'd normally be suffering on, but if there was a game, that came first."

In the 1989/90 season, saw an injury that could have been the end of Macca's career. Four months was the diagnosed 'chill and rest' time for ol' Frank, and this was surely a time to collect his thoughts on an alternative career, if the worst was to come. So if he wasn't a footballer, I think we'd both agreed he'd be happy to be a football fan!

Frank- "Well I've always been a fan. I'll be honest, when I bought 2 season tickets for Celtic, and I only watched 'em twice, it was probably the worst football I've ever watched in my life, I mean I won't go and watch that. I went and watched a few West Ham games, and it was great."

Surely, we have all seen or had a favorite on the pitch. Maybe even at times you thought 'oh, mate, for fucks sake, get in there, son, missed again!' Sure enough, Frank had some thoughts on this. In the past, Frank said Alan Devonshire was one of the best players he had ever seen, but was there any player that he felt never reached their true potential?

Frank - "Well only one name comes to mind and that's me (laughs). Kenny Dalglish said I should have been one of the best players ever to come out of Scotland, but it's just one of those things. Now when you talk of Alan Devonshire, I just simply liked him as a player. To play beside him was just awesome, honestly it was, his balance and everything about him. If Alan Devonshire could score goals, undoubtedly he'd be the best player in the world. He used to beat 3, 4 5 players around the goalkeeper. He was simply amazing to watch with the ball. I'm not kidding when I say he didn't have 2 players mark him, he had 3 players on him. He would take that ball and take it around 2 then 3 players, past the goal keeper and into the goal, and this was after he came back after an injury, he was just unbelievable. Kenny Dalglish was my idol and I was fortunate to play beside him."

You have played, trained, watched and know some quality players. What is Frank's all-star team?

Frank- "Oh, fuck me. You've got me thinking there. OK, George Best, Jimmy Johnson, Diego Maradona up the middle. Alan Devonshire, Roy Keane, Christiano Renaldo, Jurgen Croy. I mean, I could name many others. Kenny Dalglish was my idol growing up, and it was something to play on the same field as him. The lads I mentioned though, all have that something special."

Being the eye catcher with the ladies, ol' Frank surely turned heads when he was out and about. With this though, comes the same amount of attention from the local sweat-head, beer gut, and all knowing loud mouth. Known for being quick witted and a bit of a silver tongue, was there any situation he thought 'oh, shit, it could really come on top here', but a bit of his charm, it all turned out good?

Frank- "Well there's only one time that one guy came up to me, and was giving it all that. You know 'McAvennie, you're really shit', and all that, you know. You know that there's nothing you're going to say that's going to get this guy away from you. So he's really going on about how shit I am, so I go's up to him and say, "Yeah I know, but no one else has fucking noticed." Well all his pals busted out laughing. He wasn't happy about it, and I knew I had a few minutes to get out of there. Sure enough, I got out of there. His pals gave him a hell of a time about it as I'd brought him down, but it was that that gave me enough time to get out of the place. I know there was nothing I could've done to have stopped this guy from having a bop at me."

With an off field, reputation as a regular feature on London's party scene- It was built rapidly until it became legendary. At any stage did Frank think 'This is all too good to be true?'

Frank- "Yeah, every night I was out (laughs). I was out with some of the most gorgeous women and with all going on; I just couldn't stop enjoying myself. I would often think this could all end tomorrow, and now looking back, I wish I could have thought more about my future, but again it could have ended in more ways than one the next day. I have no regrets about living the good life or anything I've done."

Not the type to kiss and tell, Frank respected the rules of the 'game', but were there any other players out there that were as much as a rogue as himself?

Frank- "Oh yeah, but I can't mention them, but there's a few of them still out there, even some on the telly."

Frank, you partied like a rock star, blew a small fortune, birds, booze, a roller coaster of a ride, anything but the best of times!

Frank- "Well with some of these newspaper guys, I mean there's one of them that told me I kept him in a job for years. It was like whenever I got caught doing something I'd just put my hands up and say 'yeah'. There's no sense lying, you've just been caught. I mean, it was one of those situations and when I got into trouble, a lot of the press stuck up for me as when I'd been in trouble in the past I always put my hands up to it."

Surely a cult classic, the infamous Saturday morning show Soccer A.M. You heard or saw the incident. A ball hit one of the ball boys in the head! Since then the car park has been known as Frank McAvennie car park. Would Frank, if given the chance, have called it something else?

Frank- "Well the funny thing about that is I was doing that with a great pal Ray Winstone, and we were having a laugh, and you know you're making a comeback when you have a car park named after you (the famous Frank Macca laugh is there)."

The press known by many other names, these 'reporters' do football players no good at most. If left alone, does Frank think players would stand a much better chance of survival in the world of football?

Frank- "Well, with me I always put my hands up when I got caught, at the end of the day they're just doing their job. I would not trust them as far as I could spit, but as they're always working, and players need to get that through their head. I've been told by a few players "Nah, they're alright", and I've told them they're not all right, they're always working. They're always working, and it's come back to bite them on the arse. I mean, they're taken for a couple of beers and the next thing you know it's fucking headlines, and then they wonder why. Now the footballers are so far from the crowd and so far from reality with the money they earn, it's frightening."

With the politics involved (sponsorship has an influence too) what does Frank think changed in terms of how the clubs are run or managed and how the players need to be looked after?

Frank- "I think the foreign culture that's been brought into the game has taken away the way it used to be. When there was a drinking session with the fans and the players, the good times have gone away. I never really had a local drinking place. For me it was just about going out and spending money. We knew it wasn't right, but we did it anyway. Now they have dietitians, they have certain people looking after them 24/7, and because of the money involved, they even have minders with 'em. It's different from when I was there. Some of them are really too far from reality. Some of them are arrogant, some of them are OK, some of them simply don't have time for their fans and it's the fans that fucking love 'em! I just don't like that, not having time for their fans, they should always make time for the fans."

Name one thing in football that if you had the choice and overall vote would you change for the better of the game?

Frank- "They should give all their money to ex players like me (Once again, the famous Macca laugh is emitted), but seriously, if anything it should be the technology in today's game. There seems to be a lot more mistakes in today's game. I think there should be a buzzer when the ball crosses the line. With the difference in what one point can do to a team in terms of relegation and promotion, and there's a huge difference in the money involved in today's game too. So if anything, because of human error, get technology more involved in the ball crossing the line."

Rounds of champagne were in bottles not glasses, a great night. It was a testament to Frank's good times, as much as when he says, "to watch him play was just amazing", giving credit to another player who shares the same passion for football. For me, "Sure, Jase, you're always welcome" is another example of a fella' I know as Frank Macca, my pal and yours, from north of the border.

A long path lay ahead of me in finding resolve, but Frank was certainly a good first step and he remains a good pal and valued person in my life. Everyone at some stage has had egg on his or her face. Frank will laugh and simply say "me too, pal." He takes the good with the bad and never holds anything more than an experience. Above all his time spent playing professionally he looks as a blessing and even though it was cut unfairly short, Frank remains grateful for that opportunity in his life. He is humble, honest and one of the old school. Someone if given the chance I would recommend anyone to him to gain some insight into loss and strength.

Bill Gardner

The name sets a standard, a man amongst men. If you ever have the privilege to talk with Bill, it is both an honour and a walk down memory lane, with what has to be said as one of the greatest names in terrace history. Bill always the modest man that he is, declines such a title. "I'm just me, Jase", is the answer I will be given, when we chat about the glory days, and those that tried to take what simply was not theirs.

There is no shortage of truth in Bill recalling the decades as both a fan, and as someone that you could always be count on being there. The merits of Bill's character are largely due to his belief in what is right and wrong. A combination of influence from a childhood hero of his, who was also called Bill. An uncle that was as a positive person in young Bills life as any one could have wished for. The other character building experience was a less friendly one as it was the many years of hardship that Bill experienced as a child and as a young man. However, Bill being the person that he is looks upon this as a part of his life, and as much as it was unwelcomed one, was a building block to make him into the pillar of the man he is today.

From Bills unhappy childhood, where he would always speak the best of people that he cared for, right through to his early beginnings as a football fan, Bill always treated and accepted West Ham as his real home. Bill found something that could not be put into words at both football and the West Ham football club. It was more than family and bonding and more than kinship with fellow hammers: it was a sanctuary.

For many, football was the weekly gathering and the friendship, which is a quality equally seen with some family's blood related or through year's reliance and time invested together. Football remains one of the best disciplines in a boy's life.

I honestly think Bill found calm on the terraces. It was a place where he could mature as a man and somewhere that would later be the very place that promoted Bill into one of the most respected of men in terrace history.

People go to football for different reasons, to follow their family's example by joining the same supporters club, to be amongst a gathering of fans holding the same liking or simply as a weekend event with neighbours and friends. One thing that few people may know is that Bill, apart from his introduction to football through his dad, (who was a Tottenham fan) actually became a West Ham lad through his own deciding. There was something that called Bill to West Ham. Even in the start, it had nothing to do with violence (again, this was never Bills outset or agenda). It was to find his place in life. A place Bill that filled him with great pride and he will always says he was amongst his family at West Ham.

With technology came the computer. In the heyday of football hooliganism the p.c. and all the other trimmings of modern technology (mobile phones etc.) not forgetting the mouthy wannabe hard man and infamous keyboard warrior had no place in history or chance at any tear-up. These loud mouths were all too often easily caught out, as the football fights in their day were based solely upon the strength and sheer courage in standing, not leaving your mates and holding your own.

Where Bill differs from so many self-decorated terrace top boys, he would call it like it happened. "Credit where credit is due" Bill would say.

I'll tell you this one for fact! ANYONE, that claims never to have come un-stuck whether it is a home or away game, is either talking total bollocks or has never even been there. I've been caught out more than once. Living in West London, it's as sure as the day is long you will cross the other team's supporters. This was inevitable for yours truly, as this part of town is known for being a Chelsea and Q.P.R breeding ground. I've had my fair share of run-ins. This I will also give, in the times I've been in a fight that was away from my pals, it was typically a one-on-one. Tools? No! The most I've encountered was a piece of scaffold out side Baker St tube, but being out numbered you sometimes have to improvise, but never a knife! That weapon is despised. Only once was a blade pulled on me, and that was up north (European away games is another story) and the pal I was with foamed at the mouth in anger. I didn't even get in on that one. My pal was in like flint."

Like-minded people like Bill will tell you your test was as a man by using your fists only, and your feet if all else failed.

There is a lot that is missed with Bill. If you were to look away, and listen to the knowledge he has, he should in all fairness, be an ambassador for West Ham United. I am not far from fact when I say he breaths, lives and has every bit of information on the club, players, history, and without any doubt the best formula for running the club.

Our conversation started off as it ended, just a couple of lads, chatting about our beloved team, the way it's being run now (I opened a can a worms when I asked his opinion on 'this and that' on today's football) and the history surrounding the Hammers. Not once, even at the height of our chat, did Bill ever show any aggression (there goes that newspaper reporter's theory out that window!) or malice towards any football teams players. Simply places of loss and win, constructive points on the others teams, the pals from other clubs and above all, his love for the game. The time and places for our chats had to be conducted over a few separate conversations. Meeting up with Bill was an easy choice; it was our home and our place of worship and church to anyone with claret and blue running through his or her veins. Bill caries a standard that is welcoming to any of his friends and again, there for his own. The time Bill invested will always be something I will hold in the highest regard and have gratitude for.

So, If you have not read Bill's book "Good afternoon, the names Bill Gardner" (Why not!) it should be only fair we start with, who is Bill Gardner?

Bill - "In my youth, I was homeless for a year, lived on the streets of London, worked for gypsy's (travelers) doing paving, driveways, drove a lorry at 14, still went to football, loved to watch West Ham. I didn't have a happy home life. Football was my life. I was going to West Ham on my own for a few years, I met up with a few people, and from there on I decided and found that I wasn't going to turn my back and run when the chips were down. It was as simple as that really. I wasn't a very confident person as a youth, but as I grew up, it seemed to grow with me. Back then, it wasn't like it is now. Then, it was a case if you went, the other teams knew where you came from. They used to wait for you at the railway station, or at the coach park. They knew by how you dressed where you came from, the police were nowhere to be seen, and you had two choices. Either you went to the game, or you didn't come out of the railway station. I used to like watching my football, so I went to the game. Now, I still go to every game, but I now go with a different type of person than I would before. They are no better or worse than the people I used to go with before, just a different type of person. I've got children now, so I'm more of a family man. I just simply still kept going every week, I love my football, now, when I'm there, and if shit hits the fan I'm still there.

For me, the name Bill Gardner was a much of West Ham as the club itself. Bill's reputation for standing and being there was a trademark that he never faulted or swayed from that of a true general. The qualities of the great East End were woven into the standards of the I.C.F as much as their predecessors, the Mile End Mob. Now, being that Bill calls it as it is, I was curious if he ever saw what I could only ever see in the I.C.F, in any other firm.

Bill - "No, I never saw any of the qualities that we held in West Ham's supporters in any other firm. I do think that's what is lacking in today's society, even in our country. Honour, comradeship and maybe even courage as the youth of today fight with knives. In our day, we fought with our hands and if you beat a man and when he had enough, he'd had enough. Now they want to stamp on your head until your eyes bleed. It's a different type of person you're dealing with today they don't have any honour today. They're two-bob and I've got no time for those types."

One memory that stuck with me all these years, was at a certain railway station (exact time and place, cannot be given. Sorry O.B), and a healthy number of Cardiff's Soul Crew bumped into said firm, and the look and intent on Bills face said enough. The words, if memory serves me right were "Fuck off, you mugs!" The reason behind such intent was that Birmingham's Zulus had stabbed a pal and the mere fact that it was a stabbing sent Bill to deal with this cowardice incident. (Funny that Bill and I could remember this all these years later!)

Bill - "I also think that with the whole comradeship thing was more a West Ham thing than an East London thing. I know there had been a few times when Canning Town and Stratford where at each other's throats, they were the same team but different areas. It was a simple case of when one man went down, you picked him up, and you never left a man behind. This is what built confidence in us, this spread like wild fire, even with people that had never had a row. I knew if I went down, our boys would be there for me. Many of the other firms never had that. They'd look over their shoulders, and think who's going to be with me, and I know for a fact, and having spoken to other former firms members that had the numbers, little gangs within them, and some of them had good little gangs but they were weary of each other. We were a solid unit and they never had what we had.

Now, mum had her hands full with two Chelsea and a West Ham lad all living in the same house. Many an opinion was shared whilst the telly was on, and it did not matter what team was on, we had our opinion and sometimes there was an 'off' as a result. Our poor mum's living room was never the same after this. Bill having a strong passion for our team, and having a dad that was a Tottenham supporter, was this a similar event also in the house of Gardner?

Bill - "In all fairness I had the choice of the two, and it was always West Ham, always! I was only ever going to be West Ham; the football never came into our home life. In my own family, we're all West Ham, every one of us, through and through. We're lucky we never have any conflict in our house" (chuckles).

Bill is a modest man, quiet and never one to brag on things. Unlike so many that have had their way of telling a 'story' and in some cases in books too. The said books made 'claim' in an attempt to either save face or inflate their egos, but we both know who this, and at one incident Bill really set the record straight with the so called brave person.

On a return train from a game, there was a station that a load of cockney-reds (Manchester fans based in London), boarded the train. Very soon, word spread through that one of these so-called hard-nuts top boys, was on board. Without a word or mention of back up or follow me lads, Bill simply proceeded through all the carriages, asking for the tuff-nut by name. The same person who had been saying all the things he was going to do Bill Gardner. When Bill got to the last carriage, the so-called hard man was pointed out to him. Bill confronted this 'hooligan', and asked for a one on one. Declining the offer, as it was thought the mere 10 people that had followed Bill, might jump in! I simply questioned the fact that there was only 10 West Ham fans in the middle of a carriage load of opposing supporters and being out numbered should have been enough to question this person's real courage. Bill told those behind him, that no one was to interfere and he still declined. The hand full of West Ham lads that entered that carriage walked out with something that the person left in the carriage didn't have to begin with. Read Bill's book, it says it all.

In one interview, Bill was asked why did he leave it so long to write a book seeing as there was so many out before. Bill said, "It was about time that he set the record straight." Nearly every book I have read on the era gone by of football hooligans, the name Bill Gardner, and the I.C.F is mentioned. So, with the book release and the success of films that surrounds the life of hooligans, had much changed in the life of Bill?

Bill- "I like to think I'm the same person I always was. I'm much calmer now, but that comes with age anyway (laughing). You know, as you get older, you mellow (I'm still young at heart, Bill). It doesn't mean you get weak, you just think a bit more, and I think that's what I do, and I still enjoy my life, and with my book, they say money changes you, and I didn't make enough money to change me (laughing).

The book was really to settle the dust. A lot of things were said about me in other publications, and I wanted to let people know the truth. I've read all the football books and to be fair 90 percent of the 'stories' are shit. One that really wound me up was the Manchester boy's one. Somebody I've never heard of, I honestly don't think any one had ever heard of him, made comments about me, and when you read my book, you'll see the truth."

He's seen miles and miles of train tracks, many a service station to and from a game has been visited, more than his fair share of cold and rainy days on and off the terraces. Did it seem like a lifetime ago for our Mr. Gardner?

Bill - "Seems like yesterday. When I see any of the boys who we may not have seen each other in 10 or 12 years, we always greet each other like it was last week. I saw one lad the other day that I hadn't seen in 36 years. After 2 minutes, we acted liked we hadn't ever been apart. There's a friendship built there, that can last a lifetime. That's something that can never disappear. When you've stood alongside someone, and they've stood alongside you, those friendships last a lifetime."

I go on to comment to Bill, that with the few pals I know, that are spread over other firms, that I never saw the bonding or the loyalty that I'd seen in West Ham and I've never seen anywhere else.

Bill- "It's something that only we have. It's special what we have."

We all have our memories, our favorite times that we may have shared with pals, growing up in around the ones that also help build those memories, and seeing as Bill has seen a lot of what has been written, what was it that he remembered the most when traveling with West Ham's fans.

Bill - "Ah, I've got so many memories really. I used to love the European trips, and let's be honest, we never really made that many (laughing), but those were great. We used to play many tournaments away, I loved those experiences and those were special. Italy, Russia, Sicily, Sweden, all those places were terrific. Where you would mix with your mates at football, doing your traveling, you're doing your friendship; you're doing your football, all special days."

They have been spoken of more than any other firm has, and they are mentioned in nearly every footy book, seen on the telly and in films. Many firms speak in respect of the standard and code, set by the I.C.F and their top faces.

Bill – "I was around before the I.C.F was about, and even after they formed, I just kept going. I won't take any credit, and truth be known, 95 per cent of the people that really know me, will tell you, I was never a member. I had a few people that I would go with, the I.C.F came along, and when the shit hit the fan, we would just join in. I had my group of mates, if you like, but we had no name. We didn't have to broadcast who we were, people knew. The code of conduct has been lost, definitely. It's not like it used to be. I mean, you could have someone working for you, and they could be ripping the arse out of you, nicking things, there's people that'll call you a mate, then they're nicking things out of your house. Things are different now, I've got a few mates that are supporters of other teams, and I've found there's a mutual respect amongst the older element, even though they was at it when they was younger. We now have a respect for each other, but you don't see that amongst the youngsters I'm afraid. I'm not here to put the youngsters down as I've got a lot of time for the youngsters, but at the end of the day they've lost something that was very special to my generation. Today, the drug culture has changed a lot of it when a person has to have something up his nose to give him bravery. In our day, we didn't need anything up our nose to make us brave. A lot of research at Universities said the reason behind a lot of the hooliganism was due to alcohol. This is absolute nonsense. If the truth be known many of my friends that went along, never drank. There's a saying that I believe to be very true. A drunken man can't fight the same as a sober man. Anyone will tell you, that if there was the possibility of a fight, you didn't drink because you'd needed to be at your best. With alcohol, it can give a man a false sense of strength. After working on the doors, you realise that certain people will get drunk and become very mouthy and a bit flash. When they haven't had the drink, they're not all flash and mouthy."

Now for all the books I have read, there has been very few that when re read, I came to a different conclusion, maybe missed a bit and thought "bloody hell, never thought of it that way." With Bills book, one thing that left an impression each time was that he was a fan first, and that he simply acted in the way he did, as he could not tolerate bullying. Had I read it right?

Bill - "Always, Always! West ham was the family I never had. The football has always been a big thing to me. I've coached for a number of years and I'm still involved in football now to a certain degree. I Follow my boys, as they both play, and I just love football. It's as simple as that. Football has always been first for me. The rowing was second, but there was no way I would miss a game, and they weren't going to stop me from seeing my football. If they said 'no', I was going. To me I wasn't going to turn away, not from anyone."

We touch on the media classing of football fans that get into a row, the whole 'hooligan' title.

Bill- "If you look up the word hooligan, it actually dictates that it's someone that go's around smashing things up and a disruptive influence. I didn't ever consider myself as a disruptive influence to anyone, only the people that wanted to give me or my mates a clump."

When you read into the reasons why there was a 'hooligan', it counts to certain reasons, and many can be justified. Bill was a person that could not and would not stand for bullying. Visit any away game, and be 'greeted' by the fans and see if you share the people's opinion!

Bill - "I suffered bullying as a child at school, I wouldn't suffer from it at football, and I don't suffer from it now. I hate to hear about children suffering from it at school. I know where they're coming from, having to suffer from it myself at an early age. It's something I hate. Driven, I was very driven. I would never let them beat me. When I used to go to football, and the others will tell ya, I was always at the front, never at the back. If I was going to 'ave it, I would 'ave it with their top ones. Now when I watch all these silly programs on the telly, and they're joke programs. Any one will tell you, friend or foe, that I was always at the front. I was never at the back. I was never a back marker; I would never stay home because I was worried what might happen. If I went, I was at the front. Those that claimed they looked for me couldn't have looked very hard, because if I went, I was at the front."

No way could you talk about West Ham, and Millwall would not come up in conversation. There was a story told about how loyal and patriotic Bill was for his West Ham. Upon the threat of those across the water coming up and supposedly painting the Bobby Moore statue, Bill took guard on his own, against anyone that dared come near this place of 'worship'. He arrived single handedly and waited until the early hours, only to go home and get an ear full from the lady indoors.

Bill - "Ah mate! What a night that was. The old woman told me off something rotten for that. I stood guarding that statue 'till the early hours of the morning. Obviously, nothing was going to happen. I've heard that it was going to be covered in another colour, but that statue, as you, will always be claret and blue."

Touching back on the book, it was really about setting the record straight. As bill will tell you, he is a regular man that stood up for what he believed in and stuck by his morals.

Bill - "There's nothing flash about me. I will always give respect to people with me and to people I've faced. That's how you'd survive all the years I survived. I had respect for everyone, for friend or foe, but both were treated in different ways and without a doubt, the book helped set things straight. It achieved what I wanted it to. Just our conversation shows me you read the book and got the message that was in there. What it meant to me? I was a football lad that took no shit, and that's basically what it is."

OK, it means many things to many different people. Let us face it, people are going to have a different view on the game and seeing, as it is the most watched sport in the world. So, what did it mean to our mate, Bill?

Bill -"Football then was a game where people met, friendships where built for life. A friendship that was made back then lasted a lifetime. Now a days, football is a money making machine. The football teams and the players back then seemed to have more time for you. I get the feeling now that the fans are there simply to make up the numbers. The money they make from telly vision coverage etc. The money is more important than the fan. I do believe the arse will fall out of it. The clubs will need the fans again, there's not the bond that we used to have. You see this when the players are walking into the ground, and then you see one of the older players sitting in a cafe. It really is a more of a 'them and us' and I do think it's down to the money they earn now. If you look at the players in the '70's and '80's, the players were earning well, they were earning maybe 6 or 7 times what the man was earning in the street, but now they're earning such fantastic amounts of money. Let's get it right, Ashley Cole made a comment when he left Arsenal asking how did they expect him live on £62,000 grand a week! That just about sums it up really. You can't blame a man for trying to earn as much as he can in a short career, but I remember when you'd drive all the way to Sunderland, get up at 4 am and driving all the way there to be ready for a lunch time kick off. You would be standing about all day in the pissing rain and then lose. Then you would have to go back home and you would not get much sleep there or back. I'm sure the players never gave a thought about it, but it's a different game now."

The great game of football is every lad's right to play the national sport of our great nation, which is kept dearly in our hearts. It shows courage under fire, and being there for your pals on and off the pitch, so that someone is there for you no matter what the odds. In Bills opinion, what did it mean to him?

Bill - "For me, football is a great game. It's our national sport and it's a game I've loved since the age of five and it will be a game I'll love to the day I die. I like all levels of football. I like both non-league and league football. I just have love for the game, you know! Football can mean something different for each person. Some one might say 'I'm not going to watch them tonight; they're not having my money as they've lost 3 or 4 games in a row'. I go because I support my team, and I keep that in my heart because that's who I am."

Bills integrity and honor can be seen in many ways. His actions are proof that he has stood toe to toe for his mates, and in the hardest times were clearly visible by anyone that was there. Whether it is alongside him or facing him, countless times people have said that he simply would not back down, if there was the possibility of trouble and a pal could come unstuck. Integrity again, not one to be any more than just a humble man, he can be seen when I ask him about films and the like. What did he consider a good watch or read?

Bill -"'El Cid'. The man just had plain honor. Film wise, that would be one I'd say was a one. Books, I've read 'em all and liked them really. 'Steaming in' was the first I read. I did enjoy that. It was not a bad read, again all good really. As for T.V, I know a lot of the lads like shows like 'Hard Bastards' and I was offered to be in it, but that's not for me."

History, like the lessons in life has a habit of repeating themselves. Much like things in our ever-changing society, things do come around for a second or third chance. Clothes, music and certain aspects of culture have a way of rearing their often-embarrassing heads, so what about football hooliganism. By popular belief, it has never really gone away. A different level of hooligan now exists, but is it soon to be a thing of the past?

Bill- "There will always be a football hooligan, in the sense you'll always have rivalry between people. I don't think anything will ever change that. Obviously, the cameras, the police, the punishment in terms of crime vs. the time, but I always think you'll get the odd incident sparking things off. It may be at a service station or train station, but what has changed is that you can't show any passion or get too excited anymore at football. We have to take all the shit that they throw at you and once the passion goes out of the game; you've lost the game of football!"

OK, opinions are that just that, I have mine, you may have yours, but I do not need to be a fortuneteller for this one. Who is the best firm and I have seen a few. Bill certainly has been up against all of them. So, who is the best firm out there?

Bill - "West Ham. The rest are two-bob, and they know it. When they made noise, we shut them up. We'd hear comments about what all the others firms are going to do, and this and that, and they never did."

Bitter rivalries can still be seen today. Being that Bill has long retired from the terraces, did he still think there was any chance that he would consider an enemy?

Bill- "Probably all of them (laughs) not a lot will change there. I've made friends from all over; Chelsea, I'm the godfather to a Tottenham pal. I've even got a pal that's Millwall, but only one, that's enough." (More laughs from both of us).

OK, some politics and did Bill share my opinion on this? If there were more money spent on programs and less on CCTV and added 'security', would this be more of a positive step in the direction of a greater football nation?

Bill- "Absolutely yes and I do believe that. I think there should be sport for all, even disabled kids. I used to run a primary school football team and we had some kids there with special needs, and it was great to see how all kids can enjoy the sport of football. I used to do it every other week when West Ham was at home. I think there should be a league for kids with disabilities just to see them get involved would be great and even veteran footballers for those that just wanted to turn up and play the great game of football."

Touching more on whom Bill Gardner is and the reason he was so respected, Bill shares with me, for my understanding, what is lost in today's culture.

Bill - "In life, some people are born to be shepherds and it's as simple as that. Some people are born to keep control of a situation when the shit hit the fan, but I always kept a cool head. There's times when you'll see someone down on their luck, and that's when you'll see if some ones got eyes in their head. Help that person out and throw them a few quid. I'm lucky that I was born a Sheppard, so I could help people out. When a mate is down, you can honestly put your arm around him and say 'what's wrong, mate'? That's what the difference is between a Sheppard and a sheep and I was born with a set of eyes in my head."

The following statement can sum up the conversation I had with Bill. How do great generals win wars? Throughout history, great generals have done what their enemies have least expected or feared. Bill's book is a collection of actual events that most firms will, if being honest, will tell you that is how it really happened. Much like generals with their troops, Bill was there for his mates. He would not send a mate in to a situation without his willingness to go first. Great generals do not repeat what has failed before, nor did Bill leave a mate behind or when he went down. A great general did not send troops directly into a battle, for which the enemy is prepared and waiting and nor would Bill think to save his own arse at the expense of another. Most successful moves are made against the enemy's flank or rear, either actual or psychological. Bill was a master at taking care of the lads at a game home or away.

The impression I gained from my conversation with Bill was the admiration and kindness that is clearly missing in society today. There are some blinding people in today's world and I think in fairness as many as there have always been. However, people are not and for good reason, as generous in their giving today as they were in by gone years.

Bill is of the frame of mind that is a representation of a good character, honesty and above all, he was there for anyone that truly needed some help in the world. To this day, I still remember the kindness and strength Bill gave to someone that was on the brink of snapping and taking on the world. Some would say guidance, but I guess it could also be interpreted as generosity. For me, it was an important part of the path in finding resolve and closure to the loss of my baby brother.

Carlton Leach

The first thing that comes to mind when you say or think the name is going to be different for each and everyone. For me it was a name that stretched back over 30 years, when the name was infamously known on the terraces. A name, along with the face was a sought after target by many firms and their own main lads that where looking to have a crack at one of the I.C.F's top boys.

Carlton's humble beginnings started in the great East End (so there is some bias!). Good parents, schooling, and a fair environment should promote a lad with enough to lead what most in society would consider a normal life. However, fate and the man had other ideas. In what would be enough to cover three life times, Carlton managed with a mixture of pain, loss and pride, to have a life that would not only help others, but also mine. The code is a word infamously known within all levels of crime and the criminal fraternity. A code that holds value, merit and above all, an unwritten set of rules that as much is it respected within the underworld as it is despised within the corridors of law and order. Someone once told me "show me the written code and ill show you a liar." Actions speak louder than words my pedigree chum! One particular event that springs to mind, was when a known heavy-duty drug dealer, a no-bars-hold fella decided he was going to test his weight with Carlton. The aftermath was the same person clutching for his life under armed police protection. Now this was not a simple person that fancied his chances, this was a person, who at the time, held very little regard for both Carlton's life and those innocent people standing close by. Under the order of a court summons and police questioning, Carlton still followed the rules. Carlton accepted that if you live by the sword, you die by the sword. The same person was lucky to survive and walk again and approached Carlton some years later, to pay tribute that if Carlton did identify him, he would have faced a large part of his life in prison. Although a criminal by all standards, these rules are by far better than no rules at all. They save taxpayers money and separate the criminals from animals. That lone gunman's actions could have very easily taken an innocent persons life. Wild bullets whizzing through the air do not discriminate their victims, and it's a common belief amongst both Joe public and the Old Bill that if a criminal is killed by another criminal, then that's fair justice. Tell me if I am wrong!

This code or rule prompted me to seek counsel with the man. If it was advice and experience in both self judgment and experience in fighting demons of past, then it was a wise choice to have a sat down with someone that carried over 30 years of hardened troubles, stretching from the shared terraces across the country, to the murky underworld of London's organised crime scene.

At West Ham, there is a phrase that is as well known as the days of the week. 'A bruva from another mother'. No truer word has been spoken and if Carlton heard of my troubles and a simple word from a shared pal gained an invitation to spend as much time as needed to 'get what was needed' an investment for my cause.

One phone call later and I am on my way to spend some time with the man. There was a little jaunt from East London to the leafy suburbs of Essex, to meet a man of stature that contradicts many people's thoughts or impressions of Carlton. He is not an over powering or intimidating animal of a man, instead he is someone that was there for my cause. Anything that was needed or could be done within his power was emphasised from the get go. "West Ham is family, Jase." That is still a comment that promotes why the club is unique in both its structure, and why it justified my regular journeys from west London to Upton Park to be with my pals. More than pals, in fact they were 'bruva's from another mother'.

It is still a task for me to justify to my septic pals, the bonding and relationship with a club like West Ham. For many, football is as much as a home and a gathering of people, as is the weekly ritual to some to go to church on a Sunday. We go to pay our respects to a bloodline of people that are interwoven within the history of who we are, and what we consider the value in life.

Carlton is a representation of the term 'there for his own'. Carrying experience beyond any arrest sheet, more than what could be said in any interview or shown in the multiple documentaries based on his life. It is something that a word from a shared close friend permitted Carlton to invite me into his very private and personal life. I am bottom of the totem pole. Carlton has all levels of violence in his past and he once said, "I believe there's still a bullet with my name on it!" What was important was the guidance and input for one to another. Trust was never a question here. Blood makes your related and loyalty makes us family.

Carlton was once a member of the Essex boys, who made a serious amount of noise until their brutal gangland style execution. Carlton carried the loss of a best pal within the group. The murder of a close friend cannot be justified by the all too common phrase 'with notoriety comes a price' nor can the questionable loss of the youngest person within my own family. Here I know I will find some rationalism to the premature death I had experienced.

An express ride from East to West, in one of the finest imported German sports cars the Kraut's had to put on the market, got me there in style. The welcome and hospitality extended by Carlton is again contradictory to the lemmings that read too much on the very little they know. It was an important part of the puzzle I was building to help fight my own demons.

So let us start on the terraces! To dispel any myths or guessing, and to and give insight to the reader; who may have missed the whole real beginnings of the football hooligan era, in what was the real story about the legend, the man and the I.C.F.?

I was lucky. Not only did I get to spend a lot of time with Carlton, but also got a chance to hear firsthand what would only be written in his own book. The stories you normally hear and the questions they would promote, Carlton kindly shared in benefit of my late brother. For this alone, I am indebted to a legend I grew up watching in the beginning days of the great I.C.F.

Traveling around the Essex and London borders, I faced a man that held answers, to questions I have had ready and only hoped would also be have been asked by my late brother Junior.

My first was thought was, why did Carlton think the I.C.F was so strong and successful in terms of its menacing of other football firms. The answer I got seemed easy and obvious. Neither boasted nor exaggerated but instead the reason was, as Carlton pointed out, that the I.C.F was unique in that it had many top boys who were very strong and solid members. It could in fact be compared to organised crime. Next, we get into the real story and why did he think the I.C.F was such a household name? As any one will tell you, in the days of the top firm, the I.C.F. was at the forefront in running the show.

Carlton explained, "Being the underdog against so many of the 'glory teams', like your Arsenal's, Tottenham's and your Chelsea kind of spurned us on. West Ham fans, because we've always been underdogs had to make a point. We had to be the hardest and the scariest firm in England! If we couldn't be the best team on the pitch, then we would be the best firm on the terraces."

Now, if it's thought I'm being a little biased, let's just check what firm is spoken of most today, remembering that the press has put a 'lid' on football violence? Why after all these years, is a team without the numbers in terms of supporters like your 'glory' teams, still have such a strong bond with a lot of the original (old guard) hooligans within the I.C.F?

Carlton - "It's history and it's like a family. Any person you have a shared a passion or interest with is the same thing. Put that with 20 or 30 years and even if you lead different lives, come from different areas, that Saturday afternoon and shared with the love and passion you have for that team along with that hard class working mentality will make a bond that can't be broken."

So, I now have to ask, what was some of the best memories being a west ham fan? Like most lads, their dad was the stepping-stone to their life on the terraces.

Carlton goes on to explain, "Going to watch West Ham with my dad and sitting on his shoulders in 1965, the year after we won the F.A cup. Then at the age of 15 or 16, I was getting to see a lot of the older boys regularly at the matches, the train rides, the atmosphere the '75 cup final at Wembley."

Of course, early games were 'sponsored' by your parents. Most of us had to rely on a few quid from mum, and accompanying of the old man; but when you came into your first wage packet well it was a whole new world with just you and your pals. We did not have to endure dad or his mates and the organised routine there and back. This opened up a completely new adventure and this was true for Carlton.

Carlton - "If there was a home game, I'd be able to go out during the week, and still being able to afford the Saturday match. But an away game meant staying in, saving my money, so I could go."

Now here we go with a question that would be asked by every one that ever experienced witnessed or heard of two firms meeting. What was the best ever 'meet' or tear-up?

Carlton - "Around '84 against Everton away, we had between 8-10 thousand supporters there. Many were hard-core supporters. It just blew my mind away to see that many people there and we took over the grounds, the pubs, and the whole area."

Now a little shared laughter on the subject. Having a mum with an East London background, I was always curious if there were any shared memories or similarities with me going home after a tear up and having to justify why I was asking for new clothes that was near impossible for my mum to keep replacing. Also having to face what was an equal amount of aggro' from the old girl as the fella that had just kicked me into next week and my clothes into a condition, that looked like the week after that. A smile and a look of 'oh, yeah' came about Carlton.

Carlton - "I was 15 and got a West Ham tattoo on my arm. I was pissed, and managed to hide it for about 7 or 8 months and then one Friday night I came home from a night out with the boys and passed out in the bathroom. The next morning, my mum couldn't open the door, so with the help of my dad, they pushed it open. Then I heard the cry from my mum 'Norman, he's got a fucking West Ham tattoo on his arm'. That and the coming home with black eyes, the kicking's, being nicked, sometimes not coming home. Yeah, we've all experienced that" (also a chuckle at the end).

Looking back, at many of the days of 'exploits' that at the time seemed like a real disaster, I was surely not alone with some of the thoughts of 'oh, fuck me, this is gonna hurt' or 'I'll laugh about this later'. Did Carlton have his fare share of 'it hurt then but can laugh about it now scenarios'?

Carlton - "Yeah, I was about 15 or 16 and we were in Brussels. I got completely smashed, and ended up having a fight with a load of Belgium fans and getting an injury that led me to being in hospital for three days. All the nurses talking to me in Italian, as they thought I was an Italian, and my mum and dad walked through the door. I didn't have a clue where I was. Did I think that was funny? Well, now, yeah! What was funny, was hearing from my best friend from school. His family saw me there on my hands and knees, crawling outside the stadium. I was so drunk I was not able to walk and was just crawling along. Listening to other peoples stories about what I did was always funny."

Being at the forefront of one of the country's most feared firms, must have made the normal, ever day fallouts over either a bird or another team, more eventful. Or did it?

Carlton - "For me it was simple. At the time of leaving school, I'd just got in with a whole new bunch of mates from football. I'd met what would be my first wife, Karen. I told her, that no matter what, if I go out with you, I still want to be able to go West Ham when I want and where I want. I told her West Ham would come first. As for us being the most feared firm, I never really thought of it like that. I mean I knew it was happening as I'd read about it. For me, I was just thinking about my mates, the crowd I'd get up to meet every week, the planed meet at the tube station with the same crowd of people and having a laugh all the way there. I liked having a tear-up and coming away laughing about it, the ride home and then going home to your old woman. Then when Saturday had finished, Sunday 'till the following weekend, all week I would be at work and I would be thinking who we got this week, where we gonna' be?"

There are many opinions about what is football culture. So, let us hear it from the 'horse's mouth'. Football culture as per Mr. Carlton Leach: -

Carlton - "Football culture was invented by a Englishman. We gave the world football, and we'd suffer for it. That's how I look at football culture. We invented the sport and everything that goes with it good or bad."

OK. What about the game of football?

Carlton - "Football is an English man's sport!"

Now, a word that is synonymous in society and is heard in nearly every conversation when you talk about football is the word 'Hooligan'. Again, each person has his or her opinion or interpretation of the word. What does it mean to a man that was at the forefront of hooliganism of our time?

Carlton - "A hooligan is someone that went along to football on a Saturday afternoon, had a row with another teams firm who was looking to do the same to me as I was going to do to them, and see who came out as top man. It's no different than two boxers going into a ring and seeing who's the winner. So if me going along and doing what I did makes me a hooligan, then yes, I was a hooligan. I was doing it for my team's colours."

Now the question that always has to be and always will be asked is who is the best firm?

Carlton- "The I.C.F for 30 years, we were untouchable. Now for rivalry, passion and violence it's Millwall and for notoriety and numbers Chelsea. Up North, you had to give it to Man - United just due to their sheer numbers and support. But it's like anything and on the day any dog can win. I mean you could turn a corner and it could be a hundred of you and a thousand of them and do 'em, but again, you could get caught out and get hurt. But for week in week out violence it had to be West Ham."

Now every fan or hooligan has to have a favorite player. What is yours from any team, any player anywhere in the country? Now to be fair, there are some blinders out there, so How about naming three of your top players? Mr. Carlton Leach picked Ex-West Ham striker Paulo De Canio, for his sheer passion for the game, Billy Bonds who epitomized West Ham, and wore his colours on his chest, and the greatest player we ever produced was Booby Moore.

Now a shared question, as I think it only fair that I include those two urchin brothers of mine, even though they are Chelsea. What are the football / football hooligan related movie that Carlton considers a favorite?

Carlton - "I liked The Firm (original), as this touched real points. I.D, based again on the I.C.F, but if I had to choose a movie simply based on the true underdog theme, it would be Scarface."

He carried 3 decades of experience that allowed me to better comprehend the loss I witnessed within my own family. No matter how many people I spoke to in the 'normal' world could help me understand the loss or reasons behind Junior taking his life. It even went as far as someone suggesting that I speak with a 'professional'. I understand and I have studied psychology. For eight years, I used the chosen subject to train any animal put in front of me. To be told about something that I could have simply read from a book was a waste of both their time and mine and to be frank it was a load of bollocks! Two days with Carlton allowed, me to realise there was a puzzle that simply needed to be put together.

Club Land

In Carlton's book 'Muscle', it describes a man that by no short can be either your best friend, or a fucking nightmare. Now, let us all be honest here. Before you point your finger or suggest this man is a raving lunatic, unhinged, or has no business being on the same streets as the 'normal' bearing folk of our beloved England. It is this man and the likes of Carlton Leach that many a respectful businessperson has been to regarding unsolved business issues. Understand a little more boys and girls. A lawyer will charge you 6 - 9 months of procedures and paperwork, not to mention additional thousands of pounds of your hard earned money.

The brawn brigade as they have been dubbed, gets it done in 6 - 9 hours and at a fraction of a cost. Of course, minus a few teeth and some embarrassment at the cost of the worthless toe rag that tried to rip you off in the first place. But, before you point your little middle class finger in my direction and claim that I am condoning either violence or menace; I'm sure that your activity at your local video store won't only reflect Disney DVD's on your rental history. I am sure you always change the channel when they are broadcasting boxing or a 'sanctioned' form of violence on the telly. Get my drift, Skippy! Anyway, back to my point. It is just that, it is a way of life, whether you like it or not and it is something that exists in our world. Ask the fella that Carlton saved or recovered 20 grand of their money that some dodgy no good mongrel tried relieving him of. Without Mr. Leach, he would now be serving burgers or working at a supermarket chain as his business has just gone down the toilet. Thank you!

My interest was just that, who was this former gangster I had heard of? I had seen Carlton the hooligan, the football menace and terrace legend but not Carlton Leach the hired muscle or the man that had run some of the toughest doors in London; including some on enemy territory; South of the river. "Fuck with me or my door crew and I'll smash you to bits. Just enjoy yourself tonight, boys." So here we go, into the perils and truths of hired muscle.

Where better to conduct this chat? Carlton and I pondered just a few days before, while hurtling down one of London's outer motorway in a supercharged imported German Sports car. Not a nightclub that could boast some of the hardest men in London to enter through their doors, not outside a reform center for naughty boys, but instead the comfort and tranquility of Mr. Leach's home (And you all thought he was pure evil) and our chat begins.

The first thing that will strike you (not literally, thankfully) is Carlton himself. He is calm, well mannered and above all honest about himself and his past. I described my interpretation, to Carlton of both my own and my brother's visits to a club. Typically, the first person you would be greeted by would be the doorman or bouncer as some still call them. Normally he was a mountain of a man (or woman, if you are in the wrong part of the country), a 'grizzly' sized fella' that would more often than not have a scar or two from his (or her) time in the 'field'. They normally demanded respect by their sheer size and posture and that would normally be enough to keep order on the premises. Something that I had experienced as a compact fella' (5'7 is not short, thank you!) was that, because I was typically the shortest of my pals, I always seemed to be one to be a target of some moron that fancied his chances. Considering that, my brothers and I had seen our fair share of clubs, being minded by doorman and the like, had often noticed a fella, of not as tall stature as other doorman in their crew (there can only be so many grizzlies out there). So my first question was did any of his crew for whatever reason no matter what always seem to attract aggro'? A kind of 'Oh shit, Dave's been clumped again'

Carlton - "Well our lot, when we used to go out, was me, Vick dark, Keith Lewis and a few others. I think it was a case of the not so powerful ones became a target.

The places we went people knew, like some of the older lot who could handle themselves. Not a particular person, but if there was a fight it was one of my old school mates that seemed to get it more."

Now going back to Carlton's book it mentions that he ran some of London's toughest clubs and doors. With that came certain privileges and rewards. There were certain types of woman that were attracted to the head doorman. Even though that lifestyle and part of his life was long behind him (I will not share Carlton's age, but he is still a young chap), I was curious that if that was part of his past and still raises it's ugly (or attractive if you are there) head?

Carlton- "No, as I'm no longer in the door business, the security game it's all behind me."

Now, I am sure you, the reader, have had some friends or family that's have been out at a club and have experienced some aggro from 'Johnny loud mouth', the all too often larger lout who was sometimes a bit of a bruiser, which has raised a bit more than his glass for a toast. Being a person, that attended some real tasty venues and events, Carlton has seen a lot or not to assume, maybe even heard of a fight or two. My thought was I was glad when I was out and had some real mates with you. I knew I was not going to be at the end of a kebab knife in bandit country as my mates where there. The pals that thought along the lines of 'sod the birds' and a bit of thing Jay's come unstuck'. So I asked, were there times at the time of aggro', he was glad he had some real pals with him.

Carlton - "Yeah but one thing I want to point out about doormen, it wasn't always the 6 ft. 6", 28 eight stone ones that I was glad to have with me or by my side. It was the smaller ones, the ones that had the heart. If you had the lineup of my doormen, it was always the one you didn't expect. You'd have your big lumps or the muscle bound ones but it would be the one you'd least expect. He would be the one with the courage; he'd be the most dangerous one due to his loyalty, not his size. Now one of my memories of going to a club in Essex was with a local girl who got completely out of her tree and threw up all over my new Armani jeans and Gucci shoes."

Being that Carlton had seen more clubs antics than most of us have had hot dinners, did he have any memories he would like to share? Now when

I asked him this, he not only leaned back with a huge grin, but also let out a little chuckle. I think I may have 'opened a can of worms here' boys and girls.

Carlton - "This is fucking great this, as it was the 'Old Paradise' rave club in Islington. We had the security there and everyone of the security were beefed up on steroids and went in at 16 or 17 stone. I was wearing a white polo shirt. You know, rolling up your sleeves your muscles are bulging and I was walking through there, early hours of the morning. I mean it was absolutely mobbed in there. There was a three tier flooring system with at least 1500 people in and I mean it was just heaving in there. So there I was just walking around, with my radio. During this, I started to get all sweaty. So, by the time I'd walked all around the club and got to the main door, I noticed I was really sticky all down my back. It was then that I realised that someone had puked up all down my back. So there I was, this big muscle man with a pure white polo shirt, and there it was all down my back. It was not a good image.

Another time was about ten years before that. I was in the old dickey bow set up and doing my rounds, when this fella' came running around looking for the toilets and just threw up all down me. Being alcohol sick is not the best, especially when you have to stand there for the rest of the night with someone's puke all down you. It's not very attractive towards the females and not a good pulling point, so definitely a downer."

The Essex Boys.

Now in his book it also highlights the drug scene. This, for the best part of the '80's and '90's was part of club culture. I commented that the drug industry went hand in hand with clubbing and asked was at best or worst a dicey game.

Carlton - "When the drugs started in the '80's, it was more of a laid back mentality. Everyone was there to enjoy himself or herself, it was like a new world had appeared. But during the late '80's, what started with E's, cocaine started to come back in. Then people realised this was a moneymaking industry. You had the potential where you could get 10 thousand people in a warehouse and each person would want an average of two E's each plus they're drinking bottles of water or Ribena whatever, but again you're talking 10 thousand people and that simply means 20 thousand pills and that's where you make the money. Crime comes into it, it attracts it, then you'll get your darker side of the element, it's nature."

This led of course, as time will reflect, to the life of Carlton in the most feared organised crime syndicate in the whole of the south east of England, and what was known as the Essex boys. Rise of the foot soldier, Carlton's life on film. We have already covered terrace and club life. The movie that my brothers and I enjoyed (Oi, Mr. no violent DVD rental goer you, you know the truth. You watch 'em) was a certain part of his life that I wanted to talk about and being that I was welcomed into his world, I thought it only fair I finish the trilogy on Carlton's life respectfully. 'Rise of the Foot Soldier', not your Hollywood glam and glitter approach. Defiantly true to life, grime and grit on the reality of the price and cost of the drugs underworld. This lead to the untimely death of Carlton's best pal Tony Tucker. Carlton explains, a little more on the subject.

Carlton - "Was Tony's death drug related? Yeah, I mean it was related to drug deals and yes it was because of his involvement in that scene. Although, I believe he was dead before he was killed physically in my eyes."

Now the conversation that followed I will take to the grave, as it included his thoughts, on why my brother he took his life. That conversation not only hit a real nerve with me, but also allowed me for the first time to find a little bit of closure on the subject.

He detailed the dangerous world of mixing both class 'A' and a whole cocktail of drugs. How he watched his friend dying in front of him over a period of time and how that with one step forward of progress, the drugs took his friend two steps back.

Carlton - "The Tony Tucker that was killed in the Range Rover was already dead, and I couldn't save the man."

Recapping on his film Carlton explained that it is not a gangster film; it's about an East London kid having to fight for everything. He did not want a film with all flash cars and high-end motives. He had the luxury to command that but he wanted the film that people could relate too. He was not a godfather just a human being caught on the roll and the ride and the spiraling effects that made history. Carlton also explained what I think is easily forgotten and not realised. With the great success of the film came a price. I think Carlton would have rather not experienced what the film carried with it that was the memories, loss of friends and pain. The movie allowed that anger and frustration to surface to the top and the people that cared for Carlton noticed. He was not a violent man, but a man that was a human being with emotions and most importantly feelings. The photos of the victims from the Range Rover shootings were seen for the first time by Carlton. Reliving some of the memories on set and of course the one thing that stills remains is there a bullet with Carlton's name on it.

The Carlton Leach I had heard of or seen in my youth at football, was the same man sitting in front of me all these years later. What he carried with him now was not a lifelong worth of lessons to hand out, but instead a man with experience in what most would have given up if life had thrown at them. Some of us have experienced that first hand. I am just thankful Carlton was there for me to help piece reason and logic to a brother I only wish he could have met.

The I.C.F

The name ICF at its very beginning had not yet matured. No one outside of our group really knew what it meant. It was not until the early '80's you would get the odd one shouting out ICF, as most within it preferred discretion. We were the first organised firm with leadership and goals that were recognised. This was after all of the internal disputes between the different firms at West Ham had stopped fighting each other, and came together. The success of the I.C.F. was not just gained with different areas coming together, but also specific regions in the ICF. By this, we mean firms would unite only from a few selected areas. Mainly Hornchurch, Upminster, Elm Park and Cranham would consolidate their masses. Some would meet up with Carlton and some with Cass, but it has been agreed that without this coming together there would not have been the notoriety or success. Again, it has to be said that it was not just the ICF, all West Ham firms made one powerful unit on the day. Carlton without the help of Hornchurch and Cranham didn't have the numbers. In the '70's and early '80's the pillars of West Ham were the old Cranham mob, which Bill Gardner liked having around. How is this known? It is known because we stood on the shoulders of giants. Some of us were still kids, and we ruled the terraces, made history and we started it all and it has not been matched since.

John Turner & Dave Rayon- Hornchurch

The I.C.F

As most lads in their 40's and 50's will tell you, (yes, that's me getting on a bit now) the I.C.F was a favorite name in the news, along with a few other big stories in the '70's-90's. They boasted style and a quality that not many firms could measure too. An era of the top firm and the top boy were created through their notoriety. The I.C.F created a completely new order of football hooligan. They did not only employ the working class from the East End, but there was also bank managers, clothing designers and lads with more than a few quid in their pockets. The I.C.F boasted of one of the first firms to arrive at matches in designer clothes. Often expensive imported French and Italian gear, instead of the once scarf wearing, singing fan that was the norm.

Attitudes and an aura of confidence, often confused as arrogance, was another trademark of the I.C.F. Their name appropriately given as the hooligan at West Ham would mean boarding higher priced intercity trains, instead of the specials put on for the away fans. In addition, buses, coaches and other means of transport were used to avoid the ever-watchful eye of the Old Bill. If the police attempted to interrupt the travel plans of the hooligan, then another means of travel would be arranged 'By hook or by crook' as it is said.

For the visiting fan and especially the hooligan that fancied their luck against West Ham's boys, will tell you of the nerve-racking walk from Upton Park Station to the stadium. Once safely tucked away in the south bank section, or at least in the eyes of the visiting firm, it was only a matter of time before the "off." This was the I.C.F's manor. No one was ever going to get a steady foothold inside the stadium, or not at least get too comfortable. Another I.C.F favorite move would be to queue up with visiting fans, buy their tickets, and at the right time would cause uproar within the ranks of the visiting firm and this is a method used to this day and is attributed to be a creation of West Ham. More so with the predecessors of the I.C.F, the Mile End Mob. The two firms that are largely missed in most conversations but were known as key elements in structure along with the I.C.F, were the lads from Hornchurch and Cranham. They were hard as coffin nails and always there for anyone within West Ham. West Ham's numbers consisted of several different groups from different areas. Whether it was Mile End, Teddy Bunter's Firm or those already mentioned, everyone knew their place and who could be there to watch each others backs

Outside the ground was no easier. Local favorite meets were only a stone's throw, and could easily have many a "member" ready for what would be become a painful day for the once brave outsider wanting to have a go at the local lads.

Now something often considered by an outsider, is why the hooligan acted in a manner that could be only interpreted as mindless, barbaric and selfish. One of many ways could answer that. To the passionate man, it was supporting his team in a way that would allow him to exert energy and a voice in something that was his and his alone. It was a chance for someone to elevate his existence to another level. Self-promotion if you will. Ask any fan of the countless times, whether they are from the north, south, east or west of the 'aggro' they experienced as a traveling fan by 'welcoming committee'. That being said, there were many an honest hooligan identified with the violence and power that could be gained from running with the pack. By interpretation, this was not something that had to be bought. This was something that he was in control of. This was his voice, his team, and his way of life. His passion and love for the team would be demonstrated to anyone else who questioned it. The team was his to protect and above all, to be proud of. None of the hooligans, in their time of affiliation, ever considered their actions as anything more than a way to tell their story, their love for the game. This was the I.C.F.

In later years, they would generate a cult following throughout the whole of Europe. Now, if it is thought at any stage I am exaggerating, ask anyone involved or part of a firm in the height of football hooliganism, and they will tell you the necessity to organise for a game against West Ham. Even more, look at the years after the once thought 'era gone by'. This top firm generated books, documentaries, movies. Nevertheless, what was equally as important, was the respect that was generated amongst other firms, and this still remains many years after their retirement. This, of course, does not mention the fan base that continues throughout different parts of the football world.

West Ham Steve is as much a brother to me, as can be found in any true friendship. Not someone that I'd hold hands with whilst taking a walk down the beach on a spring morning, but someone that's always going to be there as a brother, a mentor and one of a few people in my life that I would trust, not only my well being but those within my own family. He is someone that over the years has corrected me and stood by my side in my darkest hours. As it has been said, 'I'd rather walk with a friend through darkness than alone in the light'

When the decision was set upon me by my demons, I only saw two options. Seek retribution for the loss of my brother's life or seek what was suggested as a more constructive path. I will be honest; I would have happily taken the first! Steve was one of two people that were there from the outset. No matter what decision I made, Steve would be by my side. The one thing that slowed me down is a comment he made to me. "If it goes pear shaped son, your mum will be burying two sons instead of one!" That hit me more than anything in my life either before, or after.

Steve rationalised the options I had and spoke in a way that simply made sense and he added "Whatever path you chose, I'm with ya'! If it seems like its coming on top, remember you've got family around you." I could not have argued with that advice. In addition, I know I would have been kicked up the arse if I were doing something I should not have. What could have been interpreted as a negative, he had gained in his former experiences from being a once known face following West Ham home and away. This was now the voice of guidance, reason and logic.

Steve remains one of two people that are top of my tree. He is as much family, as the bloodline of my own kin. Much like anyone that knows of someone that has always been there for her own, Steve encapsulates what a 'bruva from another mother' means, stands for and represents.

Ladies and Gentleman, I give you, story of a foot soldier:

Now many of you may well think, or go as far as to say, that the football hooligan is a thing of the past which was safely put to rest by the Thatcher era, brown bread, like a dodo, 'sorry, luv' not seen 'em in a while'. Well, there is a rumor that those boys in heavily clad designer gear, ready to upset the Saturday afternoon shopper and put certain authorities overtime schedule back in full swing (like their truncheons), are here. In fact, it has been said that they never left. Due to the introduction of C.C.T.V, they have simply moved their chosen social interaction to another arena away from the ready eye, as to say, but again this is all rumour.

What better authority on the subject than our very own West Ham supporter West Ham Steve; who was a former member of the I.C.F. Now for those that shudder at the sheer mention of the chosen firm, let me suggest that I could not think of a better choice. Seeing, as the I.C.F is one of most hated, feared and yet respected firms in the land. So they are much like any 'organisation', with such limelight and public attention, they must have merit in the 'field'! (and on it, boom, boom!)

OK, OK. So there's some bias. Other firms around the country may well object that they deserve and mention. Well, I am claret and blue, the East End is in my veins and well let's just trust my judgment. No sense incriminating myself is there! In terms of a chat with a former soldier and a voice, well boys and girls you have just that.

Deep in the East End, I have the luxury of a chat with a former 'player' in the firm of firms. So sit back and enjoy what some have put on the line in terms of passion and enjoyment for you to accept this as part of history in the world of football. My questions are what could have been asked from an outsider. Some already covered, some not thought of covering, some not dared, but we're not here for dancing around the subject. So as they used to say 'lets 'av a meet'.

So, I asked- Although it would seem that football firms have been a thing of the past, and they have typically have been out of the press, they are in fact alive and 'kicking', the answer was as many have guessed.

West Ham Steve- "Yeah there are many in fact that are still alive and kicking, it's still going on. There are many of the hooligan elements, mainly your northern clubs and your smaller clubs, but not so much your larger clubs, like your Man-United's or your Liverpool's."

So this being true and with our friends (yeah, right!), in the main stream media catching a recent event, I thought it only fair to ask a little more on a the event that caught many an eye, when it was reported that a plane was charted by supporters of West Ham.

West Ham Steve- "Yeah, there is a story behind that. That was a couple of years ago, when we played Everton away. They'd stopped all the trains from London to Birmingham. Repairs, leafs on the tracks, you know the usual bollocks! Well, we go in luxury. So to go one better, if not first class intercity, then let's fly! So this particular Saturday, one of the lads arranged a flight from Stanstead. When we got there to the airport on the Saturday morning, there was a good 300 hundred of us waiting for the flight. We were waiting for the announcement for the flight when we heard "would all passengers for Con Air flight 1 please approach gate number blah de blah." So I thought that must be us, and as the truth of it was, it was us! So we flew up to Liverpool, we came out of John Lennon airport. There were a good 300 hundred handed and there was another 200 plus boys that had traveled on coaches. So, there were at least 500 hundred West Ham supporters. We just strolled through Stanley Park without any hindrance, no one said a word, and it was at least 500 hundred East End boys walking through Liverpool. That says it right there, it took me back 20 years."

Now if that is not ringing any bells, that this was a strong and well-respected firm, why not ask the obvious. Why is it that the I.C.F. has had by far the most attention in recent books films and documentaries to the dismay of other self-proclaimed top firms? Legends have been born from this brotherhood of great East End and the surrounding areas of Essex. Why is that?

West Ham Steve- "Because, well we were the best and we went 30 years undefeated. That's 30 years of being the most feared firm in the country and the reasons you've got books, documentaries, films i.e. The Firm, Hooligan, Green Street and even parts of Rise of the Foot soldier is because we're the best. The I.C.F is still thought of as the number one firm in this country."

Now with the consumer market always calling for films on life and such, it was inevitable that some would be made on the game of football, and more specifically the attention that the naughty boys brought to the streets before and after the game. 'Green Street' was marketed at the American audience. It was one of the newest and contained some former members of the I.C.F. in the cast of extras. So, as our friend and a former member of the I.C.F., can you tell us about that.

West Ham Steve –"Well there is a really good story there. I was employed to do some C.P; close protection work. The fella that hired me wasn't a football minded man, boxing or anything like that, and kicking a bit of leather around was not his thing. But he's phoned me up and said I've got a bit of security work which involves a film crew coming over from America and they're making a football film. I need you in on it with me. I asked what type of football film it was. Do you mean a hooligan football film? I then said well first and foremost what club are they basing the story on and where is it, because I have to be careful where I end up because of my history.

Now to my man's sheer delight he gets an answer that makes it all possible for the film producers. It's West Ham so you know that's right up my street. I know the terrain, the people and if I've got to walk around with 50 actors and extras in front of West Ham's stadium, the last thing I need is a bunch of actors singing songs that West Ham fans aren't accustomed to. The fans might think it's a rival firm. Then I've got all the actors and extras all over the pavement, with their heads hanging off. So, off I go to meet director at the studios in Bow, and I had my I.C.F. baseball cap on and this director went a bit wobbly at the knees. I'm thinking 'ello, I've got half a chance here. I knew it wasn't my good looks that attracted her. But unbeknown to me, it was my I.C.F. baseball cap, because this director Lexi, has two brothers that are quite high profiled football hooligans. As soon as she saw my cap, straight away we clicked. Anyway she had a little bit of research done and it was said I was a former member of the I.C.F. and had association with some known members and the like.

It was all intriguing to her that she had come here to do a film and found someone here on her doorstep, that was originally just hired to do some close protection minding for the actors and stars and now is a football hooligan consultant. I mean I'm just a fella out of East London. I do C.P; but if you said to me 10 years ago, I was going to be in a film I'd said you were fucking mad."

Now there had to be some fun and games?

West Ham Steve – "Well yeah, we were doing the very last fight scene first and they had 5 days to film it. Well, we've had a crash course in how to fight people without hitting them. Well, fuck me, we were once in the business of hitting people, you know, that's what we did. So we've got Pat Johnson; that was the fella that was the fight choreographer for all the karate kid films and I mean this man is an absolute legend. We're standing on this dock at the East London docklands, and we're taking our positions. West Ham extras this side and Millwall extras that side. This guy has come up to say 'ello and I've just been told I'm going to be fighting him, so he says I he just wanted to introduce himself, so when we ran out and meet in the middle we both know who we're fighting. I thought 'oh, OK'. But he said that he's so and so and he's actually Millwall and I said well yeah,

I know you're Millwall and you're over there, but he said that he was really a Millwall Hooligan! The all I've heard my brother say is 'oh fucking 'ell, why'd he say that?' So I thought right yeah, I'll see you in a little bit! Oh fuck me; he made himself a right target and it was best he stayed schtum. I think he realised his mistake a few minutes later because as soon as they shouted 'action', I've gone running in and 'bang' I've knocked him right out. He's sparko and I've got to fight this guy for about 2 or 3 minutes, then all I'm doing is standing there, everyone's got their partner, so I saw my brother fighting another fella, so I just went over there and helped my brother beat him up. The funny thing was that we've all gone in the next day to work and Lexi came running up to me and said she doesn't know what to do as she's got a problem. I asked what it was the and she told me that between me and my 3 mates we'd beaten up 30 extras and they wasn't coming back as they didn't get paid enough for the injuries they got. She then asked me if I could bring in some of my mates. Well I asked if she was serious and had she really thought about this, but she said she was and wanted to make it look real. I made the call and within an hour and a half, I had boys from all four corners of London. So there you had it, within an hour and half I.C.F past and present, boom!"

Now because of loyalties within the East End and its former members namely Carlton Leach, only the loyalties would be stretched from one production to another. Here, in Rise of the Foot soldier, former I.C.F. can be found in addition to the main lead Carlton Leach.

West Ham Steve- "Well he's one of my best friends. Carlton Leech is a brother from another mother. That involvement for me was just for love and respect."

A question typically asked and I am always hoping that I will hear a different response is that I want to hear the fight in someone's voice. All too often, I hear a tame reply, a response that accepts defeat in the responding tone. If someone has the oomph in their answer it's here in front of me. I wanted to hear from someone that has put their time in, that feels the 'game' in what they do and has been taken away or cut short. I wanted to hear if the role of the foot soldier, what with C.C.T.V and extra policing of grounds with added measures in terms of anti football programs had really changed.

West Ham Steve- "Well that's big brother, ain't it! They say it's a free country, well that's bollocks. I've never heard so much crap in all my life. It's a fucking police state. When we were running around, there were no computers; there were no mobile phones. It was a case of we know where we were going. We knew where to find them, they knew where we were coming from, and it happened. Now you've got the Old Bill that infiltrates these web sites. They have blue tooth phones and a small spike camera in their collar. I mean you're talking about the biggest gang in the world. They were fucking cavemen, when we were originally running around causing havoc. Now they're on the penny!"

Fuck me I got the answer there!

A common phrase I hear a lot from my predecessors, is that the new school are not of the same breed as what I knew in the old school. The loyalties and the old school code are gone especially in the underworld. Was this code lost with hooligans, old and new? Is the code and loyalties that made the I.C.F so strong still there?

West Ham Steve- "From what I've seen in the I.C.F., absolutely! I mean that's what made us so strong as there's a lot of little firms that were made up from different areas. Then when you get all those five or so firms together and make one big firm, it wasn't a case of all the top boys; it was just simply the I.C.F."

Now I have to mention it for no other reason than respect. It never gets old hearing it, if it does to you, than you are not claret and blue. We all know who one of the most respected men was.

West Ham Steve- "Everyone's dad at West Ham and he's like our big brother, it's someone we all look up to and that's Bill Gardner and Carlton Leach."

With the growth of 'A Night with.... and Gangster dinner events', curiosity may lead you to ask if any of the once mayhem and havoc dealers can tolerate each other's presence considering at one stage in life, the hooligans of old were out for blood, whether you were East, West, North or South.

West Ham Steve- "Well there are some that I can socialise with, a few. Remembering that just 10 or 15 years ago we'd be tearing each other apart. There's Mack from Cardiff and you've got Jason from Chelsea. I consider him a close friend."

Now if you want to hear some more on the movies and if they are of standing. Well, I have my opinion and you have yours. Even though you'll deny ever watching them as they condone violence (What was I thinking!), but if you was to pop down to your local D.V.D store, and if by chance you dared to enter the world of football hooliganism, and wanted a pointer, let's get a few ideas for you here

West Ham Steve – "I.D. for a fictional film and for a film that set a standard, it would have to be 'The Firm' with Gary Oldman."

What with the ever growing list of wants and needs and let's say you've got to get a pressie for one of your nephews or maybe a friend's son. I would suggest a book. Again, it is only fair we give you a pointer or two. So what would our friendly former hooligan recommend?

West Ham Steve- "Bill Gardner's book. It's like reading a bible. When you read that book, it's coming from the legend."

What with Top of the Pops out the window and our chance of West Hams best players ever getting a chart of their own, why not list it here? Only fair and to fucking right mate! So my list is mine. What about a fellow football fan! Oh look, by chance I have a local authority here with me now. So, me ol' mukka share with me your favorite players if you will please.

West Ham Steve- "Alan Devonshire for his silky skills, Bobby Moore, that man is a saint, and without a doubt Paolo Di Canio. What that man brought to West Ham, well, it's pure passion."

The positives that can be gained with being involved on any level of football can be clearly seen here with Steve's story. From a simple chap out of East London following a shared dedication and love for West Ham, he has gained more than an experience in the opportunities given with his involvement in both film and media production. There is without question a silver lining in every cloud. The doubting Thomas' can be assured of the old saying 'a positive from a negative'

It also helps to see that the memories we have from being a footy supporter keeps us alive and prompts the kid in all of us. Hooliganism will never fade. The characters it has produced have for me, allowed real people to be part of my life during and after their involvement. Even after the modernisation of our game, that kindred spirit has left the terraces but remains with the fans and this can be shown when a call goes out from within the ranks from one fan to another. 'Never a loner' is produced from the once over crowded concrete steps we called home. The only separation found back then, was in the terrace handrails and dividing fences and can only witness a gathering of close-knit communities that cannot be catalogued and sold through any online club store but can still at what we call family.

Since my time writing this chapter, I have faced what I had considered buried demons. The bitter battle of guilt, that I know I'll carry to the end of my days rears its ugly head now and again. Typically, I look for resolve by channeling that energy, and frustration through violent means. The strength and resolve is there each and every time from someone that has my best interests at heart. The consistency in support that Steve gives is a true measure of friendship. I once read that friendship is not about whom you have known the longest; it is about whom never left your side and that is my pal West Ham Steve. I continue my fight, but with the pals I have I dare any demon to share my path. Those around me are always at my side.

Under 5's

Djelal 'Jela' Ispanedi

I wanted to belong to something, but not be part of Margaret Thatcher's establishment. That world did not exist for me. It was a dead-end no hope society for many and football allowed us to escape reality. We were against the system but were united by West Ham and for me that was everything. In the beginning, it was hard, real hard. No clothes no reputation and a tough time being a kid. It was the start of the casual era, which was associated with football hooligans and like-minded youths. We stole, robbed and borrowed. We wanted to see the world and this was for most of us the only chance. A lot of firms claim they started the trend, but it was progressive in its making. We traveled around Europe, which was ideal for exclusive brands and easy thieving. Being the top firm was our goal and we gained notoriety through our actions. We fought them all, and became as notorious as the I.C.F. We were just kids but we stuck together. The older lot did not want us around. They felt kids would just get in the way, but we were together at times separated only by generations. It was the best time of my life. I was 13 years old when I received a serious head injury resulting in me being in a coma and on life support for three months. I had to rebuild my life and my world had changed forever. Even though my life had stopped, the football violence continued inside of me. The only substitute to replace the buzz was drugs. That was another battle all in itself. What didn't kill me made me stronger?

Jela

The challenges I encountered certainly weren't unique to my own story. A pal at West Ham had also gone through a series of challenges but instead of the loss of life it was a loss of someone that could have been part of his own. Thankfully, he found structure and resolution at Upton Park. Dean, had once been the main chap in the under 5's which was West Hams youth / younger firm.

It said that we are a product of our environment and I think in all fairness Dean was an example of what was and what can be another positive example of there for those that need the support and clearly demonstrate the process of fighting through the challenges life can unfairly throw your way. Like most inner city youths, violence is an answer for the questions that no one else can give you the answers. The same fight for recognition from a society was in Dean's early life and the introduction to the youth element at West Ham. Some might say that it was a matter of interpretation; not giving up I would reply. The disciplines needed in a young boy's life can be easily found at football. The pride in a club, the dedication in following both your friends and a team, and the social structure found and represented best at your club of choice.

My trip out east was the same as any other. A Carriage load of people sharing not much more than a few minutes of shared elbowroom and the all too common brat with the earphones letting out the annoying high-pitched tones. On the odd occasion, I that would be treated to what we English are proudly known for which and an old aged pensioner would call their stiff upper lip and spirit. The breed of old gents are what once served proudly and are amongst the most respected bunch of people within the UK. These pedigrees are the ones any decent human being will offer their seat to, or tip their hat in passing. It is sad to say, but this is a dying breed. A shared opinion by all working class is that these chaps have more spine and courage than any politician does. On one journey, I witnessed one such gent who at the bequest of both his wife and the incessant grumbling of one of London's snotty no balls of their own upper middle class city workers to challenge the youngster and his less than personal iPod music. Wisely, the urchin lowered the volume. That fighting sprit put the great into Great Britain. The old man may be out of breath but not out of courage. In addition, if the little twat had given the 'ol' boy' any lip there would have been at least three or four sizable people that would have stepped in and made mince meat of the degenerate.

One thing you are always aware of is the closeness of you and your chosen team's arena. The feeling is electric. Anyone that goes to football will tell you of the same excitable feeling and atmosphere, as you get closer to your home ground. The same passion and dedication fills the air. The songs and banter from predecessors and pals take over the airwaves and with the right team, this noise can easily mask out city traffic and commuting noise.

A few streets to cross and bang on time there is my pal. Dean expresses all gratitude for being part of my request to be involved by welcome smiles and the familiar "All right, Bruv, what can I get ya?" It makes sense, as we are deep in East London in the heart of West Ham country. The crowded bar makes space as a few more come over to make sure all is in order and everyone's good, to some, friends; to us, family. After some simple chitchat Dean spends some well-invested time talking over the ideas he has and the story he has to share.

The rest herein is Dean's story. I have been pals with him for some years and witnessed firsthand the dedication, which is missing in today's society along with the fact that Dean is clearly part of the norm with my pals. It is not an expected or requested action but more instinctual to be there from those that hold merit in your life. It is much like the retired chap on the train; courage and loyalty were there when needed. Known for the naughtiness are the great I.C.F. 30 years undefeated and a style that boasted and never beaten. Many a top face and firm came unstuck without an explanation but more of an excuse for the day's loss and humiliation against this once notorious East End firm. What is seldom written are the exploits and adventures, if you will, of the once famed under 5's. The youth structure of the mentioned firm was a tactical unit within the infrastructure of the I.C.F. Sometimes given a mention here and there, but for the first time, we think it only fair you get a word from within the ranks. I give you the under 5's:

Under 5's

D. W.

For the under 5's, there were always 3 things that stood in their way at West Ham and they were in this order. They had the opposing firm, the Old Bill and the most difficult object they encountered and still encounter many years into their inception was the older faction of the West Ham's firm.

The old heads of the original Under 5's and even some proper old heads from the I.C.F. of old which some of these cunts had been around since the '70s, didn't know how to take a backward step when it came on top and were horrible bastards. It was therefore understandable that a bunch of kids, as a lot of the Under 5's were back at the start would not seem to like the type of people they had want to share a battlefield with.

Some of the Under 5's finally gave up trying to gain respect from the older faction of the firm at West Ham. It was as though they were flogging a dead horse, but that never stopped them getting together and trying to achieve things off the pitch.

Not everyone was against them, in fact a fair few old boys took them under their wing, as they knew they were the future. Even if some of them knew deep down that these kids would never be on the level they once were over 20 years prior.

The boys were in their late teens or early 20's, West Ham was facing relegation into the soon to be formed Championship, so the football was going to be pretty shit for a fair while and was manifest as trips to Preston, Walsall and Rotherham which would be on the cards. Not to take away the passion that these lads had for West Ham as a club, but as a whole, it was still going to be a massive part of their lives as it always had been and it always will be.

One of the biggest misconceptions about lads who get involved in this side of the match is that they do not care about the football, or their chosen club. That's the biggest load of bollocks ever spouted, by the clueless media and all the fucking idiots who feed off everything the media said. There are the ignorant and moronic people who cannot form opinions of their own and assume that if it is in a weekday or weekend tabloid rag. Then it must be the way of the world and all of its inhabitants think.

The boys all came from relatively decent families and family backgrounds. They all had jobs or were just out of school or college. Some were using the Under 5's as a stepping-stone into the greater scales of violence and a step up from the violence of pubs and clubs. Others were using it as an extension to their need for violence. One thing all the lads shared was that of an insatiable thirst for chaos and an overwhelming passion for West Ham United, despite what certain people say.

My uncle got me involved in football at a very early age. I was about five when he first told me I had to support West Ham and by the time, Italia '90 came round I was bang into my football. My idols of the time were Gary Lineker and Paul Gascoigne. It is somewhat ironic that they played for a team I should have hated, a team I fully understand the hatred for now, but I was young then and they were both fantastic footballers and a massive part of football at that time.

But it wouldn't be until 1991 that I'd go and see West Ham play a pre-season friendly against Southend United at Roots Hall. From then on, I was hooked on the spirit the West Ham's supporters had. I sat there and watched the West Ham fans in awe. I recall my uncle telling my mum when he took me home that I paid more attention to the nearby West Ham fans than the match itself. I was in with a bunch of old farts and other kids, but in the next stand, it was mayhem. All the security and stewards left the stand, as they could not keep the West Ham fans calm and I wanted to be a part of that. As the years went on, I only went to few matches, as I was young and my uncle stopped going as much as he had previously because that dreaded thing that comes to us all in the end happened to him, he fell in love and got a mortgage. It was bad timing for me really, as none of my friends went, and my dad was not around. Anyway, from what I had been told was not even into football.

As the late 90's came the time, I lost interest in football. As I was at this point in my life I was fully indulging myself in hating the system that I felt was ripping me off and trying to mold me into something I was never meant to be. I had fully embraced punk rock by the age of 15, so it was not until Japan and South Korea 2002 that I got interested in football again. It was quite annoying as I felt I was starting again, but it re-installed the passion that I had as a child.

Personally, I was never interested in football violence at first. I wanted to get back over to West Ham on a more regular basis with people I could enjoy that time with. I had led quite a violent life style and would fight almost once a week without fail. I had grown tired and angry at the world and I felt I was losing touch with my friends at the time. I had grown away from them or they had grown away from me. I had ostracized myself from everything I once loved.

My father walked out on us when my brother and I were 1 and 2 years old. I went out of my way to meet him when I was 16 and my mother warned me that he would hurt me, that he was no good etc. I did not listen and I went ahead with it and everything she said turned out to be true. If he ever tried to get in touch with me, again I know for a fact I will end up doing something to him because what he did was unforgiving. He met me, promised me the world, well, he promised to involve me in his world and that is all I wanted at the end of the day. He was going out with a much younger woman. She was only 10 years older than I was and she became jealous instantly. He arranged to meet my brother and my dad did not turn up. We never heard from him again. It does not take a genius to figure out what nor should I say "who" made him stay away.

My mother remarried and had two more kids, both of whom I adore greatly and it is something I never had a problem with. My now stepfather had taken my mother in as well as my brother and I. Something like that is admirable quality in my opinion. Raising another man's children is something not many men can do, so I have always loved him for that and will always respect him for what he done and any man that does the same thing for that fact.

As the years went on and I was leaving my teens and entering my 20's, I felt more distanced from my family. I felt like an outsider and as my older brother led a life of crime and was heavily involved in drugs, he was not really a part of the family at this point. It took him many years to get his head together and clean his act up. Something we are all proud of him for. Back then, I spent every day thinking that he would not be with us much longer because of the life he was living.

I then became a father at 17 and I ran away in fear from what I had done. My girlfriend left me and for selfish reasons of my own, I took a step backwards and stayed away from her and my daughter, which is something I have regretted ever since. The last I heard was she had got married, moved to Bristol and had another kid. I was nothing but a bad memory. By the time, I had decided what I wanted and what I had turned down it was too late. I was not about to upset my daughter's life as I could only imagine that she was happy with her life that life did not involve me. So, I ran away for selfish reasons and then I ended up staying away for un-selfish reasons. It is somewhat ironic but nobody would understand that unless they were in the same situation themselves, I suppose. I have never really spoken of this to anyone before except for a couple of very close friends. Nevertheless, things need to come out eventually.

What with all this going on in my life, I was pissed off with being a lone warrior. I needed some friends around me who thought the same as me and who were as angry as I was. Anger is not something to be taken lightly. As Aristotle wrote in The Nicomachean Ethics, 'Anyone can become angry - that is easy, but to be angry with the right person, to the right degree, at the right time, for the right purpose, and in the right way - this is not easy'.

I did not want to be angry with blameless individuals anymore. The people I was fighting did not share my views or my anger. So why fight them? It became pointless and made me feel pathetic and like a bully. Sometimes it was something out of nothing, sometimes it was war, but it all became pointless.

September 2007

West Ham v Arsenal

The Under 5's had started the day early in the City. They were evading the 'Old Bill' for obvious reasons. The majority had tickets for the game, some only left the house because they were on a promise from Arsenal that they would repay the Under 5's for turning up, firm handed and taking the piss over Highbury Fields the previous season. The lads were meeting up in The Crosse Keys, which is a grotty Wetherspoons pub at Bank in the City.

The boys sat and waited for a call for a good few hours. Contact was made days previously, but today the contact had dried up. Arsenal Youth had bottled it; it seemed to the Under 5's.

Only 2 weeks previously, Arsenal had a major result against Tottenham's youth lads over Kings Cross. Arsenal Youth had been making a slight name for themselves from the previous season. Arsenal had been a pretty much defunct firm throughout the 90s and into the early 21st Century. They had older heads that would be about, but you never really heard of anything that involved Arsenal. Considering how active they were in the '80's this was a bit of a phenomenon.

With nothing but doubt in their minds regarding today's activities, the Under 5's split into 2 groups. One group with tickets made their way to Upton Park. Another group, which consisted of lads on FBO's (Football Banning Orders) lads and who could not afford to get tickets and the lads, who had tickets but were so pissed off that they had been given the run around, were prepared to miss the match and hold out for Arsenal to find their bollocks and come good on their promise. The lads that were holding out headed towards Liverpool Street. Plotted up in a boozer, the name of which evades me and even with doing plenty of searching, I cannot find any evidence of this pubs existence.

5pm comes and the lads who went to the match had made contact with Arsenals youth. They had told the Under 5's to get to Bethnal Green and they would make a call when they had shaken off the 'Old Bill' and were plotted up in a boozer in Bethnal Green. So, with this the two groups of West Hams Under 5's hung around in Liverpool Street for a couple of hours to let any football related business on the tubes finish up and then headed to The Old George, which wasn't too far from Bethnal Green Tube Station. A couple of the lads were local so they knew the area like the tops of their dicks.

After a few hours they got wind that there was another group of about five younger West Ham lads drinking in the Camel, which is a walk back up the way they'd come down Bethnal Green Road, down to Roman Road and into Globe Road. So The Under 5's were looking to be 25 handed and yet again waiting on a phone call from Arsenal to confirm they had shaken off the Old Bill and or got into the Bethnal Green area.

It is probably a good time to point out that the Under 5's had successfully managed to avoid the Old Bill detection all day by purely staying out of their usual haunts. Arsenal met up first thing in the morning at the pub they meet in at every home game, and every London derby game. So they were obviously going to get wrapped up with the Old Bill early doors. Nonetheless, while on route to the Camel, Arsenal finally made contact. By this time, it was getting on for 10pm and they confirmed that they were in the area and that they were in 'The Hare' on Cambridge Heath Road, which was only about 10 minutes walking distance. It was decided that there would be two lads sent up to take a look at Arsenals numbers. Upon walking past the pub on the other side of the busy road it was apparent Arsenal had a good-sized mob of lads in the boozer of around 20-30, as agreed.

While one of the lads was on his phone outside the boozer, he recognized one of the spotters from the previous season at Highbury Fields. He called out and met the lads over the road and he said they were there and they were ready when West Ham was. A shake of hands and the spotters returned to The Camel and gathered the Under 5's outside the pub. If you walked down Roman Road and over the cross roads past Bethnal Green station, you can walk on the other side of the railway lines down Poyer Street and Clare Street, undetected from the bustling streets of East London's Saturday night. With 25 young lad's hell bent on a spree of violence it made more sense than to walk down the main road.

The group split up into two or three groups numerous times because of piss stops and certain lads wanting to be at the front. These were all hungry young lads who had been waiting around all-day and felt like they had been fucked about a lot. As you come up to Hackney Road there's a train bridge and a row of shops just before 'The Hare'. As the lads had just pop out of from under the train bridge mob handed, one of Arsenals lads was outside the boozer and was clearly on the lookout and despite that, he was captured with his pants down. This was because they probably did not know the streets like the lads and expected to see 20 odd lads from a mile off, down the Cambridge Heath Road.

Suddenly the Arsenal pile out onto the street down the side of the boozer, which is a tiny little street called Hare Road. Holding the pub was of absolutely no interest to them and as it was not one of their usual haunts, so they had nothing to defend and I suppose they knew that West Ham were not going to try and attack it or put the windows through. This line of thought worked for both sets of lads as they were now on both the street and charging into each other. The Arsenal lads had come out with bottles and glasses and were raining them down onto the young West Ham mob. All West Ham could do was wait for the hail to stop and then charge Arsenal and back them deep into Hare Road. The Arsenals lads were dropping like flies but they were picking themselves up as quickly as they were going down. At one point, they even backed West Ham off to the top of Hare Road and almost into the oncoming traffic of the Cambridge Heath Road.

West Ham gathered themselves and prepared to go in again when a bottle came flying from one of the lads and down into the mob of Arsenal only about 20 yards away. The bottle landed square on the bonce of one of Arsenals lads and within what seemed like 2 seconds, his face was covered in blood as if it was something out of a film and the blood just poured down his face in one sweep like a sheet red silk had covered his face. He did not seem too happy and swiftly retired to the back of his mob to feel sorry for himself.

With that, it seemed that Arsenal were a bit pissed off and made a sudden charge into West Ham trying to push them further into the road, but it was like they had hit a brick wall as the West Ham were tired of fucking about at this point. One last surge into the opposing firm and Arsenal literally had no back foot to go on and they were getting fucking battered. Arsenal's lads were littering the street outside the boozer and even the Landlord came out asking West Ham to give em a break, saying, "They've had enough, you've done 'em." On hearing this, one of West Hams lads told him to get back into his pub before he was slashed with a broken bottle.

For interfering, one of the lads picked up the Landlords advertising board with his 'watch live football here' written on it which was chained to the wall (well it was until it got ripped out the wall) and it was launched into Arsenal lads knocking a few over and backing a few more off. With this West Ham seized the opportunity to steam into Arsenal again punching them back into Hare Road once again. The advertising board was once again was picked up and thrown onto the Arsenal lads who were on the floor. It was not so much to do them more injury but as a warning to them to stay where they were. They did not get up after this. A couple was seen trying to use their mates legs to pull themselves up but they were like baby giraffes with their legs all gangly. One lad looked like a baby taking his first steps and his legs were completely bowed!

There was no remorse or sympathy as the Under Fives were not letting them off and continued to charge knocking more to the ground and backing more down the Hare Road. It seemed like an hour, but was probably only a matter of something like ten minutes (a result itself in terms of football violence these days). The onslaught had to be cut short there as the Old Bill had been called and there were three meat wagons scattered around the 50 lads from both sides. The only difference was that the Arsenal had ended up on the floor of course.

A lot of West Ham jumped on trains at Cambridge Heath Road Station or jumped on buses. They arranged to meet up in Plaistow. They arrived in dribs and drabs and everyone recalled their views on the fight as well as what they had just seen. One of the lads managed to walk all the way to Whitechapel Tube and round the houses to Plaistow, unbeknown to him, with someone else's blood all over his face.

After a couple of phone calls to Arsenals boys, it became apparent that they were not too impressed with the Under 5's result, claiming they had brought older lads with them and claiming they had 50 lads and various other bollocks. The fact was that West Ham had out classed Arsenal and they just could not take the shame. Well, they had done the infamous Tottenham Youth only 2 weeks before. So they couldn't have been done by West Ham's Under Fives, surely not eh. It was soon revealed, reluctantly by Arsenal that three of their lads were in hospital and two had been arrested. West Ham soon noticed that they were a man down and it became evident that one of the lads was also banged up.

Until this very day, Arsenal still claim that it was West Hams older lads that turned up that night in Bethnal Green, but anyone who knows anything will know that West Ham's old heads won't leave Plaistow to go to Bethnal Green for a bunch of Arsenal kids. In fact, it still the case that Arsenal did nothing to redeem themselves other than turning up 2 nights before we played them in Dagenham and then calling it on. The mind truly boggles.

D.W

Looking back on this and many conversations I have had with Dean, I have thought if it is better to have loved and lost, or lost knowing there is some one out there that could have been more in someone's life. The families we have all found at football helps us maintain a sense of belonging and are the reason for the day-to-day hurdles we all call life.

West Ham Away

J. P

Another story and experience comes from a close pal of mine at West Ham. This short story in my opinion shows the closeness and friendship that has been gained at both home and away games. Here is another example for your own.

"I have always had great pride and passion being a West Ham fan and this night in Palermo just endorsed that feeling as we were massively outnumbered but stood together as a group.

When challenged with intimidation and defeated the Italians top firm Palermo on their own manor, I doubt any other team in Europe could or would have followed our example.

This adventure started with a flight from Stanstead airport, which was packed with hammers supporters who were all in good spirits. Even the air flight attendants joined in on the fun and sang a few songs including bubbles. As soon as we all landed and passed customs, we were greeted by taxi drivers with attitudes and vastly inflated prices. We checked into our hotels, and went to the square in Sicily where all the West Ham was in a boozer. Many of the usual faces were there. Just as I was about to put my lips to a glass of larger, it started. Someone shouted "They are coming they are here the Palermo's boys." Italy's top firm wanted the scalp of England's most notorious traveling army. This may have been their wish but it was not going to happen without a fight. They were at least 1000 coming in from all corners of the square and they were launching flares, missiles, bottles and bricks. West Ham was 250 - 300 handed and I personally felt like Michael Caine in the film the Zulu. This was not the usual battle that was going to happen, as these Italians were well organised and must have planned this in detail after they drew West Ham in the competition. My own personal view on West Ham fans are that they are not liberty takers, nor do they ever attack anyone who did not want to fight and only went for the people who wanted trouble or violated their rights or attempted to intimidate them. This was an attempt to intimidate in my opinion, and there was only one way of dealing with intimidation and that is fight or be destroyed. All the West Ham stood together and then charged at the 1000 Palermo. As per usual, the most feared and dangerous firm Italy had to offer dropped their weapons and ran for their lives. They then came back with more flares, bricks and bottles. This battle went on for over an hour and under no circumstances would Palermo's firm stand and fight toe to toe with West Ham as they knew the outcome would have been a West Ham victory. We even came under fire from citizens at high level throwing bricks and bottles down onto us and finally the local police rounded everyone up outside the main boozer and made us all get onto buses. When the buses drove through the town, more bricks bottles and missiles were thrown through nearly all the bus windows. We were taken to an army base and were kept there for over 5 hours. About 80 West Ham were arrested and unfairly in my opinion as they were only defending themselves when confronted and violated by the Italians. On the day of the game all West Ham met in the same boozer and this time they were 500-600 handed with all the faces there as always. Approximately two hours prior to the game, we all walked through the town towards the stadium. The local police stopped all traffic and all local Sicilians came out to view this unbelievable march to the home of Italy's top firm in the home of the Cosa Nostra. Even the local major came out, was hostile as well and aggressive. He was whacking West Ham with a large truncheon. I will not ever say who finally cracked and through him in a bush, however he deserved it in my opinion. When we got near the ground it all started again this time it was not only Palermo's firm, but also local gypsies who were tooled up to the eyeballs with mallets, baseball bats and kosh's. Yet again, the West Ham army charged at them and the battles started all over the place on a large open wasteland. This was like a battle in the film Last of the Mohicans (Daniel Day Lewis). The Italian gypsies had planned this and attempted ambush us, which was unsuccessful I am pleased to say.

West Ham lost the match 3-0 on the night, which was 4-0 on aggregate with well over 3000 West Ham fans attending the match. Just over 3 weeks later Newcastle United which is known as 'The Toon Army', played at the same venue. They only had 50 fans at the ground after seeing and reading about the battles of Palermo. It is my own personal opinion, but I think West Ham United has the most passionate supporters in Europe and this trip just confirmed my opinion once again.

Chelsea

Now when you say the name, you are automatically talking about a sizeable mob. Being that I also lived in Chelsea country most of my life I would say they had fair numbers. Both my little urchins of brothers were Chelsea, did not bother me, they had to support someone and if it was not going to be West Ham (still can't figure out why they didn't) then I suppose Chelsea it was. One thing I noticed with this lot from the West was that they always had a decent sized mob even when they went away. They also boasted a top boy in each generation and had some half-decent books written. These books never really hit the film scene to the same degree of another said top firm! Is it that Football factory boasted a Chelsea theme, but so did it carry a Millwall theme as well? It is a good job West Ham's lads were there to carry the flag!

OK, Junior had his team, no worries happy days. So as I have mentioned a decent amount of books. I have read 'em all and nice to see them give credit to other firms, including the top firm in the country, I am going to' throw it in there! OK, it is biased, but I am sure you would be the same way if you were in there.

Chelsea, Chelsea Junior's team! I think he really was a Chelsea boy, simply because most of his mates were. Jun' always liked his mates and he had a load of 'em, but never swayed with the influence of me or a few of my pals. He was a loyal fella' and would stick by his mates and those closest to Jun' knew he could be blinded by his loyalty. I honestly think he also supported them because I was West Ham, the little shit! Yet, that is what makes brothers. As much as boys will have their difference of opinions, they will always be brothers. The colour of a shirt does not change your bloodlines. So you're here for the naughtiness aren't ya'? No! So let me ask you, do you buy the newspaper just to read your horoscope or do the crossword? Like fuck you do! You see the front page, 'Hooligans' and wallop! You are in like flint pal, of course you do. Chelsea hit the front page, more than once. Even in recent events, it is said the fans get a bit 'noisy'. The little sods even came top of a chart bless 'em.

With the Premier leagues release of the 'behavior of fair play acts of 2007/2008', Chelsea fans topped the naughty list. Moreover, they have certainly shared the headlines in the days of my brother's younger years and my days of footy and what went along with it. Now let us 'ave it right, Chelsea did have some rivals. Along with some other football firms Chelsea's football hooligan element made their mark in history in the social event we call football and in turn claimed a place in football hooligan history. With other firms like the 'Chelsea Headhunters', was it liked or hated to receive the notoriety about firm. With harsh punishments being dealt out by the powers and administration of the Thatcher era, what was once a planned and well-orchestrated event by the firms most passionate members became a hard lesson to be learnt if any of the firm's members were caught in the act. Now the fella' I had the chance to talk to came by the recommendation of one of my own and this was as good and solid as far as I was concerned.

Now to touch on the lengthy 'investigation' and what was pursued in terms of his punishment was a joke. It was an insult to the person even having to read what surrounded the whole thing. I will not take away from what was written by the man; as his book is spot on. It shows, in each and everyone's opinion involved or around the 'element' of the time, that this man was a 'scape goat', but we will get to that in a bit.

If there was ever a case of injustice and a blatant stitch up it was with Jason Marriner. It was like those involved in the same practice or like-minded fans you would take the good with the bad, but this was a total fucking liberty in what was known as the lie of the year (or 6 in terms of Jason's experience).

Much like my late brother and in fact most of my footy pals, Jason accepted the outcome as best he could. With me, and again a shared opinion is if you do the crime be prepared for the time. However even a saint would have sworn like a sailor. Six fucking years for a total fit up. Frustration is looking at it lightly! Wrong uns get found guilty and get less. If its time and a chat I could do with from someone that has dealt with an unfair hand it is Jason.

Jason is a likeable person who is full of banter and energy in each, and every conversation. In the days of old, there was less chance of a word as the rivalries where still part of the game. This certainly would have been the case here. Jason had long retired from his terrace antics, but this did not make him any less of a fan. My questions were certainly welcomed here as Jason had been fitted up royally, but simply rolled with the punches. He clearly displayed an 'it is what it is' attitude. I have seen many people completely come off the rails in similar situations, and I honestly believe the powers to be were expecting that with Jason.

When I heard of the lengthy sentence Jason received, I like many, thought it was down to one of two reasons. He was either involved in heavier circles than football hooliganism or the old scapegoat routine which was another example of Thatcher's iron fist against troublemakers. As it turned out it was the later, but with lies being the main ingredient. Anyone will tell you this extreme punishment and the new measures in place were the worst thing that could have been introduced. Anyone with half a brain will see this as not a way to stop fighting at football as it will heighten both the need and necessity to inflict as much damage as possible in as short amount of time, and simply try not get caught. This was another clear example of people trying to involve themselves in something that they could just not comprehend. To put it into perspective, just because I can walk into a restaurant and order a meal does not mean I know how to run the place. Anyways, the lies videotape and fabricated 'evidence' were enough to land Jason a lump of porridge and a greatly unfair amount at that! I have been told, for legal reasons, I'm not allowed to mention names or incite any malice or ill fate towards a certain reporter, but out of sheer principle I'll simply say McCunt, McLiar, McWatch your back prick!

The thoughts sitting with Jason from this prison term must be something I could draw from. Again, Jason is a liked person and being that there was 'history' and rivalries between West Ham and Chelsea, I decided to see if there was a chance that I would be able to meet up with the fella. The wonders of modern technology and a simple phone call later, I was set up for an evening around the man's home.

Now there is a lot of this and that going along with the myths around football and some of their 'fans'. One common story was that the Chelsea's Headhunters was an all-racist affair! Combat 18 and right wing and Jun' was of mixed race. With that being the case, if you have ever been to Chelsea or any of the away fans gatherings and still say racist, then I have a different opinion and so would many others too!

Admittedly in the '70's and early '80's there was a prejudice against certain minorities, but I'd just say look at some of the firms and fans up North and their opinion in comparison to the attitude of the South. Fuck me, it didn't matter what firm or team you represented, you could be in the same clobber and singing the same songs from the North and they'd still have issues with you if you was anything darker than Eskimo white. Typically when people talk, you'll hear 'oh this black bloke this or Chinese fella that, but it means no more or less than you will hear that fucking Northerner' and 'those fucking Southerners'. Jason Marriner seeing my brothers photos and having the support for this book, as well as me knowing some of the 'fans' at Chelsea knew that this opinion of hate against mixed race, black and the like was simply bollocks! I cannot think of an easier way of saying it than that. It was not racially motivated; it was another team's colours or team's name that motivated. Select a negative quotation or label something in a way to create dislike to a group, and you will sell a story. It worked for Hitler when he needed the support of his own! It was just another excuse for the media to slam anything and everything associated to the way of Jason Marriner. Jason was a smashing fella' who made time for me in a way that welcomed the efforts needed. Like I said, I was given a couple of options for a Chelsea 'word', and Jason was it. He was sound as a pound and if he was not blue, he could have been anyone. It did not matter though for one simple fact that I was welcomed in this man's house. Prior to my arrival and invitation at Jason's, he knew I was claret and blue and I would not change in the presence of a former top face from Chelsea. He even invited mine and Jun's other brother James around being that he's Chelsea too. A little protest from James, as he had a pal around at the time, "Ah, fuck it, mate, bring your pal too" was the word from Jason. Jase is a good man who loves football, plays football and he even has good to say of others team's players. He is in it for the love of the game. If you ever sit with the man and talk about football, you should be prepared for a fucking good laugh and some history lessons, as Jason knows his stuff.

Jason made the headline news for all to believe and was the digest on the facts on the inside scoop on the football hooligan. A naughtiness and mischief go along with the traits of the hooligan. Jason will be the first to admit to his exploits on the terraces, but this is not something new. What some would have said is a turning point in a now family friendly game, have surely missed the dates and facts of football and the fans of the past. It has been a game that has been banned by none other than the Kings of our great land. Football is a sport that has had so much commercialism rammed down its throat. This was once a working person's affordable game, but it is fair to say that the family and scarf wearing fans right through to your terrace trouble maker that was this all really just a ploy to control the income of our beloved sport and squeeze a few more quid out of us all. Not to incriminate anyone, but in times of the 'naughty bunch', not once did I ever see a scarf or non-hooligan ever included in the 'mix'. This in fact was sneered upon as weak or bullying. However, for the non-educated and the guessers of the hooligans it was just an excuse. This is a shared opinion of Jason and many others in an effort to make a platform for the 'bad ones' in football. This referred to certain organisations that made a 'product' of Jason as a scapegoat. Give yourself half a chance and half a thought, and ask how many times something has happened. You read about it or hear about it later from a third party and think 'fuck me that is not what happened at all'. My favorite is when I have overheard a 'journalist' speak of the standard make-up of a hooligan. 'They are a terrifying bunch who are all drug dealers and out of work anti socialists.

They are thieves and the dropouts of society and all come from single parent families'. One of the best statements is 'the tattoo, oh yes they have to have one of those'. Great entertainment that was, but it is this absolute crap which put Jason away for 6 years. I do not have to defend Jason as he can do that for himself because he is a smart fella'. I have time to sit and talk with anyone on our great sport. I might not be able to give you every player's name and time they played for my team but, I'll not be the sort to sit by and give a gentle clap and a little 'yeah, nice pass', and a little nod in appreciation when that piece of leather hits the back of the net. It is my god given right to scream and let you know that I am a fan and shout, "blinding fucking effort, pal." You want reserved then go and play Tiddlywinks! Right, I have made my point, or at least shared an opinion and I am not alone in this. Football comes with a price. It has fans, and some are good, some are noisy, some are troublesome but they are all fans though. It is not for me to discriminate on the colour of a man's skin or their choice or 'style' of fan, and for those about to jump out of their imported IKEA arm chair and say 'but not all fans have to be violent' well again I never witnessed a football fan get involved unless he wanted to. You have to look passed a stereotypical image presented to you to at least understand the reasoning why these 'fans' act in a way to cause aggro'. I will make one last point and move on. In the animal kingdom, three sub species of animal kill or harm for fun. Humans we know, because we have just to read the bloody paper. The other two that we have a great deal of affection for are chimps and dolphins. (See, I'm a bit of an educated fella', so be careful how you accuse the once supposed drug dealing, out of work anti socialist tattoo sporting and supposed uneducated hooligan)!

Jason Marriner, former Chelsea Headhunter. My first impressions were that he was passionate about footy and honestly if he was not a footy lad he would be a standup comedian. He would be the first fella to buy you a pint and he is open and sincere. One of the things that still impressed me was that he did not hold a grudge! Many men would, if they had 6 years of their life taken away from them. In fact he just bloody shrugged it off. So come on, you wanted to meet this evil thug didn't ya? Well, I am not one for believing the press as I know how they work. Like most lads though, the plan is to sit and reminisce about some fun and troubles of the past. So we'll pop over to Jason's house and have a chat, with the evil tattoo sporting terror of the 80's and 90's, and of course Jun's team leader.

The evening's fun and games started on route, and if recorded would have made a classic comedy. Picture this. I had Jason on the other end of my brother's friends mobile (cheers, Tel). It was not the clearest reception to begin with but Jason was trying to give me directions to his place and my brother James was insisting that we had the fucking windows down on the car at 9 o'clock at night. We were screaming around London in a little girly car (sorry Tel'), and I was sitting in the back and trying to read the road signs in the pitch black. The car winging along at the horrific speed of at least 60mph, and it was bloody struggling at that. I could not see a thing and both of the little shits in the front were more concerned with what C.D was playing and were missing every turn we should have taken. Jason was trying to hear me and I was calling out a dozen road names at a time with Jason saying 'What was the name of that road? Slow down ya' nutta'. We then went back to at least half of the roads I had called out in turn to hear Jason then saying, "Oh no, that's not it. Keep going down that road you called out about 5 minutes ago." On top of this, we had an endless supply of winging from the girls in the front of the car, that we should have been there by now, and these little shits wonder why I nearly clumped the pair of them!

Eventually we arrived at chateaus Jason Marriner. Now, one of my own and a close friend to both Jason and myself had told me that Jason had a wicked sense of humor. When I said to both my brother and his pal to behave and show manners as we was in another man's house, I think I set the pair or at least James up for a disaster. No sooner had Jason welcomed us in his place when he saw James and welcomed him with a "Fuck me you need a few more burgers mate!" Now James is as thin as a broom handle, so with this, I just rolled about the gaff. Jason is just one of the lads, treats you like a pal in the pub and all the laughs that go along with the normal routine that would normally unfold with a bunch of mates out for a beer or two. "Drinks all round and make ya' self comfy, boys" was the overall welcome.

All around chateaus Jason Marriner is football memorabilia covering different players and events. Like I said, he is a real football fan and even as we chatted he got in a lot about football and opinions on the sport. Not all Chelsea stuff either and he gave credit and insight to players that covered different football eras. I had a list of things I wanted to cover with Jason and each question, like all those people involved I let Jason read and say ya' or nay to.

Jason just wanted to do anything he could do to help the book. (Oh, and I did look under the bed and behind the curtains for that scary mindless racist thug that the media portrayed, but could not find him, so I guess he had popped out to the shops)!

Jason was originally from the same 'neck of the woods' as my brothers and me and that is West London. This created some conversation about shared neighbourhoods, although his family was from south London (not a Millwall fella', could have been an interesting chat!) Now if you were to talk about Chelsea, the names of players, some history and the like would come to mind. To the lads of London, and even further afield, namely some rival firms and the name Jason Marriner would eventually crop up. This was to me a prime time to ask a very passionate football fan what was and what is Chelsea?

J.M- "Well back in the day when it was proper supporters who were old school, it was good. There was the 'fun factor', not as it is now. A lot of the fun in the crowds has been taken away. Now look I'm not a smoker and can't fucking stand smoking, but if you go to watch your beloved team you should be allowed to have 'an in and out', you know what I mean! Now you cannot stand up you have to sit down. I mean I'll give you a prime example at Chelsea, I've just come off a ten year ban at Chelsea and I was at the game and I saw a fella' selling Benedict rolls. I told him he was at the wrong gaff and that Tottenham was thirty miles that way mate. I mean, what happened to cheese and tomato? What happened to ham sandwiches, what happened to hamburgers? But, let me tell ya', he had a line as long as the milk rounds. Then I thought he's doing something right is this geezer, you know what I mean! That is how the times have changed. I mean yeah, Chelsea is a good side now and they win trophies in this that and the other. I mean I prayed for it as a kid as they were my life as a youngster. If you want me to be honest, I would have the old times of standing on the terraces, cunting each other off and having a laugh. Not necessarily, the football violence as that obviously went hand in hand, but you know; now there is nothing at all. There's no atmosphere there."

Now what come next is clearly the passion and flare that your mate and mine are famous for. Jason shows his humor and a laughing side that is without question, what got him put away by lies and miss interpretation of how any lad from that era that would display his passion and pride for his team, his players, and his voice.

J.M- "The other day I saw this geezer and a bird holding hands and they were walking to the game! I said where was you in 1982 with Millwall ya cunt! I even questioned it and then was told that he loved his bird. I told him I love my mum but I never took her!"

I see the funny said of it now and I am sure in the days of windy terraces, with the rubber food disguised as overpriced burgers and the madness just made a Saturday afternoon. Now the reason, yes the reason that a good few papers are sold and the name Jason Marriner helped fuel a 'product' for all to criticize, was that I wanted Jason's story on the name The Chelsea Head Hunters.

J.M- "Well in the '80's everyone adopted a name for their lot. You know what I mean. You had Millwall with The Bushwhackers, the C.B.L had the Cold Blow Lane and West Ham had The I.C.F. To be honest, I don't know who come up with the name but it was a blinding name and whether you like or dislike a team, I do like the names as it gives them a bit of character you know. The I.C.F were called the Inter City firm because they traveled on the Inter City and the names were good. So anyway, we adopted the name and brought it to another level."

Different areas of the country drew different fans from areas further afield than the walking distance fans. The Cockney reds were Manchester United's following from London for example, but we have some blinding teams especially one in London. So why the fuck would you travel all the ways up there mate! What lead Jason to Chelsea? Like most, the influence and camaraderie of a pal or family member and the typically father and son relationship was the norm.

J.M- "It was my dad. My dad was Chelsea, so you know the man you love and respect and look up to. I think every kid should follow the father's example." (I was thinking where's the Journalist that made that pseudo intellectual claim that all hooligans came from single parent families. Total dog shit, right!)

My opinion, my thought and most of all something my brothers and I would talk about a lot is this. Being part of the football culture, football and what went along with it; I rarely saw any other sport that boasts such a rich avenue of history. Even years after the supposed closure of the firms around the country, football hooliganism is still a much talked about subject as the players and the clubs are. Did Jason agree?

J.M- "Yeah totally and if I'm being honest it's taken them 35 years, but I believe the Old Bill have won. I mean I have just come off a 10-year football ban, right. My ban was a little bit of a joke ya' know. It was stated that I was not allowed within a mile and a half of Chelsea's ground. So when I got sentenced, I asked the Judge if I going to be resentenced as he'd just told me I'm was allowed within a mile and a half of the ground. That meant if Chelsea were playing at home and I was being put in Wandsworth Prison, I would be breaking the law every time they played at home."

Again, I was treated to a great line that cracked a laugh and a smile (Jase, mate. Consider stand-up, you would be a belta!).

J.M- "Now, I'm on a worse ban as I recently got nicked in the game between Chelsea and West Ham and I got into an argument with some fucka'. Now in parts of South London some can't speak a word of English. Me, I get one that is fluent, so bang I am nicked, and it's not even football related. So the deal is now I'm not allowed in the town, the city, the borough, and the district, four hours before the game and six hours after the game. I'm not allowed within 2000 meters of wherever Chelsea's playing and, I'm not allowed to enter any sporting event!"

We had a chat about 'what the fuck is going on, but you can build and come to your own conclusion. Mine is this, you get these nonces and cunts walking about prowling the streets on innocent kids and they are on less of a ban, but that is only my opinion though!

Both Jase and I got patriotic here NOT racist! We have a chat about 'fairness' and a topic that is discussed around the corner, with mates and around the world and it is this. You have a protest march, a demonstration against English soldiers fighting to protect our freedom and rights and people are allowed to cover their faces. You go to football match with your covered face with a scarf and you will be arrested for conspiracy to commit affray. A bit of good ol' J.M, humor is thrown in as he really has a positive and funny look on a lot of crap in the world.

J.M- "Well I was just protesting against Tottenham!"

Here again, I give a laugh. I add that every English lad's right is his to football as that is a religion to us.

J.M- "If I'm being totally honest football and football violence is a religion to me. It's the best drug in the world and it is a religion!"

Football, the fantastic fucking game of football, English lads breath it, love it. It is born and bred in us and football is all around us. Something you grow up listening to and being a proud part of a country that invented the game. For my brothers and me it was boxing too, but let us have a chat with Jason about, if it was not football then what would have cured his passion for in terms of a second sport.

J.M- "I can't see past football. It is in your fucking blood. Look, if you cut me I'll bleed fucking blue, if I cut you I'll see claret and blue. It is just the way we fucking are."

Here we come to make a synchronised statement confirming hundreds of years of passion and making.

J.M- "It's part of who we are and our identity."

You watched the telly and you have seen what was 'made' in terms of a 'view' on Jason Marriner and his terrace antics. It may have been a sensitive subject but I believed some people are made scapegoats for the football hooligan era. One politician said 'We need to make an example of these people'. I feel that some paid the price for the collective! It is unfair that someone nicks some sweets from Woolworth's and a fella across the county does the same and gets my deserved punishment as well as his, don't ya' think? What were Jason's thoughts and feelings?

J.M- "To be truthful, I'm one of these fella's that believes that if you play with fire, you're gonna' get burnt. What they did and how they did it was outrageously wrong! I was offered 20 kilos of cocaine, 20 stolen cars and more and I said no! They even went as far to take a friend of mine out, wined and dined her. She is just a pal but she is switched on and they're started to ask her all sorts of questions about me. They even offered me a contract with their supposed courier company as they had a fleet of cars that were also supposedly bringing in all the dope. I owned a tire company so I gave them a price and got the contract. Why wouldn't I as I had a straight business. Now when I was in prison, I knew a brass monkey (Junkie), a smack head. He told me a story that he was with some 'Cozzers' who were also doing gear. He thought they were sweet, served them and got nicked. So the point of my story is this, it happens to people every day of the week, but mine wasn't the Old Bill it was journalists! Now I will say this. When they did me I wasn't that active anymore. Those days had been over really. Yeah, I used to turn up at Tottenham, West Ham, good cup games and some Stoke away. You know, boom-boom good day and have a good crack. Now, I am asked this question a lot about this MacIntyre and this is it, what I've been told is the best answer I could give. I hope he has twins both are blind and keep bumping into each other."

I am pissing myself and so is everybody in the room. It was London humor at its finest (I hope there is an agent reading this, as he'll give the likes of Jim Davidson a run for his money).

J.M- "I mean the bottom line is that they are not allowed to ask leading questions. I mean, we absolutely slaughtered them in court and we won the case. Make no mistake about that."

Then Jason made a comment that reinforces a statement I had made to some pals and the thought that I carry to this moment.

J.M- "Look, people ask me about this MacIntyre. He doesn't bother me in the slightest and I don't give a fuck about him. They drive themselves mad about that. This is my thinking though. All the time he lives in my head rent free, I'm not getting a pound note! So he's not living in my head for nothing it's as simple as that!"

Jason still has his love for the game. You sit with the man and can talk about fucking Eskimos playing the game and he'll tell ya' about their game of football. He's an ambassador for the game. He knows the game. He breathes, eats and was bred for the game that we call football. What is it like for Jason after all these years and after what many attempts people would say they tried to take away his game from him?

J.M- "It is still 3 fucking points. I think though, as you get older you accept defeat a little bit better, probably because you are older and wiser as well as having more responsibilities. I mean I'll give you a prime example. I was with a couple of our top lads that didn't go to Moscow for the cup final. I got to Chelsea to watch the game by two o'clock in the afternoon and by this time I was like John Wayne looking for his horse, you know what I mean. I am half lagging. I tried to pace myself and I'd had a good light ale and I do remember it. I mean Ballack, proved he is a world-class player and took the piss out of Man-United's mid-field. I honestly thought they, by right should've won the game, but having said that Man-United won. I will say this right here and now that I honestly believe Man-United are the best team in the world, not in the country in the fucking world! I have my opinions about football and feel very strongly about my football. I mean, when Chelsea lost the cup against Man United, we were in Chelsea watching the game in a boozer across the road from our normal spot. Well, there were some in there smashing the place up. They were not from there and likely never to come back, and I heard they got it. I mean that is our front room. Now back to the defeat, I mean I think we deserved to win and I honestly do think we deserved to win.

When we lost 6-0 to Rotheram and I remember that Tuesday night was pissing down with rain as I do the Champions League, you know!"

Football has changed no question about it. Ask anyone that was there in the '70's and '80's and even the first part of the '90's. The whole face of what was once a working mans sport. The lads waiting for the Saturday to arrive, just trying to get through the endless week, this was painful to some. To seek the excitement of the game and for all to see their heroes to dance about the field with such grace and skill has been lost over the greed and control of the clubs. What did our pal feel about the changed game of football? He was no longer allowed to get into the 'mix', to seek adventure in the way he used to enjoy and allowed himself to express his passion for his mighty blues. How did he honestly feel?

J.M- "You know what, this may sound terrible but apart from me having to hand in my passport and sign in at the police station when Chelsea or England is playing abroad, I couldn't give fuck. But if that had happened to me back in the day then I'd have been devastated and we never used to win! Best we did was winning the second division!"

They are out there; sold a few copies, some I have even heard gloated on the fact that this was the bible (fuck me, you are kidding, must be that journo' again!) about football hooliganism. What did Jason think about the films out?

J.M- "In 'Green Street' I fell asleep. It was not because of any other reason than I was tired. The 'Football factory', I was never in a rush to go out and watch that because I was at the forefront of all of these things. Those films are fictional. Even though they say that, it was based on me and the fact that I had a flower stall and all that. I'll tell ya' though what does fucking annoy me, is this. There's a bit where this fella' burgles this house and he's then on the back of the coach. This one fella' calls his mobile that's been nicked and then there's the bit where he pulls the gun out. I mean, they have always to go one over the top. They should've had real people. Not saying me, just real people in there, you know. At Chelsea, there is no Danny. If you're a respected lad, if you're doing a left, you're doing a left. You know what I mean! It is as simple as that. If you say, we are having a meet at 10 o'clock at Earls Court, then that's where it is and there's no changing it. They just had to go over the top with things, and they should have kept it on the level! Get people that have been at the forefront and that are clued up about it, although they got a bit right. The dressing, this, that and the other, and it's the nearest they've ever come."

I wanted some more on the subject. For a few pals and me 'The Firm' with Gary Oldman was a great start. A London based fella that knew the culture, knew the ins and outs of the scene and surely a better choice than an 'actor'. What was Jason's view?

J.M- "I think if they did a film like that today, someone like Ray Winston would be a good choice. More so, get some people off the street. You know, even kids off the street."

Things have changed also in terms of rivalries. 'Borders' have been broken down and the once 'destruction on sight' has been calmed down. A few pals from other firms have been made in the process. Is there any worth a mentioning?

J.M- "Absolutely, I mean there's Boatsy from Nott's Forrest, Gilly from Wolves, Brains, Tate from Birmingham of course and Steve and Carlton were the West Ham faces. To be honest I know 'em all. They're some good fella's, and at the end of the day, we're all the same, we just support different teams."

A very patriotic fella', Ol' Jason and so should we all be. So here's an easy question. Which comes first, England or Chelsea?

J.M- "I'm very patriotic, love my country and I'm English and proud of it. I'd love to see England win the World Cup and I've been to many a World Cup, and have even been there when some lot came to our hotel to give it. We got our act together though and gave it to them and that's what I'd like to see; England firms together, standing as one when we go abroad."

This thinking outside my home field was defiantly a plus. Jason has a comical and light- hearted attitude with the unfair decision he was giving to live. I gained another valued persons opinion in loss and frustration. I have decided that more outside opinion and experience would not be a bad thing. It was time to put the feelers out and see if I can get some more, if not a little further afield opinion on what has given me resolution and sanity in this situation. I started this chapter with Jason as the theme and obviously so. Finishing, I have got a proud English man that should be in politics, giving the best interests to the St. George flag. This may be interpreted as a site for prejudice but I see pride. I see a man that is proud of his roots and what is involved with that respect is football and being a Londoner. Respect to my mate Jason Marriner who was once a member of the Chelsea Headhunters.

Black Danny

Northerners speak proper English, are you having a laugh? This with the usual stereotypical assumptions by us Southerners, that the only pets kept by those up North of the border were whippets and ferrets. The only drink available would be brown ale, which would be served by a caveman in a flat cap, smoking a pipe with brass band music to march to was also a common belief.

In a conversation with one lad in the confines of our 'city walls', He asked me if Potters Bar was a pub on the way to football match! Such comments will always make me laugh (as humour my friend is just that. It is there to provoke a laugh from the exaggerated or in this case, the assumed and unknown).

These views are typical of the footy lads in London. Well, what would be any less of a thought on the journey to visit the clubs outside the comforts of our glorious city limits of the South? Cold, dreary, wet, damp, and nothing less than an Arctic breeze and a miserable inbred O.B to greet the traveling fan. Different fans hold as many opinions and memories of their own journeys to the desolate north. One thing that does hold is the welcome I always got from Aston Villa's Black Danny aka Danny Brown. Many a conversation held just as much a laugh as the memories we both held for visits of both clubs to each other's respective grounds. "'Ello, Jase! How ya' doing my friend?" was always the start of the conversation with Danny (and yes, they do have phones in that part of the world). Very much a contradiction to my first assumption was that everything North of Watford was cold. With as much love for the game as any lad, Danny was as much for Junior's cause as those North, East, South and West of the border. Over the course of several years I got to know the fella that shared the same amount of passion for the same coloured kit, as Danny was always reminding me who was the true claret and blue, and to hear of Danny's experiences which were very much the same as Junior's. The bullies and ignorant masses are in each corner of both our beloved game and country. The North / South divide is nothing new, nor is there any less bullying from those in question. We are not here to promote one aspect over another, but to share stories, awaken the northbound traveler of at least one known lad and his warmth, and welcome in the land that time forgot.

North of the Border

My name is Danny Brown AKA 'Black Danny' and I am the author of the best selling Aston Villa F.C. book, 'Villains'.

I was born and originally brought up in Gloucester, though I have lived most of my life in Birmingham. I am a black Afro-Caribbean, who was the son of Jamaican immigrants that came to England in the 1950's. I am also British. British culture, values and ways of life are an intrinsic part of my identity, when abroad, I am even more aware of how my 'Britishness' defines me. In Jamaica I am referred to as 'the British guy', black, but British nonetheless. My Brummie accent sets me apart as a 'Brit'. On the other hand, there are Jamaican customs, traditions and pride that run through my veins.

Having spent my entire life in England, I am as much immersed in the British culture as any white British native. I am not particularly different, apart from on the most superficial basis: the colour of my skin; although my two older brothers were born in Jamaica, and have maintained more aspects of the Jamaican traditions than I have. Even so at home, we all speak with an English-Jamaican pronunciation, eat Jamaican food and socialise with other Jamaicans. In spite of this and the fact that my brothers came to England as kids, they still find it hard to adjust when they go home to Jamaica because they have unwittingly, become accustomed to the British ways. Other black British who have decided to go back home to Jamaica or the Caribbean after living in Britain for many years, are realising that they are now much more British than they could ever have imagined.

Britain is full of culture and traditions from the Commonwealth countries, which have been around for well over a hundred years. British customs and traditions are famous all over the world. When people think of Britain, they often think of people drinking tea, eating fish and chips and wearing bowler hats, but there is more to Britain than just those observations. We now have English and British traditions within sport, music and food that are the diverse cultures of twenty-first century Great Britain.

The disappearance of many local British festivals and recreations is down to local councils cost cutting exercises and refusing to fund these events. However, in recent years the popularity of St George's Day appears to be increasing gradually. So much so, that M.P's have been putting the arguments forward in the House of Commons to make St. George's Day a public holiday. The most significant development within the black British culture has got to be the Caribbean Carnivals. Carnival is the most powerful contemporary symbol of the right to mass assemble, eat, drink and dance. The most important one has been held each August Bank Holiday since 1966. The Notting Hill Carnival is the largest festival celebration of its kind in Europe. Every year the streets of West London come alive with the sounds and smells of Europe's biggest street festival. Its survival and growth therefore have a special place in British cultural history.

Reggae music has always been particularly popular in Britain as it quickly emerged from Jamaica in the 1960's. The appropriation of Ska and reggae music by skinheads and Mods and other disaffected white youths in the 1960s and early 1970s was superseded from the late 1970's / 80's by a new generation of working class black and white youths in Britain, who were now going to clubs together and listening to Ska and reggae music. The two Tone genres were named after two 'Tone Records', a Coventry record label that featured bands such as The Specials, Madness and The Selecter. You must recognise that reggae even had an effect on punk music with its politicised lyrics, rebellious attitude and message. In the 1970's, Steel Pulse was an up and coming reggae band from my childhood neighbourhood of Handsworth, which is situated in North Birmingham, home at the time to Britain's largest Caribbean community. Steel Pulse politicised lyrics, musical experimentation and a rebellious attitude that had a far-reaching influence on the black youth from the area, more than mainstream South Birmingham reggae band UB40. Steel Pulse was the only British reggae band that really mattered to followers of reggae music. Steel Pulse's first single was "Ku Klux Klan" (a call for resistance against forces of racism). It was released in 1978 and five months later, their debut album *'Handsworth Revolution'* was released to critical acclaim.

Steel Pulse broadened their national appeal by performing at Rock Against Racism at Victoria Park, East London in front of more than 80,000 fans. Steel Pulse always gave a master class performance in winning over impressionable youngsters of all races with their raw power, their masterful melodies and harmonies. Their energetic and hypnotic stage performance complete with costume changes and white KKK hoods were impressive. When Steel Pulse performed their powerful version of reggae with lyrics based on their Handsworth roots, within just a few beats from the stage would be enough to get you hooked and in the groove. Handsworth has produced some notable popular musical acts such as Joan Armatrading, Pato Banton, Benjamin Zephaniah, Swami, Apache Indian, Rub Turner and Bhangra group B21.

Other significant developments occurred in popular music, with the uniquely British 'Lovers Rock' a reggae soul fusion invented by producer Dennis Bovill, with singers such as Sandra Cross, Carol Thompson and Janet Kay.

British reggae groups like Aswad were innovators of the 1970s and '80s and continued their studio experiments in dub, still influenced by sound systems such as Saxon, Jan Shaka and Coxsone. These sound systems' mobile units of sound engineers, selectors and DJ's are well known for their high decibel output at blues parties.

Hardcore reggae, the powerful dub plates became the rallying cry at Blues Parties. Mixed with the race riots and the Police' new powers to stop and search, although West Midlands finest only seem to be interested in stopping and searching the ethnic minority groups. Things were brewing for trouble – big time! Blues Parties became a significant focus for confrontations between black youths and the Police.

With symbols of Rasta culture and reggae stars such as Bob Marley, Burning Spear and U. Roy whom black kids saw as their heroes, the Police were harassing them on the streets and putting many of the brothers behind bars on trumped-up charges as they could. A very interesting observation of what I suppose The Clash band member Joe Strummer meant when he was describing the extension of the UKs race and class system and how its establishment works.

40 years on and from the investigation that concluded London's Police of being institutionally racist, we have heard a great deal from politicians and the media about the Police bigoted canteen culture. Now canteen culture along with its dogmatic prejudices is still here in its covert format though institutional racism that goes much deeper than just the Police canteen. Racism is inherited by people in power and with their own prejudices, based on insufficient knowledge of others.

Young, gifted and British

Respectfully I feel I have a duty of care and a responsibility to promote to local teenagers of all colour and race (though predominately those of Black/Asian minority ethnicity backgrounds, whom live in the North Birmingham region of the city) that Aston Villa are their local football club, and they shouldn't be supporting any other club but the Villa.

Just like most inner city areas in Britain, Birmingham has a gang crime problem. Many young people do not realise they are in a gang, they will just think they are in a group of friends. Being in a gang is not illegal - only the criminal offences committed are illegal. The problem with street gangs is nothing new even though the media would like us to believe. That it is a new problem that manifests from the importation of American TV shows and street culture. Gangs in fact have been on the streets of Britain pre- the days of the Kray brothers, back in the 1950's and 1960's to the Mods and Rockers of the 70's. Being associated with a gang is not the overall problem, as not all gangs and crews are criminals or Street thugs.

The sublime message is making sure these young boys come together at an early age for the right purposes, not to destroy their community or their identity. For those young men caught up in criminal activities my message is basic. Eventually you will get caught and go to prison. It's inevitable. On the flip side of the coin you could make a list of what of what you want to do with your life and piece it together one step at a time.

Brummies, Cockneys, Scousers, Mancs, Geordies and Yorkies

The Cockney seems to have this concept that any city or town past Watford is NORTH OF THE BORDER. Insults of, 'Don't these northern inbreeds have electricity or running water in Birmingham?' and 'Stone me, lucky if they can get cooked food up there,' plus many more have all been heard in my time you Cockney brats! Though that is not a true geographical concept of the North-South divide, I have never considered Birmingham as either in the North or South as it has always been in the Midlands. Those Cockneys without the geographical intellect to read a basic map tend to forget that the Midlands is a region in its own right and includes Birmingham, Wolverhampton, Leicester, Derby, Coventry and Stoke.

I consider the Midlands to be the heart of England with its cities and towns of great cultural diversity. I find the Midlands accents a lot warmer and friendlier than most regional accents. There are certain accents I dislike, though I could not even imagine being rude to someone simply based on hearing their accent. My accent changes a lot depending on where and whom I am with. I am self-conscious about it because I've found that people treat me differently when I talk with my normal Birmingham accent, though it isn't always wise to talk in my more English / Jamaican patois, which can only be understood by Jamaican Afro-Caribbean people or their first & second generation offspring.

Birmingham: My native accent is from Gloucester, which is much harsher and lazier-sounding to the ears than the nice rural burr of the

Gloucestershire County. I can say that, because I am Gloucester born though Birmingham bred. Gloucester is a beautiful part of England and I am glad I was born there. I first moved to Birmingham at the age of nine, though my Birmingham accent is not that strong. People from outside the region seem disappointed that I do not sound like Barry from 'Auf Wiedersehen, Pet.' and they take the piss with comments such as, "Considerably richer than yow" from Harry Enfield. The likes of Ozzy Osborne, Cat Deeley and Clare Short have helped to make the Brummie accent famous and there are specific words that are typical to this city.

The word 'innit' has been used around Birmingham for quite a while now - but I would say it was originally almost exclusively an Asian thing. It's a mispronunciation of the word "isn't it." The Black Country accent is so different to the Birmingham accent, in the same way that the Geordies and Mackem's accents are dissimilar. The Black Country is also known for its distinctive dialect that differs slightly in various parts of the region. The accents are very broad; in particular hearing words like Walsall mispronounced as War-sall or Wor-sull is hilarious. Overall, I would say it is an inoffensive accent.

In summertime, short skirts in Birmingham are the best. Birmingham women are by far the best dressed in the Midlands, maybe even the UK. I really can't think of a better pastime when it's 30 degrees than to be drinking outside the front of a cafe or wine bar in the Mail Box watching the good stuff walk by, it is very interesting!! Ladies, despite what blokes say to your face, we all think the same thing. Birmingham is famous for its ethnic diversity manifesting itself into scores of communities. This is exactly what makes Birmingham such a great place. I hate to use old sound bites, but it is the diversity of its people, males & females, which makes Birmingham such a strong and unique place. We need the new arrivals, the Asians, the blacks, the whites, the colourful and the eccentrics... They all add their own influences, cultures, styles, skills and wealth and without them we would not be where we are today, which is one hell of a fine city.

London: Most Southern accents can come across as very aggressive. Though the East End people are the salt of London and are true working class, the twang is not too bad, though you would be pushed to get a word in edge-ways. A Cockney is literally a person born within earshot of the bells of St Mary-le-Bow church, in what is now the City of London. However, technically speaking there can be no Cockney's born after 1945 since German bombs destroyed the bells during the second world war. Today the term has expanded to encompass not only those from East London specifically, but from London in general. The latter tends to be attributed to by non-Londoners stemming from their ignorance of the true meaning of the word 'Cockneys'.

The fake rhyming Cockney accents of Luton, Watford and Milton Keynes are just awful and highly irritating. My dilemma is that their efforts are perceived as worse than silence. Just like the MK Dons, no one will take them seriously.

Liverpool: Too much nasal business going on there. A lot of them have very funny personalities. You will need earmuffs because once they start rapping and screaming in a high-pitched voice, they will send you mentally deaf. Right wing toffs and the gutter press, who have never visited Liverpool, usually reinforce the myth of scousers being all criminals.

Manchester: Greater Manchester, the broad accent is a good regional sound, excluding Manc's who jabber on, like glue sniffers. Just listen to the Mancunian Gallagher brothers. Apparently, in America they have to be subtitled, as no one understands a word they are saying. Apart from the fit barmaids on Coronation Street, the show bores the crap out of me. I cannot stand that awful accent, especially that Janice Battersby. She reminds me of someone who has got off the special needs bus and has been promised a cream cake.

Newcastle: Great nightlife and the women are on another level. The Geordie accent has been voted the sexiest in Britain thanks to celebrities such as Cheryl Cole although you will need a translator on arrival.

Yorkshire: Most regions in South & West Yorkshire are fine, though I cannot tell the difference between the accents of Leeds, Sheffield, Doncaster, Rotherham and Barnsley. They sound pretty much the same to me. Other regions in North Yorkshire are awful, places where old farts drink brown ale and talk about fishing and Rugby League.

London's rich, reckless and shameless

What can I say about London's rich, reckless and shameless? A few things have already been mentioned but that is only the tip of the iceberg. I am particularly pissed off with these middle / upper class farts in the City. They really get up my nose. They proliferate in the cities posh areas, turning surrounding neighbourhoods, which were once nice places into lavish real estates. Born and reared in the City of London and other luxurious hamlets now know little about the rest of Britain, but habitually look down on the rest of the country. Thankfully most of these aristocrats are only exclusive to London and do not really saturate the rest of the Midlands regions.

Do not be fooled for one second. Take this from someone who has visited and worked in the borough they call Central London. The streets are littered with dog shit and chip wrappers, which blow around under grey skies. Central London is a region with the highest crime rate for fraud in the UK. Yet the journalists in the media will make you believe that Central London and its luxurious hamlets have become the New Jerusalem, a center of regeneration and Europe's capital.

It is not until you have spent any length of time with this middle / upper class farts that you realise just how false and deluded they really are. They think Chas & Dave has made London the culture capital of Britain as well as thinking that all the government subsidies that bought them the Olympics Games make them the sporting city of the world. They always show up to business meetings over-dressed in Selfridges clothes thinking it will impress the people they are meeting and sadly it makes them look insecure. The middle / upper class toffs are something else. They are so parochial it is unbelievable. Just mention The Midlands or The East End and they will start foaming at the mouth and going mental. It is laughable.

October 6th 2007
Villa Park – Aston Villa 1 West Ham 0

Today is the day I have been looking forward to for months, because today is the day that I am meeting up with my old rival – Cass Pennant. Anyone who was associated with or was involved in football violence over the last 30 years would know who Cass Pennant is, and therefore would have experienced him and 'The ICF'. Cass, is no longer involved in any form of football violence is a respected author and publisher, and following the success of his bestselling autobiography "Cass", he is now involved in the project 'Cass the movie'. The movie will tell the incredible true story of an orphaned Jamaican baby who was adopted by an elderly white couple and brought up in an all white area of London, to how he became one of the most feared and respected men in Britain.

I was thrilled to be offered a part in the movie and I played a convicted prisoner in the scrubs. From what I have seen of the cast, there is a list of stars ranging from 'The Football Factory' to 'East Enders' appearing in the film and even a few of my old sparring partners from yesteryear. One of my mates has a corporate facility at Villa Park and in fairness to him; he has never forgotten his roots and invites as many Villa old lads as he does customers on match days into his box. He invited Cass and me for today's game. Unfortunately, Cass rang about a week before the game to say that he couldn't make it due to work commitments but he would be sending on the sub! Fucking hell!!! Can you imagine the shock waves of delight when I realised whom Cass was sending as his replacement for the day! It was only the Godfather of West Ham football hooligans the legendary Bill Gardner. Bill has been around for a long time and is now retired from football hooligan activity. Bill goes far back to the days of the Mile End boys and is renowned for his one-liner whilst steaming into his rivals, "Good afternoon gentlemen, the name is Bill Gardner." That introduction itself was often enough to provoke sheer terror in his opponents. To this day Bill is still a terrace legend at Upton Park.

Match Day

I had arranged to meet Bill and his son outside Villa Park at the main Trinity Road Stand at 12 noon. Even though I was 20 minutes late, I have a philosophy that when you meet your guests for the first time you keep them waiting for a while. Those 20 intended minutes gave Bill and his son the chance to have a look around Birmingham's first Cathedral, Villa Park and when I did finally turn up, they had a good insight of our proud history and bright future. I approached the Trinity Road Stand, and spotted Bill from the distance. He had his back to me, but I could see he was smartly dressed in a suit, looking like Tony Soprano. I tapped him on his shoulder and as he turned round to shake my hand, I said, "Mr. Gardner, that's the first time I've ever seen your back in 30 years of confrontation." The ice had been broken and not my hand. Bill had an equally warm welcome from the box holder and the rest of the lads. We were drinking a few beers and reminiscing about the good old days. Bill pointed out to us where his firm had entered the Holte End back in the 70's and I asked Bill about the infamous 1980 FA Cup game at Upton Park. He confirmed the story of him being the steward who let the West Ham firm into the Villa end of the ground. Unbeknown to us there was a group of my mate's customers who happened to be West Ham fans in the box with us and they knew who Bill was but at the time nothing was mentioned about his past. He was introduced to them as Bill the West Ham fan; we talked about football and how West Ham stole our club colours nothing else. However, Bill was spotted by other West Ham fans at half time, and even recognised by our very own Dennis Mortimer and it was probably a little embarrassing for Bill having to sign autographs and pose for pictures with fans.

First class hospitality was the order throughout the day with ex Villa player Charlie Aitken presenting Bill with a framed picture that read "Good afternoon Mr. Gardner. The name is Danny Brown; welcome to the home of the real claret and blue," with a caricature of me holding the Villains book. Bill had remarked on the day how much he admired Villa Park and our football legend Dennis Mortimer as a player. What really impressed me about Bill was his understanding and knowledge of the game. It's second to none.

My mate's customers definitely knew who Bill and I were and did not say anything on the day but on the Monday morning emailed him asking how he got Villa and West Ham's top men in his box on Saturday. Deadpan as you like he said we worked in his finance department; me covering customers in the Midlands and Bill in the South of England, who he was having problems with getting payments. They replied thinking what he was saying was true. "Do you have many problems getting paid, now?" He replied, "Not since Danny and Bill went to see them!"

At some point, this story will do the rounds, but whilst it's very funny; Bill Gardner and I are not working in any Finance Department for a very well known Birmingham company. Despite my mate's mischievous sense of humour, I told him politely that the only figures Bill and me are doing are the sales of our books. It was a great day out, first class company, top class hospitality and three points.

The Original Claret and Blue

Despite many hard-fought battles over the years (on and off the pitch), I've got to admit that I've always had a bit of a soft spot for West Ham. This is partly because, in common with many black kids of a certain vintage, Clyde Best was one of my first heroes. At a time when I had cricketers galore to look up to, black footballing role models were a bit less prominent. There were the brilliant Brazilians' of course, but in the days before 24-hour sports channels we only got to see them every four years.

When another opportunity arose, I was one of many eager disciples who wanted to see Edison Arantes Do Nascemento (that is Pele to you) when Santos played a friendly against the Villa in the middle of a power cut. Doug Ellis hired a generator at a cost of £5,000 to get the game on, and the decision paid off as more than 54,000 attended. Much more common for a young black boy hooked on Match of the Day and the Midlands' own version of the Big Match, Star Soccer was the sight of Clyde Best bustling through the uncompromising defenses of the day. If you think the defenders were tough in those days, you should have heard the fans! As well as his undoubted ability, the stick Clyde got from the terraces helped me to relate to him even more. I am all in favour of the 'Kick Racism out of Football' campaign, but I cannot help thinking that the need was greater when poor Clyde was doing his best to brave that abuse! Another point in Clyde's favour was that he was wearing the famous claret and blue, albeit that of the Hammers rather than my beloved Villa, but as every Villain knows and every Hammer should know, B6, Aston, Birmingham, is the home of the original claret and blue.

There are many theories as to how we adopted the colours in the first place. One is that club committee member and founder of the Football League William McGregor, brought down kits from well-known clubs in his native Scotland and specifically Hearts and Rangers. This seems unlikely however, as at the time of his move south; both sides would have been unknown in his native Perthshire. Another suggestion is that Villa took their colours from the decor of local pub called 'The Barton's Arms' and this is exposed as myth by the fact the pub was built in 1901 which was many years after the Villa began wearing claret and blue. It is widely accepted that McGregor did make the decision to adopt the Scottish symbol of the Rampant Lion as the club's badge (the first club in England to do so), and his first design was a black lion on a claret shirt. This, for obvious reasons, proved hard to see, hence the change to a light blue lion and the adoption of claret and blue as the club's colours. The club occasionally experimented with different colours, most notably chocolate and light blue, but settled on the familiar claret body and blue sleeves during the mid-1890s. Then, in the summer of 1899, the story goes that four Aston Villa players at a fair in Birmingham challenged Bill Dove, a sprinter of national repute who was involved in the coaching of the fledgling Thames Ironworks side, to a race. Dove won but the Villa men could not pay the wager so one of them pinched a set of claret and blue shirts from his club (he was involved in the laundry) and gave them to Dove to settle the debt. That is the story of how West Ham adopted the colours of Aston Villa, and why, if you ever venture onto various Villa websites, you will often see the Hammers referred to, somewhat unfairly in my opinion, as 'The Kit Stealers'.

-Danny Brown

Lower league football violence

When you talk of violence, frustration, anger and its origins, people typically think of things that may have been an influence or an experience in their current consciousness or a memory that simply will not budge. Psychological practice suggests that this anger or frustration goes back as far to your infancy, which is long before youths subscribed to a visit to the social gatherings on the terraces.

Therefore, if I was to practice what I preach and find further resolve, then surely a bit of thought should be put into the days on the terraces and where it all began? There were no sponsors or over saturated commercialism. There were no new age plastic upper middle class influence and certainly no chinless wonders allowing their limited over paid country club living knowledge of the working mans sport be a contributing factor in my journey of resolve. Through a mutual pal, I was put in contact with a younger chap that could also invest in yours truly and hopefully place another piece of the much-needed jigsaw into my personal unfinished battle.

If there is anything to be said about football violence and hooliganism, it is that it is universal throughout the entire lower league. It is not just found amongst those that held headlines in the '70's-'90's, but also as far as your Sunday afternoon teams. You can find the competiveness and social structure-questioning gene in all fella's throughout the sporting spectrum. Of course with those in question, took it to a cheekier, higher, less socially accepted level.

They are not household names amongst the premier team's hardcore element, but the hooligan medium that follow Rochdale F.C (the Young Chosen Few) certainly are an active one. As recent as in 2009, the Y.C.F gained the attention of the local press for promoting what is thought to be as active terrace trouble, in the lower leagues hooligan family tree. In the infancy of terrace mayhem of the '70's-'90's, the premier clubs had lads promoting their fun and games around stadiums that were once filled with the lost and forgotten terrace style set-up. With the lack of interest from major sponsors and low attendance crowds, have allowed many lower league clubs to hold a firm grip to the style of stadiums that is often missed by your father and son attendees. Nevertheless, the rawness and character filled terraces, which made way for the price inflated; crowd-controlling' arenas can still be found north of the Border, but not for long though. So while the chance is still there, let us 'ave a word with a lad who's in the infancy of what he believes is a sport worth fighting for.

Everyone played football as a kid

My birth as a football fan came as it does for many kids and none better than the welcome I was given by my family who enacted their roles well. My brother and dad played the parts that many kids allowed their football idols to mold and dictate. They helped the formula needed for any lad to enjoy the fruits of the world's most loved game. Not forgetting another great person in my life, our mum. Many a time she would get us to school early, allowing us to form a team and alliance with our squad. The always untimely and unwelcomed sounding of the school bell only cut short the game we loved for a short time. This was not anything more than a break and allowed me to formulate a dream and goal for the next game. The game became part of my identity as a person, and it would be part of who I am today.

Being a youngster around Rochdale, most of my mates supported the big teams such as your Manchester United's, Manchester City's and Liverpool's, and being at an impressionable age I was dragged into following them as most people I knew. One day, for the better, that all changed. I remember an elderly man walking past me as I was kicking a ball against a wall. He asked me whom I supported. I told him United and asked whom he followed, he replied West Ham. I paused for a second then asked why, and he said it is where he came from. Always support your local team he added. This provoked a thought. I generally checked how Rochdale F.C were doing, and living round the corner from them allowed me to hear the fans singing and the big roar go up when they scored. That night, I asked my dad if we could go and watch Rochdale play, and as a result, shortly after I was converted to a blue heart. I remember it quite well, it was a sunny Saturday afternoon and my Dad, my younger brother, and at the time, his girlfriend came with her two sons to the game. Hull City came to play Rochdale at home. Our ground was a testament to the archaic style of grounds of yesteryear; full of character and as many memories as there was cracks and blemishes in each of the terrace steps, all that once held company with fathers and sons. The atmosphere was electric, accompanied with loudness and excitement, enough to charm any football fan. There were 3 stands for standing fans as Pearl Street was in the process of converting to an all seating stadium. What echoes in my memory is the fact that I lived within a stones' throw of my place of worship, and after the seeing the home grounds of other teams on T.V, I expected our home ground to mirror those too. But thankfully our ground and the terraces within still held real fans, fans that were filled with both individuality their own stories and indented hard working people that all came for a shared common interest, our team.

With the allure of any football ground, the neighbouring housing estates filled with lads flooding the bordering streets, and it was inevitable that there would be some fun and games, but this all came later. The game finished 2-2 and it felt good inside of me as I had gone to watch a live football match, not only that, but I had followed my home town, it made perfect sense. I was around 9 years old when I watched that match, my parents had split and my feeling and wish was to simply play football all the time. During the summer holidays and living close to the ground allowed my brother and me to watch other kids play football at the back of the Pearl Street end of Rochdale's ground. One day a coach walked up to us and passed us some leaflets from the club about the football, and so I got on the football schools. My brother and I went to the soccer schools and at the end of the week, we met all the players, had autographs signed, watched them train and got match tickets to watch them again. The foundations had been laid I was now a full fan. My family's involvement with the game did not stop with my parents'; I even made my Grandma buy me a kit. I was going to games on my own by now and shortly after my brother and Dad started to watch them, as Rochdale was all I ever spoke about. I had watched Rochdale now for about 3-4 seasons, however I could never go to away games, as my family is working class, and we always will be. I do not care about how much money people have and how they would walk around thinking, they have the world at their feet. We are honest hard working people and that quality remains with all those I have as family. I had no income, I was still in school and my dad could not afford for us to go both home and away. My first away day did come along though, and it changed me in a way I never would have imagined. My Grandparents usually asked me who Rochdale F.C was due to play, and when I told them Halifax Town away, they had alerted me to the fact it was not far. I looked on a map and found that it was roughly 30 minutes drive away. I begged my Dad but he could not take me, and like all kids if we never get something we go in a mood. With it being football, and not the usual about wanting sweets etc. my Granddad said he would take me. We got a club coach and we finally got there about 2.45 that afternoon. In a car, it is no problem at all, but these coaches struggled all the way up the hills and as a result, we were nearly late for the start. It was a good day, it was my first away day, it was special for me, and my Granddad, who I do not think had ever been to a football match. We were dropped at the ground and my Granddad and I immediately went straight in, bought a programme and found a place to stand on the terrace to watch the match. It was a completely different experience for me, being away from Spotland for a Rochdale match. The atmosphere was very different. The grounds were as well. The goals behind the net were not roofed at the time, they had a stand that was being built and opposite is what I now know to be the Skircoat Road End. The weather was nice, and when the teams come out it was very noisy. Every time Halifax attacked, there would be a huge roar from around the ground, a really old feel to it. Halifax never found a way through and neither did Rochdale. The game ended 0-0, however something that day caught my eye. Half way through the second half, the game had gone a bit dead, the atmosphere had died down a little then all of a sudden, and we heard a massive chant. Dale! Dale! Dale! Which was coming from the home stand in the Skircoat Road End? All I could see were about 70 men fighting. It went on for several minutes. The police came into the ground and all the Rochdale lads went onto the pitch and were marched back around towards the away stand we were in. It was ruthless! It had an impact on me, it definitely did. There were about 40 of them walking round the pitch and once they stopped fighting, they looked untouchable. All had similar clothing on, were all jumping on each other like they had achieved something, they was buzzing, it was something else.

The next home game I went to, I noticed all these blokes again. All had designer clothing on caps, scarves etc., and sat well away from normal fans. Obviously, I never knew why they did not wear club shirts, but it was all a process that would be unveiled to me. The more home games I went to, the more I noticed them. They kept together like a gang and kept quiet most of the time throughout games whilst other fans were singing. I started to sit close to them. We played Coventry City in the FA cup, the ground was a sellout and I was very fortunate to get a ticket. I noticed as I went to go into the ground that day there was a heavy police presence. A lot of roads had been shut off and fans were being marched to the ground by police. The turnstile I went in was right besides the away stand. The police had formed a line and it all seemed very heated. In the ground, I went in and the first thing I saw was these blokes again to my left. The atmosphere was awesome, electric and every hair on my body stood up. Spotland was bouncing and jumping about, and this time these chaps were loud as fuck. I have never heard anything as loud. It grew on me. Everything that day was perfect. I took my seat behind the goal at the top of the stand, and as the teams come out, the roar from the both fans went up; there was no better feeling at that time of my life. During the game I kept looking over at these men, all their faces were twisting in unison with the 'feel' and 'play' of the game. Their heads were turning from the match to the away stand. The fans were singing all sorts of songs, but my concentration was this unknown army within, and all I wanted to do was join them. Bang! 1-0, we scored just before half time, Coventry were in the championship and we were struggling in league 2, everyone piled down the steps to the corner closest to the away fans and abuse was flying their way. All the Coventry fans were gutted. The second half-begun and we scored almost immediately and went on to win 2-0. Towards the end of the game I went and stood near these men again, all I could hear was "outside! You're having it you cunts!" Both sets of fans were goading each other and then the final whistle went a big roar from our fans and then everyone piled out of the ground. Outside the police had blocked the road off to separate fans from clashing. Everyone was trying to get at the Coventry fans, I was about 17 or 18 at most, I cannot really remember, but what I do remember is that the adrenaline was pumping! I wanted to get stuck into them, but the police had it on lock down and shortly after, everyone dispersed. I went back home and but could not stop thinking about the buzz and what had happened. Everyone stuck together and the buzz was unreal, I just wanted it again. I couldn't help but keep going on about it to my friends, I wouldn't tell my family as they'd go mad so at the time kept it to myself. The following week all this was still on my mind. The next home game came and I thought I would sit close to them this time as it was back to a normal league match. I had noticed some of the clothing and decided to look it up. I wanted to be one of them and decided to save up. As it happened, I had a few hundred quid from Christmas still saved and I got the money off my dad and went straight into town. I bought a Burberry jacket that cost £250 quid; this shopkeeper looked at me strange and must have wondered how a teenager could spend such money on a jacket. I did not show my dad the jacket, but bought a few other things such as jeans, a few shirts and jumpers. I also bought a pair of shoes, I showed him them and he seemed happy. Little did he know what I was up to! I used to go to games with friends or sometimes just meet them in there. On one occasion they came in and noticed I had no team shirt on and asked me why I was dressed smart, I began to explain. Within a few weeks my other mates followed my footsteps, started dressing smart, it was 'casual'. We would be served in the ground for beer and we started to go into a few pubs around town before the games and then after. The older lads we had seen started letting onto us, and conversations followed soon after. They started to tell us a few stories it was now about heart, presence and pride.

Home

Some of the other teams sung songs hurling abuse towards us. This is our town, our place, our people and our pride and nobody gets away with taking the piss. There was about 15-20 of us some weeks and we would go looking for a row with other firms. We would usually meet up in the town centre, have a breakfast and get on the beer. Then we would see what were knocking about, get up to the game and get behind the lads. It was the way forward for me. I was now football coaching for Burnley and had weekends off. I would work hard during the week; go to the gym a lot and then just could not wait for Saturday to land. We began to sit near the bottom of the stand in front of our older lads and try to catch their eye. It was a direction and a new life. It is very different from simply knocking about on the streets drinking with people. Here you earn respect; you feel good, create trust from one another and become good friends with good people. My mates and me were all really close. When we are not working, we are always in contact with each other. We are a band of brothers, and we are proud of where we come from. Meeting your mates on a Saturday is such a buzz. Getting ready to go to the football, ringing each other to see what you are wearing, the banter, the brotherhood, togetherness, the thrill great times.

Graduation

Being a lad in the lower leagues, unless your club has been somewhere like the premiership or the old divisions 1 and 2, unlike Rochdale, it is not easy. We have never really had success on the field as a football team, so it is one of them situations in our town, where there is a lack of interest, because basically we had been shit! We aren't going to get the numbers like some other firms do, although we would like 100 lads week in week out, we'd much rather have 30-40 keen as fuck lads, that won't budge, that will stand, doesn't shift, and can give and take. Maybe the numbers game can work in some cases, but again you cannot beat being outnumbered, doing the business, and emerging victorious, it is all on the day for a lot of us.

Sometimes there are 30 of you, sometimes up to 100. Then you get the lads that are escorted about whilst others are having a tear up, shit happens. If you are done on the day, hold your hands up. The grounds are league apart. With the modern day ground, you will get your all seater stadiums, where as in leagues 1 and 2 you get your old school type stadiums that give you that really old feel. There has been so many grounds that you feel intimated in. Your Millmoors (Rotherham), the old Booth, Ferry Park (Hull City), Swindon, Halifax, The Shay, Lincoln City, Sinical Bank, Bradford City, Valley Parade, Port Vale, Darlingtons, old Feethams ground, Chesterfields, Crewe, Chester city, Wrexhams, Burys, Oldhams. Walsall just gives you that tension. Then there is the areas surrounding and leading up to them that start getting to your nerves as you patrol through their areas with their towns and with their lads in. Turning the corner and bang hello here they are, straight into them without a single police officer in sight, battles taking place in back alleys out of town centres. There is too much CCTV in the town centres and police have it on lock down as soon as you land in them. Getting out of the way, entering the ground at the last minute, you can bump into other firms and the games begin. More times than most, we have had it well out of the way of CCTV and the police. In your back alleys leading around the ground and side streets, out of the way, depending on how your towns set up you will work it to your strengths. Around Spotland there is plenty to choose from so it would be no problem catching out the opposition en route to the ground or when their leaving town. I love it when you turn a corner and bang, groups of lads are there, and you go steaming in. There is no other place on earth you would want to be, once that's hit you. It is better than taking drugs, the adrenaline is something else, that feeling hits you and you are a very different person, and after the row, you are buzzing with your mates. Even when we get done, we hold our hands up and laugh about it, as you can come unstuck many a time in this game. It is all part-and-parcel you just have to take the rough with the smooth as the saying goes. Your friends are the family you choose to pick, and I would say if you get 20-30 lads, you can rely on to always stand your corner, stand side by side regardless of what is thrown at you and stand toe to toe and not back down for each other you will be very hard to break down. Trust plays a massive part in our lifestyle and it's all about knowing each other inside out and knowing no matter what come at us we stand as one for each other and for our town, as the old saying goes "he who dares wins!"

Rochester vs. Everton

Bang! It was like being born again. The new season was upon us, everyone was wearing out their new gear, the banter was flowing smoothly and the beer was going down a treat. The sun was out it was 10.30 in the morning, and 20 of us were out for the Scousers. It was pre season, and Everton were in town. A city lad had been in touch, had sorted out a contact, and had told us they were coming to town for us. It was the first game back and we could not wait to get things rolling. The season prior we had many rows, won a few and lost a few but this time the big boys were coming to us, in our town, our streets, our manor, and it was time to put the word out we are a growing firm. A lot of good firms in our division had started to rate us and our reputation was growing. Our lads were aged between 15 and 25, and for a few it was something new, a rollercoaster of a ride they were about to embark on. More and more lads come to the boozer we meet in, placed nicely out of the town centre, and away from CCTV and allowed us to get it together. Time moved on and it was now about 1.30 in the afternoon. We were now about 50 handed, none of the older lot, simply our younger firm.

I remember a black BMW pulling up outside the boozer we were drinking in, the window came down and a bald chap with a scouse accent said "'e ar, mate, where's the footie ground?" Fuck me! This was something else, how he never seen the ground on his way to us I will never know. He must have gone past it and been looking around the area to see what we looked like mob wise. One of our lot shouted back "you know were we are, go and get your lads and lets ave it!" The lad smiled and replied, "The county road cutters are here, dont you worry yourselves, you'll get a call soon." At this point, everyone was itching to get on with it. We were geared up big time. We simply could not wait for them to come round the corner and both of us go steaming into each other. However nothing come our way, and people were getting naffed off. We sent a couple of our lads up to the pubs around the ground. Not long after our lads informed us, there was roughly 60+ Everton about.

It was approaching kick off, so we got together and marched up taking all the backstreets and alleys. As we got there the time was now about 2.50 we turned a corner and the police were no were, a few Everton come out but the rest must have gone into the game. We called it on but they did not want to know. I am not surprised to be honest; a few of our older lads had met up with us on our way and when they go, they simply are untouchable. A few of us walked over to their lads and asked what the crack was. We told them were to go after the game, or if they wanted to come and meet us whilst the game is going on. A lot of us are banned from home games; the police could not get us banned via the courts initially and so went directly to the club who issued us with letters. Where is the justice in that? Anyway, as this was happening a police horse came in from the side and used its head to hit mine, it must have been trying to knock me out. The officer on the horse got on his radio. About 10 others and myself went back to the boozer we originally were in, the other 40 lads went into the game. During the game our lads had bumped into a few of them in our home stand, only 2 of them but instead of kicking fuck out of them and bolloxing it up, they told Everton that when the game was over, to walk down the road opposite and the pub nearest to ground is were we would be waiting. I think it back fired it must have done. The lads in the game messaged us to let us know the score. So, with 10 minutes to go we walked to the point and waited. One of our lads phones went off and it was Everton who said they were on their way down to us. There was 10 of us waiting at the side ginnel, and we was thinking were the fuck are the rest of the lads, they should have come out abut 20 minutes before the end. Then about 40 of them come down the road and one of us looked round the corner. They are here! Fucking stand, come on Rochdale stay tight together. Smash, in we went to them. Well outnumbered, and up against some big blokes I remember taking a step back pretending to throw a punch as one came at me. Crunch down this lad went, the adrenaline was flowing like never before, I recall fighting with 3 blokes and another I must have caught under his chin, he stumbled back and one of our lot came in from the side and one timed this big bald cunt. He down he went and everyone was punching everyone. I was been hit about 20 times but had thrown about 40 punches. Not everyone landed but most did. All I could make out was their lads on the deck, I had a quick look to my right and saw one of our young-uns getting smashed by a couple of older chaps and so went straight over and got stuck into them again. It was crazy as fuck. All our lads were fighting mad and more of them went down. Then there was a stand off and back again, we went. It had been going off for a few minutes and when the police horses turned up. There were only two of them, but it did not end there. Our 10 lads were holding it together; we had been bottled and pelted with bricks that come from rubble on the way down to us. Why we did not use them to our advantage was beyond me but it did not really matter, everyone was roaring. I could begin to see a couple of ours getting a kicking on the deck and a few of us stayed close and got them up fighting off the Everton lads. They must have thought we were crazy as fuck for not backing off and going straight into them. More police turned up and we spilled into the main road. The same officer as before tried to grab me, but got nowhere near. Our lads were still scrapping but their numbers were starting to prove to much. A few of them come into the road with us and punches were trading left right and centre. Bloody faces, black eyes, claret tops, there was no better feeling!! This lad stepped forward with a few of his older mates and screamed at me, "Come on you fucking Rochdale twat" I must have taken about three attempts at trying to hit him and finally caught him. He flew to the left landing on his stomach. Bet he felt a right cock and the rest of us steamed in at the others and before you knew it there was about five riot vans pulling up. Everyone scarpered and decided enough was enough, had the other 40 lads come out earlier and been more organised, I doubt the Old Bill would have stopped it but shit happens. A few lads were arrested but within an hour, they were let out. There was no C.C.T.V and so it was not captured thankfully. Although it would have been a great watch, and maybe would have put a stop to all the bull-shitters on the net that dont tell it how it went. Back in the pub everyone was buzzing, did you see that, did you see me; did you see fingy knock that lad out? Someone shouted, "Did u see Matty clean that lad out that screamed at him?" Everyone started laughing. About an hour later, one of our lads got a call. The Everton lads said fair fucking play to us and said they thought they had the better and asked us what we thought. To be fair they brought a decent outfit, game as fuck, but with more of them on deck than us, I doubt they can claim any result. Anyone that was there knows this is how it happened. We put up a performance though, but it just goes to show what you can do when you dont back down. Being a small tidy firm we are close with each other and being cheeky like that is what we are all about. Other firms were in touch saying Everton's' claiming they ran us ragged. Total bollox! No matter what you do, sometimes people choose what they want to believe but we know the score. It was a great experience. You dont have to be hard for football, just show no fear and pick the people you're with who will back you there's only so many I would go with, it's not numbers it's quality. Its true, that's why we were called the CHOSEN FEW because were a small firm but stick together and know each other, that's how you get results. I learned with the older lads they took me every were I love it but had to get stuck in but I never regretted any of it

Where am I with this?

There are people in this world that wouldn't understand why we do what we do. They get doctors and researches involved and try to make us look we violent etc. What a load of bollocks. There are lads in not only our firm but also many others that as well as being working class people all have a respectful jobs, fantastic families and know how to live life the way it should be, enjoyed! We are not criminals! We do not run around and hit people that dont want to get involved, we have it with like-minded lads. The criminals are your rapists, pedophiles, murderers, drug dealers, thieves, fraudsters; people those mug old women, child molesters and people that carry guns etc. People that attack people for no reason are the real criminals, but I guess we make easy press targets, as what goes on behind the scenes kept well away. We all know that the papers and news talk about is what they want us to believe. I for one will not get misled by their lies or corruption, the systems bent we all know, there the first people to stop us fighting in the street but are the first to send us to war, hold your head up high. You only live once, we all die one day, where when and how we do not know. Live with no regrets, do not look back and think why didn't I do that? Why didn't I say anything? Always remember to do what feels right, say what you want to say and live life to the full. The heart, presence, pride, brotherhood, banter, that feeling, its part of our way of life and part of our culture

The A-Z of firms around the country

England

Aldershot – A Company

Arsenal – Gooners

Aston Villa – Villa Youth, Steamers C crew

Birmingham City –Zulus

Blackpool –The Muckers

Bolton Wanderers - Cuckoo Boys

Bradford City – The Ointment

Brentford – Hounslow Mentals

Bristol City – City Service Firm

Burnley –Suicide Squad

Carlisle United – Border City Firm

Charlton Athletic – B Mob

Chelsea - Headhunters

Coventry City – The Legion

Derby County –Derby Lunatic Fringe

Everton – County Road Cutters

Fulham –Thames Valley Travelers

Grimsby Town – Cleethorpes Beach Patrol

Huddersfield Town – Huddersfield Young Casuals

Hull City –Hull City Psychos

Leeds United –Leeds United Service Crew

Leicester City –Baby Squad

Liverpool – The Urchins

Luton Town –The MIGS

Manchester City – Guvnors

Manchester United – The Red Army

Middleborough – The Frontline

Millwall – Bushwhackers

Newcastle United F.C. – Newcastle Gremlins

Nottingham Forest F.C. – Forest Executive Crew

Norwich City – Norwich Hit Squad
Oldham Athletic – Fine Young Casuals
Oxford United – South Midlands Hit Squad
Plymouth Argyle – The Central Element
Portsmouth – 6.57 Crew
Preston North End – Preston Para Squad
Queens Park Rangers – Bush babies
Rochester F.C-Young Chosen Few
Sheffield United –Blades Business Crew
Sheffield Wednesday – Owls Crime Squad
Southend United – CS Crew
Stoke City –Naughty Forty
Sunderland – Sea burn Casuals
Swindon Town – The Aggro Boys; Swindon Active Service (SAS)
Tottenham Hotspur –Yid Army
West Bromwich Albion –Section Five
West Ham United –Inter City Firm
Wolverhampton Wanderers –Subway Army

Scotland

Aberdeen – Aberdeen Soccer Casuals
Airdrie United – Section B
Celtic – Celtic Soccer Crew
Dundee & Dundee United F.C The Utility
Falkirk – Falkirk Fear
Heart of Midlothian – Casual Soccer Firm
Hibernian – Capital City Service
Montrose – Portland Bill Seaside Squad
Morton – MSC
Motherwell – Saturday Service
Rangers – Inter City Firm
St Johnstone – Fair City Firm
St Mirren – Love Street Division

Wales
Cardiff City –Soul Crew
Swansea City – Jack Army

Northern Ireland
Linfield – Section F

Something extra for your mince pies:

Hooligan- The origin of the word 'Hooligan' is unclear at best. Although one story that seems to spin a common circle is, it derives from the Irishman Patrick Hooligan, who terrorized inhabitants of London with his youth gang in the 1890's.

Football History:

Here are some real examples of the hooligan when we were all but a twinkle in our daddy's eye.

1314, 1315 Edward II bans football!

1349, 1388, 1410 Football was banned from the city of London due to complaints from merchants.

Two hundred years later, no Sergio or Fila. Not even, bit of Stone Island. But, it's still kicking off....

1576 Middlesex County Records reports that 100 men assembled unlawfully to play football.

1579 After the start of a match against the students of Cambridge, the townsmen of Chesterton proceeded to assault their visitors.

1740 Football match in Kettering turns into a food riot and local mill is destroyed.

1797 Kingston-upon-Thames. Traditional Shrove Tuesday match turned into a riot after a few participants were arrested.

1843 Soldiers and police officers were needed to patrol the ropes at a Preston North End v Sunderland match.

1846 A match was stopped in Derby. The riot act was read.

1881 At Wigan station two railway officials were knocked unconscious by a group travelling to a Newton Heath v Preston North End game.

1884 P.N.E fans attacked Bolton Wanderers players and spectators at the end of the game.

1885 Aston Villa v Preston. A mob of "lads" attacked the visiting fans.

1920 Birmingham City football fans use bottles as clubs and missiles.

1921 Bradford Park closes the boy's section for three months after the referee was pelted with rubbish.

1924 After a match in Brighton the pitch was invaded.

1961-1968 An average of 25 such incidents per season reported.

The rest is history (And fucking C.C.T.V!)

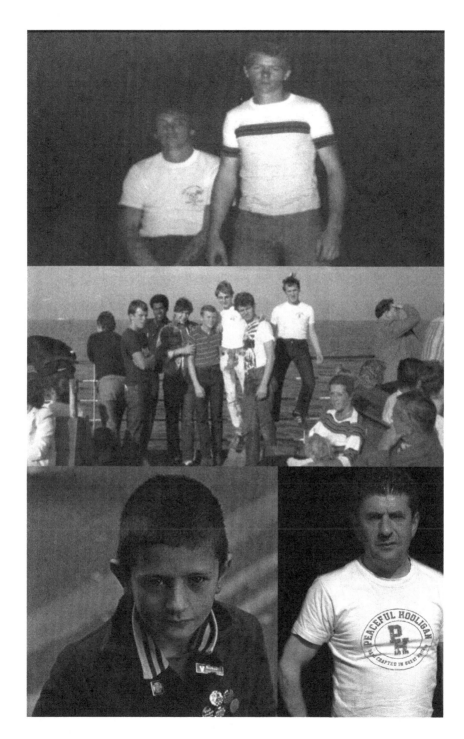

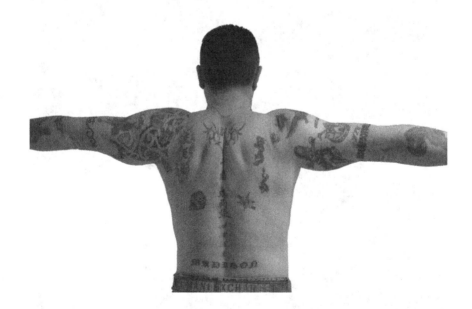

Who is the real Hooligan?

Lager Lout:
A person (especially a young male) who
behaves in a violent manner when drunk.

Scout:
There for his own.

Danny Dyer

Casuals

"I'd rather any lad to spend the money they
did on clothes instead of drugs"
- Mum 2009

"My pals from up north, when traveling to mainland Europe,
brought a whole new meaning to the phrase duty 'free'
shopping"- A phone call from me, to my younger brother back in London.

J Allday 2009

For me it was the early '80's that saw the birth of the casual scene, not that
I could afford fuck all. A measly ten quid earned from the weekend milk
round hardly warranted a trip to Harvey Nichols or Selfridge's (I later
learned a way round this). So, for me the start was a slow and frustrating
one. There were a few of my pals that had a bit of a result though. One
of my best mates was never to short of a bit of decent clobber. His dad
was a London cab driver, and not your MK 1 Cortina special, but a black
cab. So he was treated to a wardrobe of Hugo Boss and Fred Perry polo's,
Lyle and Scott, Pringle jumpers and some nice Lacoste numbers. Not sure
if his dad was aware of the newly acquired clothes by his youngest, but
nonetheless, he had a better result than some of us and credit where credit
is due, I sometimes got a bit of gear thrown my way.

Early memories and the relationship with my younger brothers also tempt
a laugh many years later. When you have two younger brothers growing
up in the same house, it just cannot be avoided, that at some stage, the
little buggers will 'dip' into your collection of highly prized cotton and
threads. At least my collection of trainers was saved as they had feet the
size of basketball players.

Back in the beginning of my world of clothes, all too often I was spending mums last pound note on a Fred Perry polo, a pair of Dr martin boots and of course the 'tight enough to see your nuts' faded jeans. So, when the said mentioned brothers came of age, mum thought it only fair I make an effort to cater to their needs and help get the boys some new gear. What was once OK in terms of a run of the mill T-shirts was quickly replaced with a more expensive item to emulate the big brother and his pals look. This coincided nicely in favour for my little brothers, as the birth of the casual scene had firmly arrived.

A sunny afternoon, coming back from a little shopping spree, revealed my worst suspicions and nightmares that the little shits had been wearing my gear. I was walking from the tube station, with both swagger and flare and was proudly displaying the bags with department store names across them and in an effort to gain a little more common knowledge by passers-by of our in the know peacock display. We noticed flying past us with a look of pride and panic, my two brothers, fronting the new wears from Liberty's and Harvey Nichols, I had only acquired just the weekend before. I never knew two kids on B.M.X's could peddle so fast and the peddling and panic that followed generated roars of laughter from my pals, who had been my traveling companions up from town. In an effort to emulate, a combination of Daley Thompson and the roadrunner to catch them was at first a valiant effort but sadly wasted. Shouting while in chase "I'm going to' fucking kill you ya' fucking pickeys" warranted a reply in almost chorus type fashion by the thieving pair. "Mum said!" and then faster peddling in an effort to reach the safe haven of both mum and home. After reaching home and passing the getaway vehicles strewn across the front garden I walked in the kitchen to find the thieving duo standing as close to our mum as possible. I entered looking for both reasoning and justice to prevail. What I got was two brothers panting like an aged porn star, sweating like a fat kid in a chip shop (all over and through my clothes) and a simple "It's just a couple of tops and some shorts, Jase!" reply from mum. "I'll throw 'em in the wash later" was another reply. If it was not adding insult to injury now, they had been seen in the gear which in the 'street jury's' opinion was now theirs. It also did the clothes no credit, as it was insulting to see the latest and greatest hanging off them due to it being four sizes to big for them dripping in both their sweat and tears. Again, this was the joy and luxury of growing up and sharing a house with two brothers.

Looking back on this and many other incidences it gives me a great sense of pride they both looked up to me. At the time I interpreted their actions of thieving little shits. Now, it is clear as day that I was the big brother, the trendsetter. A reference to two young lads who were proud of the older brother that donned his gear they just wanted to be part of. Another memory and a well plan lead took a few lads on an excursion to some golf clubs just outside London. This newly found treasure trove was not prepared for half a dozen teenagers from a housing estate in West London. Normally, at most it was an old girl, with her head buried in a paper back or romance novel, not worrying about the over whelming number of teens that just popped in for a present for a dad or an uncle (that story seemed to always divert the unnecessary attention). Shortly after, the Pringle jumpers, Lacoste rain macs, Slazenger wear and on one occasion an entire unopened delivery out back was all mysteriously gone! And if the unthinkable happened, and your newly hard earned imported sportswear was handled in a way other than what the care instructions on the inside label gave, by a opposing footy fan, then back to a new outlet for some more must have cotton and threads.

The funniest story is when a pal stayed behind in a department store, waited for closing, thinking to empty the store of the desired goods. This was of course when the stores best line of defense was heavy bars on the windows, solid locked doors and shock sensor tape along the glass windows. A car jack would work easy on the bars, prying 'em apart allowing any teen the opportunity to slip out. This in our opinion was easier than daytime shopping. The only question I had was why the bottle of Jack Daniels for such planned adventure. "A bit of Dutch courage" my pal insisted tapping the side of his nose with one finger while giving the all-knowing wink. One failing fact with my pal was it was known that when he started drinking he could not stop. In what should have been, an easy take resulted in him spending more time drinking the 'Jack D' instead of throwing the planned loot out of the upstairs window. My much-wasted efforts of shouting up to see if all was still on were fruitless. Instead, he fell asleep on a pile of clothes and was discovered by the cleaning crew the next morning.

Then another pal, his approach, well more of a 'Robin Hood kind of deal'. Nick from the whereever and keep for him self. A few trips across some of the nicer neighbouring houses off our housing estate's back gardens, to have away the odd top and jeans from an unguarded washing line worked in his favour. This was all long before the now self-proclaimed hooligan who can simply walk into one of a thousand choices of outlet and simply whack it on the old credit card. My early days, lead from scrimping and scraping and 'by any means necessary'. A few schemes more often than not, were the way for a few to ensure, the latest and most sought after gear.

There are stories that the Scousers, with Liverpool being in Europe, were the only reason for the unseen French and Italian sportswear now taking over from the DR. Martins and faded Levis. Being a Londoner, and watching the clobber before this claimed story, I kindly have a opinion that wouldn't say it was all because of my northern pals, but will say as much as this. I had a few Scouse mates, and what wasn't tied down; they bloody took in great numbers. My pals from that neck of the woods certainly set me up with a few nice Sergio Tacchini and Fila track tops. Cheers, boys, and however it started this is true to this day. The English terrace lads set a standard that has not demised down its own back path. Nor has this standard from the start until now, let the smart and often seen as cultural leaders in the way of terrace wear throughout the whole of Europe become any less.

Typically known for the start in smartness is the Mods who throughout the '60's and '70's, also an opposite to the 'greasy' bikers, claiming not more than a leather and a pair of jeans as the 'uniform'. Completely taking the clothes to a whole new level, the then 'French and Italian invasion', and the only time so many French have ever been welcomed into the U.K, was by way of clothes, and not forgetting some blinding Italian numbers too.

One thing that I have said to a number of pals throughout the football world is that it's amazing, such a culture spread like wild fire, without the help of the all now powerful internet. The technology of today, with mobile phones, internet and publications spreading the 'word' far and wide, it's quite a thing for the names to spread like they did, from simply seeing the opposing 'fan' at a station or ground back in the day. Word of mouth is truly a power full thing, eh. One thing a few pals throughout the U.K have all agreed on with me is this. Your trainers, was typically the most reason to be exclusive. A lot of the lads started with, what is still considered one of the best brands Adidas. Reebok made quite a mark in the late '80's through until today. A few others including Diadora, Kickers, Nike and Puma all too played a part. Now I know there is a boatload more, but these are a few of the favorites between my brothers and me. I would go on to say, back then it was rare to see any real terrace wear mentioned in any of the mainstream publications. A fanzine here and there, may boast a new brand being displayed by a local firm, but nothing in terms of the deserved recognition to the efforts made by our friendly hooligan and the 'not yet seen' item fresh off the ferry.

One fella', that did make a cracking effort, and a well documented collection of stories, names and places came by mention of a pal up north. If there were a reference, I would give to anyone that promoted the memories from the casual era in a book it would be Phil's. This chap was north of the border, but I would go ahead and say he had it 'spot on'. His name is Phil Thornton. His book was Casuals. Football, Fighting and Fashion. A tribute and compliment to the casual era. Certainly promoting memories of my own, like all those in here, he stepped up and gave some insight to share. So, I'll leave you in the capable hands of my mate, Phil.

Fix Up Look Sharp!

We'd been for a quick scoop in town in the Brunswick, by Piccadilly station. As usual, it was a mixture of Cockney Reds off the shuttle, moody Mancs and small town wannabes like us. Rossy, our wheels, had a curly perm, a Jerry Dammers grin and, even though he was five or so years older than us, wore the latest clobber. A proper fucked up character to be honest, his dad was the local Labour councillor on our estate but he shared none of his socialist principles. As one of the Doc's Red Army brigade, Rossy was our guide to notorious characters such as Paraffin Pete, Eddy Beef and Sam Spade.

Last season we'd came out of Hurley's golf shop and walked slap bang into the biggest mob I'd ever seen. This gang was a thousand or so strong and were silently mooching up towards Piccadilly, to welcome West Ham. It was the silence that made this crew especially un-nerving, no ballooning about, daft chants or hard-man posturing, but just a quiet determination to confront the most notorious mob in the country at that time. If United's Red Army was the most notorious hooligan crew of the 70s, then West Ham's ICF had literally carved out a niche for themselves as spearleaders for a new type of hooligan mob in the 80s; smaller in number, yet tighter, more organised, independent of the main fanbase by necessity and design.

This was the beginnings of the so-called 'designer thug' era and although there were many myths spouted about this time, there's no doubt that the ICF were the catalyst for many other copycat crews; from United's half-joking 'Inter City Jibbers' to the apparently serious 'Lincoln Transit Elite', the ICF became the model for away fan organisation and etiquette during the early to mid 80s. The clothes of course played their part and again, this was largely misconstrued by the media who felt as if the donning of golfing, tennis and other leisurewear was a form of 'disguise' instead of a return to pre-bootboy standards of working-class 'sharp' dressing. Let's not forget that it was on the terraces of football grounds that male 'street fashion' was paraded and copied. 'REAL' street fashion not the stuff thrust upon us by The Face, I-D and other ludicrous style mags.

In Liverpool and Manchester the scaly / Perry boy look had developed in the post-punk era and even though I was still listening to The Cockney Rejects myself at the time, the Cockney 'Herbert/ Chap' look shared the North West's desire to look beyond the stereotypical skinhead/bootboy hooly cliché. Of course this debate has raged ever since; Cockneys argue that London soulboys were the template for the 'casual' look and scallys claim to have invented it after watching Bowie sing 'Sound & Vision' in 77 – whatever the influences (and they were many and varied) what cannot be denied is that by 1985, the day of this crucial FA Cup game between these two United's, Manchester and West Ham, the casual sub-culture was at its peak.

So here we are sat in the Brunswick a few hours before kick-off having missed the other kick-off. The rumour was that the ICF had already been in town and walked to Old Trafford a few hours earlier. Only the main 'scarfers' were yet to arrive and reports of running battles along Chester Road were filtering back to the Brunswick. Disappointed, we decided to sup up and do a spot of shopping before driving to the ground.

By this time there had been a definite split between dress codes, not only north and south but also within cities. The 'scruff' look had taken a hold of Manchester (scruffy northerners? Never!) As a reaction against the 'sports casual' look that had dominated for a few years. Today I'm not mooching around Hurleys Golf Shop for Cerruti or Australian Tennis trackies (soooo 1984!!) but Dunn & Co for suede and cord cardies and the Oasis centre for 24 inch flared jeans and Adidas Stockholms.

Rossy parks up by the cricket ground and the three brown bitters I had earlier have caught up on me, so I'm stood pissing on the wasteground that passes for a car park and West Ham's double decker busses offloading the specials from the station pull up alongside me. I cut my piss short and give it toes as they disembark walking alongside the escort towards the ground as they mock my 'callards' chanting 'Flares! Flares! Flares!' and generally take the piss. I'm stood there thinking 'I'm not the one still wearing Pierre Cardin pal' but it's to no avail.

Amongst the usual post-Pringle leather blouson and bleached shit-stopper brigade are a strange bunch of spiky headed and slick back merchants and this confirms the rumours we've been hearing about the new Cockney look; 'they're wearing fucking paisley shirts, wedding do kecks and slicking their fucking hair back, the divs!' seemed to be the general consensus.

Needless to say a few months later, I'm wearing a paisley shirt, a pair of pegged 'wedding do kecks' and have my hair slicked back. But this day, I'm still resolutely in Manc Mode and the game is going well for us with ten or minutes to go and United easily winning, the ICF decide to jib it and what happens next is captured on the now infamous ICF 'Hooligan' documentary.

The excitement amongst many of the casual / hooligan fraternity when this documentary was screened cannot be over-stated. Only the seminal 'Harry The Dog / Millwall F-Troop' documentary from the 70s had approached British hooliganism from a half-objective perspective and this film got to the heart of 80s football culture in a way that a thousand University of Leicester sociology studies could only dream of.

Showing the ICF 'on manoeuvres,' both at home and away gave an insight into inner city British codes of masculinity and urban life that had been long ignored or brushed under the Thatcherite carpet. Here was a generation for whom the buzz of the match, the visceral thrill of violence (or at least the threat of it) and the solidarity of group identity flew in the face of accepted Tory myths; working class sloth and self-imposed poverty.

Whether consciously or not, wearing the best clothes and 'spoiling the good name of Britain' stuck two fingers up to Maggie and co and by refusing to bow down to the 'short sharp shock' tactics that attempted to counter the 'mob' threat to her policies.

Areas of traditional poverty such as East and South London, Manchester, Liverpool and Glasgow had always responded by becoming proudly self-sufficient and the so-called 'criminal classes' flourished both as a social necessity and as a way of bypassing the 'class structure' that aimed at keeping Cockneys, Scousers, Mancs firmly in their place.... away from the 'un-deserving rich!'

Seeing thousands of young lads, mostly unwaged, in poorly paid unskilled jobs or blatantly on the blag zapping up and down the country and abroad, wearing ski-ing, yachting and hunting clobber, taking the piss out of the police, out of the football authorities and out of the government couldn't and wouldn't be tolerated.

1985 was Year Zero; Luton v Millwall, Birmingham v Leeds, the Bradford fire and finally Heysel! Hooligan was filmed in the run-up to these events and was screened a few months after Heysel. This tragedy finally forced both the Tory government and UEFA to take harsh action against British clubs, even though their own part in the horror was conveniently whitewashed, incompetent planning, blundering police, rotting stadiums, greedy clubs, corrupt officials, foreign hooligans? Too close to the truth that, so blame it all on 'The English Disease.'

Of course we played our part too and it's easy to look back with rose-tinted Armani shades but there was no two ways about it; the 'glory days' were over with CCTV, hoolivans, undercover Police operations, banning orders, jail sentences and an increasingly brutalised atmosphere inside and outside grounds making it almost impossible for hooligan gangs to operate (at leading British grounds at any rate).

The ICF heads interviewed as part of 'Hooligan' seemed to sense that the game was up as they assessed the repercussions of Heysel and indeed the general pessimistic feeling amongst many fans. I went to the '85 Cup Final against Everton with ten or so mates. None of us had tickets and expected it to be tough getting into Wembley. No worries! It was a piece of piss and

Heysel or no Heysel, old school terraces were always easy places to bunk into and hide in. It took Hillsborough to finally put an end to that.

With the rise of acid house and the associated drug boom, some of the crews catered for a different audience, set up new avenues to exploit. The clothes went through a more dressy continental phase (Ciao, Chipie, Chevignon etc.) then another 'scruff / hippy' phase before settling on the neo-casual uniform of new and re-discovered classics in the 90s; Lacoste, Stone Island, CP, Henri Lloyd, Barbour, Burberry, Paul Smith, Adidas, Prada, Paul & Shark and gradually the dark ages came to an end.

Maybe it was Italia '90, maybe it was the beginning of the premiership and Murdoch's millions being pumped into the game, maybe it was lads getting older and a younger generation failing to come through the ranks priced out of all-seater grounds or just sidetracked by other outlets for their energy. British or rather English football became a much nicer 'product' and grounds became safer and pleasanter places to visit and yet, something had been lost.

We now watch the terraces in Spain, Italy, Turkey, Argentina and we realise that we'll probably never experience anything like that again in our own grounds. The odd European game, derby match or cup tie provides the odd flashback to our idealised past. Let's not romanticise the 70s and 80s, in many respects they were horrible and ultimately self-defeating. In the 90s many hooly enemies began to realise they'd played tit for tat for too long and there were bigger enemies to fight or easier ways to make a buck.

The casual sub-culture, always umbilically tied to football has undergone something of a re-birth over the past decade too. Like hooliganism it never really went away so can't be described as a 'revival.' It was never a 'movement' in any case, it was what it was, no more, no less, just the clothes we wore, the way we acted, the language we used, the separation of 'us' from 'them.' The ones who knew the score and the ones who knew the train timetables off by heart, West Ham, Chelsea, Man Utd, Everton,

Leeds, Celtic – there will always be rivalry and competition between cities, between colours, between east and west, north and south, red and blue, claret and green. That's just the way it is, but finally at least we can all agree on something casual was NOT invented by Brummies!

Phil Thornton

The Italian Job

It would be unfair not to include the innovators of the casual scene that took the terraces by storm.

There are few places that you cannot go or a routine you have, that does not spur a memory or two. This of course includes the clothes. The revival of terrace wear has seen at least two rounds with the terrace regulars. With the re birth of Sergio and Fila to name but a few it has to be said the conversations spawned as a result of the re spun favorites is a trip down memory lane that can't be ignored.

Sometimes it was more effort than what is was worth trying to explain to two younger brothers the origins in what they would happily wear, as it was the social norm. 'Dodgy perms and flares' was a comment from the urchin brothers of mine when they saw early photos of the '60's and '70's Hornchurch, Mile end and Cranham mob (pre-ICF). Looking eagerly for a Lacoste or bit of Burberry was the only chance they thought of gaining a small slice of credibility of knowledge in photos of past. Instead, they would laugh at the donkey jackets, thick-soled shoes and the undeniable flares. Of course, way back then it was a different type of label that was the standard. Little did they know that your willingness and reputation was worth more than expensive brands and Italian imported clobber. Later on, it was the local chaps and their favorite outlets for designer gear. Some of the boys had a few exclusive hidden away places they would frequent for the most sought after casual gear. The necessity of exclusive and not seen before wears was as much of the days planning as the meet between the familiar faces.

Amongst some, arriving to meet the lads in a new bit of clothing and in turn a reaction and conversation relating to said items was an extra stripe earned with the 'in crowed', but caution had to be part of the equation. Turning up and if what you are wearing was considered unfit or unacceptable, well that is it! As much as you could be remembered for what could be considered an all exclusive, could easily turn into something that would earn you an undeserving, unforgettable, timeless nickname. The golden rule was never wear copied or snide designer clothing. If you were sussed, no matter what efforts you made there after would be wasted. You were now a pikey, suicide by casual failure.

The Italians took their clothing and support with the casual scene to a completely new level. As it is many of the ultras, that have started successful clothing brands of their own. Who can fault the investment shown by the Ultras! I think there is as much dedication with the Italians support with their clubs and passion as there is with preserving a large part of the country's cultural identity with the game. It goes without saying that there is a hooligan element throughout all Italian clubs, but it is a very small in percentage compared to the large amount of fans that actually go to a match.

With an equal amount of oppressive policing at their games as with English football, it's agreeable to say, it's an unwelcome one but none-the-less it's as part of the parcel. One noticeable difference between us English and the Ultras, is their clear protest against the unacceptable presence and attempt at the modernization of the game. No one in the whole of Europe displays their opinion and opposition against modern football (A.M.F) as strongly as the Ultras. Here the political part of fans and their organisations step in and protest en masse, at the attempts of cooperate takeovers and their influence. With the passion displayed that is comically confused by the media as violence, it is almost embarrassing when you know the real motive of their display. The Ultra Italia's and their passion at each and every game is a true reflection of this and it is without compromise. It is simply a show of support, with the mass ensemble and the efforts and show that is put on for a game by the fans. Some English firms will display numbers in an attempt to intimidate the opposition. Ultras typically show numbers, impressive amount of noise and banners, flags and flares. So we've had some influence from our pals on the main land of Europe. One said firm that has claimed notice throughout the great shores of England is the Ultra Italias, and as luck would have it, I got some connections in the land of

Vespas and pukka clobber. So, only just that we have one of the most well known from over the water give their little bit of 'asserzione gratuita'.

To Pedro, Old Lion forever

"Just remember this - in this country they drive
on the wrong side of the road."
- Johnny

The year 2009 marked a final year for the Italian Ultras movement. And it doesn't stop there, also in general for all the football firms in Italy, and it's likely to be measured as Ground Zero: rubble everywhere! In the last two years, the death of the police inspector Filippo Raciti and the murder of the Lazio Rome supporter, Gabriele Sandri, helped finalise the Ultras history that lasted 40 years. The decline was already well in 'view' from the last decade. An increase in police suppression of the terrace troubles through more reporting and arrests and the introduction of the banning orders that they have reduced the numbers of crews' members, including the notorious ones. Moreover a lot of the firms' members have begun to divide the crews of the same team. In 2004 Fossa dei Leoni of AC Milan, the first Italian ultras group, established in 1968, was disbanded, and for many people that's really the end of an age. And this is nothing new, the same thing happened in the United Kingdom several years before. Now, the many fans prefer to follow the teams of the lower leagues, where the chance of trouble is higher and the presence of the police force is less oppressive than in the Premier and 'glory teams'(U.K) and 'Premie A'(Italy)

How about a bit of clobber, Italian style?

In previous years, the 'casual fashion' exploded in Italy too. Yes, fashion, because actually the 'casual style', even though the term used was 'Cani Sciolti' (free dogs), was well prior to the '80's, when on both the streets and the terraces, you could see the first members of the only youth subculture, born in Italy, that has influenced the youth in the UK; a subculture that has more than a single point of contact with the casual style. We are speaking about the 'Paninaros'.

Born in Milan at the rising of the '80's, as a refusal to a decade of exasperated politics in the '70's, the first Paninaros met each other in the first fast food area called Burghy in piazza San Babila, a collection of both lads of the city center and inner city. From there the phenomenon spread to the rest of Italy and in some other foreign nations. The Paninaros became obsessed by fashion, so brands like Monclair, Stone Island, Armani, Levi's, Timberland etc. had a large success in those years. In the mid '80's a part of the subculture had a political change to the extreme right wing, although more in a street life style than in a real political knowledge. On the terraces, the Paninaros had a huge presence in Curva Nord of Inter Milan in the Boys San (and some of the lads created the bases of the notorious group of Skins), in Curva Sud of AC Milan in the Commados Tigre (the first Italian casual mob) and, in Rome, in Curva Nord of Lazio Rome. Thanks to the away games of British football teams in Italy, the British youth remained fascinated by the Paninaro style and reported it back to the UK, where the casuals assimilated it with more consciousness. In 1986 the famous pop band, the Pet Shop Boys called a song 'Paninaro' and the video was shot in Milan. A new version of the song was reissued in 1995 as 'Paninaro '95.

The famous French brand Moncler was a popular brand amongst the football 'fans', but due to the demise of the mentioned subculture, this in turn lead to a decline in sales in the Italian market. In recent years, it has seen a healthy return and made its name amongst the other big brands as an Italian favourite amongst the hooligans and fans alike.

From the '80's, the Italian Ultras changed from a politic look of casual terrace wear and switched to a specificity of his own; an initially all Italian prerogative rise. The Ultras look is born. Here you also see all the crews begin to produce and design their own merchandise and labels.

Aiming this new 'home grown' product of clothing line to their own members and supporters; the lads then started to wear the ultras stuff not only on the football days but also as a form of local support. Near and sometimes together with that of a recovery of British subculture like the mods (they often wear Italian suits), the skinheads, the Herberts and, in less measure, the punk grew up. These subcultures caught on at first in the big cities like Milan, Rome, Bologna, Turin or Genoa and then spread all over the country.

Towards the end of the '90's, also in Italy, grew a more marked desire by the ultras to distinguish themselves from the mass... The ultras and skinhead fashions render the crews too recognizable by the Polizia and in fact there was a return to the past; the explosion of of being casual. In Italy, it can be considered a second era of the Paninaros: next to the old guard, maybe Paninaros in their teenage years, a generation of youth comes side by side, a generation that, a little for fashion, a little with consciousness, (re) wears Stone Island, Timberland, Sergio Tacchini, Fila, Ellesse, Burberry, Aquascutum, Lacoste etc. The same thing happens to the following of the National team: no more flags of the clubs and skinhead look, but a search for expensive gear, also encouraged by the birth of the low cost airlines that permit the trips to England at competitive prices.

The future? It is difficult to say... When something becomes to be the mainstream, usually it is already only a revival and it is already a step behind. However, mixed in the crowd, on the terraces or on the streets, someone always will be, as Madness sang, 'one step beyond'. Maybe a new style will grow, maybe the good old days will rise again... and the ultras movement will never die, maybe not in the same ways or with the same numbers of the past, but maybe a new Italian Job will be, not a sad remake, but perhaps a surprising sequel.

Roberto 'Johnny Boy' Vacca

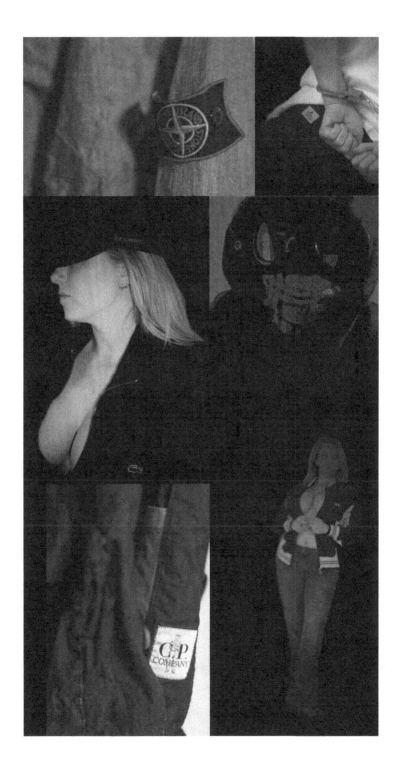

Faces, villains & bank Robbers

"You're a good bloke, mate and as the saying
goes water always finds its level"
- Richie Reynolds chatting with Jason Allday- 2010

B ank robbers and blaggers, in many parts of London; the place my brothers and I grew up in, boasted some real stories and players, that helped us identify the roles we'd play as young adults. Each of us had a story that when shared was simply to out- do each other. Here that very story could earn points, not in monitory gain but blagging rights in who knows what, a simple game that allowed points to be earned if you heard about a job, or blag before the other. Points if you guessed the story before it hit the headlines, and you was considered the mutts nuts if you knew someone on that score. The social ladder even between brothers prompted a laugh and friendly competition amongst us.

We all agreed that the villains and their actions gave us hope. That the mundane life we was dealt with in London's working class communities, could be helped, if we took the dare and our boy hood escapades to a higher level. Where we grew up, your image and attitude was something that you were in control of and not having to compete with those that looked down on us. This was something we could have, our culture and an identity that was something of ours and of our own making. We related to the ones that took from the very system that held us down and gave conversation between the three boys in London. I think the appeal was a simple one. The rascals and liberty takers that took the headlines were a voice for all lads across the country. The anti establishment attitude and the result that ensued gave us something to marvel and cheer for.

Why should anyone put a bank robber in his or her thoughts? The mere thought of a person committing a crime of such 'ante-socialism' surely, shouldn't be allowed to be graced within the pages of any book? Yeah, bollocks! And let's be honest, everyone has at one stage liked to read or has enjoyed the 'escape' these scoundrels' have given us. Either the lottery or a story of someone making or getting a 'result' from the very system, that would otherwise only allow them stay at the level of mediocre, to see them through the week is an example. And if you want to consider that I'm justifying the lads' actions, then at least consider this, we have all at some stage found entertainment within those few that do have the courage to stand up and take a little extra. If you say no to this, then I'll give you the name of the most famous of robbers. That has been seen on stamps in other countries, songs have been made about his 'gang' and his exploits, and his stories have reached as far as Asia. Yes, our very own Robin fucking Hood.

How about some famous capers!

The Great train robbery.

It wasn't called 'Great' for nothing, a favorite amongst rascals and villains. Even Frank Fraser said to me "I'd like to have been in on that one!" This event spawned several films, a great read, something to be marveled at by all lads across the country, and talked of for many years after. At the time, the amount of money taken wasn't only what made the headlines; the fact that the daring villains took from the royal mail train is something that most said was the reason for such hefty sentences, for those caught. In today's' money it is estimated that it would be the equivalent of 38 million quid; back then just under 3 million. A gang of 15 made the historical dawn raid on the Glasgow to Watford mail train, and to date it is suggested that the bulk of the money was never recovered. Bruce Reynolds, Ronnie Biggs, Buster Edwards and others took the record amount ever taken without the use of a single gun.

The longest on-the-run member of the gang, Ronnie Biggs, remained on the run until his voluntary return to England in 2001. His ability to stay one foot ahead of the law allowed him to gain not only fame through the public's eye, but also entered into the hall of fame for greatest escapes and respect within the underworld. He enjoyed the spoils of his new home in Brazil for 35 years.

The Baker Street Robbery.

Lloyd's Bank has some size able deposits at the branch located on the corner of Baker Street and Marylebone Road, but little did they know that the biggest 'un authorized withdrawal would take place on September 11th 1971. It is 'theorized' that the amount of cash taken, could be in the area of 16 million. It isn't a 'concrete' amount, due to a lot of the valuables was never reported. Now what makes this a 'talk able' event is some sensitive material, was rumored to have been stolen from one of the safety deposit boxes, and rumor has it that this sensitive material could bring embarrassment to the British Royal Family.

Brinks Mat Robbery.

On November 26th 1983, six robbers entered the Brinks warehouse at Heathrow airport, with plans to take 3 million in cash. Instead, they found something a lot shinier, than a few pound notes. Three tones of gold bars were in place, and just begging to be claimed by the new owners. Unfortunately for the main men in the robbery, they got 25 years each shortly after the event. The three tones of stolen gold have never been recovered! A rumor suggested by a leading media company in the U.K, suggested that anyone that bought gold in the U.K after 1983 is probably wearing Brinks Mat gold.

Villains, money getters and faces, they typically come from families that have remained the heartbeat of the street we walk on. Many a time, it is common you have passed them and not even known of their very existence.

The rules or 'code' legalizes the everyday game of villainy and honour amongst thieves. A set of standards that allow those that chose to avoid the everyday normal 9-5 routine and to operate both outside of the law and scrutiny of Joe Public. Here the very morals of the rascals are what defines' a real 'face'. Never women or kids' is a popular standard. Never take from your own. There for your own and those in need, promoting within the realms of the local neighbourhood in terms of safety and those in need of a little extra. The actions' of a grass is a way to sign their own death warrant. Such a word in any conversation with the cast of characters is a way to either gain the story of an unwanted person, as it is advice to be given and with words along the lines of "That slag will get one in the nut...." Charities are also a favourite way of villains to give something back from their humble if not hard and disciplined upbringings. There is logic to the way the game is played, and how they profit from such an environment.

Those that live past the loss of material gain are still unyielding in their rigid morals, which was not to grass or turn on one of your own, again a test of ones real character and honesty as a man amongst men. As much as a literal partner, is often needed, in many deals or jobs, the most rewarding is not only the prize, but also knowing you have solid people around you. The chaps I talk about are amongst a few that will always hold merit when I think of my younger brother.

Danny Woollard

The story rang out in the papers and a mark in history was made as one of the most daring robberies of my time had been committed. Danny Woollard along with his crew took the headlines, along with a few quid. What was to be known as the 'Snow Hill Robbery' went into the history books. An estimated four hundred thousand pounds in diamonds and seven million in bearer bonds was the haul. Now, that was what I knew. Well, what the papers said, and we all know is that it is the truth, is it not? Bollocks! So given the chance, and an introduction from a mutual pal, I'd been granted a sit down, and a chat with one of East London's most notorious villains. Well, that is a title I had heard and seen on one of Danny's books and knowing and hearing of the name from a few high-perched people in the active scene of what you would know as the underworld, I wanted the chance to have some true insight from a man that had really been there and done that.

Danny is the real deal. He will tell you how it is, true to his word, and take me how you find me kind of fella', a person that on many different occasions gave me great insight to his life in what is called the underworld. Now make no mistake, Danny's world was a criminal world, he will be the first to tell you. It has been soaked in violence, gambling and extortion and that is how he made his living. He did not know any otherworld or way to earn a living, and he will tell you in what are now two books and several documentaries; the real accounts.

I'd read his first book 'We Dared', a fantastic real account of the life in the underworld, the glam and glitter of the high life, with all the big names I'd grown up listening about or reading in the papers. The second, Wildcats, will blow your mind. From my grandparents, stories of the late great Billy Hill the King. The Krays from my mum, and how they ruled the East End with style, and now my chance with Danny. Now to be fair there's a few other names that also ring out, when you talk of the East End. Roy Shaw, Lenny McLean, Vic dark, Les Falco, just to name but a few and as a young fella', growing up in a house with two other brothers it was great for all of us to watch and compare our favorite gangster films. Mine, up there with Scar face and the Godfather trilogy, James and Junior sharing the liking for Scar face and the new bread and in terms for entertainment it was Lock stock and Snatch. If you watch closely enough, you can see a few 'faces' in there. Here, I am sure there are those that feel I am condoning the actions of Mr. Danny Woollard. Well, it would be a shame if all I could dream of and accept in terms of history of my era, was the odd episode of the usual turn out of make believe crap they show on the telly these days. Besides, those that oppose history in its true form have not only been known as some of the worst people in history themselves, but also people that have burnt the books that the history was printed on. If you know your political leaders and real history, you will know whom I mean! OK, OK, let us keep it positive.

Danny, is real, honest and will not paint a make-believe picture. He will tell ya' the price and cost of the life in the underworld. He has been with some of the biggest names in underworld history, like The Krays, Lenny McLean, Roy Shaw, Frank Fraser, the Dixon brothers, Freddie Foreman again and the list goes on.

Now the time and place and like all those out to help with my cause Danny was an absolute diamond. A first visit got some great input for the book. "If there's anything else you need, I mean if you go home tonight and think of anything that you want to ask, just call me and pop over" was the parting word from my first meet with Danny. Well, that is an offer rarely given, and I would be mad not to take the man up on the offer as only so much can be done in a day. That night, let me tell you. I was bouncing off the walls with questions in my head. All my years, I had watched the movies and read the books that were made on the greats like Danny. First thing the next morning, I was on the phone to Danny. "Sure, pop over" was the welcome I got from the man. Like a flash I was on the blower to my friend and colleague (West Ham Steve, my brother from another mother), and the sit down was set for Danny's house.

All day, I was driving Steve mad. Poor ol' Steve, I am lucky to have him as a very close mate. So at Danny's, it was a real treat as not only was there Danny Woollard the East End legend, but a close pal of his whom I had read about Richie Reynolds. Richie was real nice fella'. He was one of your own who would sit and have a conversation about anything. Polite, in sight full and has a lot of real known 'faces' as mates. So, if I needed a little pointer he was always a good man to ask. If you can picture the setting with Richie Reynolds, Danny Woollard, a known face and a former football hooligan and me, what conversation do you expect to develop? Murder, robberies the hard face reality of the underworld. Would you believe me if I said we just chatted about the day and how my week was going? Well that is exactly how it started. Four grown fella's all just having a laugh and drinking coffee. What a pleasant bunch of chaps but as order would have it, I would want some real deal for the book. So the coffees went down and we started talking.

I will point out that I went in armed to the teeth with questions but Danny had me beat. All the time I threw a question pertaining to the East End, crime and what, why and who, Danny had a comical approach or response. This I'd seen in my family and it did not matter where my family members ended up living, their typical East End values and wit was always the first thing that would be brought out.

I asked Danny about a nickname, as all gangsters or villains had one. Either by reputation, a typical action they carried their regular duties out on a person, or just a name that stuck due to nothing more than a laugh between mates. Danny gave me every name that would make me laugh or smile. I knew this was going to be a tough interview, but not in that, I would be trying not to fall on the floor laughing (better to laugh than cry I always said!). Now what better way than to talk about his new book 'Wildcats'. I wanted to touch on the obvious the underworld was a dangerous place, filled with violence at the turn of any corner, true to his form.

Danny- "Well yeah, I'm West Ham like him" (pointing to my pal and former hooligan, Steve and laughing. Again, more roars of laughter).

Danny- "Well, it's where you live. I went to school in West Ham. I grew up in Canning town. When I was 14 years old, there was a well-known family who lived in Stratford, and there was this other fella who was the Guv'nor, and believe me he was. Well the known family out there did the Guv'nor's brother. Four of us went in there and did the known family, all grown men, with pool cues and hands. We smashed the shit out of them. It was how you survived."

Danny then talked on the subject that has been lost to the times, and that is the fact that every young boy entered the ring. Boxing! A gentleman's sport, naming some of the greats of the day, Roy Shaw, Bertie Costa, Johnny Murphy, all Canning town.

Danny "It was a hard place to be raised but made men from boys. Now when you talk, and if you're lucky enough to be given this opportunity, mention the word 'boxing'. Not only will you be given an insight into stories covering not only the generation of the gent you are sitting with, but also the greats from the forefathers. If there was a dispute over an issue within the ranks or areas that the men worked or lived in, it was typically settled on the cobbles. Real men, bare hands, until the end but make no mistake, although there was no big hall, flashing lights or pretty girls to parade with a number signifying the round and all the other stereotypical standards you'd get at a traditional boxing event, here on the cobbles there was still rules. There were unwritten, universally accepted and respected set of rules that went hand in hand with many generations of street fighters"

In a previous chat with Danny he had given me an insight into something I had never accounted for as a Londoner, and the difference not mentioned anywhere before.

Danny-. "In my opinion, people from the East End make the best fighters, East London people are known more for violence, but South Londoners know how to make money. They have a good clue when it comes to that. If you look at the Krays and the Richardson's, the Twins knew all about violence, the Richardson brothers, where very good businessmen"

Now I had mentioned I was in the company of some greats. I had planned for a sit and chat with Danny. With the conversation that progressed, I had a wealth of knowledge and history all pouring into the mix. I had a former East End football hooligan face, adding to the conversation, and Richie. This was going to be a belter' of a conversation. West Ham Steve made a valid point and added

West Ham Steve- "Well if you look at the train robbers, they were all the South London lot"

Danny carries on:

Danny – "East London all fighting men, South London, they knew even back in the 1930's, the South London lot are a different generation. Not just fruit machines and parking lots, real money."

If you want insight to a day in the life of a bank robber, well the closest many will come to such an event is the daily rag (all bollocks!), a police report, a film; close to a daily rag there, or a man that's been there. So Danny tells me about a known event, what was it like say, on a day such as the Snow hill robbery?

Danny – "Well, I'll tell you something about that robbery, and I was never officially charged with it. I was tried for murder, handling, and conspiracy to rob. The others, where charged with the robbery. That's how it went about!"

Danny being the one to share for the book answered my question on the day of an event. The smallest of details can mean either the success or failure of a robbery, a life of paradise or four walls and an exercise yard. So thinking to get more 'meat and bones' I asked well, did you get up, brush your teeth have a bowl of cereal? Danny came back, in true fashion.

Danny – "And yeah have a bunk up! (More laughter fills the room).

What had started with intentions of a serious talk and from my original plan to get real, hard-pressed issues answered was not going to happen. Instead, I got something better, the real deal! Along with a person that had been there and really lived the life that is read about in books, or maybe a film has derived from his experiences. This all rolled into a lot of laughter with a real East Ender. Quality!

Danny adds - "Look, about robberies, you're only as good as your information. I mean, if someone said there's a security van up there, you'd not know what's in it, would ya! It's all inside work, mate. If I'd done a job, it was with inside information. Here's a bad bit of info. One time we did a job, got the lorry all the way back to the slaughter (where you off the goods) and the lot was empty! The way it normally pans out is you go down to where ever, have a chat, and out of a thousand ideas, you'll probably get one.

Now, if by chance, you may know a fella' here or there, and have the opportunity, to listen or be told of the inner workings of a job in hand or gone by. You may be told a bit on advice or standard of the modern day villain. One I had been told was to never get cocky, always treat each and every job as a new one. If you got a touch on a previous job, that was it. New job, new approach, do not get sloppy or lazy."

Did Danny have similar thoughts?

Danny - "Absolutely, no question, but again, inside help."

Richie also gives some insight and thought:

Richie- "Well what you have, as well, is if this one doesn't pan out, then you've got that one. There's always something on the go."

Danny- "Back to the 'Snow Hill Job'. The driver got 50 grand for his whack."

A statement made on a press release for Danny's new book; 'Wildcats was that for all the bad, we learn of the qualities of these hard men'. I asked Danny about that statement.

Danny- "Well when people don't grass, they're great men." This again promotes a room full of laughter.

Danny –"Look, I was put away for murder. I got eighteen months on remand, I didn't do it, but I didn't grass the geezer that did it either." In the underworld, there are two things that make you the lowest of anything possibly put on this earth. A nonce and a grass and both are dealt with by very harsh measures. If you read any book worth its salt, look in the chapters on the men doing some time. If they are inside, and there's a known nonce or grass. Well, they're in a world of pain. If they're not, they soon will be! I would've rather done life than grass, that's the old rules! This is where the rules of the game come in. It's very much the same deal across the board. Mafia, Triads the Russian mob, hold your tongue. Or it'll probably be cute out, at least! These days, you get some one that does one or two drug deals, they think they're villains"

When you read or hear of the 'old school' you hear some common quotes and sayings, loyalty, trust, respect, honor dignity among others. Was this all gone?

Danny- It's not all gone, but I know if I got nicked, my circle of friends know they can sleep well. The same goes for me. Trust, reputation and knowing that there is no grasses, that's what I have"

All three men in that room gave me accounts of the differences between 'wrong-uns', and how easy it is to be 'fucked-over'. I had three very intelligent men, that many a crime writer would sell his soul for. The insight and knowledge had me on the edge of my seat. There was no Hollywood here, mate. There were no scripts, or listening or watching a DVD on the ins and outs of the fearsome and clued up. This was real conversations, real experiences and above all, three men sharing the real value of men from the East End. Fucking quality! The three fella's were all hitting me with different stories, and it could not have been timed better. All came to the close of their own stories, and they all said exactly the same thing at the same time "when asked, no comment!" If I was to close with a question, it had to be in tune with my afternoon with Danny. What was the funniest charge he had ever been charged with?

Danny- "Well being charged with an apparent murder, and the charge also attached to that was the denial of a proper burial. Because they couldn't find the body, they tried to attach anything to link me with it. None of my lot would say a word, no fucking way"

The rest of the time I spent in the company of these greats was a mixture of lessons', advice and stories that would help any person understand how to discriminate between right and wrong in their world. For as many a story with a moral or a lesson, there was one right after with a disastrous out come with a room full of laughter. Stories going back to the start of their careers and how they survived, how the basic principles of the East End made them the pillars of their worlds, that of respected and honored individuals.

The lessons I learned from an afternoon with Danny, beat any book or insight I had ever been given by any one claiming they knew the about the Snow hill or the like. I left with a head full of lessons and morals. The same as my family from east London had already raised me by. You cannot be both sides of the fence; fucking hates grasses and be a man. Morales and your dignity are some of the only things you cannot have taken away from you, and one that still rings around my little old head. Danny" when and if you get nicked, you want to say 'it was him', and to get yourself out the door, but you can't!" This was not a make shift conversation. I had met Danny before, the same lessons, the same principals. Seldom is the qualities seen in the old school, in that of the modern day era of criminal. This is something that I have come to learn and that if it is seen in a new school or new face, then this is golden. A prize of an individual, someone you want in your corner, a person that can be respected and trusted.

Several months had passed; and I am back in the land of the 'Septics' and things were starting to fall into place. All the right faces, all the right moves had made an impressive list in the book. Then one palm tree, sunshine filled day and I got a message to bell a pal back in the smoke. I was to call Danny Woollard. "All right, Jase" was the friendly and always inviting voice I got when Danny answered. "Listen, pop round when you're over next, pal." Well, always there for me, so the least I could do is spend time with one of East London's finest.

My day of departure arrived and it could not have come soon enough. A few demons had surfaced. Time is the only healer it is. Bollocks! A much-needed conversation with people that have lost more friends and loved ones is what I needed. The endless lines of kid-crazed families filled the airport but knowing I had been given the opportunity to have another sit down with a known heavily respected person in East London was justification enough. Boarding the plane, I set myself to some reading and a few tunes on the iPod.

When reading back on the lessons and time Danny invested in me, I thought back to something a late friend once told me. 'With the criminal elite, trust is everything. The relationship you build with them is typically started by an introduction by the right people. Over time, your actions, if carried out in an acceptable way will allow more time and also open more doors to open with the heavy hitters. If an invitation is given, never turn it down'. The same friend was grassed up by an outsider and as a result took his own life so as to avoid at least a life term in prison and his partners doing equally as much time. Another memory that sprang to mind is when upon hearing of the company I was keeping someone, commented that "These chaps are hardly knights in shining armor." My reply is if the knight has armor that is still shiny, it simply means he is a man that has never had his armor tested!

Arriving back in London, I was greeted by a pissed off under paid, over worked passport shuffler that has the personality of a half eaten waffle and a face with an impression that it has been hit with a wet fish. The boat on it would warrant any sniper that took aim at it to miss and save a bullet. My parting comment of "chin-up, mate, there's always tomorrow!" Was as welcomed as a fart in a phone box. His shrug and wrinkled jacket suggested tomorrow was just another day in paradise.

As always, I am welcomed into Danny's home and life. A bit of breakas' and Danny sits and listens to my trials and tribulations'. Then as always, looking to help he says, "look, I'll tell ya' what isn't normally discussed outside of my most trusted pals. Going back to the start, Billy Hill was the boss. He was the guv'nor. The Kray twins worked for him. He was absolutely top of the tree. Everyone knew the rules. It was not because of Billy, but he was the boss. He had a lot of good contacts, very good contacts. He even had the blokes that fitted the safes in the post offices and they would just give him the keys. He died a millionaire. He was the first to have a boat, he had clubs in Morocco, was fetching all sorts back from there. Clubs in London, and do not forget he started with nothing. I mean he was international before any of them. He lived out in Tangiers. The Krays worked for Billy. When he retired, he put them up the ladder a bit. He was a very good man, Bill. I liked him. Bill had a fella' working for him called Eddy Chapman. Now, Eddy was a safe cracker, much like what Bill used to do when he first started. Anyway, he got nicked up in Scotland, and broke out of prison. Well, he came down and went to Guernsey. While he was out there, he was nicked again, breaking into safes. German occupation came. Eddy Chapman could talk fluent German, and he became a double agent. He then was coming back to England, making out he was working for the Germans. He even got a German medal but he was really working for Britain and this can be proven. He said to Churchill that he could get close to Hitler, but Churchill would not allow it. Now, after all these years have passed, you can actually read those files. Eddy Chapman told me that they dropped him behind enemy lines and he actually got the plans to the atom bomb and gave them to Britain. That was Billy Hill's right hand men. Billy's minders were George Walker; Billy Walkers brother, he was a multi millionaire in Russia. These were the people he had round him, he had no mugs around him ol' Billy, Proper people.

There was many smaller firms working bellow Billy. Again, the Twins started with Bill. The Richardson's, south London, they were not violent people. They could not have a fight, but were businessmen and money getters. The newspapers had stories about them electrocuting people, nah! Just money people, I know Charlie Richardson very well. If the twins went over there, they (Richardson's) would not have wanted to know. They were money getters. The Twins, I never had a problem with 'em, always paid me and paid well as well. I liked Reg' and Ron'. Never had a crossed word, I think they was real gentleman. I did quite a bit of bird with Reg', he was a good pal. I did bird with him in Wayland prison he was a good friend of mine. I looked after him, again good friend of mine. I was more friends with Reg' than Ronnie, both was nice fella's. Paper talk got out of hand; they did a lot for everybody, looked after everyone. The twins' was as good as gold, I mean they weren't Jesus, but they were as good as gold, good men. George Cornell comes over to kill Ronnie. Ronnie got to him first and killed him, there ya' go.

George Cornell was originally from East London. He moved over there and went to work with the Richardson's. Well, he did come over here to do Ron, and he was telling everyone he shot Freddie Mills, as Freddie was knocking about with Ron and, well he got himself shot didn't he. I think Ron was a fool, to just walk into a pub and shoot someone. You're gonna' get nicked whoever you are as someone is gonna' grass.

He should've waited and done it outside and he wouldn't have got caught. You know what I mean! Reg' of course killed Jack 'the hat'. Jack was only a bully, a proper bully. George Cornell was a tuff man, a very tuff man. Would've probably beat Ron in a fight. Ronnie was an ex boxer, but I think George would've beat him. I think he would've been his guv'nor, but you don't work like that do ya'! I mean in that sort of situation it's not a boxing ring is it, not the same rules.

I've still got good people around me today. Mickey Gluckstead, Angelo Hayman, Richie Reynolds, all good men. We've got a few round us. You know what I mean? I could get on the phone and loadsa' help is there if I ever needed it. We all respect each other, like the old days. Good days they were really. Weren't that much money around really, but all good days, there was no grassing, nothing like that, but that's part of life these days, they say grass on 'em, and that's the end of it.

Things have changed, it was easy in the '60's, and there were no trackers on lorries or cars. There were no cameras, you were able to smash a jeweler's window and you were gone, before the Old Bill showed up. It's been slowed right down. You have to do other things, don't ya'! You'll always get a living. It's not as easy as it used to be, I mean it was easy really, weren't it. That was Billy Hill he would smash windows and all that. Billy told me "you should always be into different things, don't just do one thing. If they get used to you doing one thing, they'll soon cop-ya."

Mickey Gluckstead does cornering (conning) people. He loves it. He's either selling fresh air, or services he don't do and he'll fight anyone. He's had loads on the cobbles, me too, I'd fight anybody. I've never lost a fight and I never will. If I did, I would kill 'em. Bartley Gorman is another good fighting man. Matty Attrell, Ernie Harris, Jackie Right. Teddy Hunt was another great fighter, great fighting men. Roy Shaw, tuff fukka', good fighter Roy, he was a hard man to beat out in the road. Mickey Gluckstead was a tuff man out on the road, tuff, and very tough. I'll tell ya' another very tough man, and you will never hear about him. A fella called Freddie Botham; I think he was the best. Cor, he could fight! When he hit someone, they were gone. He boxed, never got beat. Another good one was Del Croxson. He would fight for fun. He challenged Roy and Lenny. They didn't want to know. He died at the age of 32 in Belmarsh of a drugs over dose, a wonder full fella', Del. Barry Dalton another, I could name a hundred. When I was prize fighting, you could get a bill together just like that. I could ring up 20 geezers. You try to get a bill together today! There ain't any fighting men about. All they'll want to do is stab, or shoot ya'. There ain't any fighting men about like that anymore is there! There was a lot of fighting men years ago. Reg' and Ronnie both fighting men, Reg' used to say to someone "Would you like a cigarette?" and as they reached for it he would give them a left hook. That's what he used to do. Saw him do it loadsa' times. Break their jaws he did. I liked 'em. Did a lot of deals with 'em, they were all right with me. I used to get hold of a lot of one-arm bandits, sell 'em to them and they'd put 'em in clubs. They were good fella's, the twins, I think so anyway. They never grassed no one when they were nicked, did they, they didn't put anyone in it, they were good boys, and they made a lot of people a nice few quid.

They upset the wrong people though. What actually happened in the '60's, Harold McMillan was the prime minister, and his wife was having an affair with Lord Boothby and then she had a child. Anyway, Ronnie Kray was hanging out with Lord Boothby. Well there was a big fuss and it was all in the papers. Well if you have an association with Ronnie Kray, the prime minister's wife and the fella she's having an affair with; Lord Boothby, well it ain't gonna' go down to well, is it! Not only that, the Queens cousin had a club in Kensington, called Esmeralda Barn. You couldn't have bought it for no amount of money. Well, they went up and stuck a gun to his head, and made him sign it over for a few quid. You can't just go an upset the Queen's relations like that, you're gonna' get plenty of bird aren't ya! Well, they never came out did they! I was in with Reggie when he got his parole papers. He'd done 32 years and I was in the next cell to Reg', there was some people that did him no favors. Celebrity types, no good! He lost his parole because of them.

When I was living around Manor Park, Billy Hill lived there in them days. Well there were two brothers that run all of London for Billy, George and Jimmy Woods. They was the two that did the gold bullion at Heathrow airport, they made a film of it after would. Now, they were two good men. Cor, I know them well, they was good people. With people like that on your crew, if they were turned over, you know you're going to sleep at night, don't ya!

Let me tell ya' about Manor park. There was this little estate, and all the streets were named after prisons. There was Parkhurst, Walton, Grantham, all prisons. There was the roughest of the ruff on there. That's where I lived, that's where a lot of villains came from. All the Wood's, Billy Hill lived round there. Gypsy Riley also lived round there. Let me give you an idea how much Billy Hill had. He gave Mickey Riley, that's Phyllis's brother, the equivalent of 6 and a half million pounds in the '60's. He had millions that geezer; he was the cleverest man alive. And you know how he died? He met up with another woman. Well, she overdosed and died. Billy just pined away and died. He had a flat in the Moscow road in Bayswater. I went up there. He was a good man, Billy. He used to have a razor, and what he did was have some black tape round it. He would just cut you to pieces. He wasn't a big man, but I tell ya'! He was lethal with that chiv (knife), I tell ya'. Gypsy too, she would take out a sailor's eye right out too. She had a gang of girls round there. Ivy Taylor, Olli Taylor, Vera. She had a gang of about 6 women working with her. Jack Spot was against Billy Hill. Yeah, Billy finished him off.

One of the gamest women you'd ever see was Linda Calvey. They did that T.V show based on her. She was called the back widow. Her husband went on a bit of work, he only had a sawn off shotgun. When the police got out of the Range Rovers, they had high- powered rifles, shot, and hit Danny and the geezers in the motor drove off, Ronnie Cook and Leslie Joyce. They drove off and left him. Danny died. Lynda palled up with Leslie Joyce, got him out to Spain and he was never seen nor heard from again. When she came back, she then palled up with Ronnie Cook, who had 380 grand. She spent that, and when Ronnie came out, she shot him. Killed him and got 20 years. She is a game woman that Lynda I tell ya', very game. There ya' go. Some people I know, and there's many more that are just as good, a lot of have since gone, but there are a few still around. Not a lot, but a few and they are always there for me, like I am for them."

Finishing my time with Danny is always a tough one. His charm and honesty can bring light into a person's darkest of times. The time Danny spent behind the wall would have put many a man in an early grave. Danny and his personality, demand much more from life to let something like time slow him down. Concrete, in both his word and actions Danny has welcomed my troubles as his own, and seen me through many an obstacle. Danny remains one of two people that are top of my tree. Nothing is ever a problem or an unwanted request. There for a friend, as much as it is always a pleasure to be support in any issue that has tried to question my well-being. The old guard! Retired from the underworld and criminal activities has not stopped Danny from helping and being there for his own. Not one to fade into obscurity but remain as a pillar for the ones he calls pals.

Late 2013 I learnt from another friend that Danny Woollard is longer with us. Danny Snr passed, leaving many people with a part of their lives missing. He was a true friend and family member.

R.I.P Danny. I will miss you mate.

Vic Dark

Vic Dark has lived the life you could place on the sides of a coin. One side the action, loss, suffering and pain. The commitment needed to be feared and respected within the underworld. The other side of that coin being able to look back and tell you the real story of crime, the true meaning of loyalty, honor and respect, the story of a real villain; bad to the bone.

When you speak with Vic, there is calmness about him. There is control and confidence. With the reputation he carries, it is almost contradictory of his calm nature during conversation. There is truth in the saying 'power is nothing control' and Vic is a representation of this statement.

Being amongst London's criminal elite, Vic carries a respect for what is well known and considered as the 'Old Guard'. His name is rarely mentioned and even less is known of the group. Blue bloods have their Freemasons and secret societies, the underworld and criminal fraternity have the old guard. The code is standard within the crime families. Again, here Vic carries the rules to the letter. One of the best examples of loyalty and there for your own was an armed robbery that Vic was on were things simply did not go to plan. This in short resulted in the second member of the robbery being seriously injured and Vic making the policeman he'd taken hostage carry the man from the crime scene, risking not only his own life, but not knowing the extent of his crime partner's injuries his life too. What ensued is legendary in known circles. Hostages, car chases and his life were being taken in a direction Vic had not planed for. The ending result was a shoot out with the police armed response unit. This division of Police does not fuck about. In response to an armed robbery, the unit replies with automatic weapons and a tactical almost military approach. An every day person that walked this path would have fallen apart in this situation in a heartbeat.

In one of my first conversations with Vic, there was a matter of principle and rules to his involvement. 'The company you keep, Jase, is an important one!' Proud to say I followed the request, as a result he was happy to contribute. No matter of my standing or friendship with those that opened certain doors for me, Vic is careful whom he allows in his personal life and for good reason. Since his release as a double 'A' category, prisoner the slightest blemish or involvement with the wrong people could land him back in trouble.

From his early days and as a known chap at West Ham, to his progression as a money getter, Vic has led a fearless no-back-down approach to anything thrown at him. At the age of 17, he was a main face within a group of armed robbers. While many he once fought alongside with on that remained on the terraces twisting people's heads, Vic was on the pavement earning more than a shiny penny. Vic has had his metal tested on more than one occasion and come out stronger each and every time. His fearless approach to earning money from armed robberies allowed him to make as many as 3 hits a day.

So, who is Vic Dark?

Vic: "I was just a working class boy who had no money. I had a Maltese father, grew up behind a junk shop, and had a bit of a chip on his shoulder, Psychology wise. I mean if you look at physiologists and me being in prison for such a long time, and there (in prison) they have some of the best psychologists in the world, they'll sit you down, take you back in time and they'll try and work out all the reasons why you turned out to be the person you are today. I mean I didn't realise that because my dad was Maltese, mum was English and living behind a junk shop, I had a lot of issues. You know, I had people looking down on me, so I suppose that's the Vic Dark and that's what started the ball rolling."

Integrity- Part of the make-up for this man's identity, and also how he carried himself within the day to day running of his life and former career. Much like a professional banker, except here Vic was robbing them instead of running them. For those that consider an individual as a primary source of information, consider Vic's life and experiences as both a lesson in life and an education. Vic's start in life developed into a multi-layered meditation on loss, hardship, his right for respect and yes, violence. Known for bank robbing, his convictions also include violence, stabbings and shooting. What is not known about the East Ender Vic Dark?

Vic: "I look after the old; I stick up for the working class people. I do a lot of work for the old people and those that are bullied like women and children. I step in and stop a lot of people getting bullied. It's kind of like working behind the scenes. I'm not a copper, but I stop a lot of things before it happens and that's one thing I just can't stand are bullies."

I mentioned in our conversation that there are some great pro grammes for those needing help in the community with bullies, and typically its run and organised by the people in the community, and not by higher authorities.

Vic: "There's a break down in the communication. There's a huge melting pot. You have all these different cultures, and different cultures have different attitudes. I have a completely different attitude to a lot of people, and those that wasn't born in the poverty and the brotherhood of the East End as we know; it's the East End villains. We stick together. I can get on the phone and get say a hundred people, easily a lot more. It's all about the East End and where I got brought up. Our people trust each other. It's respect. Respect is the big word really. Unfortunately people easily follow the pound note today, they don't follow principles, they don't follow the principle of the person, and if there's a person who is a good guy and hasn't got a penny, and then you have a person that has a lot of money and he's also a bad guy, a wrong-un, I'll help the good guy. And that's the difference between most people and me. People haven't got the principles any more like they used to, when it comes to a pound note. This is where you have to get answers to the questions. It's not about money, it's about loyalty, and a lot of people haven't got that today."

From here, I'm given some insight and lessons on the principles and how they've changed. Personal advice from a man that was tested and never folded for his principles and code, an understanding that makes a man from the East End and what it takes to be respected and how it's gone from a lot of the villains of today. From this I thought when did Vic realise; age or situation, he was destined for a life of crime?

Vic: "When I was growing up, and seeing the difference between the rich and the poor. My dad was working for Ford, I was working on the railways, I was doing my martial arts, and I was going nowhere and with the abilities and the arsehole, I found it was easy for me to earn money really."

Life for Vic was like a trapeze act, but without the net and there was no better place to mold and test your minerals than the East End. Here Vic explains why.

Vic: "I turned it to my advantage. I learnt with the mask and the gun, and I know it's a bit wrong, but I've never robbed a working class person in my life. And that's the difference between a lot of us, and that's why we're called the old guard. The old school. Now I want you to hear about the old school."

O.K, my chance to have a real face, genuine, not imported or copied, a man that's not a celebrity, not plastic and can provide insight what the old school and old guard is really like and all about.

Vic: "It is the people that was from the '60's and the '70's, the Kray's and Freddie Foreman's era who gave us the beliefs we had that you don't inform on your fellow companion, you don't have it with wrong-uns, stick with the way you was raised and principles, it's how you was brought up, that's the old school. And when you bury one of the old guard, you see thousands turn up. When Joey Pyle died, there were nearly seven thousand people there. When Reggie Kray died, there was about twenty thousand. That's the old guard. There's not many left now. There's thought its dead, there isn't many new kids coming up, that follow our principles."

Again, I am given some advice that is golden. A generation that is slowly dying, one of the old guard warns me and tells me more on what is seen and easily accepted as good advice by others out there, but in fact is total bollocks. Vic explains to me, that there is a breed of person and exists in our society. With what would seem as 'the way' and some that claim to be 'in the know' that are in fact a total waste of people's time and space. I don't have to quote here boys and girls or repeat some personal advice Vic gave me, Just understand that this man is of the breed and class of knowing the score and really was part of what you only see in the movies read in books and hear of what a real villain was all about. It has further explained and shared.

Vic: "There are a lot of us; we're a quiet army, an unseen army. We're not seen all together. Where you have football hooligans that mass in numbers, we're not like that. Again we are a quiet army. Say there's a problem, some one's getting hurt, I'd meet up with the people that would do what they have to do, and then things are obviously done, aren't they! Most people when they get found out, I mean people don't get killed for nothing, but the youngsters today do, if you looked at someone wrong, they would kill someone. Now in my world, people would've got ironed out because they're either wrong-uns, or done something seriously wrong. Going back to football hooliganism, for me it was a learning curve. You had your numbers, and that you had the arsehole to fight. For me it wasn't really anything to do with football. It was London fighting Manchester, or London fighting Liverpool it was territorial. It was about thousands of them coming down and trying to take the piss, and us meeting them head on. It was never about the football, it was about the tear ups. For me, it started with having a punch up on the road, then in the neighbourhood, then football, then I took on half the police force, and they're the biggest gang in the world aren't they, and you can't underestimate them. I've been in 5 major battles, that's 5 major trials, and I was a 'AA' cat prisoner, and I've been acquitted twice, by a protected jury, now ones ever done that. And that's where I also help people."

On one phone conversation, Vic said he was in the middle of trying to save a young girl from a lengthy sentence. Apologizing to cut me off short on the phone and he will catch up with me later. A few days passed and we carry on the conversation bringing me up to speed on the situation he was involved in

Vic "I'm helping a young girl right now, and there's certain things that aren't allowed. When I give advice, some of the people look at me as if I'm mad. Any real top criminal should know Archibald backwards (the book on definition and terms in law; what can and can't be done). In my game you have to know the book. I spent many years studying it. This was the type of world I ended up in. It's a different world, a different class; there are not many that are really in this 'world', there's very few of us left. I've learned my lessons, not because they beat me, but because I was in the box for many years. I've got a family. Now, I want a quiet peace full life. I'd done ten years two weeks out of the original fifteen years. I did eight years five months and three weeks out of a twelve-year sentence. I've never had parole; I've done it the hard way. When I went back, where all these scum bag heroin addicts, arguing over their telly's and radios. Using their phones, and I think what have I fought and lost for, all those years, with these sorts in the prison system. And that again is why I'm different. Some of these people out there claiming this and that have never even been arrested. I'd be inside and on the wings, I'd see all these self claimed gangsters, then I'd see some young fella' from up north, rolling around on the floor having it with the screws, and he's got more arsehole than these cunts standing up there put together, who claim they're all that. I've been to the worst places in someone's life. I've seen people hanging from the bars in their cell. And that's why the bond with my own children will never be the same, and it's still hard. When they'd be on a visit, I wasn't allowed to touch my girl friend; I was a double category 'A' prisoner. And then when you come out, you've got to pick the pieces up. It's very hard, even now. It's hard. For all those years, they made a wall between you and your family. You don't realise it, but that's how they do it. Sometimes I see a family all happy together kissing and hugging, and I think fuck me, I wish that was me, they robbed that from me."

It's been said to me by some pals 'in the know', that aggressive behavior can be quite rewarding as long as you stay in character. This intrigued me, much like why are we as humans are attracted to crime, the naughtiness and the day to day run-in's of the feared and sometimes unknown, with Vic, who has a criminal record that would keep many a crime buff in awe. What is it about the life of crime, does he think attracts Joe public?

Vic: "I think they just like the excitement. They don't like the rapists, the nonces and the like. You turn the telly on and watch shows like East Enders and they have to have a villain in it. It's just something people like. Your action films, they love 'em, don't they. They just love their all action hero's, but again in crime it's not your child sex offenders or your nonces, your rapists, those are a different type of criminal, they're not in our league, they're scum."

Apathy! Not a word in my daily vocabulary, but you would agree, wouldn't it be boring if we earned this title? What have you experienced? For me, and my two brothers, we set the dares amongst ourselves. A life without the adventures and exploits would have been a boring one, especially if there was nothing to talk about. So if I was to ask on a specific time or memory within Vic's life, It should be was there a situation you was in that made you think 'fuck me, this could be the end of it all?

Vic: "Well there was this one incident. I'm the only man to ever get away, carrying a mate, surrounded by armed police. Well, I got away, and I was having a bit of a gun battle with the armed response unit of the police, I got myself in this field, and I buried myself in the earth. Well, they (police) came through, missed me the first time, but the second time they had a dog and it was sniffing all around me. It had been raining, and laying there in the earth and I could hear my heart beat. Anyway I was watching the dog, that was about 7 feet away, and when I looked up I could see them all just standing there, so close I could see their numbers and as I'm laying there with a hand gun in each hand. One down to my side the other in the mud. Now, where they'd followed the footprints into this potato field, and he'd come right above me, so close it was just inches away. They was just standing there, and I thought if they see me. Well, in my mind I was thinking if they did see me they'd either try and iron me out, or I'd have to iron them out. If they were just one, maybe two inches closer, they would've stood on my leg. I think that has been the most critical moment in my life. When they went, a few hours passed I crawled out of the hole and wondered into a pig farm where they was held up and looking for me, there was 30, maybe 40 handed. It was also there, that I thought what could happen next, a shoot out? In their minds they could've shot and killed me, and in my mind I knew I wasn't going to not go without taking some of them with me. That there was also a time when I thought I'd never get out of prison alive. If you kill a cozza and you go in prison, you are at the mercy of the guards. I honestly think not many people would've come across a situation like that. And again, looking back, that was seriously fucking heavy. If I'd been found, they'd killed me, if I came out of the ground too early I could've killed them and I'd never came out alive."

They say that you always remember the best and worst memories in your life with equal conviction. Was this true for Vic, and if so, what was his best memory from being a key figure or being involved in the underworld?

Vic: "It's funny, but there is one thing that sticks in my mind. I was facing a serious sentence and I thought to myself, as I'm standing there, and the Judge said I'm sentencing you to 24 years today. Go to prison, 18 years, blah, blah, blah, he read on read on read on, I waited right to the end of it, and a Welsh cozza was standing next to me, and as it was read out he said "Justified" and I just said, "Fuck you!" The whole court gave a gasp of disbelief. Well then, I got back to Brixton high security and then the next day I got moved to High Sutton. There I got a copy of the Sun newspaper and on the front was 'Dark shouts fuck you at the announcement of 18 years'. I thought to myself at least I got myself back on track, you know, and it's one thing that just stays in my mind. I was proud of that, and kept that copy of the Sun in my cell, a kind of inspiration. Thinking about it, I was given a serious lump of porridge and I stood my own, do you see what I'm saying? It's just that I'm a proud person, not necessarily proud of being a criminal, just that I'm a proud person."

We see the stories in both the newspapers and on the telly, prisoners making a bit extra on the inside. Typically, it is played out in the movies. (You know, the ones you do not watch as this would only glorify the violence you so whole heartily disagree with, Mr. I don't watch them, I don't know what you're talking about!). Being Vic was a bit more under the ready eye, than your average man, was this true in his life behind the concrete wall, in his opinion, was the villainy involved in prison, as hard as the outside world of crime or harder?

Vic: "It's hard, no question. I mean for me, I was an 'AA' cat prisoner, in fact it was fucking terrible inside. You've got so many nut cases in side. It's like walking through a minefield when you walk out in the morning. You could have the I.R.A. I mean I was in units, it's totally different, and you've also every worst case physcofrenic in England, that's been put away and he could have, killed maybe 4 or 6 people and they're on your landing aren't they. It's not exactly a way to expect to wake up with a smile on your face is it! There could be some of the biggest mass murderers you could think of, and I'm the next cell. I wouldn't say prison is a fucking happy place, you know. I've had some laughs in there. Having a drink, partying things like that, but most of it is depressing, and if anyone says prison and being a category 'A' prisoner is easy is a liar. You're locked up 23 hours a day, you can't work, because you're high security, it's a fucking absolute nightmare. Again, if you're a category 'A' or 'AA' it's not easy at all. It is in fact double hard. Always searches, they drive ya' mad the cunts."

So would Vic have preferred to be a criminal in or out of prison?

Vic: "There is no criminal activity as a cat 'A' prisoner. All you can do is get your canteen and live really. It's an existence, prison. It's not about being a criminal on the inside it's about being banged up for 23 hours a day as a criminal. You're not a criminal on the inside it's just about being a name in there, especially us. I mean, walk into a bathroom, take everything out of it, put a bucket in the corner, that's what I had for most of my bird, no telly, and imagine that for 20 years."

Many a film and book dictates the way of a gangster / criminal day goes this way, that way. Can Vic share a memory of a day on one of his more famous known of activities, were the memory of that incident sticks with him the best?

Vic: "It was fucking worrying about where you were going to get your next pound note really, that's how it basically was. I mean we was big spenders, especially when I was young, I mean you lived it, it was different, and I lived it, and I had to live that life. I mean I didn't give a fuck, man or beast, I could tackle a man, a bank, a main post office, you know what I mean. It was where the money was, my everyday life, was looking where the pound notes was really. And it's a nice feeling when it's over."

He has many titles, and he is known as a terrifying man. One that surely puts chills down the average person and second thoughts to some one that should know better. Is he / was Vic a dangerous man? Here Vic answers very calmly, no second thoughts, not a pause in his answer, but instead very calm and relaxed. It is almost as if I am being taught lessons, and being given invaluable advice from a man that has been there, and more.

Vic: "Everyone's a dangerous man aren't they? Anyone can be a dangerous man if they're pushed. It's like everyone can be a hero. Hero's in my life are firemen, fighting fires every day, ambulance people, saving lives. They're unsung heroes aren't they; they're the ones saving lives. That's how I look at heroes, they're my hero's."

Looking for an answer, Vic gave an extended answer touching on personal beliefs and feelings. From a man, that some may say is cold and shows mall ace due to lengthy incarcerations. Instead showing a sense of respect and gratitude to some of his own personal collection of saved thoughts. If a film was to be made on the East End fella, we know as Mr. Vic dark. Who would play the lead role?

Vic: "Well there's not many that come to mind, that would play me, but I'd say one that comes close is Robert De Niro, especially when he did that film Heat, for me that was the closest to reality, where he has the shoot out with the police. Then he goes back to do the police informer at the end. He then had to decide, either to go with his bird and get away with all the money, or should he go back and do the guy that grassed them all up. For me that was one of the best I've seen."

Appreciating Vic is a very humble man, I wanted to ask, if there were a film to be made on Vic, where it would be filmed. Here the answer is given without pause or hesitation.

Vic: "The East End!"

As many a young man, my brothers and I always watched the gangster films of past. Who is some of Vic's all time top gangsters or even from the real world some of the best underworld figures?

Vic: "The ones I look up to are the old-guard. That's where I'd leave that, simply with the old school. And they know exactly who I'm talking about. They are and always will be the leading lions in my life, the old guard. My beliefs came from the old guard."

Having a former life in the underworld, what remains with Vic from his humble beginnings in crime?

Vic: "Codes, principles and respect. And I'd like to think that I've earned respect, for the codes I've lived by."

With a code of ethics that the underworld was once famous for, has it changed a lot.

Vic: "It's all changed everyone's for themselves. No ones for each other anymore."

What underworld ethic if you like, does Vic see as a good moral standing in today's society?

Vic: "Anyone that helps the old girl across the road, someone that's looking after the working class, someone that picks up and carries the banner for the working class people."

So, what made the East End so great?

Vic: "It's the people that came out of it. I mean, you had the Purely Queen, with all the buttons sown all over themselves, all the old grannies laughing out in the street, it's an era that's been lost, a great era in fact that's been lost in today's culture. It was an absolutely fantastic era, everyone helped themselves, helped each other, you'd see the laughter you just don't see that no more. What is needed in the East End, is someone who has been educated and lived the life. The lessons needed, can't be learned from a book or classroom, only from the school of hard knocks."

Vic's life has been a mixture of what the great East End boasted strength, respect and plenty of colourful characters and villains. The pals my brother and I had go back as far as I can remember all quality. Vic, being the man he is, working on a standard of basic principles and ethics, must have promoted quality within the ranks.

Vic: "Yeah, I've got quite a few friends about."

You appeared in the film 'The End', documenting the faces in London. If you were to send a message to anyone watching you, either film TV or a book, what would that message be?

Vic: "Follow the old guard, follow the old school. Stick to the old school beliefs."

If a message had to leave behind, just one thing known about Vic, what would it be?

Vic: "I'd like to be buried upside down, so the whole world could kiss my arse."

Is there anything that Vic would have like to be involved in from other famous so-called criminal activities (that hit the press or telly)?

Vic: "Nah, I think I've been on enough (chuckles). You name it. I've done it. Been there, bought the T-shirt. The life of crime isn't what it's cracked up to be. One second being who you are, and it's not been easy for me, it's been fucking hard. I reap the rewards now, because I've met someone I love, got my family, live in a nice place, it's all come right for me, but I've had to pay my dues for it."

Now this does not mean that Vic has forsaken his fondness or natural ability for crime, but instead of living it or doing it, he simply directs his efforts into the working class and their needs. When you speak to Vic, there is still the same power and confidence in his voice of the man that was once an active member of the underworld. Some would say a face, a legend and one of the greats. Vic will be his modest self and tell you as he did me:

Vic: "I'm not great, I just understand what respect and loyalty is all about."

East End villains are known for their famous sayings or often a classic one-liner that has some meaning lesson or a code woven into the words of wisdom. Does Vic have any to share?

Vic: "You can't be wrong and strong, and you can't be wrong, if you're right!"

Vic has retired from his former life but will continue to be a reliable measure in the world of the real East Ender and those in need. In the world of entertainment, we imagine we are the bank robber, action hero or even playing the villain. We marvel in awe at the culturally unaccepted or frowned upon acts of those playing the role. I personally always backed and rooted for the villain pulling the heist, the bank robbery or simply trying to get a result. I always thought this was a bit more daring and interesting. How about you? Closing out this part of the puzzle in my journey, I recall something Vic said to me. "Jase, I've hit 'em all and I've hit them hard but what I respect the most is the family man."

Angelo 'Festus' Hayman

No sooner had I reached West London and I get a voice mail. Gotta' love technology. We can put a man on the moon. Receive and send signals millions of miles away but go into a tunnel on the underground and you are outa' luck! Once again, Danny has come through. Listening to the voicemail I had been left was golden. Before leaving Danny Woollard's that day I was asked if I would like to speak with another chap that'd be a very good contributor to my cause. Absolutely, if it is from someone that comes recommended by Danny then it is without a shadow of a doubt worth it.

The following morning could not have come soon enough. I am on my feet lively and heading out to deep Essex. This time I have the luxury of a chauffeur. My girlfriend has offered to get me there and back. Bonus! Save on the shoe leather and by far better company than the hustle and bustle the underground has to offer and besides, someone to give stick to being she is a chelski supporter. No sooner than we arrive at Danny's then I am meeting and sitting down with a very trusted and close friend of Danny's. Angelo Haymam.

Angelo was convicted for his part in the 'Snow Hill Robbery' and in turn received a 21-year sentence. His life has certainly been an event worth documenting. This known fella was once high perched within the criminal empire and had real life experiences within a field that was a worthy investment in my cause.

Sitting with Angelo, you get a sense of 'been there, done that'. Calm, respectful and above all well mannered. Angelo is of the money getter villains' era. Not a simple snatch and grab merchant by any means. Like all those involved, Angelo was welcoming and accommodating. Before I even sat down to build some questions and consider what and how to approach the questions, Angelo opened with "how can I help, mate?" Again, another quality person from the ranks was more than willing to come through, give his life long hard lessons, and experience from a world of hardship and struggle while maintaining the code.

A man's journey through life can reflect the shifts and changes necessary to survive. Angelo's most famous conviction was the infamous Snow hill robbery; that landed him some serious porridge. Like those that are known and respected within the underworld, Angelo plays by the 'rules'. Again, not to be confused with the purse snatching, two-bob petty thief, Angelo was guided by the 'code' that dictates what is simply right and wrong.

Angelo - "For me, like most in the start, it was a means of survival. It was different back then though. When you were younger back then, it's not like it is now. You survived more for yourself. Now you have the care system, this system, that system. You can't get away with now what you could back then. When you are younger, your family breaks up, you know, your mum and dad. Now, my dad was Maltese. They can be vicious tempered fuckers, believe me, especially in them days. I give him his due he was a hard workingman, but he was fucking violent. Well, my mum and dad separated. It was a case of they've gone their way, I've gone mine. My brother stayed with my dad. So I started squatting in a little council flat. No toilet, no fucking nothing, you know what I mean! I think I was only 13, and you've got to eat, haven't you! The first thing I nicked was a hamburger stall, and a tin of hamburgers. Done that, but that's not going to' last forever is it! So, I've got all my mates. Now I was bought up in a gang called the Chick sand gang, Brick Lane. Even to this day, it's generations that have taken over, the same brothers and cousins. You know gone from one down to the other. So, you start off burgling, warehouses, dis, dat and the other.

We'd burgle warehouses at least four or five times a week. It was like forever. When I was 14, I was running down the road with mink coats. If I'd had the brains or the knowledge, I'd earned a fortune, but you don't, so people just come and they're mugging you off, you know what I'm saying! I remember we did a jewelry shop once. We got up on the roof, and we knew how to get passed the security, and this was by the time I was 14 years of age. Don't tread on the mats. Don't do this you know. I knew what to do. I'd carry ammonia, that way if someone grabbed hold of ya' 'bang' Straight in their eyes, he's gone! I don't care who he is. He's had it. I never got pleasure in hurting no one. When you're young, you don't want someone grabbing hold of you. You don't want to get nicked. So you will do what you have to do. I'm not saying it's a great thing, but you do what you have to do. Now I'm not going to' sit here and tell you I'm not going to' hurt no body. You know, I'm like the old time villain, I won't do this and I won't do that! If I have to do something for money, I'll do it for money. I can sit here and tell you I've never done it out of pleasure. It's always been about money, because I think that's a bit muggy, I mean why do you have to hurt somebody if you don't need to! And that's the first thing, give me money, and then I'll change my mind. It might sound horrible, but I'm being honest. So, after all that, I mean you get a bit older and a bit wiser. You then learn what you want for your stuff. My ol' man used to buy the stuff from us. I knew he was mugging us off with some of the stuff, but you know. It was when I was about 15 or 16that I went back home, with my foster brother. This came about when I was squatting. I met up with this bloke, that we 'come such good friends, that he become like my brother. His dad had died. His mum had left him. So I went back to my mum and dad with the condition that he comes with, and that they foster him legally. And that's what I did.

Shortly after, I went quiet, I joined the army, was there for a few years, done a bit of soldiering as you do. Left the army, and what's about! I mean, really, what's about! There was nothing about, and I've got all this knowledge, and I can't earn a pound note. Then I started doing small stuff, here and there. Nothing regular, Just enough, you know what I mean! Got with my wife, had twins, I was about 21. Things are hard you know what I'm trying to say! Things are really fucking hard. Living in Brick Lane, doing a bit of work here and there, nothing fully though and it was always in my head, 'What's all this bollocks work!' I remember saying when I was a kid to all my cousins and my family owned all the speilers and the gambling. That's why I've never gambled in my life. My ol' man would've murdered me! I was never allowed to use a machine. Even now I don't gamble. I don't drink, I don't smoke and never took a drug in my life. I've got other vices, but not them. So what it is in that area and you had some right nutty people.

I remember once the Kray twins came to the Maltese cafe, as someone owed them money. I was only about five or six, but that stayed in my head forever. Believe it or not, those people are your idols. It's like for me now, I go certain areas, and kids look up to me. When I came out of prison, I went to pick my daughter up from school. So I pulled up in a Range Rover, I'd only been out of prison a week. My little girl was about 15 at the time. She's came out of school, and as I've pulled up there's kids everywhere! So, she's got in the car and I've said we'd better wait, as it looks like there could be a bit of trouble here, and I pointed out. I then said there's a lot of boys standing over there and pointed at another bunch of boys somewhere else, and she told me that they was here because of me and they wanted to see me and who I was! That took me back to when I was a kid. Going back a few years, I knew Charlie Kray very well. I got a letter from Reggie saying "Good fella" and all that. So I can understand how kid's minds work. Some might think that's a shame but, then I've never regretted anything I've done in my life. If I wanted to work in Sainsbury's, I'd worked in Sainsbury's, I don't regret anything and that's the truth.

So, you get older. I've got my wife, my kids, and you try and get a job, don't ya'! You know, you've got to do the norm'. I just don't think I'm a normal fella'. I think that's what it is, you know, but you do the normal, but then you know, you're still 'duckin' and divin'. Now, I'd started up in a security company. I was the manager of it, no one's above me, and I'm earning about 600 quid a week. Now, this was about 20 years ago. So 600 quid a week is a lot of money. Well, that's not good enough! Now, I've so many guards, and so many that don't even exist. I've got ghost guards on sites all over London, and I'm taking their wages. It's not just about the money. I'd love to just sit here and say it's about that, but I think we get a buzz out of doing different things in life. It's just that little extra bit of 'villainy' that gets ya'. Well, I did that for about 14 months. You obviously get caught don't ya'! I'm asked, "Why do we have all these extra guards that we don't have!" Well, I resign. Then I start on the proper stuff. You know vans and that kind of stuff. Armed robberies, some heavy-duty stuff, and a lot of pavement stuff. It's bringing in a living. You've got a nice car, a nice house, shooting off here and there. Sometimes you haven't got any money. If you speak to anyone in crime, and they tell you they've had money all their life they're a liar. One day, I'm not joking, you're driving around in a XJR super charged Jag', 52 thousand pounds. A month later, you've got a MK 1 Escort.

I don't know anyone that's always had money. Even now I have god times and bad times but that's life in any trade. Well, I started doing that and that was my main thing. As for the violent side, I've never done violence for pleasure. Half the time, there's no need for it. If you set up a robbery properly, the chance of violence is, well if it's done properly, it's hardly there, and those that have to, well it's muggy. Again, I'll be honest, I'm not going to' say that I feel sorry for the person, this, that and the other. In that situation, I'm after the money. And I won't the fucking money! If I've come that far in what I've done, I want your fucking money. If you say you're not going to give it to me, well, listen, you're gonna' give me the money, or I wouldn't be standing in front of ya' risking getting a life sentence. If I've got that near to ya', I'm walking away with the money! So I will use violence. I can't honestly think though, an occasion I've used it. If you do it properly, there is no need to do it. Muggs do it. Muggs will go in shouting and throwing people about. Someone wants to know that when you go on him or her that they're not going to be killed. They've got a chance of walking out with nothing wrong with them.

This geezer, this robbery, the last one I got nicked for, he was so worried about his wife, the poor fucker, "Oh, my wife" ya know. Well, I said "I can't leave ya' here", because where we put the motor, we covered it, leaded it. I didn't want to leave this fella' rotting away there. He looked like an old fella'. So I said "That's alright, mate. Give us the name of your wife and the phone number and you've got my word nothing's going to happen to you." I asked him if he'd been treated fine and he said "Yeah." I said, "Well, I give you my word, you'll be treated fine." He then showed me that the cuffs/

quick clips were hurting him. So I asked for a blade and cut them right off. During the event I had to simply cover his face, as the plan was to reverse the van up, but he said he was scared of that. So what we did was smash all the mirrors so he couldn't see what's behind him. Now we could simply reverse the van up to the armored van, so when we were up top cutting our way in, he could not see the motor's number plate. So, what I'm trying to say to you there's other ways of doing something. If he's all claustrophobic, don't cover his face, the poor fucker. We're there for the money, not his life. So we did all this, got away, phoned up his misses, explained the situation, that he's perfectly alright, but get someone 'round there to pick him up. When we got done, his statements said that these people looked after him. He then gave a description of the person that come up to the van window. When I jumped up to the window; it was right outside the police station. I put it right up to the window, and said, "Open it or I'll blow your fucking head off." He saw me a few inches away! His description was nothing like me. Why? It must have been something! You understand what I'm trying to say to ya'! He really did have a bad memory, or he thought 'hold it a minute'. What's right is right. If you have to cause violence but most of the time, there's no need for it. You leave it to these arsehole kids, with their trousers down to their knees, with their arses hanging out, screaming and shouting, waving guns about shooting lamp posts and fresh air. If you do things calmly and planned there's usually none. I mean I could take you off the street without a noise, without nothing. Just walk up to them and walk with the person. And while you've got them, their brain isn't functioning. He will turn from a big man, to a sheep in about half a second. This you can do with any man, unless they're a villain. The villain knows the game in his head. A straight goer won't. Now for that, I got 21 years.

When you come out, what are you going to do! You do what you know. It's as simple as that. What would you want me to do? Become a schoolteacher! If they had half a brain, they'd pick someone like me to go check out their security and their banks or their vans, but they won't do that, as they think we are there to rob them. And they're probably right, we would! They pick monkeys to do it, who don't know what they're doing. Scary! Here's one that sometimes crosses my mind. When we was being bugged, we come out one time, all shootered-up, if I'd turned right, I'd been shot-up by the O.B as they were waiting for me. As when I got nicked, I saw the statements from the SO 19's. They were waiting for us. Let's be honest. They're not fucking around, but then neither am I. They'd shoot us, and I'd have shot them. They're not straight goers. Not someone that works in Sainsbury's. You've got to treat people the way they treat you.

Another one that taunts me is when the three boys were shot in Essex. Well, one night we were out and up to no good, and they actually nicked us for what we were up to. Now if they hadn't had nicked us, we'd been fucked! Anyway, we were around the area, shootered-up, and lucky that we did get nicked. The O.B was listening in and they said we were out to hijack a lorry. So, if they weren't listening in, they'd nicked us for the Essex boy's murders too! Those boys used to come down the office, so the connection was there and it could've been really shitty. Another time is when the O.B alleged that we went to shoot another geezer. What they said was we went up through the garden, went to the house, as we got to the window the O.B reckon we saw a geezer, black helmet, black outfit, firearms, ready to shoot the geezer in the house. Well, that's what they say. What we saw was the SO 19's and we fucked off. That's on the record. They were waiting there, that's another time they could've shot us.

You've got other circumstances where you fall out with people, monies involved, and they're trying to fucking shoot ya'. It isn't always the police that are trying to shoot ya'. You've got the baddies trying to shoot ya'. When they (SO19) come for me; well it's been twice. The first time they come for me, I was lying in bed and it was quarter past six, boom, boom, and boom! Now, I can name that tune in one, I know who that is. They'd put the ram on the doorframe; and it's a sixteen hundred pound door, solid steel frame, thick oak wood, blocks that go everywhere. Bloody great big door that was, and they took it off in six seconds! Marvelous bit of machinery that was. They'd rammed it with hydraulic rams and I heard the shotguns go. Boom, boom! They'd shot off the hinges off the door. I'm one flight of stairs up; sitting room and kitchen down stairs, you know one of them one-flight bed room upstairs, bathrooms. So I've jumped out of bed, looked out of the window, and they're all there. Laser sights everywhere, through the window. I thought "Fuck me, must me something!" you know what I mean! Then one of my kids came out the bedroom, and I heard them (SO 19's) scream, "There's someone in the passage, there's someone in the passage." I literally booted my kid back in the room, because they saw her, the sights and lasers were coming through, you know what I'm trying to say! So she's gone flying back into the bedroom. I've then gone back into the bedroom and dragged all the kids into another bedroom. I've then said, "Sit here and don't move." Now all I've had on is a pair of underpants, and I'm not going out showing how well endowed I am, you know! So, the SO 19's are screaming, "Come down, come down!" I'm thinking 'I ain't coming down yet, mate!' So once I've got all the kids all right, I'm shouting down there "I'll come down, but my kids are up here." They continue to shout "Come down." I could hear the fear in their (SO 19's) voices. I think if I'd acted like that I'd be a dangerous person on the street. They were shaking and I'm thinking what the fuck are you shaking for man. So I just did what they said, with my hands up, I went down the stairs, Let me tell you something, I'm 5 ft. 6 and my hands where so far up, they were scraping the ceilings. I'm giving them no chance. I come down the stairs, hands up, walking towards them. They do the same thing as they always do. I walked towards them, they had their shields up putting their guns through the shields, and they ram you, smash you on the head a few times with the butts of the gun and they always do that, every single time. Two sets of hand cuffs on me, took me around, helicopter outside over head, ambulances blocking all the streets, I'm in the car, and they took me to the nick, helicopter following the Range Rovers like I'm a terrorist. So they got me to the nick, I'm sat there, and I never make a statement, ever! I don't ever make a statement, I never say anything, ever. I do not even say "no comment." You want something out of me, try and get it out of me. You know what I mean! Once you say something, you're committed, that's it. They've got nothing on me. 6 days later, they let me go on bail. So I'm in doors, about 6 weeks later, and all of a sudden 'boom', the doors are blown off again. I thought 'Fuck me, here we go again!' And the doors, they cost a fucking fortune. And they still take 'em off in 6 seconds, and always with the shotguns, on the hinges. Doesn't matter how many you've got, always all of them off, exactly the same routine as before. The same as before, I got the kids in the bedroom, but now I've got myself ready, you know, shower, trousers on, a bit smart. Not going out again for all my neighbours seeing me. So same as before, this time I came down when I was ready, but this time when I went down, there's a dog there, a little box on his head, a camera. They're watching me through the dog. I've gone down stairs, and I know what's going to' happen, and again they rammed me. Hit me again on the head, and what the fuck do they have to do that for every time! And when I'm looking at this one's face he was so nervous, he was spitting when he was shouting as his mouth was so dry. He's screaming and his hands are shaking. This must have been Roger from Norwich; he's probably never seen a real villain in his life. I'm honestly thinking 'You're dangerous, you are fucking dangerous'. He had no control, his hands were shaking and he was holding a gun. He should have been as calm as me. Exactly the same routine as before, down the station. The funny thing was, my kids. One was 2, one was 7 and the twins were 14. Saddest thing was, they nicked my wife, and left the kids in the house on their own with no door on it, and they actually had my kids lined up with machine guns pointing at them. That is the gospel truth. What are my kids honestly going to do? So, my dad's gone around there, and he's a mad Malt', isn't he! He's going mad. Anyway, they let me go again. They've got nothing, nothing! 3 weeks later, I've heard a tap on the door. I thought, fucking funny, must be O.B, no one else would knock at that time of the morning. So, I've opened the window and shouted down "What do you want?" They've shouted "Hello, Angelo. Come down and open the door, mate." "Yeah, all right, mate", I've said. So I've looked out the back, and they're fucking everywhere out there. So I've gone down, answered the door and they've said "Hello, Ang'. Listen, we're serious crime squad. We're not gonna' mug you off like we did before, and bullshit with ya', we've come to search ya' place, we've come to arrest you on so and so charge, and we'll put a woman copper to put with ya' kids and ya' wife and explain you're not in trouble, we'll put the handcuffs on you outside the door. And you'll admit we're being total gentleman with ya', aren't we?" I said "Well, I'll be the same with you then." And that's all cool. Now you have to ask yourself, what's the difference! So they've got me in the nick, and they've said "what we are going to do, as we know you don't talk, we're gonna' ask you the questions, you're not gonna' talk, and then we are gonna' give you bail. We aren't going to' try and stop your bail, as we know we can't, as you have no bail conditions.

There, you have to question on the whole approach. Gentleman and fucks! I understand a real dangerous person, and how they are going to' come at ya'. That's fine coming at me like that, but, my wife and kids! Then to nick your wife, and say to her "We have enough to nick you and send you to prison and all your kids will have to go into a home." What has she ever done! She's a straight goer. I mean, if I've got a problem with you, I'm going to' come see you don't make no mistake about it. I'm not going to' go see your brother, or see your mother. Fucking yella' bellies. If you're a big fuck of a man, I might not and come and see you now, but I'll see you when you're getting into your car. And I will come and see you. So by them coming to see my wife and my kids! There's a limit for everyone. I'm not here to have people think the O.B are arsehole bastards. Listen, the police are there to catch people like me. And I don't have a problem with that. You can't have people like me just running about around the streets. The world would be chaos.

You've got to have balance, if the policeman did his job, no problem. The Judge does his job, no problem. Get in prison, the screws, do your job mate. Don't try and be a big man, and I don't have a problem with them. I don't have a problem with the whole system, not at all. You see with me you've got to be straight. Like me, if you're a criminal, just be a criminal. Don't you be a double fucking wrong-un' or something like that. Don't play both sides of the fence. Be one or the other. You can't stroll around being jack potatoes, full of it, then turn around and be a fucking informer. Take your bird! I did my bird.

I was in Spell side for nearly 6 years, and I was on the worst wing, C- wing, where all the trouble starts. I was with Eddie Richardson, Sid Drape; everyone was given a little spur. And you'll never meet any one that's got a bad word to say about me. If there was any trouble, I'm there for trouble. I don't give a fuck if you're 6 ft. 3, 7 ft. 3 or 2 ft. 3. It doesn't matter to

me. If I am going to say it to you, I'll simply say it to you. You want to'
make something of it, than make something of it. I'll be standing right
beside you, in front of you. Anywhere you want, as long as I win. I'm not
one of these people that'll let you win. I will fucking win, but, I will be
the person I am. Not anything I'm not. The other day, I read the paper.
And this made me sick. When I was away, there was this person that
killed a kid. Anyway, I'm reading the paper, and I see him in the paper.
What happened was, he used to run around vacuuming our rooms up and
cleaning our floors. He was a real mug. He was a no one. Then one of the
screws walked up to me and said "Ang' listen. He's in here for stalking
and bashing women." Now, before you're told all this, you might get to see
some paperwork. His card, what he's in for, his photo, and that's the kind
of people you've got to deal with in prison. I'm glad he was dealt with! All
my years in prison, I never had one single photo in my cell. I even made
an official complaint, as people could simply look at your file, and see
your address. When you get your letters you have to sign for it. Well I put
a stop to that. You could have a real nonce see all your addresses. When
you're in prison, you're surrounded by them kind of people, and they treat
me like I'm some sort of monster. Who's the monster! I nick money. If I'm
going to' hurt somebody, it's going to' be another criminal. I'm not going
to' hurt Mr. Smith that runs a shop.

I've been in places, and I know I could beat someone. Here is a good
example, I'm in my car, and someone shouts out "You cunt, use your
indicators" or something like that. I think 'or what, I've been shouted at
by bigger people than you, ya' mug!' that doesn't mean nothing to me. If
they've got me trapped in a corner, then I'll show them what, you know. If
you're in a pub and you spill beer on me, I'd probably say "For fucks sake"
and I'd even go and buy you a pint. It all depends on the circumstances.
What does it really matter? Or do you think that if you spill beer on me
and you'll lose your temper at me, that I'm going to' fucking kill ya'. If I
don't kill ya', I'm gonna' pull your eyes out of your fucking face, bite you
nose off and do your jugular vein? Or, you're gonna' do it to me? We may
as well go and buy each other a pint. These youngsters think it's makes
them somebody, to go around stabbing some body, to be vicious to people.

It doesn't make someone a big man if they beat somebody up if they know they can. It makes them a bigger man if they beat someone they think they can't. That makes a tough man, as you know you can get hurt. It doesn't make you anything more than a bully if you get someone you know you can beat. I saw kids of sixteen and seventeen doing serious time for kicking someone in the head 'cause some one looked at his bird! My boy has never, to my knowledge, had a single fight in his life, and if he goes through life that way, I'll be the proudest dad alive. If he has to defend himself, then he's got to defend himself. That's why I find it hard myself when I see it going on. That's why I'll never be a bully and people know who you are. I tell my boy as I do my girls, that you must avoid trouble if you can. If you can't, you have to go all out. If I ever had to fight, then I'm going to' do my best to just kill you. If I don't, then they could just get up off the floor and kill me, and that separates a lot of us from simple bullies."

Shortly after our conversation ended, Danny came back in the room. Smiling with great content, I honestly believe Danny saw a look that suggested I was one-step closer to my goal. In the conversations including this one there's a sense of understanding I'd come to understand that for all the crime these chaps had committed there was without a shadow of a doubt a line that was the same throughout the whole of society. Rules and conduct was as much a part of the survival of ones self and coexisting with everyday life. It the same as either being on time for work, opening the door for someone, or a multimillion-pound heist. You had to know the rules of the game, when to turn it on or off and above all know the difference from right and wrong. Danny led me outside to the back of his house where were greeted by the rolling lawn, trees and a sizable property that stretches beyond my sight. "Look at that, pal!" He said looking again at me, he points out to the horizon and moving his pointed finger from left to right Danny says something that to this day has me laughing. Chuckling he says, "Now tell me crime doesn't pay." True humour and a good pal.

Frank Fraser

Francis Davidson Fraser, more popularly known as Frankie or Mad Frank, was firstly the "minder" for 1950's London gangland king Billy Hill and then, in the 1960's, quite literally the hatchet man for the South London brothers Eddie and Charlie Richardson. Along with a title and common knowledge, or so it's said, that Frank has killed more than 40 people not 41 as he hates odd numbers, and he is said to have been certified insane 3 times. That's quite a worry for any one being Certified 3 times! If would be like-minded criminal tried to cross Frank in his business, then there was a price to pay. Those that did reportedly came under the man's Axe (literally in one well-known incident) and some lived to take not only a warning with them but also a memory that would hopefully keep them and others at bay. Like most of the professional criminals of the time better known as the 'Kray' era, there was a code of conduct. Even those that where enemies of Frank will say he, like most in this chosen profession, always kept to the basic rules.

So how would someone like Frank play a role in a house of 3 brothers? Easy really, a gentleman through and through! He was one a few that was highly respected by us all. A scoundrel, a man of both honor and code, stood up for what right and never changed his morals or ethics, even if deemed mentally unfit by the 'powers at be', someone that could be relied upon and went the distance through 3 decades of crime. When I tried to explain to a septic pal who this fella' was, I was cautiously asked, "is he a hero or a villain?" "Fuck me", I thought, he's both. To me and a lot of pals that mix in the same circle, there would be discussions to who was really 'in the know' or a total wanker. Frank was of the old school, and if I was asked on Frank it would be simple. He was at the other end of the phone, when I simply asked if I could pop down to his side of the water and have a chat. "Sure my friend one condition, please turn up and don't let me down" was the request. Sharing an afternoon in a local battle cruiser, we chatted about the greats of an era gone by. Like-minded pals and proving the world really is a small place, well London anyway. With an edge on any comedian and still holding a grace about him Frank shared some old and some new memories on what made Frank such a liked fella' in the eyes of mutual pals and 3 London brothers.

Frank Fraser-

An Age-old argument. In passing conversation, someone commented to me that my glamorising and rising on a pedestal attitude towards criminals should be re thought. They added that there are plenty of role models that I could seek counsel with and find direction from far less questionable characters. To some this may be logical reasoning. To me, if I wanted the advice or 'role model' influence from drug fueled, spoiled little millionaire heiress's to hotel chains, maybe a person that was given a talent that in turn became an influence to millions of kids across the country and decided that over dosing on a cocktail of drugs was a worthy contribution to molding young minds. Or Even maybe entertaining the thought of a chat with someone that despite the fact she finds it a nuisance that she's arrested for driving a luxury sports car down a family filled busy street while on a combination of prescription drugs and heavily over the alcohol limit only to escape prosecution due to her 'popularity' a good idea. I'll sum it up very easily and justify my ideas in one sentence. Honestly, ask yourself if you would trust any of those 'popular' stars in your child's life? That the care and influence in the morals and integrity needed in life would be given. That your children would be taught the difference from right and wrong. If I was given the choice of the well-being of my children, or my families lives in someone's hands and I was to chose from the pop stars of today that end up across both their sports cars bonnet and the daily rag describing how they found the pressures of millions of pounds and everyday life too hard. Or a person like any of those listed in this book I'd chose the latter - NO QUESTION! END OF! (Sometimes common sense is a flower that does not grow in everyone's garden)

When the opportunity was given to speak with frank it was as if I'd been given a golden opportunity too good to turn down. Accepting the fact Frank had served more time than most criminals in his time and taking it on the chin (not crying and begging for mercy like so many modern day self acclaimed gangsters) over the entire length of his criminal career, frank displayed a clear understanding and representation of the infamous 'code of conduct' amongst the criminal elite. From his early days working with the true king of organised crime Billy Hill to his relationship with some of the best money getters south of the Thames; the Richardson brothers.

From a local battle cruiser, I made the call and spoke to frank. I was welcomed to spend an afternoon with frank but it meant traveling into bandit country. This sacrifice I'd be willing to make. So with my loyal traveling companion and girlfriend (needed someone to carry my packed lunch.) we set off to battle more sunshine travelers and the shared morning commuters on the underground. No sooner had we arrived in what was once the swinging south London area of the Elephant and Castle, (only thing swinging these days are a pair of Primark specials from an overhead cable line) and we were greeted by our host. Right off the bat Frank displays two of his famous trademark, his manors and personality. Nicky is taken by the hand given a kiss on the cheek, and greeted like a long lost friend. A True gentleman! Then a firm hand shake for yours truly. Drinks, simple chitchat on how things are going were the start of a real history lesson on one of London's greats.

Taking in my surrounding it was easy to see why frank was still a known and respected person in south London. It was obvious he was entertaining two guests and for as many people that came in to what was clearly one of franks locals, not once was we asked, approached or interrupted during our afternoon chat. In fact on once occasion frank stopped in mid conversation excused himself with a "Sorry, please give me a moment", stood up and gave a good afternoon to an elderly lady that past. Top man in my book!

Franks opening comment to me was asking after how my family was managing with the loss of my baby brother. It was said in a tone of sincerity and care. Generosity in his kind words is more than anything I could have wished for. I got the impression Frank was not happy to pursue the conversation for my book until he was convinced that both my self and my family was o.k. Our wellbeing took priority. For both my younger brothers and me Frank Fraser was as much a positive influence, as he is respected by us all. He started out with the best of what London had to offer in the criminal world. Frank chose his associates carefully and equally as careful as those around him. Frank worked his way up, through the known villains, including the true boss of all heavy hitters Mr. Billy Hill. Frank has never made excuses for any of his criminal activities. Equally as much as he would never stray from his principals of how crime is played out. Never women, never kids!

When we were all settled frank calmly sat back and asked, "What would you like to know, son?" During this time, Frank asked my girlfriend on several occasions if she was comfortable and if she wanted another drink. After which Frank would add "Ok, my girl. Just let me know ok" with a reassuring pat on her shoulder. Sitting with Frank it is hard to imagine that this polite well-groomed gentleman, was once one of the most feared men in London. I started as I did with all those that granted me an audience. With that, was with the added assurance that I'm a person of my word. Whatever is said always gets their personal looking over before it has saved, stored and printed. Again, Frank shined with his all-powerful smile and mannerism, simply lent forward, winked one eye, and said, "You're a good lad, you're fine." I sat back and prepared myself for time with an underworld legend.

Frank- "I'd like to start off if I may and say that my family was a large part of my life. My mum was a lovely lady. Never saw bad in anything I did as a child. Felt blessed that she had the children she did. Times were extremely hard for us growing up. My sister Eva was my best pal. My dad was Canadian, his mum a Native American, my mum, Irish. Now my dad went to sea, in the navy at a very young age during the First World War, then in the merchant navy and come over here. That's how he met my mum. Fell in love and got married. Back then it was again very hard. I think more so for us as we didn't really have the family that was typical around other families. As a boy I'd go over Waterloo Bridge and buy some cheap bread for mum. There was a bakers shop at the back of Shaftsbury Avenue, then walk back home with it. And that's how things were back then. Mum was always ever so great full. Mind you, she'd never tell our dad though. He was so proud, and it would've hurt him to know I'd trudged all the way over there for bread, you know what I mean! Mum, bless her, never ever told him. And that's how life was them days. Now me and my sister Eva were the only two thieves in the family. We were the only two rascals. We'd sometimes come home to mum and say we'd found a pound or two. Then of course it was a hell of a lot of money. Being a strict Roman Catholic she would do the sign of the cross over her body, you know, and say "my god, what lovely children I've got." She believed us and never cottoned on that we were rascals, it never entered her head. She never told dad though. She knew how honest dad was, and being dad would've marched us down to the police station and would have told them that his children had just found the one or two pounds and would you please try and find out who had lost it. If you'd told dad when he came out of the police station are you mad dad, the coppers will have that themselves and he would have given us a clip round the ear and said "how dare you say that." I mean mum was not that daft, as she never told him; that's just how it was. Those have to be my earliest memories of childhood, my family. You don't forget things like that.

Now it didn't take me long to figure out I could make money. I'd say from the age of about 12 years of age and upwards I was getting better at the game. You know, a rascal. Back then as well, all that really mattered was a meal on the table, survival. The basic comforts were appreciated. I knew from an early age there was a living to be made of from being a scoundrel. I sort of sensed it back then. Now for me it wasn't the 'excitement' that made me a villain or a scoundrel. I do understand it, but it was never that for me. For some people that was a big plus. It certainly wasn't in my case. It was all about getting a few quid, it was a money getting game. Remember, money was very hard to get in them days. I do remember my first decent earner. It was a smash and grab on a jewelers. I think I was about 14 then. That put me on the road. That there put me on the road to fame and fortune. It was about the same time I got my hands burnt. Approved school (Borstal), I never regretted my time. It never even entered my head. I was there, and dealt with it. When I came out, it was as if I'd never been there.

I remember some of my first pals in the game with me. Some were very, very astute. Me, I was dead unlucky as a thief. People were always asking for us, we had the bravery to do it. I mean, I'd have a go at absolutely anything, it didn't matter what it was. Now, going back, Billy Hill was the boss of bosses. I went through the very same as Billy. He was highly respected. The only difference was he had a family that had come from a criminal background. His older sister Maggie was a top shoplifter and she did Harrods and all the best shops. There was one time in 1935 that a policeman had upset her, and Maggie wore a hat with a large pin that went through the hat one side through the hair underneath and back out the other side of the hat. The pin acted as a way to stop the hat from blowing off. Well, she took the pin out, stabbed the copper through the eye and got nicked. By a miracle, she got bail. She was in front of the old Bailey, and was asked to plead guilty or not guilty. She said not guilty and was then found guilty. The Judge announced she was an evil woman, and that an officer has lost his eye. And as a result you will now go to prison or a long time, 4 years penal servitude. Now in 1935 for a woman to do penal servitude for four years, and having to do every day of it was 'nuff a long time. Then the Judge said, "Take her away." As she was being led away, she shouted back "you didn't say that last night, you dirty bastard when you was making love to me." Years later when I knew Maggie very well, I asked her "When you shouted that back at the old Bailey, was it true?" She said to me "Frank, I wouldn't have said it if it hadn't been." I mean, you couldn't of made that up, could ya'? I've never forgotten Maggie. People like that, you never forget.

Now, solid pals, in any game, any earner? My first pals were the Murrays. They were always there, no question and were 100 %. Now before I moved in with the Richardson's, I was already known. I'd already made a name for myself. Now while I was in prison, some thugs had beaten up my sister's husband Jimmy. Well, The Richardson brothers liked my sister, Maggie. Well, they found out who did it, and gave them a good bashing. So when I came out of prison, I went to see them, and thanked them. It was then they said, "Come in with us, Frank." I told them I'd think about it. I then went to see the boss, Billy Hill and asked him what he thought. He said they was 100%, and to go with them. And that's how I started with the brothers. I'd like to say, Billy was terrific, a real gentleman. A pleasure to know and he was the best, always dressed in the best. Impeccably dressed and well presented. He was the best role model, for everybody. He knew and upheld the codes, the rules. And what made it special for me and Bill was our birthdays. We shared the same birthday. He always thought was something special.

Now, the Richardson's weren't out and out thieves, they were businessman. They always had their eye open for a good move. I mean, they wouldn't say no if there was a safe with a hundred thousand pound in it. But, mostly they was just very good businessman. And that's how we got in with the one-armed bandits. Billy had introduced us to the right people. We had them in clubs all over the country. We were doing marvelous. Atlantic machines was the name of the company, and quite rightly we were really getting them from all over the world. Now there is a common saying that east London villains were known for their violence. South London villains were known for being very good businessman. What that really means is we are very good thieves. The great train robbery was all south London fella's. It can be said we was the best thieves.

Another one is George Cornell, a good man. Always smart, an all round good fella'. Now, what isn't known is he was originally from east London. He actually fell in love with a south London girl, Olive Hutton. She was a top shoplifter. Anyway, George fell in love with her, married her and moved over to south London. The twins (Krays) in their eyes could never forgive him for that, and that's how that all started. They felt George had deserted them. That was the real upset, I mean they grew up with him. But, by George moving away to marry a girl in the Elephant, that was it. It had nothing to do with anything else.

The thing is in the thieving world villains and scoundrels it was all about money. If someone had a fall out with someone from East London or had a row or upset someone from South London, and it wasn't unheard of, the individuals would see each other first to sort it out. It was a money getting game. It wasn't an all out war over something simple. Each 'party' would let the other know what the interests on each other's manor were. It was as simple as that. That way everyone knew what was going on and then you'd come to an arrangement. You know what you can have and what you can't.

Going back to my earlier sentences, I started in approved school, the Borstal. That's where I got the birch and then the cat at 18. The home secretary of that day had the power to convert my Borstal to 3 years penal servitude and that's what he done. I was at Portland Borstal and then transferred to Dorchester prison. I got in more trouble there and was then transferred to Wandsworth and got into more trouble at Wandsworth. Then I was transferred to Chelmsford. Now the Governor at Chelmsford had the reputation to be able to handle people like me you know troublemakers, or whatever they wanted to call us. I got in trouble there, but the Governor gave me a good job. Well, by prison standards anyway. Now, I wasn't an idiot, so I didn't get in any more trouble. Now in about October or November of 1942 I was took out and handcuffed for a medical for the army and the war. Now, they said are you fit? I was proud of being fit and if I'd had the proper brains of a thief then I would have said no. But, when I was 5 years of age, I got knocked down by a lorry and got a fractured skull. I also had meningitis, which was true I did. I had some bad injuries growing up. I'd then have been given grade 3, which was unfit for military service. So, when they did say I was fit I was so proud of being fit, I said, "Of course I am." I could have kicked myself later. I came out in January 1943, as I did every day of my borstal, and I was only home a week and mum came in and said, "there's a letter for you." Well I ripped it open and it was my calling-up papers for the army. So I told mum to light the fire with it. Then I was on the run from then on and of course I carried on with my criminal activity.

Now, my older brother, he was decorated with a very high honor for bravery in the war, very high. After the war, he said to me "You would have made a good soldier, Frank." I said, "Leave off, Jim. I was the best deserter they ever had." He told me that once they got you to the desert, and of course, you couldn't just catch a train home then, there was none of all that saluting and all that out there, it was more comradery, you're all fighting together and I'd been a good soldier. My brother was a dead straight man. Same as my son, great man but he too let me down. Never did a day of prison, let me down, and I never forgave them for that (laughing), again very high amount of respect for them.

Now going on to my prison again, when I did borstal, where I first hit a prison officer, and I did every day of borstal. I then went to prison and everything was on my record. Well you can see how small I am and the screws saw how small I am so you could literally read their faces. Thinking 'look at this little cocky so and so. We'll put him his place'. Well, I wouldn't have that, would I! I fought it all the way and it got worse and worse. That's where I never broke my code or my morals. I stuck with them every day, all of the way and everyone knows I kidnapped a prison Governor and I hung him out there on Wandsworth common. Where I wasn't strong or tall enough to hang him from a high enough branch, his feet managed to touch the ground. Years later, his son was a Judge who I appeared in front of and my council brought all this out with his father and me. In today's world, he would have had to abandon the trial, but they got away with it.

The longest time I did inside was 20 years, and I did every day of it. Originally, I was only doing 15 years. That was when I lead that riot at Parkhurst prison with about five others and me. They were taken outside for punching the prison officers and all the rest of it. Well, I was found guilty and got 15 years. The Judge said to me was there anything I'd like to say before he passed sentence? I said "Yes, my lord. I realise that you'll have to increase my sentence. I'd like to request that you make up sentence up to an even number as I really hate odd numbers." Now, he had a smile on his face, and I thought 'oh, this is handy'. He might only give me a year and make it 16 or 3 and make it 18, you know, even numbers. He then replied, "I've taken into consideration your dislike for uneven numbers, and I will have to increase your sentence and make it even numbers. I'll give you another 5 years consecutive and make it an even 20 years." I shouted out "You dirty bastard", and then his parting words were "Take him away" and I did every day of the 20 years.

Now there's no easy way of doing 20 years. I've certainly done more bread and water than most men alive. They don't have it in prison now. From a young age, I was always in trouble. When I was in prison, it was hard. If I was 6 ft. plus it may have been a bit easier, but being as small as I was and very thin, the screws thought they'd put me in my place. No way was I having it. Everyday was very hard. I took each day as it came, fought all of the way. As my release date was approaching, it never entered my head to go straight. All I thought of was how to earn some money. How quick I could get into something a bit hooky. When I did get out, everyone had been so good and fair to me; they had all put into a pool and got some money together for me. I came out to quite a lot of money.

Villainy has changed more now than it has ever done before. I mean internationally, you have people from more places than ever at it. You have a different criminal population all together. Albert Dimes, formally Albert Dimeo, changed his name because of the war. You may remember that when Mussolini sided with Hitler, it got everyone's backs up towards the Italians. Then the Italians were living over in Clerkenwell, London. Well, what Albert's family did was to take the 'O' off the end of their last name and replace it with an 'S'. Hence Dimes. Now you couldn't beat a better man than Albert. He was terrific and Battles Rossi was another fantastic man. The Jack Spot attack that I was done for, well Battles was completely innocent. Again, great man, Battles.

You know Frank Warren the big boxing promoter, well his uncle Bobby Warren was as innocent as you in that incident. He got seven years with me over that Spot incident, nad was absolutely innocent. Spot new it and swore his life away. Even when we got sentenced at the Old Bailey and were being lead down from the dock to the cells I remember saying to Bob "Never mind, Bob." He simply turned to me and said, "No don't worry, Frank." He was terrific and 7 years was a very long time for an innocent man in 1956. This remains the same since the day of Billy Hill. The codes will always be there with the real villains that is, the ones that really matter."

Words had escaped me! I had sat here listening to Frank and for one of the very first times in my life I was lost for words. Frank calmly lent back in his chair, sipped on his drink and smiled. My older pals that move in criminal circles who will remain nameless, all spoke of Frank with the upmost respect and from my time with Frank it was easy to see why. If I was to go to any corner of branch of the criminal world, one of the first words spoken when you say Frank Fraser is 'gent'. Those closest to me say other words that also give him merit like he's 'An absolute diamond', 'Top drawer' or 'One of the old school', 'The code', 'Old guard', 'Don't make 'em like that anymore', 'Solid man' Ol' Frank!, the list goes on.

Frank and I carried on talking. I showed Frank a photo of my late brother and myself the last time we were together. Frank smiled and said something that remains firmly with me. It was with reference to my brother and shows how empathy manners and respect are a part of Franks making. He lent forward in his chair speaking calmly with warmth in his voice and said,

"People joke about if you wanted to try and pull a proper job you could play the race card! I, of all people can relate to that and I know how that can feel. In my upbringing as a child, I was very much alone and my sister was my best pal. Having no family around, made me feel I had less than the other families that had each other. So I understand and know what it feels like to be treated as an outsider."

The way it was said and interpreted to this day, reminds me the level of compassion and respect Frank has for those around him. Leaving South London I felt emptiness, where there was for a few hours a genuine person who gave his time in conversation and heart. I felt a contribution to a simple London lad and his family's loss of a young lad.

Jimmy Tippett Jnr.

"**I**f anyone was going to lead the life of a gangster it was me"- A conversation between Jimmy Tippett Jnr. and Jason Allday in 2010.

Through mutual friends, I was introduced to Jimmy. Being of the same era there is a lot I understand and relate to with Jimmy and that is a person that was raised by standards that are clearly missing in today's criminal world. What a lot of people witness today with all that exists in the new breed of criminal and their activities is the complete opposite of Jimmy's style and approach. So often the comment is put out how, 'The old school is long gone' along with 'Back then there was honour amongst thieves'. Well I can honestly say, if there is ever a standard or measure to be used as reference to the code and rules within the world of organised crime in today's new breed, then Jimmy is just that. When speaking with Jimmy we would often talk of mutual pals and comment on our relationship with them. Jimmy always had me beat with the lengthy respected time in with all I knew and so much more.

It is a very difficult world to live in. Either crime can have a strong positive effect on a person or it can be the most destructive force that will eat you alive. When and it is inevitable it will that you come under the spotlight, your true colours will be tested. Here Jimmy has been tested many times and honored the rules of conduct within organised crime. This standard was the education he received from an early childhood. One shared opinion that Jimmy and I have is all too often some one will comment how offensive it is to use bad language but yet back stabbing, lying, stealing from your own and fucking people over is more acceptable in today's society! Twisted, upside world we live in but again this is why the rules where put in place.

Thoughts and anger along with frustration as much can be mice nuts to some, but are issues that target an individual. When amongst heavy-duty people and the world they live in, their daily role within the underworld and the dangers that go along with it can over shadow any issues you may be carrying. Who better has had to overcome situations of mass loss and troubles more so than villains do? I lost a brother and more recently a cousin. One of my pals within the world villainy has lost no less than 30 friends! Violence and the world of crime demands sacrifice and only the strong survive in this world. Every-mans reign is questioned and challenged and whilst everyone was feeding upon the luxuries of life, I was left with indigestion. Jimmy has been a strength I was privileged to draw from.

When Jimmy learned of my brothers death, he was there and willing to contribute. On one phone call I assured Jimmy I was all-good but the accommodating nature Jimmy possess he insisted "Even it's a chat, pal." Following the advice from a late pal on how never turn down friendly advice of help I accepted in some advice and insight that could help anyone that might need it. A person of merit and high standing within the four corners of the English underworld for his integrity and morals, Jimmy is respected by all those I know and within my family.

Jimmy Tippett Jnr

I was born into a criminal aristocracy, with boxing legend and feared but respected south London enforcer Jimmy Tippett for a father, infamous cop killer Freddie Sewell for an uncle and the Richardson's as close family friends so it was inevitable that I would be drawn into a life of crime.

My first encounter with crime was the incident when my uncle Freddie Sewell shot and killed a high-ranking police officer after a botched robbery on a jeweler in, Blackpool. That got front-page news on every national newspaper. The police were hunting him and no house with Tippett attached to it was going to be left without a complete search. All of our homes in and around South London were turned over. So this took my diary of childhood right off the scale with the flying squad kicking down the door.

"Yeah, I was literally born into the 'life'." The characters and villains of past are often termed the 'colour full characters' of an era gone by' and also 'the honest criminals', more of a time when there was honour amongst thieves, today it's without question a different type of criminal. This is also a true reflection, of a society that we live in.

If you are going to succeed as one (a criminal), you have to learn to adapt and find new resources to new or untapped opportunities before they become known trends. What was once a simple smash and grab later evolved into smuggling of people, guns and drugs to more newer unknown acts of criminal activity. You also have to be very careful of the company you keep. What was once a trusted business partner changed also with the introduction of drugs. The latter changed a lot of what was once a universal rule or understanding and of what goes on in the underworld. In some situations, greed took the place of trust. Certain types of criminal business will dictate a type of business behavior. A simple beating or warning escalated into loss of lives. What could be possibly made in a business 'venture' was nothing in terms of the profit and money involved with drugs. Drugs were a new era for many of the old school. Even the new school or lower ranked criminals would be tested with this new trade. The underworld and criminal fraternity had a new mistress. She demanded violence and lust the very soul of those that entered her world.

Many have trodden the 'path of life's miss adventures', and you would be unwise to think of entering this type of world if you had just finished reading the latest crime book or watching the latest episode of your favorite gangster TV show. There is no class for late beginners or thinkers in this world of organised crime. It really is a world of dog-eat-dog. It isn't a case of you make a mistake and you take two steps back. It can be as simple as you make a wrong decision and you take a life term in either prison, or six feet under. There is also no 'right of passage' you have to earn what you want.

Gangland killings, infamous robberies, serious violence and scandal of my life cut no corners and takes you to the very heart of the criminal underworld. When you grow up with the lifestyle that was on offer to me, it was as simple as do I want to live a normal life and hope for fate to deal me a lucky hand, or do I want to go out and take it all? The answer as many of you know is now part of underworld history. I've seen and had more than most could dream of. I also spent it as soon as I got it, and why not, I knew I could always get more; easy come, easy go as they say.

It's funny when you watch films that show someone introduced to crime as a youngster and then in a blink of an eye they too are part of the criminal world. Well, I started much like that. My life story has been likened to an English version of Goodfellas, from the tough streets of southeast London all the way up North along with my dealings with the northern underworld. It didn't matter what corner of the country I dealt in, death and murder had the potential of being only a step away.

I went straight from school to a driver of many of London's biggest names in crime that soon lead me to embark on my full time criminal career. My first 'lesson' was when we got nicked for armed robbery. I was 20 years old.

It was with a heavy-duty firm out of Greenwich. In the police interview, they started to pull out machine pistols they said they got from a pals house during a raid. "No comment!" There's a lesson for anyone to read!

I had all the right ingredients and makings around me to become a successful gangster. My dad was a legend and strong arm enforcer of 1960's South London, I was educated by quality, real heavy duty people, that knew what loyalty and honour meant, and those I had around me are as dangerous as the world we lived in. These men set the rules for the world we played in and I was schooled by some of the best. Both my family and I hold the men I speak of in the highest regard. Respect isn't a strong enough word. My dad, the real deal! Charlie Richardson, Terry Adams, scouse Norman Johnson who wrote the book 'Black eyes and blue blood; definitely a good read and my pal black, Sam Dundas.

Murder, fast cars, dangerous times and women, gun deals, cocaine, Rolex watches were all part of a daily conversation and lifestyle. I had it all, but paid a heavy price. Many in what was once my chosen profession have paid with their lives. Others are serving and will tell you the cost wasn't worth the price they paid, a life without freedom, but you can't run with the pack and then complain if things don't go your way. Everyone knows that if you can't do the time, then you shouldn't do the crime. It can't be any simpler than that really. A cocaine and crime lifestyle led me to H.M.P Belmarsh. Far from the stately home and playboy lifestyle, I was accustomed to, I took it on the chin and the rest is history.

History that includes my run-ins with the notorious Hull City hooligans and the Dutch Hells Angels to being on the run with escaped killer Claire McDermott in Ireland, which hit the headlines on the front page of the Sun newspaper in Ireland. I've breathed, lived and shared time with some of the most notorious crime families and names the U.K has had to offer.

After numerous court cases, a number of psychological assessments and a harsh prison sentence for defending my own life I have turned my life around. I am the main person to feature in Tony Thompson's number one bestselling book 'Gangs, a journey into the heart of the British underworld'.

At this time of writing this, my own autobiography 'Kill or be killed' is ready for publication and I have already sealed a deal with Allen Davies at 'Cast You' to turn it into a 6 million pound budget film.

Kill or be killed

"Jimmy Tippett Juniors story is totally unique. If anyone was going to lead the life of a gangster, it was him. Born into the criminal aristocracy, he was the archetypal gangland face of the hedonistic nineties. Living the life of a playboy, drinking champagne with London's criminal elite at all the glitzy West end clubs with expensive tastes in women, Gucci shoes, Rolex watches, fast cars and cocaine, there is nothing Jimmy hasn't seen."

Jimmy's life is like something straight out of an episode of the cult American TV gangster series The Sopranos. Connected to the world's biggest ever robbery, which involved 292 million pounds worth of bearer bonds. Friend to the most infamous gangsters in British history, The Krays', Jimmy was once sponsored to fight on an unlicensed boxing show for Reggie Kray.

Still in his thirties he has lived an action packed life full of wonder full adventures with the most colour full characters London and the U.K has to offer. Uncompromising in its language, pace and style, Jimmy's story is the ultimate ride into the exclusive power driven world of the gangster. This is an English Goodfellas, the inside story of the cartel that dominates modern British crime."

This story I dedicate to my pal Jason, his family, and in memory of Junior Palmer.

R.I.P. Your Friend Jimmy Tippett Jnr.

Joe Pyle

Old school? New school? All school!

Taking the path of least resistance, I doubt anyone would turn this option down, if given the chance. Considering the choice most of us are given, we have to deal with the hand we are dealt and the lessons and pals we get from it are our own. Many have told me, that the stronger the 'situation' you go through, will be a better lesson learned, and equally as much, those that stand by you are your true friends. Along life's path to the inevitable, as one makes his or her way through the trials and tribulations, we make choices that undoubtedly affect not only ourselves but also those around us. "The friends you keep, Jase", "The legacy a man can leave behind, can be an impressive one." I'm told these things by friends 'in the know'. All parts, of what will determine the kind of person we will become.

When you speak to those that are really 'in the know' the old school way, that aren't earned through a program but more so through an unwritten 'school' of respect and 'moral's, than you're also talking of men of such respect that when their untimely passing comes it can bring thousands to pay their respects.

By measure, this was demonstrated, when legend Joe Pyle Snr, left us in early 2007. Joe was a respected, and understood as a businessman, that for all his years working in London, he was able to walk amongst East End legends Reg' and Ron' Kray, and their bitter enemies the Richardson brothers; south of the Thames. His countless contributions to many charitable organizations also allowed him to be noted and respected within the community. An impressive boxer, savior to those that were in need, and above all a man of honor and morals, This is a man that so respected, that even at the time of his passing, some of the top and well known faces within the underworld, all put their differences aside, so as to come and pay their respects.

Born in 1935, raised in Islington; North London, Joe worked by a set or morals and standards that always kept him one step ahead of those trying to put demise to this London lad. Always calling it like it is, a phrase Joe is known for, that typically always brings a smile to my face is "Crime doesn't pay, but the hours are good." In addition, the type of business that Joe kept was that away from the everyday person. "Stealing from people on the street, well those types are no good." Another example of the old guard is shown here looking after you own.

Always speaking with courtesy of his friends, keeping things simple, many a word spoken with honesty and integrity, these ways can be seen in certain circles. The circles Joe kept where trusted friends and businessmen. One man that was in the circle, was respected and feared Roy Shaw. Whatever your opinion may be at this stage, this fact remains that at one of the lowest times in a man's life, those that stand by you, and not only see you through the thick of things but also ensure you come out on top, truly deserve the title 'friend'. For those that do not know, when Roy was in Broadmoor at one point we thought that Roy might never have seen the light of day. One of the contributing factors in the saving of Roy's life was Joe. Not only did he ensure that Roy was taken care of, but he saw that Roy was helped onto the road to recovery. Saving a life is something very few people can say that they have done in their lives.

My brother was someone I'll always put on a pedestal. No one loved junior more than our mum did. Everyone within my family knew junior and his real motives and agenda in life. His premature death is something I know I will never accept. The passing of a family member can never be justified or condoned. I never had the luxury of meeting Joe Snr but have had the privilege to speak on many occasions with his son Joe Jnr. If there's one thing that rings true its Joe Snr was there to lay the foundations for his family that proudly show they're of the same quality stock that was once amongst the greats. I could write on all I have heard on Joe Snr; but I think no one knows someone better than your own family. A great man will always be remembered and so it is true with Joe Pyle Snr.

Joe Pyle

By Joe Pyle Jr.

I have heard many names spoken about my father, old school, boxing promoter, gangster, mobster, friend of the Krays', tough guy, drug baron, extortionist and legend, but to me he was my father, the man I loved adored and looked up to. I have heard many people called legend and it seems a word that is used somewhat too easily today. What is a legend, is it someone who achieves legendary feats, or someone who writes a book or even a pop artist? Maybe it is just in the eye of the beholder. Out of all the well-known facts about my father and one, which is often, spoke about is the Pen Club. My father was a young man and was arrested with Jimmy Nash and Johnny Read for the murder of Selwyn Cooney. What happened then was criminal folklore. The case fell to pieces amongst Jury nobbling and witness accusations of threats and all the men walked away from the murder and the Judge to his dismay stated that 'Cooney walked in the way of a stray bullet. In a way, the trial brought my father into the big league of the criminal underworld. My father was the youngest of the accused and by doing the right thing and keeping his mouth closed he found himself being respected by the old guard; men who appreciated young men who stood up and kept their mouth shut when the times get rough. If you asked my father about it, he would just shrug and say we did what was expected, as there are no thanks or handshakes, as men and mates we stick together. True but we're not talking about getting nicked for some fight or burglary, when you're looking at getting life of 25 to 30 years, or worse in them days they were going to stretch ya' fucking neck, let me tell you it's a whole different ball game. Like I say no thanks were asked or given but believe me if your nicked for murder and your mate in the next cell is as staunch as you then you won't thank him for not grassing you but you will love and respect that mans integrity till the day you die.

My father he will always will be a legend to me, and the friends who knew him. He battled his way through life and never turned his back on anyone who needed his help and his friendship knew no bounds.

I saw him in the last days of his life crippled by motor neuron disease and still trying to help his friends who were in trouble, even though he had lost the ability of speech to pass on his knowledge so we wouldn't make the same mistakes as him and his friends throughout his life. One week before his death, there was a dispute around Tooting. In South London there were two fella's going at each other. One was shot at outside a pub and the other had his car torched. My father told me to get them round the house, and after ten minutes of me translating for him the two men shook hands and swore they would make the peace. Today those same men are best of mates and often tell me that if it was not for my father, one of them would be dead or one would be rotting in prison. Instances like this, as well as so many similar stories, are what in my eyes made him special. It could have been so much easier to pretend he never heard of the trouble or to say, 'It's fuck all to do with me' but that was not his style. He learnt things the hard way and did not want to see anyone in any kind of trouble.

I remember my father and me were once sitting in New York with Carlo Gambino's cousin and he said, "Hey Joe why the fuck do you wanna' help these fucking punks." My father simply sipped his drink and replied, "because before someone educated us we was just fucking punks."

Life as a kid in my household in the seventies was always a roller coaster. At best, it was fascinating and at worst, it was horrifying. You never really knew who would knock on the door, the Old Bill, my dad's pals or a film star or rock star or world champion boxer. Every single day something exciting seemed to happen. One of my earliest memories was when my dad had some of his mates back round the house. I think it was every Tuesday night, anyway I helped my dad build a card table, one day we stapled a green felt over an old table trying our hardest to pull it tight. Then my sister and I used to help him mark the cards. We used to paint tiny little marks on the back of certain cards and the marked cards would not be used when my dad was with his mates but if they found a flash harry then he was going home skint. The Tuesday game would always start late, well after my bed time but I would always stay up waiting to see who would come back. One night I crept onto the stairs and got caught. My dad called me down and laughing he offered me a pound note to start shadow boxing in front of his mates, then they asked me to deal a hand and about an hour later I went to bed with over a tenner. That was a fucking lot of money to me back then. Mum went fucking mental in the morning, but it didn't bother me, I just wanted to get out and spend the money.

Another night my dad comes home from the pub with a dog that someone didn't want, well this wasn't just a dog it was a fucking Great Dane, it looked like a fucking horse tearing around the living room smashing everything over. Mum went mad again but her mood was nothing compared to the next day when she found out the dog had fleas and had infested the whole house. We called the dog King, and we had him about a month till my mum had enough of him. He was not nasty but he was just too big for our house, he would literally drag my mum up the road and one day ripped all the net curtains down while we were out, a neighbour saw it and said it looked like a mad gorilla at the window.

One morning I remember the Old Bill crashing through the door at about 5, the bastards nicked my mum and dad and left me with a neighbour; it was another fit up job where the slags planted shooters in my dad's car boot. I then went to stay with my Nan for a while until my dad was found not guilty. The Judge called the arresting officer Hannigan, a psychopath and suggested he seek medical help.

My father also great pal with Ronnie Kray, and he would take me regular to visit him in Broadmoor Hospital. Over the years I must have visited Ron over a hundred times, at first it was always with my father but as I got older and got my own car I would go on my own and sometimes take my friends along with me. I liked Ronnie, he was obviously not well and always medicated but he had a charisma about him, always a gentleman, always suited and booted and cleanly shaved, I didn't matter who was visiting him

Ron would always be well presented. I only ever saw him once out of a suit when it was in the summer and so hot we were aloud to have our visit in the garden. Some of the things Ron would get up to were legendary; he would ask me to run errands for him all over London. I cannot talk about the things here, as it was Ron's business and not mine but I miss Ron. He always has a special place in my heart, as he was one of the few people who saved my father's life before I was born, so in a way I owe Ronnie a debt of my life and my children's lives.

Another time I remember my dad being accused of owning over 50 pubs. Can you believe it some Old Bill had rejected a publicans' license renewal saying his pub was a front for organised crime! The local papers picked up on it, and within a week my dad was front page of every paper in Britain as the Godfather of this and that. There were stories of shootings and beatings, but that went down well at my school though and half of the teachers stayed away from me for a while.

Alex Steene was one of my father's closest friends and I loved Alex. He was in my opinion a man amongst men. There was no pettiness about him and no small talk. You would never here Alex talking about birds 'look at the tits on her' or swearing. He lived for his family and friends. When my father was away, Alex came round to see my mum every Sunday for six years and gave her some money. Alex Steene truly was one of a dying breed of man, a special man and one in a million.

Roy Shaw was another of my father's very close friends and Roy and used to speak at least once a week until Roy's death. Roy used to say that he thought of my dad all the time. When my dad was in the hospice dying Roy came in really upset, he grabbed my father's hand and shouted at him, "beat it Joe fucking beat it!" I remember once when my father and I were at his restaurant in Stockwell, Roy walked in covered in bruises and a cut eye as he had had a row with a door team and fought six of them. My dad asked him what was the matter and he told him what happened "Why didn't you call me Roy, I would have come with ya." My dad said to him "Nah Joe, if you were with me mate I would be worrying about you instead of worrying about knocking the cunts out." That to me sums Roy up. He was a stubborn and old fashioned, but he was loyal and above all else 'proper'.

I remember when my dad got arrested in the early nineties. It was a crazy time. Rumours were going around everywhere as everyone was being pulled in or targeted. I found out the law were looking at me for long firms, and they tried to slip a grass into me who tried to pull me into a smuggling ring. I saw the fella and he said he had a car that we could drive to Spain and hide 75 kilos of smoke in a specially welded petrol tank, in reality he was working with the Old Bill to fit me up. Then he showed me the car, it was an old Mercedes Benz with no tax and re-sprayed, I looked at the sills and could see the cars original colour, turning to the fella I told him he was fucking mad and that customs would spot this coming off the boat. So I walked away, but the grass disappointed that he would not get his 30 coins of silver contacted some friends of mine who foolishly lured by the money went ahead with the deal. Sure enough, the car got through and as it turned up to the office the law pounced and nicked everyone, all except the Judas slag grass of course. I had another load of mates banged up and with all the heat going on I decided to hit the road and ended up in Johannesburg, South Africa with woman Janet Neaves. Janet put me in touch with some scallys from the area and once again I was back on the street looking over my shoulder, only now it wasn't just the Old Bill but the Johannesburg gangsters as well, but that's another story and what saw me being jailed in Angola. When I arrived back in England, everything was exactly as I left it. The Old Bill were still sniffing around everybody and following us everywhere and soon enough I got nicked. But it was for something stupid counterfeit currency and it didn't even belong to me but I took the rap because due to a certain scenario it was the decent thing to do. After a couple of weeks on remand I made bail and that's when everything went really crazy. Knowing I was on borrowed time I just went bang at it, and got drunk every day and had a different bird everyday as well as a punch up every day.

I remember one time where I was collecting a pension from a pub for my father to give to my mother. Now remember, this is one of the pubs that we are protecting and keeping out the troublemakers out of, and sometimes we bash someone who takes the exception. Anyway, one night my pal and I go in and I ask for the manager and the envelope. As were waiting my pal suddenly decides to start staring out a group of around ten scaffolders. What happens' next is out of a comedy film. Of course, the scaffolders start taking an interest back, so then some words are said. I pull my mate back from chinning one of 'em and start having a word with the biggest and loudest one of them. "Listen don't take no notice, he's just in one of them moods. Don't worry about it lads c'mon I buy you a drink." Then the builder gets all-flash taking my explanation as a back down. BIG MISTAKE! "Fuck your drink," he snarled. Then that is it. Crash! I glass the cunt straight in the face, and all hell breaks loose. My pal starts charging at them with a bar stool, and I start throwing glasses at the rest of them, just as the manager comes down he finds me behind the bar stamping on one of the scaffolders and smashing a bucket of ice on his head. Fucking comical and were meant to be stopping trouble. Anyway, we get our envelope and fuck off to Wimbledon, my hand has a big slash on it from glassing the first bloke and my mates got blood all over his jacket but fuck it we were hitting the town. This craziness went on for a few months until I got bored. It's funny, but drinking and birds soon lose their appeal, and anyway I had a trial coming up for the counterfeit notes. I thought I still had a fair chance even though I admitted to them, something I fucking hated doing but if I did not own up then they would have nicked someone else for them and I didn't want that to happen. Anyway, off to fucking court I go, totally fucking innocent of the charge, but knowing that if I get a guilty, then it's more than likely I'm getting some bird.

The court case was a joke. I had twelve senior Scotland Yard detectives willing to give evidence against me and I found out that on the day they arrested me, they had seven unmarked police cars following me and that they had been following me on two previous operations over the last six months. The Judge couldn't believe all of this attention was for someone who was arrested for having £500 of dodgy scores in his pocket. He even commented on it saying that either I was very lucky, clever, or the police were very incompetent and that he was not a fool and could see that something other than counterfeit currency was happening. However, the law who were on shaky-ground, smoothed it over with their usual lies and sure enough, I got a guilty. In summing up, the Judge said that if I was found guilty of manufacturing the notes, then I could be sentenced to nine years. When he said that, I thought fucking hell, I'm being set up here but in his next breath he sentenced me to nine months. After hearing nine years before I smiled and give the thumbs up to my uncle, and then I was off to stir. I was taken to Brixton Prison in South London, which was a right shithole. I fucking hated Brixton and I remember a screw seeing me on the yard one day and coming over, "Are you Joey Pyle", "Yeah", I said. The screw then said, "Fuck me, I've seen it all now. I've been here thirty years and I've seen ya' dad, ya' granddad and both your uncles walking across this yard." After about a week of eating shit food and trying to avoid the scumbag smack heads, I was lying down in my cell just after nighttime I head bang-up and I heard the door being unlocked. "Pyle, there's a telephone call for ya' downstairs in the office!" For a screw to come and unlock you after bang-up is something very rare. My first thought was that it was going to be terrible news, like a death in the family. I hurried downstairs and picked up the phone and to my surprise it was my dad who was on remand in category 'A' in Belmarsh Prison. "Joey listen, you alright son?" "Yeah good dad, what's the matter?" "Look I am getting you to Belmarsh. You do whatever you got to do there and we're doing what we have to do here. We're on protest till you arrive." The look on the screws faces around me told me just what was going on. My father, who was a double cat 'A' prisoner, was refusing to be locked up in his cell with around ten other prisoners. Four of which were convicted IRA men, until he saw the guv'nor and then he demanded that unless he promises to ship me to Belmarsh the 'unit' as it was called, would go up in smoke. When I got back to my cell, I couldn't help find the funny side of it. I'm a cat 'D' prisoner probably just about to be shipped out to a holiday camp, like HMP Ford and I got my father, and a bunch of IRA men all causing chaos to get me to Belmarsh, Britain's newest and highest security prison. Thanks DAD! But that was my father, there was never a road made which he was not prepared to go down for his family or friends.

Charles Bronson

It was his fate, and as much as his original plan, that would make Charles Bronson A.K.A Michael Peterson one of the most famous names in British history, and in the 20th century.

A man confided to darkness yet who has brought so much light to many people. His art- work and poetry is well known. What isn't known is his words of wisdom that have been given to many young offenders, on many occasions saving their lives. These young offenders are not the wrong-uns that deserve nothing less than a hole to die in, but the sort that simply made a wrong choice in life, faced a lengthy sentence and an equally uncertain future. His contributions, also given to charitable organizations, gained no more media attention that the good he did for the youths he helped inside.

For me, Charlie is a man that shows strength and resilience. There is a spirit in Charlie that can never be broken. An introduction through a mutual pal gained me a friendship that has only grown over the years. One thing I know is that Charlie is limited to his contact with the outside world. So with each and every letter I receive, I truly appreciate that is something that has taken not only Charlie his time but limited his letters to those closer to him than myself. The closing of each letter always makes me smile through the comments and words. His humor is demonstrated in his writing by witty remarks and jokes. No test of time or punishment has ever swayed Charlie from what a few close to him believe is his true talent. That is to help those he cares for through troubled times. Charlie has remained a good pal throughout the last few years and it has been an absolute privilege to call him a friend. If I were to coin Charlie to a song, it would be the closing title to Monty Python's Life of Brian. 'Always look on the bright side of life'. Stay strong my friend. Freedom is yours and there are many people that care for your well-being.

Charlie demonstrates what is typically unseen in some of the best fighters to ever enter the world of boxing, although his fights have not been seen in the boxing ring for a long time. Instead, they now stretch into a new 'arena'. Here there is a new set of rules never in his favor. The fight purse, if won, his life and freedom. The ref', changes each time he is moved to a new holding system. The opponent, the very morals he stands for are tested and questioned.

In 2008, the loss of my brother brought a darkness that would haunt me. The light that Charlie B brought to my world, would demonstrate the fight and determination for survival that not many else could display but our pal Charlie. He has many friends in all four corners of the globe. **One that he holds very close to heart and his unquestionable trust is Dee Morris. A friend and supporter like any man or woman could only wish for, Dee has stood by Charlie for almost 2 decades. Promoting the justice and fair trial Charlie deserves.**

Dee Morris

My friendship with Charlie began around fifteen years ago after our mutual friend Reg Kray made the introduction. Reg suggested that we would both get on well and that we were both very much interested in the same purpose; which is to advise, assist and support young people. Reg' was right and I am grateful that he made the suggestion as from that a loyal, respectful, solid friendship was formed.

I am lucky that I know the real Charlie. As sadly, so many believe all they see and hear in the media about him. Charlie is a very quick witted, positive and clever man. He is a man of his word and is very considerate and caring. Although Charlie can at times have eccentric thoughts, this is not something I take a negative to, as we all are capable of that at times.

Charlie is continuously looking at ways to advise, support and assist people from all walks-of-life. He has raised thousands and thousands of pounds for charity of a varied substance. He has raised money for young offenders, orphanages in India, youth boxing schools, Great Ormond Street and cancer research to name but just a few. Despite the negative outlook that Charlie has faced for the past 35 years, he remains positive and caring. I have never known someone to have so much humanity within them, especially after being treated so inhumanely for so long.

Our friendship has grown stronger and solid, as the years have gone by. I will continue to fight tooth and nail for him until he has given the freedom that he deserves. My path is not straight and it has been a long and awkward journey but one that is well worth taking. Whether I am on the phone to the solicitor, printing off leaflets, organising a protest, updating people on his well being, writing to the ministry of justice or writing to the man himself; I am doing it all for a man that

I truly believe should be freed. He has fought the system and fought for his freedom. Charlie is very much aware of his past, how this has affected him and the people around him. However, he does not deny it nor is he ashamed by it because it made him the person he is today.

Confined to a cold concrete coffin is a man with so much warmth and consideration for others, despite not being on the receiving end of any compassion or understanding by the government, media and the thousands of others. Many of who are too ignorant or shallow to take time out to listen to the real story of the person that Charlie is and not the myth that the media and system created. Charlie truly is a funny, caring, polite man. He has his principles, morals and codes the same as a lot of people do. He also has the courage to stick by them, even if he was persecuted for it. Charlie would be an asset to today's society if he had the chance to prove it. He longs to show young people that there are always options in life. As well as how valuable and important it is that you make the right choices in life and I know that I did by forming a friendship with the real Charlie.

Charlie Bronson Letter

I know how it rips you up.

I've been there and it's a fucking big empty bottomless black hole, heart and soul breaking. I can't even imagine how painful it must be for a mother or father to lose a son or daughter.

Junior had it all ahead of him, a great journey of life, a 24-year-old chap, a proper geezer but the memories live on for him especially within his family "Priceless Memories."

I do hope Jason's book will help to stop any future suicide attempts.

No matter how bad you feel about your life or how much you're stamped down it's always better to fight on even a life of problems is still worth fighting for the shit times never last.

I've survived most of my life inside a 'concrete coffin'. I know better than any man alive about the hopelessness and emptiness in this world. The isolation and coldness that chews you up but through all those black clouds of doom and gloom a light always shines through.

So let Junior Palmer's life and death be something for us all to learn from.

It can only enrich our own journey of life and prepare us for our last day on earth.

Respect to Junior

Charles Bronson 1ˢᵗ April 2009

Charles Bronson Letter

Everything in life is meant to be. Good or bad, happy or sad. Makes us all think. That's what we all need to do, think more. Now Junior's the legend and has all the fans. Not bad eh for a youngster to have so much respect from us all. Most people live and die and are forgotten. In no time Junior has become special. It's a pity the Kray twins aren't around. Cor, they would of loved to do something for it.

Junior loved his boxing. What he didn't know about the fight game wasn't worth knowing. The fight game is like one big family. We all share the same thing…. The buzz!

There is no other sport like boxing. It generates excitement and pumps pure adrenaline. My life has been one big battle. My body is covered with scars. Each scar is a memorable story. Life is a scar. Until you've been stabbed up multiple times in the back had guns stuffed in your face and had a dozen men jump on your head believe me you've never really been to hell. You have to go to hell to appreciate and respect heaven! I awake every day in my cage with a smile. I'm still the birdman. Some say I'll die in jail. Some say the birdman will never fly again. Like with junior….. it's fate. What will be will be. Jason summed it all up for me. He said "did Junior die for a reason? What is fate? Junior was a big fan of many fighters. Now all the fighters are big fans of him. That's how crazy life is. I actually believe Junior's death can be a blessing to others, especially the youngsters. Wake up and find yourselves! Go deep into yourselves and find the true you. Look at me, 36 years inside a concrete coffin. I've eaten more porridge than the 3 bears. I've ripped off more prison roof tiles than a tornado. I've had more hostages than Saddam Hussain. Yes, I'm an artist, a poet, an author, and a man with a dream. I still dream of freedom. And its guys like Junior who make me want to fight for freedom. He's an inspiration. Also maximum respect to his loyal brother Jason, what a great brother. I salute him.

Charles Bronson April 10th 2014

Paddy Conroy

Paddy Conroy was listed as one of Britain's most wanted fugitives. Newcastle's face or villain was at one stage, known as a key figure within the North East of England's Underworld. Violence and the world of crime played a daily role in Paddy's life. Gangland murders, family rivalries and the prison sentences to match, Paddy has fought wars on many fronts, some, very close to home. Here, the Tyne side hard-man will share the truth on bent coppers, the underworld and proper fit-ups.

Another trip up north but knowing the hospitality waiting from my pals north of the border it is always a worthwhile one. Packed lunch carrier in tow we head north on one of London's aging intercity trains. At least the coffee was not bad, or at least I was told that it was coffee. The face of thunder that sold me the beverage obviously missed charm class and fronted a boat that was not welcoming of questions. That and she probably ate her last three husbands dictated I keep both my thoughts and ideals to myself. I am not on board for a conversation or to give merit to the flavourless cup of piss I bought. No sooner than we arrive, than Paddy and friends greet us with warmth and hospitality.

When I first heard the name Paddy Conroy, it was surrounded with stories as the Krays, the Chinese mafia, and West London! A place Paddy was once linked to was an area not far from where I grew up. Intriguingly that a fella from north of the border had associations from East, West and back out to the Far East. What was very well known was Paddy's integrity and honour. A way of life that was clearly displayed with the villains I knew back in London.

Paddy had been part of many conversations prior to my trip back to Newcastle and was more than willing to contribute after learning of my brothers' death. Paddy is a true testament to the friendliness and welcoming of people in Newcastle. Sitting down with paddy was much like visiting an uncle. Experience a good laugh and ready to share anything he owns. One thing I was treated to was one of the best cups of tea I could have wished for. Not shy in saying, I had more than my fair-share. In good company and a welcoming bunch was the first impression. Settling in, Paddy was ready to give the experience he would pay a heavy price for. I opened with one question that was the start to some much, appreciated lessons in villainy, honour and family values.

Paddy – "Crime or villainy as I was brought up to know it, was just a way of life for everyone who lived in the same area that I lived and I mean everyone! I brought up in a rough area and my old man, were probably the roughest of 'em all, but he were a good man with it. That were the way of life for a lot of the men in them 50's 60's, and my dad was in and out of jail most of his life when I was a kid."

Can you tell me more about life with your father?

Paddy- "I did not spend a lot of time with my dad due to him being in prison a lot. He was a big hard fellow all of his life and if I were to compare him to any other old villain for being the man of the manor sort of thing, I would say he was looked upon by the local folk in the west end of Newcastle. Just like old Arthur Thompson from Glasgow were looked upon by his local folk. He was a man who was the man of the manor for decades, unlike the other ones and those who come and go over the years. He was there until the day he died. He could fight for fun and loved a scrap all through his life, especially when he had a drink" (chuckling).

What was the first 'rule' you learned or was taught as a lad in the world of crime/ villainy?

Paddy- "It was not to answer any questions if I were locked up, don't even speak. My dad taught me and I still do it to this day."

You grew up in a neighbourhood that was much like a lot of poor / working class areas. A way of life was like a way of survival in many cases.

Paddy- "I was mostly brought up in an area known as Noble St flats. Similar to the Gorbils, and it is also demolished under the same government program as the Gorbils. I believe it was demolished for being too rough even for the '60s and '70s standards; and you're right about the way of life being a way of survival. That's the way it was for me. I was put in an approved school at 13 or 14 for pinching out of a shop. I escaped the following day and headed back to Newcastle. I was then packed off to London by my dad, to his mate called Jackie Mullholland. Jackie holds the record for being the most flogged man in Durham prison. As soon as he arrived, he would spit straight in a screws face and get his flogging. We lived in Southall, Ealing, and I also stayed with my brother over at Roman Rd, Bethnall green.

In my youth, I mostly lived with my Grannie down in the flats I mentioned. She was a big old lady who liked a drink and sung in the local pubs when she had a few. The pubs were on the infamous Scotswood Rd and the flats adjoined that rd. I returned from London by the age of 16 or 17 and I got arrested in a stolen car a short while later for joy riding. I was put up at court for that offence. But due to my then age, I could not be sent back to approved school and I was giving a chance with probation this time. I worked the doors as a doorman off and on most of my younger life, and was a builder for a time. I would work the town center pubs at night and then onto the nightclub job and building during the day."

There is a saying 'a life of crime'. Having a hard childhood and having to get by and ensure survival, has the life of Paddy Conroy always been an uphill battle?

Paddy- "Yeah it bloody well has been and it still is today, only a lot worse these days. Two prison sentences where I have been innocent totaling 17 years in jail, but even that were a walk in the park compared to my life these days."

In your youth, was there a time when the small time actions of a Newcastle villain escalated into much more?

Paddy- "Yeah. When the class 'A's arrived, coke etc. I ain't been a big villain really, a villain yeah, but nowt special. Our areas were one massive criminal community stretching through miles of adjoining council estates. The West end, it is known as and it had a terrible reputation in its own right! Best people in the world and we were one big massive community. Half of Newcastle it covered, but nowadays it's all gone due to developments going on here and there, and there's hardly any community left now at all. It's all foreigners around our streets and shopping areas these days. When the class 'A's' arrived so did the trouble and those dealers went into a level of their own, due to the money being made. Like never before, the scummy families who would have never in a million years be raised up there ended up running the show or tried to anyway. That was when my battles started with the Sayers lot. They were flooding our streets with heroin, our own streets and the same streets where they were from themselves and that was the start of all my troubles!"

Is it true to say there is such a thing as a good villain and a bad one?

Paddy- "Of course there is! Ain't there good and bad of every walk of life, and I do mean every! The bad ones force their way to the top and the local community puts the others there.

Only problem I found were this, the good old ones who ran the manors before the class 'A's' turned up seemed to drop off when the real violence turned up due to the drugs and the shootings they brought. A lot of the old guv'nors did not have it with weapons full stop. So it left the bad ones to take control very easily, I found. I take it off no fucker and I'm out of it now, but still have battles going to this day. It's hit men these days though."

Reading on the listed past activities in your active days, you are listed as an enforcer, member of the West End underworld and have a reputation for violence. Can you tell me about you maturing into villainy as an adult?

Paddy- "I don't think I ever matured into a villain. I think I always were what I were (whatever that is), and it were always just a way of life from a kid, nothing out of the norm. But like I say, I don't proclaim to been an angel. While I ran the show in this town, I did my up most to keep the bad shit away from our streets. By that, I mean your heroin and crack, coke etc. There were hardly any ever about before I went to jail, not here in Newcastle. Plenty weed, speed, acid, E's, little bit coke, but little heroin and no crack cocaine. Even though all the other major cities in this country were already flooded with the bad shit, Newcastle was not."

You've earned a title as a man of violence on many levels as the papers would say, eh?

Paddy- "Oh I have a worse one than that, but you can't believe everything you hear, can you eh? Listen, I ain't been any angel, but I ain't been a bad guy neither. I stopped heroin where I could when people said that I ran the town and I stopped crack cocaine full stop. In fact, I went around all the folk who I thought would fetch that shit to Newcastle and had words with 'em before it ever did, and it never did ever. Well, not until I were sent to jail. Now it's rife and I have a few of my own relatives who use it. That's what I came out of jail to! I lost one nephew, a few months back, which was down to that shit."

Drugs in general are a very profitable market. Most cities have their 'organisations', including the control and distribution of drugs. When you was 'running the show' in Newcastle, why was your business not in the drugs area.

Paddy- "I have smoked my weed and I never allowed anyone to do what you're saying above, it was a free enterprise for everyone while I was around. We had the ones who tried to do what you say above but it came to clashes with me etc. Those people never got their way in this city, but they did after I went to jail mind, but not before. Every city has those people, the ones who 'want' to control most cities, those very people manage to succeed and do end up running the show but not in Newcastle. I myself like to see Newcastle stay cloth caps and whippets for us Geordie's."

So it is fair to say when you were in power, there was more of an honorable villain.

Paddy- "Bit of each, I just done my thing. It was all the other folk, who said that I ran the town. I think it was because they did not want the others in power so it was always argued that it were me who ran town and not the enemy (laughing). That's what happens though in real life. So after I twatted the bad guys a few times and everyone knew it, then it were me without any arguments, never me saying it mind, always ya' local people, the community. So when it was not in dispute, I thought I would put it to good use and ban crack and smack and I did a good job!"

You were respected as a known face within the underworld as it is called, obviously playing a more honorable position as a villain. Do you think it is more of a dangerous game being good villain than a bad one?

Paddy- "It is more dangerous being a decent fellow in that world these days, I would say. I find all the bad ones have police handlers these days. So you're up against that too when you fight the new breed gangsters that's about today. They get their cops onto your back too."

Being a different 'class' of villain made you a target and quite a big target, as this was a war in the making. With the money involved in drugs and your anti drug villainy, it must have been no surprise when you heard there was a hit put out on you, or was there another 'enemy'?

Paddy- "There are bent ex-cops that are involved behind my last two near miss hits that I've had. They've been cooking the intelligence books that were kept on me when they were in the job. These cops have been on the take from their informers, who they are crookedly involved with here. Their own informers have been committing murders, and then they've between them fixed all the intelligence on them cases and pointed it towards me, and its multiple murders involved here!"

A war on two fronts here, you are facing one of the biggest gangs in the world.

Paddy- "The enemy admitted in that last murder trial that they were free masons too. or their father was anyway. They blamed me for that murder to the Jury and the Jury believed them and acquitted the ones that ran that defense; the gang boss John Sayers. He then he put an official complaint in to the police accusing my bro and me for that murder. This is why we're under investigation today for those multiple murders as John Sayers is blaming us. When I bumped into the whole gang of them in the town center, a fight broke out because of these murder accusations. I ended up beating the boss to his knee's but the whole gang jumped me as soon as they seen their boss in trouble. I was kicked unconscious, but not before I were cut open with a cutthroat. With all of this happening in the middle of the main road in town center, it was all caught on council CCTV. We were all nicked for a section one affray with no way out of it. It's all on camera but the ex-murder squad cops, who used to handle this group of informers, when they were in the job came to the police station to defend the Sayers legally. Their solicitor had been getting the top ex intelligence department cops to defend John Sayers. It worked for them because the cops threw us all out on police bail and then sent us letters telling us not to come back."

The people who you were accused of murdering are?

Paddy- "Openly from John Sayers' mouth whilst he were under oath are the Freddie Knights and Viv' Graham gangland murders, but there are also more murders involved here too. I have the official crown court transcript of that evidence giving by John Sayers naming both those murders as being committed by me, and my family."

It goes hand in hand, is part of the territory it is the nature of the beast and that is Violence! With the hand you were dealt and the life you led violence was 'part of the parcel', so I am sure being a key figure of the underworld that you have seen your fair share.

Paddy- "I would not say it's been the nature of the beast or anything remotely like that where I am concerned, although I do admit there are a few idiots out there that live like that. With me, it's just been down to the cards I was dealt and the people concerned with it, and yeah, I have seen my fair share of it and its part of the territory when you look back on it. The Crowns prosecutors have described me in court as the most violent man on Tyneside, but ya' gotta' remember that I were at that time down on their murder intelligence files as a serial killer due to their books being cooked! I have never looked for trouble though, but like you say, in this life its part of the territory and is always popping its ugly head up in front of your face."

Looking back, what has to be one of the most violent episodes?

Paddy – "My battles with those muggy Harrison brothers were the most violent. There were 22 separate shooting incidents involved with it going on so long! This war, which I stood trial for in November '95 were the Conroy / Harrison war. Whilst I were stood there in court accused of that war, it were put to me in cross examination by the Crown's prosecuting QC, Mr. Paul Batty, that I were behind a number of the 22 separate shooting incidents that had taking place during that Conroy / Harrison conflict. Batty was coincidently the same prosecuting QC for John Sayers in the Freddie Knights murder trial. While it were being put to me by the prosecuting QC, while I stood in the witness stand giving my defense evidence, that it was me who was behind these shootings and 3 of the victims of those 22 shootings were still laid up in hospital with 4 legs missing from between the 3 of them!"

Any particular incident that was particularly hair raising?

Paddy- "I suppose it was when the Harrison's pulled up in a car outside my door and started shooting at me, there were 3 of them at once! I managed to get behind the wheel of my car at first to duck from the bullets, and then darted for my front door and jumped behind the brick wall built around the door once inside. But once there, bullets started to fly through my door in front of my eyes and then stopped. It was then I noticed my little girl standing at the end of the passage in my kitchen in view of the front door.

The bullets had just stopped so I took a run for it to grab her and get her out of the way of bullets, but half way along the passage the bullets started flying through the front door again and I were hit in the back! The pain was horrendous. I landed in the kitchen floor (laughing). I shouted to our lass that I had been shot and she ran over and pulled up the back of my shirt as I lay there and guess what?

The 44 bullets had only hit the big stone pillow above the front door. The bullet had taking a big chunk of stone out of it then ricocheted along the passage and hit me in the back. It was like being hit with a double strong catapult from close range, but I was not wounded except for my pride" (chuckling).

An example of death knocking at your door. Literally in this case.

Paddy- "Well I thought it were until our lass said 'Get up ya daft cunt, ya' not even bleeding'" (laughing).

Any other bullets?

Paddy- "One day we were sat in the local pub when the bullets started to fly through the windows, when the away teams of darts had just started their first game. Now that were funny."

What was the result of the feuding families?

Paddy- "Everyone knows that those Harrison family boys never ever recovered from that last war with me, due to the shame that they now carry from 'ALL' the crying that they did and mind you did they do some! Right throughout their whole trial, and right throughout their whole prison sentence, they never stopped crying once. No not once! That don't include all the crying that they had already done while spending times during that war, when they were laid up in hospital due to the gunshot lead that they were now full of from the shootings. The Harrer's never did lift their weeping heads above the parapet ever again, but hey it even got to a stage where their trial Jury were sick to death of having to put up with their crying in court and that they were pleading with the usher for breaks from it! The trial become a mockery and I myself felt embarrassed over it. I were accused of being a gang boss and having a war with these boys and here these boys sat in court like a bunch of kids, with their none stop breaking down in tears! What were people now going to' think of me! But that's your gangsters' for you though. In Newcastle the Harrison mob have never again or since been looked at as any kind of serious force or threat, and the other young youth of this city have stomped on them and treat 'em that way ever since. That was the end of the Harrison's."

You gained control, if not a reputation within the underworld. They, the shooters, must have expected retaliation.

Paddy- "No to be honest '80s Newcastle was not really into gun culture like the rest of the country was, not on the streets anyway. Everyone always knew where he or she could get their hands on one if they ever needed to, but guns were rarely used on the streets of Newcastle. Davy glover, my co accused were probably the worst around for pulling guns out when trouble started, but not many more did."

What event in your life was the most violent by the '80's standards?

Paddy- "There are a few, but for obvious reasons I can't go into them as I could end up arrested if I did. So I can only really talk about the ones which don't carry that possible, threat i.e. the ones I have already been convicted of. My criminal record is as long as your arm and its full to the brim with Section 47 assaults on Police, Section 50 assaults on Police, Section 20 wounding's on Police and Section 18 wounding with intent against police. They were all separate incidents. I had a running battles going with them for years and years and so did my dad. He had the same form for doing coppers too but never shot or stabbed anyone in my life though I can tell you that."

Going back to the trouble with the Harrison's, how did that all start.

Paddy- "1993 a little girl who lived around the corner from me had her bedroom windows petrol bombed by some local scum bags and she was burnt. A car had pulled up outside her house and two people were seen throwing the petrol bombs threw the child's window before the car sped off and escaped. I weren't happy about such an incident happening within our local community and let it be known. I sought out the people responsible and gave them a piece of my mind about the incident, hence the start of the Harrison's war. Another 3 petrol bombings later (but on my properties this time) and 22 separate shooting incidents.

Then my dad and brother's gravestone were stolen and found a few streets away smashed up. Billy Collier, the torture victim, were the driver of the van that night. He was used to ferry the Harrers' to the graveyard. In Feb 1994, was abducted from the shopping area and found a few hours later with some of his teeth missing. He had been tortured and his teeth had been removed with an old rusty set of pliers! A number of the Harrison family were shot and seriously wounded at another couple of different incidents. Hence the end of the war, but we were all nicked and locked up."

So, the famous Harrison trial... and how you saw through the 'evidence' against you

Paddy- "My last trial and conviction were for the gang war with the Harrison family. 22 separate shooting incidents were involved and three of the alleged victims were lying in hospital with four of their legs missing from between the 3 of them whilst I were in the dock defending myself against these charges! So it were a real heavy case being labeled against me by the prosecuting QC, and only ending with someone getting his teeth pulled out with pliers! I were getting no help from my defending barrister at all. I did not trust him one bit, and I knew after speaking to one of my co-defendants barristers that I were not getting away with these charges. He told me that when he passed the dock and chatted with me that I were not up at court for these charges, that I were up at court for my reputation! So I tackled every bit of evidence preparing for my appeal, this were before they told me I were guilty, when I swilled the prosecuting

QC's face with the witness stands water whist I gave my evidence did not help my case too? I pulled every bit of evidence to bits, but like I say I were not getting out of that case, the trial Judge had also been told by glovers police handlers. that my gang were out to murder his mate, a fellow trial Judge! What chance did I have eh?"

Is it fair to say there is not a justice system?

Paddy- "I just think that the ex party meetings etc. that go on between the intelligence department and the courts people, i.e. the Judge, prosecuting QC, and even you own defending QC, seals your fate before you even step foot in court. They've all got you guilty regardless if the ex party meetings are mentioning all of the murders that they suspect you of committing! Your fates sealed and I am not joking on that."

What makes you the still a heavily respected person is your willingness to stand by the morals seen in many a real villain or face. The same 'rules' as some people within the underworld the country over.

Paddy- "I view myself as no better than anyone else and only ever (even in the old days) viewed myself as the shop steward around our manor, and that were only when wannabe gangsters were laying the law down to our community. I disagree with these local wannabe gangsters who break every moral and rule in the book. Sticking to the rules is what fetches you respect I find, working for the authorities as snitches don't, and being a smack or crack dealer don't neither, it fetches the opposite by having what respect in that world that you had earned now took away from ya."

With the morals and code you live by, it must be frustrating that the justice system seems to favor the wrong-uns, almost as if you are being tested, on the very foundations you stand and live by.

Paddy- "What can you do? Turn your back because it's not you who's being petrol bombed or it's not your problem? Or do you do what's natural and join the community and shout the bastards down? That last war with the

Harrers', were a community war really and I were placed at the front of it because it were me who had words with them. I found out that the bastards whom it turned out were supplying the Harrers' with their guns were my other enemies who are blaming me for these murders today."

So, you are not a dangerous man.

Paddy- "I am not dangerous under any normal circumstances no, just a normal everyday fellow who likes to go to work. I don't ever cause any trouble myself ever! Always comes my way though and I deal with it in a way it has to be, nothing more."

There is an unwritten code, rules. We have a mutual friend in another part of the country, and it sounds as if they are a dying breed of person in today's society. They are those that will stand up for women and children. That will not turn their back on those in need. Those that are there for their own!

Paddy- "Those days of unwritten codes and rules are over and gone now and they ain't ever coming back neither."

Back to the reasons behind what has 'changed' in the attitude and society.

Paddy- "The class "A" drugs changed society. I believe the coke and the heroin. The coke hit a bigger audience than the heroin did, and in the long run it has been the coke that has changed society most of all."

The strongest always survive. You have come all this way, under a hail of bullets, attempts on your life and an attempt at getting you a life behind bars. What else can be thrown at you that you have not already seen?

Paddy- (Laughing) "Fuck me Jay, this hasn't been any easy ride that I've had! I can tell you that now; it's been real hard journey without a single day break from it. The prison sentences were especially hard and the high security conditions that I was kept under whilst I was in there (double cat "A") they gave me a squeeze at the very end and dropped me down to a normal cat "A" security status. I was released a cat "A" prisoner. Guard dogs were used to escort me to the gate on my day of release because of the cat "A" status I carried. Normally it's only the likes of terrorists that are released still as cat "A" prisoners as it means you are to still be classed as a threat to society! I would swap it all for running a little corner shop life etc.' tomorrow, I would. But due to the hit men carry on etc., it has made that impossible for me to do and that has been that way since I came home from prison. I also now find myself under the magnifying glass as chief suspect in one of Britain's biggest criminal murder investigations due to my enemies openly accusing me of these multiple murder offenses to the authorities!"

Paddy Conroy, boss, under boss or a different title?

Paddy- "Hey if Freddie Foreman is the managing director of British crime, then I can be the shop steward as nobody holds that title and it's my true one."

Your respect has stretched 'over-waters' so to say!

Paddy- "I'm a member of the Triads (sort of) only man in England to be so, that statue that were shown on Macintyre's underworld is an honored gift from the ruling family of Triads (the bosses) and it carries a lot of symbolic meanings. It's solid gold and weighs over 16 oz., the only other person that I know of who has ever received the same gift was an American I watched a show about in the 70s. The show was about him and his triad gift, exactly the same as mine! He was a mafia boss and the TV show explained all the symbolic meanings that went with receiving this gold god, it's a statue of the Triads god."

So do you think that Villainy has a place in society?

Paddy- (laughing) "Jay, I can't say that it is entitled to a place in society, but it's there with no getting away from it. Most of ya' everyday villainy has changed now. It hasn't done to pay the house bills or get you out with your neighbours and community for a drink at the weekend in your local. It's mostly committed these days to feed their addictions to class A's. Not all crime but most, and when they're not committing it to feed their habits then it's done solely because their heads are now a mash with the same bad drugs. A great number of the people from my era have died from drug related ailments, class A drugs has no place in my world in any form."

If you were to summarise our writing and your life as a villain or as shop steward, how would it be said?

Paddy- "My message is simple. I stopped all crack cocaine and done my best to stop heroin when I were about before jail. I battered everyone who ever said they run this city. Nobody else though. My way is the only way with this shit and people behind it, and it works too! I sat them Sayers down a few times about dealing that shit and talked them out of doing it, then I got 'em to agree nobody should ever sell crack cocaine and that it should be all of us who stop it too, and it worked, until they got me locked up."

The unwritten code, principles of the villains of past. The wrongs and rights of a 'real villain', does society stand a chance, with these 'new breed' of villain?

Paddy- "No, no chance! In fact I say the old way has now been taking over by the new lot and now it's all bollocks."

Your last message, a message to all villains; old and new and the working class folk of our country, something, if it was to be the last words you ever spoke... What would it be?

Paddy- (Laughing) "You git, Jay! A message eh! Well the message I would send would be to ask all the youth of today and do what I did about the class A's in your own area, regardless of the law or police just chase them bastards out of your manor by any means whatsoever. You don't have to put up with bad drugs by these people who sell it on our own manors and it's down the men from that area to sort it out. The cops ain't managing to do it, so do it ourselves I say. If ya' going to be a gangster of today then be a good guy gangster and that should be the new breed of them, not what we presently have!"

If I were to say what I gained from my time talking with paddy over this year it would be simple. He is a Good guy with a fear full background. If you are a drug dealer, specifically class 'A' drugs, be very careful of this man. In fact, keep him in the back of your mind whenever you are dealing in a substance he despises and as Paddy would say about himself, "Hey, Jay, it's all murders, mayhem and me."

Mighty Matt Legg

Matt's energy and indifference to those in authority was a driving force that allowed him to compel and progress the path of both a criminal and a fighter. Humble and loyalty also allowed Matt to keep a circle of friends that's either admired or feared. As seen in many of the great street fighters in and around the major cities in the U.K, Matt was on one of two possible paths, one of profit or peril.

Natural abilities when homed and directed can promote ones very existence. That is, if it is sent in a direction that will promote yours or those around you of survival. Luckily, for Matt his meeting of a great trainer and respected person was without question one of saving. Many youths around the country have fallen to the deeps of crime never to surface. Respective of the level and type of crime some situations have claimed not only the young criminal in training but their families too. Muscle for hire is a type of business that can be brought into all levels of crime. Ranging From C.P (bodyguard) a courier for wealthy businessmen and of course the drug trade. The latter involving a manner of violence that typically claims all those involved.

My involvement with Matt came via Charlie Bronson. Charlie stressed how respected and of good character Matt was and would be someone I should involve in my journey. One email and a phone call and I have to speak with Matt. First impressions are just that, typically worth their weight in gold. Matt is 24 carat, no question! A few later conversations with friends around the country also spoke well of Matt. Matt brings something to the table that is easily related and identified to the many youths across the country today. This is the easy route to organised crime. Matt is another worthwhile contribution and welcomed input in many a shared opinion of people that know the score.

Matt- "I would say my main memories of crime as a youngster, would not be so much crime, as it would be fights and bare knuckle fights. We (my family) lived in pubs for many years, so I would occasionally see fights in there. A few times, I would see my dad fighting a rowdy customer that would lead to one of two scenarios: they'd either be knocked out or thrown out of the pub. It wasn't until I was 12 or 13 years old that I started to see crime out on the streets. Again it was mainly fights I would see, although by that age I would have regularly arranged the fights myself against people who had either challenged me or who I'd had a disagreement with.

I have strong memories of fights and bare-knuckle fights on T.V. Do you remember the Clint Eastwood films 'Any Which Way You Can' and 'Every Which Way but Loose'? Clint played the toughest bare-knuckle fighter in America. Well I really loved those types of film as a young boy. Although, in comparison to today's films those mentioned aren't violent really, to a degree they were more family oriented, displaying ethics and honour (and of course bare knuckle fights). I liked the way that he (Clint) wouldn't start the bar fights he got into, but would always give the challenger a fair fist fight if they tried it on with him. I also liked the idea that he arranged bare-knuckle fights for money, would always win and walk away with a decent chunk of change. It's funny because, it's only after you asked me that question, that I sat and thought about it, and I realised that I must have always had a fascination with fighting, even from a young age.

It was when I was 13 that I started weight training. I was already, my full height (6ft 2in) at this age, and once I started weights I got strong very quickly. It was also around that time that I would get people at school ganging up on me. They were never alone and always four or five of them and sometimes they had weapons, like bats and knives. I would always stand my ground against these people; it was a matter of pride. On one occasion when I was at school, and about 5 lads hit me over the head with a rounder's bat, even when outnumbered and with unfair odds I still stood my ground against them, and wouldn't go down or be intimidated. At 16, I left school and I bought my first gun. Looking back, I didn't need to buy one really, because any trouble I was having then, I would sort out with my fists and head, or when it was needed a cosh.

My earliest memory of a crime that I committed (apart from pinching stuff as a kid, which nearly all of us did) was when I was 15. I was arrested for two ABH's in the space of one week. The first one came about when I was told that a new lad at school had been saying he was going to' do me, as he'd heard that I was a bit of fighter. Now this lad had just moved down to Milton Keynes from a city up north. I thought he simply wanted to make a big first impression at the school by fighting with me. So I went to find him, and after a few words he started to threaten me. I knew it was going to kick off, so I gave him three or four head butts. As I walked off, he got up and told me he would be coming back with his family and his mates, and they would take care of me. So I went back and gave him another head butt for threatening me again. The next thing is, I get home and the police turn up and arrest me for ABH.

Now I was surprised, because the lad had said he was going to' get revenge with his mates, obviously he'd changed his mind, or so I thought. The following day I'm back at school, the ink on the charge sheet hasn't even dried, I'm walking across the field with a mate of mine to my next school lesson when I saw 5 or 6 lads heading towards me from a distance. As they got closer, I realised one of them was the lad that had got me nicked. I carried on walking towards them, suspecting they must have come for revenge. Even as a young lad I have always preferred to face trouble, rather than run. I have always believed and still do, that if I stood my ground and showed that I wasn't scared, it would serve me better than running. Now this group is closing in on me, I turned and calmly said to my mate "They've come to try and do me." With this comment he left my side and walked away from both me, and the trouble that was about to occur. At the time and still to this day I don't blame my mate at all for his actions, as I know it's not a nice thing to get dragged in to a scrap, and he simply wasn't a fighter. Now this group stopped in front of me and said, "You beat our cousin up" I replied, "Yeah I did, but he got me nicked." Then one of them said "What the police do to you is nothing compared to what we're gonna' do." With that he pulled a wooden bat out of his jacket and hit me several times over the head. I managed to grab hold of him, and hold his head down by my waist. The only place he could whack me now was my legs, so he whacked them a few times, and as he was doing that all the others were punching and kicking me in the face and head. This went on for a few seconds until I pushed the one with the bat away from me. I was still standing and not looking too concerned. The lads looked quite shocked, and I think they knew then that I wasn't going be a pushover. It seemed that me standing my ground had worked, because as I stood there getting ready to punch whoever got close to me next, they in turn said "Oh Leggy's (my nickname at school) alright, he's had enough", and with that they walked off. I took it as a moral victory, if not a physical one. I picked my stuff up off the floor and carried on as if nothing happened. When my mate came back over to me I remember laughing and saying to him "Well if you give it out, you have to take it." My mate replied, "Are you O.K?" I felt fine, and to be honest, quite proud that I hadn't backed down. I actually got a few of them back in the following weeks, some of them were 3 or 4 years older than me, but I got them back all the same. One of them got repaid in the middle of the market place on a Saturday afternoon in front of all the shoppers.

The second ABH I got nicked for that week was when 3 older lads barged me into when I was on my bike. So I waited for them to come out of the shop, followed them over the road, jumped off my bike and bashed them with a lump of wood.

When I was 17 I started working for a firm who were earning good money in my area. I would get paid as a driver (although I didn't get a driving license until I was 27) and I would also earn money as 'muscle' when they had meetings, trouble or when anything that looked dangerous that needed sorting. By the time, I was 18 years old, I was 18.5 stone and very strong, especially for someone that age. I had been into my weight training for a few years, and had put a lot of work in to the bodybuilding. It was also about this time that I was asked to go with the local 'boss' to Europe for a yearlong job. I wasn't given much notice of the work and told that if I went I would be gone for a year, and I wasn't going be able to tell any friends or family where I was going. It all went well for 3 or 4 months then things slowly began to fall apart. My new work environment started to become a bit of pain. The work had dried up a bit, my family and friends didn't know where I was and the only contact that I had with them was an occasional phone call, so I decided to go back to England. My boss tried to get me to come back, but I declined. Then a week or so later, he was found shot dead in his car. The newspaper headline read 'Gangland Execution'. It was suggested in the same newspaper that several eyewitnesses thought they'd heard gunshots, and a car was seen driving away from the scene. The day of his funeral, I was suited up and just about to leave my place when my dad rang me and told me that Interpol, C.I.D and local police were at the house wanting to talk to me. I had no problem in talking to them, as I knew I was innocent of any involvement in his death, and I also knew that there was no crime in which I was wanted for. I told my dad to tell them that after I'd paid my respects to my late friend, I would come and see them. I went drinking after the funeral, got in a bit of a mess and as a result didn't call my dad back until later that night. When I did call him he said the Police, CID and Interpol had all gone. I never heard from them again. After that I was called consistently by people to help out in fights, keep people from jumping in and to allow fair play, I would also be called in to help in different types of work in similar environments.

In my late teens, I continued to follow the life of crime and found regular work in security or muscle for hire. Typically it involved being called in to settle disputes, backing people up, tracking people down for personal reasons (this type of work has got me accused of kidnapping and waiting inside people's homes) and doing various debt collecting jobs, I was just under 19 stone of muscle, so this made me ideal for this type of work. In addition, I had a pretty reckless attitude, and wasn't concerned about the police and the consequences of what I was doing. Regarding the police side of things, I was only arrested for either acts of violence or driving offenses. In addition to the acts of violence towards the police, I also had charges of threatening behavior. Although the last time that happened, was over 10 years ago in 1999. That particular incident was when I was being pulled over by an unmarked police car, which had been chasing me for a mile or so. As I got out of the car, the officer drove straight at me sending me onto the bonnet of his car. Obviously this wasn't going to go down to well with me, as I took it as a deliberate attempt to hurt me, or even worse. So as the officer was getting out of the car, I jumped off the bonnet and laid into him. I then went to walk off, but he got out the gas and sprayed me several times, once in the face and then again in the chest. So without thinking I decided to get him again for gassing me. This time though, as I ran at him he ran off around the police car. It was as I was chasing him that I heard the sirens coming from nearby. Realizing then he must have radioed for backup whilst chasing me in the car before, I decided then to try to make it home, as it wasn't far away. I had no hope of making it as three extra police cars screeched up and blocked me off. They all jumped out and I was cuffed in the middle of the road, slightly embarrassing as it was on a weekday afternoon. As I got up to my feet, two of the coppers that had just turned up and assisted in the arrest were rolling around on the floor in pain from the effects of the gas, which had come from my face and shirt. That in my head was a moral victory, as they might have nicked me, but they couldn't take a little bit of their own 'medicine'. Although I must say, of all the times I have had an altercation with the Police, I have always felt that they had caused it, by inciting me or by being over the top when arresting my friends or myself. The latter I would get involved in by helping them out.

At 18 I was sent to H.M.P Woodhull prison, which is my local nick, and also the most secure prison in the Country. At that time, the early 90's, it housed double A cats, which for any one doesn't know, are the most high risk and dangerous prisoners. I was in for various violent charges, ranging from a Section 18 wounding with intent, to ABH's and threats against police, ABH's against doormen and so on. It was whilst inside I met up with Norman Buckland, top street fighter and doorman. Norman saw I had potential in becoming a boxer, and he thought that maybe boxing would steer me away from trouble. So he started to train me in prison. Although we weren't allowed gloves, head guards or gum shields, we would still spar with a bit of cloth wrapped around our knuckles. It was good tough sparring, which I didn't mind. When I got out of the prison, I carried on with the training and started to compete in amateur boxing. I ended up having 15 amateur bouts, winning 13 of them, and only ever losing on points to the ABA Champion. I won various titles including England ABA Novice Champion, Home Counties ABA Champion and England's ABA Finalist amongst others.

My daily routine would consist of getting up at 9 or 10am, going for a run, and boxing in the evenings, which was roughly 3 times a week. Either in the afternoons after my run, I would rest, or if it were there, I would get on with various types of work. Different days could bring different types of earning potential. For example, some days it would be traveling up North to collect on a debt, or it might involve trying to settle a dispute between two firms who had fallen out. Nine times out of ten, I would know both groups in the argument, so I would always try to get a diplomatic solution to end the disagreement. I would also go out looking for people who I'd been asked to find. That was for a wide variety of reasons: for example, they may have punched a friend's daughter, they may have stolen something from a friend, but again it could have been for 1 of many reasons. I would normally be on the lookout for the Police when I was out driving, as I didn't get my driving license until I was in my late twenties. So I had roughly 10 years of looking over my shoulder when in the driver's seat. This lead to many bans, fines and community service orders. I would go between legit jobs as well, so sometimes I would be hod carrying, labouring, and even some factory work. Removal work was one of my earliest jobs. I started that at 14 years old, in the school holidays, and I would occasionally go back to that job for a few days here and there. I have to say, I have only ever been arrested for the violent offenses and the driving offenses, which makes it difficult for me to go in to great detail about other types of work I was doing, as I was never arrested over anything not mentioned. As I've got older and I now have three boys I have really calmed down a lot, and mostly focus on my boxing. I turned professional in my mid twenties, and as of January 2010, I have had six fights and won 5 of them. So, although I still get loads of phone calls about problems and jobs that need doing, I try to avoid getting myself in trouble, although that is easier said than done.

One of the things with living that type of lifestyle, and having friends who are involved in it is, it's common practice you can lose them to prison, some end up losing their lives and in some situations both can unfold in a man's life. This is the unfortunate side to the business; the nature of the beast, it goes with the territory. My pal who died abroad was only 25 at the time, I was 19 and I had been living with him only a couple of weeks earlier. We had been training together, going for lunch each day in the town center, watching films and just everyday stuff. I flew back to the UK, and it wasn't long after he was found shot dead in the car. I sometimes wonder that if I had stayed over there, would things have been different!

In one particularly bad year, two friends were killed, and two friends were banged up for murder and attempted murder. On another occasion, one friend had to move away, and one died of a heart attack. My good friend Sadat lost his cousin recently who was also a pal of mine. That was to violence as well, he was only 19. A group of men attacked him and they battered him to death on the street with weapons. This was an ongoing dispute, with casualties on both sides, which then ended up with another life being taken. The same year another friend of mine had a row with my pals' son. That ended with another death. And this time I was a friend with both groups, as a result one is dead, and the other is doing life. The same year I lost another good friend, this time to a heart attack. Kev' Evans was one of my pals from the boxing community and a local to the area. He was always helping the lads out before their fights, an all round good person and a respected man. He was still a young man really, only in his mid forties. Two more of my good mates fell out around the same time, one stabbed the other 5 times, he lived, but statements were made. So one got a big jail sentence, and another one has had to move away because he also made statements! It's only when you sit back and give it some thought that you realise most of these deaths and prison sentences could have easily been avoided! When you start to get involved in crime, the 'Underworld' or whatever is deemed appropriate to call it, you are obviously then expected to live by that set of rules which fundamentally means that you sort out all your own problems, and never ever involve the authorities. So once you make that choice, then you have to defend yourself however you can, which in most cases means getting a weapon. Even now that I concentrate on my boxing and legitimate work, I maintain and go with the 'rules' from my early start in life.

I wouldn't want to say I was recognized by the major 'Faces', although recently I have got to know many of the big names. I'm also lucky enough that quite a few of the well known ones come to support me at my fights. Chris Lambrianou is a friend of mine, and he comes to mine for a cup of tea now and again. He's always good company, and if you need advice, he knows what he's talking about. I knew his brother Tony as well, another top man R.I.P. I speak with Roy Shaw now and again; he actually came up to Watford twice especially to support me in my comeback fights. Others include Dave Courtney, Mark Fish, Big Norman Buckland, Harry Holland, Manny Clarke and many others. So I'm honored to have their support. I see Carlton Leach also from time to time. I always have a good night with him.

Charlie Bronson is a good friend of mine; we became friends a few years ago when his sister asked me if he could train at my Gym, upon his release from prison. I told them that it would be fine, and then I received a letter and piece of artwork from Charlie, which started our friendship. Since then we have spoken on the phone regularly, and always keep in touch via letters. We have helped each other out from time to time, and I'm pleased to be able to support him, as he is a unique character and has a side to him that most people don't hear about. He is very clever, witty and sharp minded, and great to talk to on the phone. Obviously we all know about his kick offs and outbursts, but he is hopefully calming down now, maybe to be released soon. I was well known in the city I lived in by my late teens. Many people would look after me in various ways, for instance the doormen always let me straight in the clubs, and things of that nature. I would always look after them in return if they needed any help. I get asked to phone a lot of people up to stop trouble that is brewing, and it helps them listen to you if you are fairly well known.

Over the years, there have been a lot of dangerous situations that I've been involved in, but I only go in to these situations if I know that morally I am doing the right thing. I can remember many times when friends of mine or even friends of friends were being bullied or had been attacked, robbed etc. In these situations, I'd have no problem in helping out, and going up against the people causing the problem. Sometimes they would be tooled up with knives, bats, and on sometimes guns. However, 9 times out of 10 the problem was sorted without too much fuss. I was first hit with a weapon when I was 13 yrs old, a man hit me in the cheek with a can of dog food he'd bought from the shop, and he cut my face. I was hit with bats and pieces of metal at the age of 15, when a gang came to find me at school I stood my ground and kept face. I've had knives pulled on me, been hit with a knuckle duster on the forehead and instantly K.O 'd the man that hit me with it, been CS gassed a few times, and had some situations against people who were armed with guns. No doubt I'll see some of these situations again in the future, but I try and avoid trouble nowadays, as I need to set an example to those important to me. I think most people view me as helpful, polite and hopefully as a good friend, so even though I've had a lot of trouble, people know I would only be involved for the right reasons. I don't know what the future will hold, but as long as it's a good one for my family, I will be happy."

JASON'
GOOD LUCK
WITH BOOK

2019

" A GReaT LaD.
A GooD SouL. "

JUNIOR   PALMER

A BRONSON TRIBUTE ... " RESPECT "

3 . 11 . 83 . . . 20 . 9 . 08 .

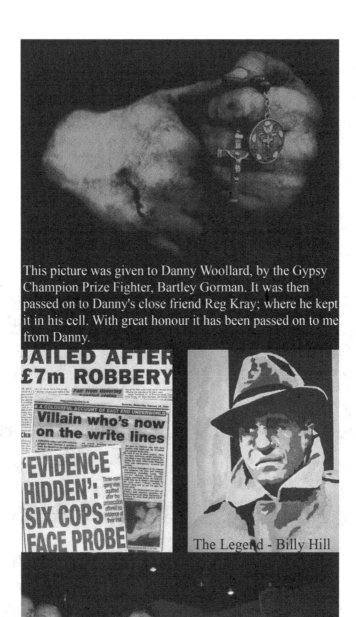

This picture was given to Danny Woollard, by the Gypsy Champion Prize Fighter, Bartley Gorman. It was then passed on to Danny's close friend Reg Kray; where he kept it in his cell. With great honour it has been passed on to me from Danny.

JAILED AFTER £7m ROBBERY

Villain who's now on the write lines

'EVIDENCE HIDDEN': SIX COPS FACE PROBE

The Legend - Billy Hill

Joe Pyle Snr & Jnr with friends

Vic Dark & Mickey Gonella   Richie Reynolds

Frank Fraser   Angelo Hayman

Danny Woollard

Matt Legg

- Wanted-

Great opportunity for the right person. High earning potential. Must be able to work using own initiative as much as in a small team. Experience with firearms and calm under pressure a must.

STODARE, every Saturday, at ·5.

Boxing

"Boxing and being a fighter was part of who
you were as an East-ender"
Danny Woollard -2009

Bare-knuckle boxing or prize fighting is thought as the origin of what is known as today as boxing, and is closely related to many forms of ancient combat sports. It comprises of two fighters not necessarily matched in size or weight going 'toe-to-toe' bare fisted (no gloves). What makes this sport slightly different from street fighting is there are sets of rules

Under these rules, fights were typically practiced with bare knuckles. The rules sometimes allowed for a broad range of fighting including holds, throws, elbows, head-butts and kicking of the opponent, sometimes known as an 'all-in' or 'anything goes'. All rules had to be agreed by both parties and or by the organizers prior to the start of the fight. Also included were the final wager and the payout. Winner takes all was a common standard. In likeness with modern boxing rules based upon the Marquess of Queensberry rules, a round ended when one of the fighters could no longer stand. Also with Queensberry rules he was given 30 seconds to rest and eight additional seconds to 'come to scratch' or return to the centre of the ring where a 'scratch line' was drawn and stand against his opponent and there were no round limits. When a man could not come to 'scratch', he would be declared loser and fights could end if broken up beforehand by crowd, riot, police interference or chicanery, dissemblance or if both men were willing to accept that the contest was a draw. While it is accepted that there was no limit to the total amount of rounds, fights typically lasted only a short time, one such fight in Australia lasted over 6 hours between James Kelly and Jack Smith in 1856.

The rules

These are the original Broughton Rules on which the London Prize Ring Rules were based.

1. That a square of a yard be chalked in the middle of the stage, and on every fresh set-to after a fall, or being parted from the rails, each second is to bring his man to the side of the square, and place him opposite to the other, and till they are fairly set-to at the lines, it shall not be lawful for one to strike at the other.

2. That, in order to prevent any disputes, the time a man lies after a fall, if the second does not bring his man to the side of the square, within the space of half a minute, he shall be deemed a beaten man.

3. That in every main battle, no person whatever shall be upon the stage, except the principals and their seconds, the same rule to be observed in bye-battles, except that in the latter, Mr. Broughton is allowed to be upon the stage to keep decorum, and to assist gentlemen in getting to their places, provided always he does not interfere in the battle; and whoever pretends to infringe these rules to be turned immediately out of the house. Everybody is to quit the stage as soon as the champions are stripped, before the set-to.

4. That no champion be deemed beaten, unless he fails coming up to the line in the limited time, or that his own second declares him beaten. No second is to be allowed to ask his man's adversary any questions, or advise him to give out.

5. That in bye-battles, the winning man to have two-thirds of the money given, which shall be publicly divided upon the Stage, notwithstanding any private agreements to the contrary.

6. That to prevent disputes, in every main battle the principals shall, on coming on the stage, choose from among the gentlemen present two Umpires, who shall absolutely decide all disputes that may arise about the battle; and if the two umpires cannot agree, the said umpires to choose a third, who is to determine it.

7. That no person is to hit his adversary when he is down or seize him by the ham, the breeches, or any part below the waist, a man on his knees is to be reckoned down.

Professional boxing

Professional bouts are usually much longer than amateur bouts, ranging from ten to twelve rounds, though four round fights are common for less experienced fighters. Through the early twentieth century, it was common for fights to have unlimited rounds, ending only when one fighter quit. Fifteen rounds remained the internationally recognized limit for championship fights for most of the twentieth century until the early 1980s, when the death of a reduced the limit to twelve.

Protective headgear is not permitted in professional bouts, and boxers are generally allowed to take much more punishment before a fight is stopped. At any time, however, the referee may stop the fight if he believes that one combatant cannot defend himself due to injury. In that case, the other fighter is awarded a technical knockout win. A technical knockout would also be awarded if a fighter receives a cut or an injury, and the opponent is later deemed not fit to continue by a doctor.

Roy Shaw

A daughter's message

A daughter's love and the bond that exists between her and her father is something that exists in most families. If it doesn't, it's a loss. There is something about the bond that has been known between fathers and daughters across the globe. It has been written about in one of the most famous of all books; the good book; a.k.a The Bible, right through to a story from a daughter to her dad in a working class city. It's also fair to say that no one really knows the man in conversation, more than his own daughter. True can be said with a man that holds high regard with my brothers and I. Roy Shaw has a daughter that has always talked to me about the fella, with such respect and admiration that it only fair I have her tell you about the good man. Pride, respect and understanding always where core points in each and every conversation Tina would share about her dad. Pride, she has carried since child hood. Never giving up or swaying in opinion, when he was thought of as less by others. Tina is always proud to say 'My dad'. Respect, knowing he always thought of his daughter, and her interests, understanding that he was always there if ever needed as any good dad should be.

When Tina asked me if there was anything that she could do to help remember my baby brother, I could only think of the relationship that exists between families, and how much we had wished we did more, or say to honour their memory. So with Roy Shaw being a favourite with my brothers, and myself I thought why not have the lady that knows Roy the best tell us about someone she only knows, as a daughter would. So with great thanks and gratitude, I will let my friend Tina Shaw, tell you about the man we all know as Roy Shaw.

My dad and me

My dad was put in prison before I was two. I can remember missing him, and my mum would take us to see him. I can remember when I hadn't seen him for ages, mum took us to see him and I couldn't understand why he couldn't come home with us. It was all very confusing at the time. My dad had made me a teddy bear [a great big one it was] the man on the train tried to charge my mum a fare for the teddy as it was so big, my mum is Maltese and a bit cranky, it all kicked off over this teddy bear. I loved it 'till it fell to pieces. He often made me things; he made me a nice dolls house (I can't remember what happened to it now) but how I wished id kept it now!! We would love going to see our dad. It was always a good day out. We would hide behind the door that dad would come in then jump out on him in surprise. He would be holding a large brown bag full of sweets and chocolate for Gary and me. One day on a visit, I was about 5. I got bored and wondered of. I was very friendly and loved attention. Well there I was standing on this table singing to these people who I didn't know, and dad hit the roof. It was the first time I can remember him being angry. He told me that the man I was singing for had killed his wife and children by locking them in the house then setting fire to it; and there was me thinking he was a nice man!! Mind you, we were in Broadmoor.

Mum and dad got divorced when I was eight, so we didn't see dad much after that. Dad got released from prison just after my 11th birthday. He came round to see us, but my brother Gary didn't recognize him, and he thought he was our uncle, but I knew it was him. I couldn't believe he was there! We lived on a council estate at the time. The other kids would tease me saying I didn't have a dad and that I was a bastard. I told my dad, so he put me on his shoulders and marched me round the whole estate I was shouting "See I have got a dad, this is my dad see!" My dad started to rebuild his life. He was doing door work up the West end and also started to get back into the boxing. We would take a lot of stick from other people for whatever my dad was doing. I was so worried when dad had the Adams' fight, as it was his first major public one and everyone was talking about it. The kids at school, the teachers, people in the street, it was crazy! But then you get the people that like dad and the people that don't. The people that don't like him don't tell him they seem to want to tell me for some reason, but thankfully there's only a few. It was such a relief when he won it though I have to say!

My dad is very different, to say the least compared to other people. He works in a different way to most. My Nan once told me that my dad hasn't been wired the same way as most. At the time, I didn't quite understand what she meant. But in time, I did. I know my dad loves me and always has, but him loving me, made him very protective at times where it was unbearable. I could never go to him with any problems, as he would deal with them his way, so really couldn't tell him anything. But he always tries in his own way to be a dad. I've had some of the best nights out with my dad. He always went to the best places to go, and we always had a good time. Then when I got too old for the clubs he would take my eldest daughter Adele. So long as she didn't call him Granddad!

He has 3 GREAT grandchildren now and I have loads of memories of my dad some good some not so well. But one thing's for sure, my dad was definitely a one off and I'm very proud to be his daughter.

Tina Shaw

Roy Shaw

'Brother' is more than a title, even after death."
James Allday - May 2009.

If ever a hard man was discussed by us three brothers, Roy Shaw was one
of them. Born in the East End of London, Roy was never short of a bit
of the action, but also carrying with the hard-earned reputation was a set
of values and code that is typically over looked and ignored by the masses
and media. This man that took on the system and in the eyes and opinion
of my brothers and me; he is one of very few to have come out on top. He
paid a heavy price for his code of conduct, and he never backed away from
the basic principles and standards that were given to him by his family.
When I wanted to meet the great man, Roy's daughter Tina was kind
enough to get the man and an icon in my late brother's book, and quite
rightly so, there are top people in here, and Roy deserves to be amongst
them. The questions are what both myself, and my brothers would have
asked, and I am lucky enough to have been given the chance to have that
connection with Roy's family.

Kate Kray did a book on Roy Shaw, and I am not shy in admitting it is
one of the only books that I have liked. I think there are few records that
allowed Roy to show himself as the character he really is. Charisma! If
an East End gent was ever to be made a textbook example of wooing the
ladies, then in my opinion and experience of the lads from the east, Roy is
one of them. Now that's not to say there's many a fella that couldn't take
out the ladies and show them the city of lights and splendor, it's simply
saying he was known for having an eye for the pretty girls and treating
them like a lady. Honour is another trait Roy is well known for. Just ask
any of the people he calls friends and they will tell you his standard for
friendship. He has been there for the saving of a friend to the simple
gesture of good will to a fellow mate. Even a young man that took his life
in September 2008, who's eldest brother made calls to friends to get some

assistance for a book, Roy's family helped, they'd been raised by the same standards as Roy, and as a result, you're reading this story.

He fought on many fronts, personal and in the public eye. Those that did get to see Roy fight never were short-changed of a story from the aftermath. He gained popularity in different circles for different reasons. As I said, for my brothers and me we all had heard of Roy. He remains with us all as one of the greatest Guv'nor's. He has had the respect from some of the most feared and respected people in both business and in the underworld. He has the heart of a lion, and the loyalty from friends that has in his own words led him from one of the darkest times to freedom. He was a successful businessman and had an eye for the ladies, but always maintained the respect from all walks of life.

Now of course the interest is there, many an interview has been done with the great man. So in fairness, he was willing to contribute here too. Like I said a gent! Roy always carried himself well when an interview was requested. Never cocky, always confident, a start in one of the best parts of London, of course we speak of East London where Roy started his life. So it's only fair that we allowed Roy to tell us how it all started and what made the man that so many respect.

After a phone call to Tina and arrangements made, the sandwich maker and I set off to a local in leafy Essex, for a sit down with a shared childhood icon of three brothers. When Roy walked up to me, I without question automatically felt a great sense of respect for the man. Taking me firmly by the hand Roy gave a firm handshake, a welcoming smile and asked how I was doing. For me it felt as if he wanted assurance I was doing well and only when I assured him with a returning firm handshake and again saying I was ok. Roy then sat down and asked how everything was going with the book. Both Tina and my traveling companion adjourned to the bar as Roy sat back and asked how and in what way he could help. My question was a simple one. It was for Roy to share some of his life's trials and tribulations, as it was from this I felt I could gain some assurance, that no matter what demons a man faced, there was a light at the end of the tunnel. Roy smiled, leaned forward and calmly began to share his life story that to this day still makes a part of me feel there's a fighter that can't be fucked with in anyone that has been through loss.

Roy- "For me, it was a tuff start. I mean it was hard for a lot of people. I was born in Stepney; within the sound of the bow bells, that makes you a true cockney, an East Ender. My family is what holds some of my best memories. My mother taught me manors, but I was and still very anti-authority. It's a matter of standing up for what you believe in, isn't it! I had two uncles on my dads' side that would take me to boxing. My dad as well, before he passed had me interested in boxing, and I would go with my uncles to boxing. They all saw I had something special when I came to that. I mean, I'm not bragging, but when I hit them they would just go over. I mean it even went as far as when I went to a dance, it could've been the Elephant and castle or somewhere in Ilford, I'd hear 'there's that Roy Shaw'. Sometimes they'd want to come over and shake my hand, other times they'd come over for something else, and then they'd get it quick.

But, it was my family that made the earliest memories for me and what made my start in East London special, sparring with my dad, him taking me to the boxing club. I loved boxing from an early age. It was part of a lot of young men's lives, my uncles, my dad and me. I was a keep fit fanatic, that's what also helped me. There were some boxers that were better than me really, but because I was so fit and strong, that allowed me to do 'em. One fighter that sticks with me the most, and it was a good fight, is the one fighter that I did and he did me was Lenny Mclean. One fight, I did beat him easily within 3 rounds, then the next one he did me. I have really met a lot of good boxers along the way. None of them was really easy fights, there's the work before hand. Most of them were knockouts; I knew I was good at what I did as I was earning the money.

I think the first time I realised there was real money to be made is when a pal asked me to come over to Barnet Fair and fight the gypsies. I went over there and done three of them and the travelers had some really good fighters, it was their game, they could really have a go. Then I was asked if

I'd fight Donny 'the bull' Adams. Well I was in prison with him, so I knew he could have a row. I trained, trained, trained really hard, and then at the fight, I went out there and 'bang', over he went. Well, I still had a lot more there. 'Get up' I'm shouting. 'Bang' again, I hit him; he was on the floor again. I remember picking him up to hit him again. The ref was saying 'that's enough Roy' and I think the ref thought I was helping him up, but I was just getting him up to hit him again so I could have another go.

After I done Donny 'the bull', not a lot of people wanted to know. How many fights? Too many for me to remember but let's say a lot. I had ten pro fights, all through Mickey Duff and then I faced prison. After that, they wouldn't give me my license back, so I entered the unlicensed boxing. Mickey Duff said I would've been a great, if my life hadn't taken that turn, and he was a great man in the boxing world, so I took that as a great compliment. Being a scoundrel took 18 years of my life, and it was all hard. I originally got 15 years for robbery. While serving, this one fella wouldn't give me my fair share of spuds, so I wacked him and was taken back to court to court, I was awarded 3 more years.

During all my time, my codes never changed. The codes and rules you live with on the outside are the same as on the inside. I wouldn't tolerate these nonce's or wrong uns on the inside. They was stabbed and cut. It wasn't tolerated by any of us. I mean there was one time they had Frank Fraser and I in at the same time, we wouldn't allow the nonce's near us. A screw let me see my records one time, and it said in there that Fraser and Shaw must never be allowed in the same prison. Frank, I really respected. Frank Fraser and Joe Pyle are top of my tree and are both great men. Joe saved me, when they put me in Broad moor. Joe was the only person that was allowed to visit me. They were treating me and where they had me locked away, was one of the worst parts within Broad moor. It was called the punishment block. Joe came to visit me, and convinced me that I had to change just enough or I would die there. Joe saved my life. Thinking back, I'd say the hardest time I did was at Wandsworth. I only did maybe 2 or 3 years there, but the screws had a much more aggressive attitude. They'd try to break you. There was no messing about there, but even there I wouldn't change my attitude towards certain people. When the screws came to my door, it wasn't just the one. It was always four or five of them. Maidstone is where I hold a record. I'm still the only prisoner to have ever gone through their cell door from the inside. Simple really, they had these really heavy metal chairs, and if you hit the door in the right place, like I did, smashing the spy hole you could make a hole. I did this until I worked my way out. Well I had a pal who was in as well and he was looking out of his cell and shouting to me 'Roy, Roy all the screws are coming for ya'. Well I run up the stairs and got myself all the buckets that were filled with sand and water. Back then, they'd have them lined up ready in case of a fire. So I pulled all these and was set up waiting for them on the top landing. As they all came running up I just poured them out and all over them, a bucket of sand then a bucket of water, a bucket of sand then another bucket of water. It was like Brighton beach. Then there was me chasing them around and the Guv'nor came in and shouted to me "Shaw, if you come down now and I'll deal with you myself tomorrow." Well the guv'nor can only give you 28 days; elsewhere you can be given 6 months. So, I shouted to everyone "did you hear that?" They all shouted back "yeah, we heard that Roy" and was all banging from their cells.

All in all I've been in 18 different prisons and thinking back it was 18 long years and a large part of my life. I was lucky that I was such a keep fit fanatic. You know pushups, sit-ups, keeping myself busy. Inside it is something they try to take away from you. Chip away from you over the years and that's you and your power. Well, me, I've always been a bit fiery, so when they tried to push me about 'bang', I'd hit 'em. It goes back to when I was very young, when my dad died. They tried to bully me then and I stood up and realizing I was blessed with the power of the punch I'd whack 'em. In the army, they'd shout and scream at me "Shaw! Get over here; stand to attention, stand-up straight" and 'bang' over they'd go. That though was when I got into some trouble. Telling them I could hear voices got me sent into a direction I didn't expect and yes, I've met some great people along the way. People that still hold a special place with me and always will be top of my tree are Joey Pyle and Frank Fraser. I mean I've met a lot of nice people, but those two boys are special. If I were to say what

I'd like to be remembered as it would be a boxer. Yeah, I did some villainy, the smash and grab jobs; like the vans, and that got me some money, but that also got me my prison. Boxing has made me my real money, and that's how I'd like to be remembered. Going back to my boxing, I always remember fighting Ron Stander. He was a big fella'. At the time of our fight, he was ranked third in the world, and a very good fighter. During the fight, I really was going at him. Bang, Bang I was hitting him. Then I hear him saying "that's it Roy, keep it up." Keep it up I thought! So I hit him again hard. "That's it Roy, and again." When I got back to my corner they said 'you all right Roy?' "All right!" I said. "I'm hitting him and all he keeps saying is good Roy, Keep it up." Then they tell me to try his belly. So when I go out again 'bang' into his belly, and sure enough Ron makes a sound as if I'd hit the target. So that's where I hit him, and hit him hard. Now I'm not going to take all the glory because unbeknown to me, not long before our fight, Ron got an injury on his ribs and this cost him during our fight. Yeah, I would have gone the distance; I was taking all his hits. And if I was to choose the fights or fighters that I liked to have it with the most, British middleweight champions. That's my weight, and again they're has been some great fighters there.

If I were to say I had a weakness it would be when I have to go to funerals. I never got over losing my mum and dad. That still hurts, I still get all-emotional, even now I get tears in my eyes. I think it's just because of the East End; it's a special place. We had heart and fight in us, simple things I carry with me even now. I always have and always will hate bullies. I've never been a bully, can't stand 'em. Happy times! Oh yeah, a lot always come to mind. One is of course when I first got married and spending time in Malta, and then of course getting kicked out of Malta. Today there are some nice times. I was at a dance hall not to long back. I'd hear 'is that Roy Shaw?' Then people would be coming over to me, shaking my hand, hugs and kisses. It's nice that there are good, friendly people out there. I mean I could be walking about in Spain, and people would walk up to me and say 'hello'. Though I do think half of the people we all know are all in Spain now. Even a trip to Las Vegas a fella' come up to me and said "Roy Shaw, just wanted to say hello." People that have done some time in prison would come up to me and say "ello, Roy, when I was away I read your book and thank you, it was really good."

I like to think of myself as a smart fighter, I have put money way, I live in a nice house, I've been on a few nice holidays, I just didn't spunk it all away. And now I just keep out of trouble, appreciate what it is like to mellow out a bit and live a nice life. Have I tried any other sports? Golf, just once though, wasn't for me. Boxing? I still think about it a lot. When I go to some boxing events, I often think to myself they're some crap fights on, maybe I should make a comeback" (laughing).

Interwoven in his violence, is his passion for the ring. With criminal activity of past, Roy Shaw also has an equal sense of values, morals and above all understanding for the rights and wrongs in our society.

When asked my opinion on Roy Shaw, it is an easy one. A Guv'nor turned Lord of the manor, a gentleman through and through, and an honor to have Roy's name alongside my baby brothers' name.

Since the writing of this chapter, Roy has passed. I've been privileged to have spent time with both of Roy's children. Gary and Tina are good friends that without question show the qualities and respect for the people they care for as much as Roy did for the people that he cared for in his life. I would like to think that Roy is up there now, wearing his best whistle and flute being the best host amongst solid proper people that he called friends. Around those events, Roy is I am sure training for a rematch with another great that was of the same era as Roy. Of course, I am talking of Lenny McLean.

R.I.P my friend. It was an absolute honour to have spent time with you.

Big Joe Egan

I am not a religious man. Well, not to the point that I go to church or pray to a god, but, if I was, the first thing I'd say about this man is, if the almighty were to put an angel amongst us sinners, his name would be Joe Egan. The conversation I had with Joe was full of warmth and an immeasurable amount of compassion. This is a man, that by most standards should be bitter, angry and looking for some form of 'compensation'. The loss and hardship Joe has encountered was a hand fate dealt in an unfair fashion to this champion, but enough of my biased opinion, Judge for yourself. To lose a brother, have a complete stranger go out of his way to offer anything within his power to heal or provide service to a fella' and that only by request of a mutual friend, and then say that's not a caring or honourable person. Joe has boxed with the best. Been graced and given commendations from the greats of an era gone by. Seen a dream held in front of him, only to be taken away. He's been measured as a champion in and out of the ring. He is The Great Big Joe Egan.

For my times back and forth from my home in the United States, I was not able to have my timetable coincide with Joe's but that did not stop him. No sooner had I arrived back in the states, I had Joe on the phone, apologising he had missed my calls as our schedules never met. This was the hospitality I had seen and heard from an uncle that had come from Ireland, always there as the host. He had warmth measured by a smile and the friendliness to match, "I'm so sorry, Jason", was the start of our conversation. Telling Joe that it was he doing me the honour by giving his time, and input into work in this book, but Joe was insistent that an apology from him being busy, and not getting a chance to meet myself was necessary. His voice carried warmth and calmness that you would not expect from such a man that carried such a fierce reputation. This was a man that had been the distance with Lennox Lewis. A man, dubbed the toughest white man on the planet by Mike Tyson, and still carrying the grace and friendliness of a gentleman, with honour and dignity.

The first thing I remember hearing about this man, was the number of fights he's had, and the caliber of fighter he'd fought but what I think makes Joe different, is not the number of fights he won or lost, or even the way he boxed. Instead, the shear fact, this man is one of the friendliest men in boxing, with the charm to go with it. Like most boxers, Joe fought, and fought hard. Often fighting opponents much older, due to the sheer size of Joe, and as a young fighter, Joe could not get a fight. He was often having the experience and age against him, but this certainly never halted Joe nor did it when he was training and fighting in the States. Common knowledge is that Joe sparred and went the distance with the great Iron Mike Tyson many times. It is also known that Mike never knocked him out and earned Joe the title, from Mike himself, as the toughest white man on the planet, along with a friendship, that many a man would envy but until you get to know the man, it is impossible to appreciate Joe's warmth, friendliness and above all love and respect for life.

OK, so I have said the man is a champion. I have said he is a great humanitarian but let us talk about things that would have been the questions my brothers and I would have asked such a fighter. So, ladies and gentleman, boys and girls; weighing in at the green corner (being that's the colour of this man's home land), holding 7 Irish titles with over 80 wins, and having fought against such greats as Lennox Lewis and Iron Mike Tyson, I proudly give you the Irish Blond bombshell, Biggggggggggggggggggggg Joe Egan!

I had to ask, with Joe being such a modest man, that I honestly think some boxers, given the title from Mike Tyson, as the toughest white man on the planet, would have had T shirts printed with that all that and more across the front but when he hears this, Joe simply gives a smile. The same title would have allowed some boxers to promote inflated egos and attitude but again, not Joe. I was, as much as my brothers would have asked why just a smile? Joe gave a response, as I had imagined, with dignity and a sense of responsibility.

Joe- "A smile, it breaks down barriers. If you growl, barriers are put up. With my size and my stature, it can be quite intimidating, but when you smile, it puts people at ease. It's a nice way to meet and great people, with a smile. When people ask for my autograph, I sign with the word happiness. That's part and part of the parcel of being happy, is a smile. You can have all the respect and money in the world, but if you're not happy, what good is it? There are hundreds of languages in the world, Jason. Everybody speaks a different language. Some people don't have a clue what some people are saying. When people laugh and smile, there are no language barriers. You use fewer muscles to smile, than you do to frown. Smiling is a very important part of life."

Like a lot of sports, there is a certain amount of outside influence that controls if not at least influence both the athletes and the sport itself, and having that Joe had been in the ring at both the professional and amateur level, I thought it only fair to ask if boxing was the same today, as it was when Joe was coming through the ranks.

Joe- "Not the amateur boxing! I think the computer judging has spoilt it. They have made it more like fencing. I don't think it's beneficial for the sport. For me, boxing is the art of self-defense, but you still like to see a good tear up. They're the modern day gladiators."

Here I have to agree with Joe. What is boxing with limitations, amateur boxing, with less rounds and protective headgear, it is sure less of a sport, if you take away the 'essence' of full contact! Let us hope they leave our football alone, boys, soon football without the ball. No injuries from dodgy tackles!

So, understanding there is now limitations to one faction of boxing did Joe feel there was anything missing from boxing.

Joe- "When you have a great heavy weight champion, the rest of the weight divisions shine as well. Everyone loves the heavy weights and because they're not putting enough small hall shows on, that are the grass roots for boxing, there's not enough boxers or boxing going on. Boxing gives a young man self respect and gives respect for another person. Television doesn't give boxing enough exposure. Boxing takes another young man of the streets."

If you are lucky to be graced with this man's presence, to share his time, to be fortunate to even listen to Joe, you will notice one universal truth and that is that Joe always has a million pound smile on his face. So what is his formula?

Joe- "Just to be happy, no matter what obstacles are put in your way, you can always think straighter when you're happy. When you go into a rage, you don't think straight. I think if you can confront things when you're happy in your mind, you'll confront them better. If you confront things in an unstable frame of mind, you'll make mistakes. Just try to be happy. Don't do things in a rage. Just sit back, relax. Think about what needs to be done and then go on."

With Joe's book, as a good source of both the lessons and the pit falls life has to offer, Joe always spoke calmly and also with a sense of 'been there, done that and learned my lesson', was it fair to say there were any more lessons to be learned?

Joe- "Oh, yeah! I mean you have to experience the hard times to appreciate the good times. If I have to draw from my life, I think that boxing is one of the best things that can prepare you for life. When you're in the ring, you go through the pain, obstacles and fear. And there are so many emotions involved in boxing that you also go through in life, it would be a place I'd advise any young man to take up boxing. Boxing gets you ready for life."

Now a thought on the world of boxers, if Joe can go toe – to – toe with some of the world's best. In his prime, I am sure he had liked to have a bit of time in the ring with at least one of the greats. For no, reason other than maybe their style, class and quality. Who would it be?

Joe- "I'd never have been good enough, but to have shared the ring with Muhammad Ali would've been such an honor for me. Just to have been punched by him would've been an honour. He would've danced rings around me, but then again, just to share the ring, would have been a sheer honour, even if I were a boxer in his era to have been a sparring partner, just for one round. I'd been dazzled by both his speed and his class. That would've been one of the greatest of honors."

Although, Junior's and my time in the ring wasn't to the degree of Joe, we both experienced the life of a boxer. A boxers' life is a lonely life, the training, seclusion, and restrictions in terms of lifestyle. Did Joe think this all helped with the pit-falls and perils along the way?

Joe- "Yes definitely and without a shadow of a doubt. A boxing ring is the loneliest place in the world. I think the training and the build up to the fight and the regime the boxer takes on help. There are so many distractions that can take them away from the concentration of the fight and that's why they have to go to these training camps. People always ask why can't they train at home. But, then they have all the problems of everyday life. So, when they are at the training camp, that's all they do. They eat, train, totally blinkered and focused on that fight. It's a totally rewarding world. Not just in the monitory sense, but also in the sense of satisfaction. The professional boxer's life can be a short one, but it's so rewarding.

When you're arm is raised at the end of the fight, it's one of the greatest feelings in the world and all the hardship is all worthwhile. It's kind of like life. All the seclusion you can experience, the hardships and the sacrifice."

Again, the boxing world is filled with great names. Did Joe have any favorites?

Joe- "Without a doubt, Muhammad Ali, I absolutely idolise him." (Prior to this conversation, we talked about another great, and a personal friend of Joe's. Of course I'm talking about iron Mike Tyson.) "Boxing just doesn't need great fighters it also needs great ambassadors for the sport and I don't think they come any greater than Muhammad Ali. The boxing world couldn't have wished for a greater man and ambassador than that man. Not only, was he one of the greatest men to ever enter a ring, he was also, one of the greatest men ever to enter this world."

Boxing is a sport watched worldwide, by people from all walks of life, including royalty. We have as many conversations about who is the best and why. Who should fight and who would win. Joe, being a local, and in my eyes a local authority would make an excellent call in terms of who, when and why. I mean, come on, he has fought some of the world's best.

Joe- "Sonny listen and Mike Tyson, there's two fighters that would just lock horns and box."

One of the greatest moments in a boxer's life is when they enter the arena, the walk towards the ring, the sense of pride and accomplishment that goes with that journey from the dressing room to the center of the ring. It is something most people will never experience. Even to accompany a world-class athlete is something some can only dream of. Our friend and hero Joe has experienced this. In one report, he said it was a great moment and it gave him a great sense of pride when he carried the championship belt for Ricky Hatton.

Joe- "Every boxer that enters a boxing ring, dreams of fighting for a world title, I wasn't good enough, but my friend Ricky Hatton gave me the opportunity to carry his belt into the ring for a world title fight and that was as close as it was going to get for me. It was a dream almost full filled, and because that man gave me that opportunity, I can't thank that man enough."

Joe has seen the world. He has been out and about and he's seen a lot in a life time. Some would even say enough to fill several lifetimes. What would some of his best times?

Joe- "Winning my Irish titles, most of my best times have come from boxing. Being the best man at my brother's wedding, my brothers and sisters having children, my family, and without a doubt, my best time has been meeting Ruth, and when I did meet her, it was just like it was meant to be. At the time I'd met her, I was at a very low point in my life, and she brought me back up. She is like my soul mate."

What about movies? We all watch them, and I am sure Joe has a few favorites. What about a film that holds inspiration, maybe?

Joe- "I know it's only fiction, but Rocky is one for me. It's a character we can all relate to. We can draw from Rocky. Away from boxing, I really enjoyed the character that was in Shaw shank redemption, Tim Robbins who played the character Andy, great movie and character."

Boxing, businessman and great ambassador to the people, what's next for the friendliest man in boxing

Joe- "To become an actor, I've been acting all my life. I just never had a camera with me."

OK, last one. Joe, the actor, what role would you chose.

Joe- "A baddie in a James Bond Movie"

The closing comment given by Joe, also gave the trademark laugh that Joe is famous for, a real treat for me.

Our conversation went on, with Joe offering his condolences to my family, for the loss of Junior. Saying things in a way that also helped mold a puzzle I had started to see, through talking to other friends and people, involved in the book. Joe had a way of explaining things that very few people had allowed me to understand or accept. Joe, is with a doubt, one of the friendliest people, I could have ever wished or had the pleasure to have spoken to. He gave me advice and some thoughts on the loss. He could not do enough. When I said that he had made a big enough contribution, by giving time and input, it was as if he wanted to make sure Junior's family was being taken care of. 'No' was not an answer he wanted to hear. Offering any help, any assistance, and above all, "Any time, my friend", was a reply I got. When I finally gave in so that I would accept that offer of assistance, for me, it was one of those times, I felt great comfort and a sense of calm, from something as simple as a conversation, with what felt like an audience with a true long lost friend. For me, an honor, for Joe, a way of showing what is in my opinion, a champion in and out of the ring is really all about. God bless The Great Joe Egan, an angel on earth.

East London

Only fair and just. These were the roots to my family, the East End. Maps and the ever-growing pace of the Internet will have it listed as The East End of London. I think it should be The Great East End of London, but who am I to complain! It is on the map, so happy days. Although it is hard beginnings was more than enough for anyone to have a grumble, getting its start just east of what was once known as the medieval walled city of London. It did not actually get 'characterised' until the 19th century. Even then, a long way from the cramming of houses and families and the start of what is known as the 'Cockneys' this was in fact a time when villages clustered around the city walls. Also in the area were farmlands and marshes. With the rumored abundance of jobs in the city and surrounding areas, it would naturally attract a large amount of rural people looking for a way to earn a penny or two. So where did the name 'Cockney' come from, and what does it mean? Again, a few different stories, but this is the one I know. Going back a few years, when the uninvited Normans arrived and had a few of their boys plotted up for a while, they called London the land of the sugar Cake! Well, I've heard worse! A name given much like a lot of names to suggest any big city had more than its fair share of luxury and splendor. In old French 'pais de cocaigne', in turn this was what all Londoners were referred to or known as. In time abbreviations and different spellings where adopted including: Cocagne, Cockayne', and in the newer English: Cocknay and Cockney. One theory suggests that with the migration of the workers from the villages out to what's known as West Ham and East Ham, this 'title' was carried along with them. Dah- Dah! The birth of the all loving, all knowing, singing, jack the lad, how's ya' father cockney boy and girl was born.

If I was to reflect back on the people that held an impression in my early years and its exposure to my current day friends within crime, than without question the Kray brothers was a very strong part of that. Of my older and wiser friends and family, the name Reg Kray was spoken with both respect and admiration. A criminal no doubt but a gentleman by all standards. Even Reg's bitter enemies will tell you of the standard and professionalism in the way Reg' conducted his business. In my opinion it would be bad manners to talk of East London and what was once an empire with the Twins as the bosses. An education received from the king himself Billy Hill and all the qualities he instilled were easily seen and are missed in what now known as the underworld.

Reg Kray

For me the Reg Kray gave time and effort in writing back to a simple London lad. The letters and the contents will never see the light of day. These letters where enough to give me some direction in my early adult life. I was not alone in this. Many people had the pleasure of Reg's company, but I will get to that in a minute. Long before the release of the film "The Krays", I was told of 'The Twins' and how they ruled much of London. How they conducted 'business' with like-minded people, and how the streets had less 'wrong-uns'. When I wrote to Reg', it was always with a sense of moral obligation. This was a man that had been raised with a set of standards and morals similar to that of my brothers and me. That allowed two worlds to exist, but never interfere with each other. The business Reg' committed was without question illegal, but during this time of the twins reign over London, there was no mention of what exists today. And if it did it wasn't allowed, especially near or around schools and those it housed. The innocence that should be by all rights should be preserved by all adults for their children, was as much a part of the twins care as the running of their enterprises. Care for their own, many of my friends and family was raised by a strong set of ethics and codes, and a lot that have been lost in today's society. Now don't get me wrong, my brothers and me had our fair share of mischief whilst growing up in London, but who didn't, and we like a lot of people that worked and lived by a set of morals and codes were taught the difference and how to discriminate between 'right and wrong'. There are things you can and cannot do. If you have to question this alone, then there are people I know that would tell you it is time for you to go back to 'school'. In the mid nineties, I read a story that an elderly lady was mugged while on her way back home from a night out with friends. The loss of her purse and few pieces of jewelry was not what it ultimately cost her. She died because of the head injuries. The two youths received a sentence of less than 3 years each, as it was classed as an act of undiminished responsibility. You do not have to be told, with the 'life' sentence Reg was given, how can the crime verses the time be justified? I know pals that got more porridge for fighting like-minded people at football than for people that take lives. To keep it positive, Reg certainly fought fire with water. The amount of people, many young lads, that got caught in the web of trouble at an early age in other circumstances would've become to a worse situation while in prison. Reg accepting these lads got into trouble for a reason at least gave them his knowledge, time and more importantly a 'paved way'. Now the criminals I speak of are not the ones you read of that have committed a crime against women or children. That is a different type of 'person'. Many will tell you they are not even criminals, they are in fact just 'scum' or 'wrong-uns', and more often than not with Reg, it did not stop with a friendly chat, and you have to remember, that while serving, Reg was a category 'A' prisoner. Simply meaning, he had very limited, if any contact with other people, but when he was given a 'breath of fresh air', he invested in other people. Phone calls to help people on release to get somewhere to stay and in most cases a job, simply helping people along the way, always educating people in the ways of 'right and wrong'. For me Reg' was a folklore hero. He was someone that the system never broke. He gave hope to so many, and contributed to saving lives, that even in the most dire of times never went against a way of life that is seen in today's society and is sold for the change in a person's pocket. He is spoken in my 'family' with respect and admiration, and I will always be proud I was known as someone in Reginald Kray's life. Like he always said at the start and of closing of each letter 'Your friend Reg Kray'

They Krays, as I knew them.

Danny Woollard

At the start of the 1960's, the East End of London was a bustling hive of activity. The streets of London were paved with gold, for anyone with a bit of bottle (guts). Everything was wide open; if you smashed a jeweler's window you were long gone by the time the police arrived on the scene. There were no cameras about, any trackers on cars or lorries; it was pure heaven just to be alive. The Kray family had two clubs, a billiard hall, a pub and 3 Spiellers (illegal gambling dens). They were also into the protection racket in a very big way. They had earned their reputation the hard way, now their name was working for them. Once their name was mentioned all sorts of businessmen quickly paid up for their services. I had heard stories about them but our paths had never crossed. Their empire started in Mile End and I was working from Forest gate onwards. We all had our own boundaries and no one encroached on anybody else are living. We all respected each other so there were no wars at all. Everyone got along just fine. The Krays had just started to move into the West End, with the real guv'nor Billy Hill's blessing and permission. They were big time and going places. Up to this point, I had never even seen the Krays. A friend of mine named Curly Martin, rang me up and said he had a bit of work for me to do, if I was interested, obviously I was interested. There was a club in the Mile End road called 'The Wentworth'. Well the proprietor 'Joe the Greek' was having a few problems there and wanted it sorted out. So me, Curly, Jumbo Connolly and Donny 'the Bull' Adams went to the club on the Saturday night and sorted out all Joe's problems for him. It was a short but very vicious battle. I knew Joe would have no more problems. Curley said, "Meet me tomorrow morning at Mile End station for your money." So Sunday morning we met up, and the four of us went into the terminus cafe opposite the station. As we sat down two very smart fellows walked up to our table and introduced themselves. It was Ron and Reg Kray. We had a bit of breakfast with them. Bobby Ramsey opened the door and the twins left with him. Curly opened the envelope which Reg had given to him it contained 250 quid for each of us which was a lot of money in those days. We had been working for the infamous Kray twins and did not even know it. Incidentally, Roy Shaw and his pal Jack 'the hat' McVitie were in the cafe that morning. I did not like McVitie, he was full of bounce and trap. I did not care about him, but I did not like him. When I think of Reg doing all that bird for a cunt like him, it is unbelievable. I did many deals with the Kray's afterwards and I found them good reliable men. Their word was their bond. I sold them vast quantities of one-armed bandits and they always paid promptly and at the right price. They were good men and I went to the old Bailey for their trial just for a bit of support. In the next court, Jimmy and Georgie Tibbs got off for shooting Albert Nichols, the very same day that the twins got their horrific sentences. Incidentally, the Wentworth club got blew up just after the case finished, almost blasting the famous actor Bernard Bresslaw's (whose catch phrase in all the carry on films was 'I only asked') house in Eric Street. Little did I realise that Reg and me' would finish spending a good few years together in Wayland prison in Norfolk. I suppose that life.

Traditional boxing style 1960's London. Jimmy Tippett Snr.

Books and those that wrote them

For some, reading is a bit of a chore. I will be honest; reading is not something my brothers and I committed to on a regular basis. All too often, mum would tell us, that reading keeps the brain 'alive'. Probably explains why the three lads in her household, often got into 'mischief'. But when any of us did get our heads into a book, and if it held our attention long enough then it was worth a read. The books that typically got our head away from the telly included those that reflected the life and times of our society. Any of the lads out and about, so to say, any one that got a result, someone that had 'cracked it', sorted themselves out, got a result. You know the fella's we talk of....

Junior, while is her Majesty's care, often got a read in. When arriving home, the book was the furthest thing from his mind. However, what else was the little bugger supposed to do while porridge was on the menu? I say, and I know a few lads that would agree, that it's a good job there's a few stories on paper, as without at least this form of entertainment, they had themselves in a lot more trouble!

Irvine Welsh

D rugs and by all accounts class A can affect not only the user but also the families surrounding the self infliction caused by the addiction and its host. Some drugs look for no merit or favours with the user only repeat business. Ask most people if they have taken any drugs and you will get an honest no! Ask those that become addicts if they have it under control and you will get an equal number of questionable responses.

Like most young adults, the drug scene goes hand in hand with the very culture that inner city life promotes and what they are easily exposed to. For yours truly it was a trip to Amsterdam and the occasional dabble with 'Lady Luck'. Through an introduction via a mutual pal, I was given the opportunity to speak with a chap that had ventured down an unforgivable trail of addiction that was paved by none other than heroin. This nasty little habit can cost you more than your dignity and bank account. Those that take this beast by the horns seldom have any positives to share from the experience. Typically, you are done and dusted. You do not need to be a rocket scientist to formulate a theory for this question. Brown bread is the answer from this equation.

An email and phone number was dropped in my lap and no sooner had I made contact with Irv' than the welcome to meet up with him and seek some solace was granted. If there was a time for a solo trip this was it. The sandwich maker understood this was a tough one for me. Surrounding Junior's death there was some question of his drug use. Knowing junior and his social activities I knew as sure as the day is long he was never a class 'A' taker. The occasional bit of Jamaican old Holburn but more a few beers with the lads was his forte. If anything a chat with someone that knew this territory and the signs to go with it would help answer some questions. At least it would help clear the air with a few suggestions the inquest promoted and supposed theories that were offered with my brother's death.

The luxury of living between California and Florida allowed me to meet up with some of the chaps that had hit the international scene. Being that train spotting hit the global film arena I knew from a conversation with Irv' that his time spent each year in the states could be pretty much on either coast. As luck would have it his next visit would land him in south Florida the same time as my own schedule.

So it was Set that I would meet up with Mr. Welsh in the swanky part of south Florida known as south beach. Three and a half hours after setting off, I arrive in the city of neon lights and over priced drinks. It was pretty much a combination of heat and flashy motors with the average club goer sporting an open shirt, thin gold chain and more stories than Jackanory. My impression of Irv' from our phone conversation allowed me to envision a combination of a literary genius and your favorite uncle, friendly, educated and above all very sharp. What was presented when we actually met was all of the above plus a man with such a comical impression on the everyday life and what urban culture presents that there is a void in standup comedy that could be easily filled by him.

The chosen spot is a little patio bar overlooking the Main Street otherwise known as ocean drive. Filled with locals, flamboyance and enough luxury sports cars to keep both gold diggers and Arabs sons entertained for as long as they pass. Between our orders arriving and the official chat, I considered my questions and my reading on the train-spotting creator. This is a fella that is feared by journalists. A chap that is admired by those that crave and seek the ingenious skills found in his work, who in turn has created a whole new way of looking at the options writers have as a result of the success and his master pieces.

When I was writing chapters, the auto spell check highlighted half the page I was typing. The difference between American English and 'traditional' English. Colour and color, flavor and flavour etc. With the 'unique' and local dialect used in his book, Irvine's screen must have looked like it had chicken pox. How did the whole writing go for him? This was my first question. Leaning back and smiling, Irv' paused and answered with a sense of knowledge and confidence.

Irvine: "It was a weird one for me, because I wrote the first draft in Standard English. When I read it back it seemed a bit flat and lacking something, so I decided that I'd be true to the voices of the characters in my head. I looked at some books where they'd rendered speech and thought phonetically, and tried to marry that up with what I was hearing and the way I talked myself. But when I attempted to do it that way and read back the first page, I almost gave up. Basically, I couldn't make head or tail of it, just because you're not used to words being like that written on a page. It takes about thirty pages, whether you're Scottish, English or American, before the voices start to insinuate themselves. I almost gave up at that point, because I thought that would be asking too much of a reader, and forcing them to stick with gobbledygook for thirty pages, or until everything became clear. Fortunately, I persevered and it worked out. It taught me not to underestimate readers. I think people will stick with something like that, but only if they know that there's going to be some kind of a pay-off in terms of the quality. If you do something like that, it had better be good, or nobody is going to take any notice of you again. So it was much more of a risk than I imagined it to be at the time. But back then I never really saw myself as having a career in writing so I was quite fearless about it."

What did Irvine feel was important for a writer to remember when he/ she are aiming their work at an audience?

Irvine: "I think you have to be a bit selfish as a writer and simply tell the story you want to tell, rather than trying to please an imaginary audience. You can't have any real concept of what some big, unrelated group of people will want. I think that for genre fiction like crime, thriller, romance, etc. there are obviously certain rules and things that the reader expects, but in so-called 'literary' fiction (even though I don't like that designation) there are no rules except the general ones of storytelling; compelling characters who get involved in interesting things, authentic dialogue, and some sort of dynamic transformation/resolution by the end of the tale."

There could have been many different options in terms of a title, so why 'Trainspotting'? It is hardly your 'anorak' kind of situation, and not a hint of what lead to this title, or is there? Irv', me old' mukka, do tell.

Irvine: "I had the title before I'd started writing it as a book. I just thought that this is a great title for a book about hard-core drug addicts and scammers. So I had to justify it to myself. When I thought about it, being a junky and being a train spotter actually had quite a lot in common; loads of standing around waiting in the cold, engaging in an activity that is fundamentally pointless. After all, you're never going to get the engine numbers for every train, and you're never going to get enough smack to satisfy the cravings as you're tolerance increases and you just need more the next time. So it's a lot of bother for nothing really. Once you actually start to conceptualize that (and you need to come to that point yourself, nobody can tell you) it's pretty much impossible to sustain addiction unless you're using the drug to anesthetize yourself against real pain. Leith, where the book is set, also used to have four railway stations. The buildings still exist, those old Victorian structures, and sometimes the place has that ghostly feel to it as a result, like I think every place has when it's not being used for the purpose for which it was intended. The old docks are pretty spooky and bleak, as they are in all those communities, like East London and Liverpool."

He played a role in trainspotting and If you look carefully, you'll see the master of writing, playing, not a junkie, but a very well played part, that by standards, is equaled in my brothers opinion and mine, as good as the 'actors' themselves. After watching the film would our friendly pal, have liked to play a different role or part?

Irvine: "I enjoyed doing the acting, and I couldn't have played a bigger role at the time, as I was very green as to what was required. The problem was that I was asked to do the same part repeatedly in different things, play a skanky drug-dealer. There's quite of few other cameos of me in films playing a drunk, a dealer, a transvestite and a pool player. I once got to play a concerned, chin-stroking yuppie social worker in one film, which I loved as it was a nice change from playing the scumbag. A general rule-of-thumb is that if I show up in a film its low budget and straight-to-video. But being on set in Trainspotting was a great crack though, and it was a real education for me. I'd always thought of acting as a poncy thing, but it's such a sweaty, physical job. I knew from that point that I was never cut out to be an actor. For one scene, I had to sit up in bed, slap my head and shout 'fuck'. Three very simple things in sequence, but I think I wasted more film in takes trying to get that right than the lead actors did in all their scenes. I've gotten a little bit better since, but it's taken a long time."

During an interview Irvine said he respected the commitment that was given by the actors in Trainspotting. Could this be thought of as the same dedication as an author (seeing as Irvine knows the dedication required in this field) and of course now experiencing acting?

Irvine: "I don't have any training or great skills as an actor, but I think it's similar to writing in some ways. I've been directing films and videos recently, and I've learned that actors give their best performances when they forget they're acting. I think writers are the same. The best stuff comes out when I'm not thinking about it, just getting into the zone and giving free reign to my subconscious. Of course, actors are rooted by the script, but if they know that and the character, the best of them just react in an honest way, as if they were that person faced with those emotional dilemma's rather than just delving into their toolbox of tricks."

Many 'themes' could have been used to carry the strong message needed in Trainspotting. So did Irvine use the heaviest of drugs to make a stronger point? Maybe get a message really stuck in our thoughts, or simply more of a way to heighten the dramatic sense or plot of the movie?

Irvine: "I first started to write about heroin addiction as a way of understanding the problems I'd had with drugs. It took me a long time to realise that I probably wasn't a drug addict, that I was simply using heroin as a way of not dealing with personal stuff like bereavement and relationship breakdown. If these things happen to you when you're younger, you don't really have the emotional vocabulary to deal with them and try and transcend or come to terms with the pain you're feeling. I think, in British working-class culture, it's very hard for men to talk about their feelings, or even express any vulnerability in any way. While part of me admires that stoicism, I can obviously see the destructive side of it. There is also the great buzz of doing something with other people. On one level its peer pressure but it's also peer education; we learn loads about ourselves through the groups we're in, be it family or friends. I'm fascinated by our culture of estate gangs, football mobs, drug and music scenes, and how we change when we get in a crowd and don't always make the best decisions, but go with it for the sake of the buzz and the camaraderie. When I was writing Trainspotting, it struck me that almost everybody seemed to be stuffed full of class A's, and intoxication in British literature at the time was all about beer, whiskey, and if you were really pushing it, the odd joint. I was wondering what planet those writers were on, because I didn't recognize it as Earth, or at least my corner of it. I wanted to write about drugs as an everyday, unremarkable part of the urban landscape. I don't think the book sensationalizes drugs, simply because they are now so ubiquitous and mundane in life that they can't be sensationalised."

Irvine's masterpiece boasted a group of lads that if thought about were much like the very lads we all grew up with. The cast of characters in Trainspotting, invoked thoughts of the pals both my brothers and I had as teenagers? I am sure like all cities across England, each and every one of them boasted their very own nutters, easy going types and smart arses, as seen in Trainspotting.

Irvine: "I think that every character a writer comes out with has to a least start with them. You can observe other people as much as you like, but you have to be able to experience the emotion and the psychology if you're going to render it effectively in print. We all have a wide range of emotions and behaviors, and we either choose or by habit play them up or repress them in terms of their suitability to the life's we live. But the characters are obviously also strongly influenced by other people, particularly the people around you. I've always been fascinated with how different characters interact. As you know from the football, the hardest boy or the best fighter or the one with the most bottle might not necessarily be the leader of the pack. All sorts of weird factors can come into play. The Trainspotting main characters were archetypal working class lads; the clued-up cynic, the psychopath, the easily led nice guy, the scam-artist and fanny merchant. Everywhere I go around the world, from Moscow to Buenos Aires, people have come up and said: 'we know a Begbie' or 'we have a Sick Boy.' I think the power of the book/play/film, was that everybody could recognize these characters, and even if they came from a more sheltered background and didn't know them first-hand, they at least had some sort of inkling that they existed. I see a lot of them in people I know. The problem I've always had is that a lot of nutters in Edinburgh think that Begbie is based on them, so I go home and get the 'is that meant tae be me, eh?' kind of treatment. The real bams though, they never see it in themselves. They stick the hundred-yard stare on you and go: 'aye, there are people like that around.' There are a couple of guys particularly that I can see Sick Boy as a merger off. They always have some sort of a scam on the go, and usually a couple of dotty birds in tow who totally believe in them despite all previous evidence to the contrary."

Much like all the films, that my brothers and I shared a liking for; Trainspotting had a few characters that always seemed to promote conversation. At least the one-liners we knew them for. Spud and Begbie were both of my brothers and my favorite characters. Did Irvine have any favorites, and why?

Irvine: "I like Spud, because he's basically a very well meaning guy, who doesn't want to harm anybody. Begbie's a nutter, but he's honest in his own way. Spud and Begbie are very much happy to be part of the community they come from, whereas Sick Boy and Renton obviously have more of an agenda. Spud is the lovable loser and that sort of guy will always have appeal. I think though that we recognise all those qualities in other people and if we're being honest, perhaps in ourselves."

Keeping true to his roots, Irvine often returns home to get his 'fix' of what only the green pastures of wee bony Scotland has to offer. With a lot of history and background in his old stomping ground, does this allow some old memories to resurface? Now, remember, a great deal of personal effort has to go into any writing piece. Memories are infused and thoughts provoked as well as personal emotional content that is required for any successful page to work. Is this good or bad for our friendly Scot, who gave and showed 'brave heart' and moved on and above the killer H that has claimed so many lives?

Irvine: "I'm home a lot, as in some ways, the older you get, family and close friends seem to mean more. It can be funny going back home, because when you're away, the everyday politics of things can pass you by. I had a big party a while back, and invited loads of the old gang. What I'd completely missed, and this is quite sad, is that some of those boys now hate each other. They've had grievances over money, women, family feuds, their sense of themselves in the hierarchy, all the usual stuff people fall out over. Being out of the loop so much, you either don't have access to these details, or because you aren't involved in the drama a day-to-day basis, they don't really stick in your mind and you always assume it's a trivial thing that's been or will get, sorted out, instead of a life-long feud or snub. So when I get back into town I often get the "great to see you again buddy, why did you bring that cunt along?" treatment. Now I basically have to check on who is on decent terms, and usually end up having three welcome home nights out instead of the one. I think when you're away you tend to see things through rose-coloured specs, and hark back to an imaginary time when everybody was all pretty tight together, when in reality, people are probably always falling out. Old junky acquaintances, I don't really hang out with so much. Even if you get along and you've moved away from that life, I think you evoke these more desperate times in each other, and there's that vibe of mutual embarrassment. Guy's that are still living that life are invariably going to hit you up for cash, and while I accept that has to be the way it is, it's no basis for a friendship."

A classic, timeless, one that will seldom collect dust in anyone's DVD collection, being a master within his field and maybe looking for perfection, did Irvine feel that there was anything that could have been done differently?

Irvine: "If we had more money, things like the animatronics baby crawling across the ceiling could have been made to look more real. But you couldn't have loads of CGI for a grungy British film of this type as its look is part of its charm, and in any case you'd run the risk of destroying the energy that sort of film needs to run on. Cast wise, it couldn't have been bettered. Danny Boyle said that it was a film full of stars. You seldom get a picture where all these relative unknowns just come in and become so big. It would be hard to cast a British movie with that level of unknown talent today."

Now, having lived both sides of the pond, there was definitely an audience that couldn't have had any more difference of opinions. Thought provoking and criticism were key words I had often seen, when reading reviews on the work Irvine had produced. Certainly, a conversation between a mutual pal of my brothers and I this side of the pond, who gave a compliment and said Irvine's writing, made him the Salvador Dali of authors! I said he was, if Irvine was to be put in a classification away from authors, and then he would be more of a Quentin Tarantino. Hard-hitting, not afraid to step away from the 'idealistic or norm', and show some balls in his writing.

Irvine: "I was never interested in being a purely social realist writer, and because I was writing about 'real' working-class people and in dialect, a lot of the posh critics thought that was what I was. I wanted to get over, is the hyper real, surreal and fantastical elements of everyday life. It wasn't just a psychoactive drug thing that facilitated me thinking it this way. I was big into house music at the time, and so much of that was based on that mood. Also advertising, television, religion all play up that sort of thing. I'm a great admirer of Tarantino's films, particularly the earlier ones. I found the dialogue and storytelling stronger in these movies, where as now I think he's been a bit seduced by the visceral power of cinema. Very talented guy though, and his movies are always a must-see for me."

During an interview, Irvine said he appreciated how well the book transferred to film. Specifically the colours and the camera work. With this in mind, has this changed or contributed how Irvine now writes?

Irvine: "The actors basically colonised my imagination. In my mind's eye, I couldn't really see the characters as anybody else but them. Begbie looked nothing like Robert Carlyle in my imagination, but now when I think of him I see Bobby's face. It wasn't a problem, till I came to write the sequel, Porno. I had to go back to Trainspotting and read it a couple of times before I got their faces out my head. It's the same now, with writing the prequel, which is based on old drafts. There is nothing more depressing for a writer than going back to an old book: all you can see are the flaws and how you'd have done it all differently this time."

When I first spoke of the film to my younger brothers, one of the first conversations was about the shit scene. Remembering my devotion to some of the greats in English TV, and hearing how a lot of the scripts and stories were based on areas of people's personal experiences, surely, or hopefully our pal from up north had not really been through this. So I dared and asked how did Irvine come about this story?

Irvine: "The shit scene was pure invention on my part. I was trying to think of dramatic ways I could expressly render the desperate need for the drug apparent, and that's what I came up with. There are a hundred more lifelike scenarios, but that was the most imposing and funny I could think up at the time. It's strange, because a good few years later, during the house music era, I was standing next to my mate Kenny in a club toilet, pissing into this latrine, when we were passing those pills to each other. For some reason we dropped them into the trough. We looked at each and laughed, but there was no question that we wouldn't retrieve the pills. He said: 'This is a Subbuteo version of your story'. You get all those old clichés about life imitating art but it does all the time."

Obviously with 'H' pointing to a past with Irv', was there any other parts of the film that carried from personal experience?

Irvine: "I can read the book back without getting narked at the things I'd do different. I just enjoy it as if somebody else has written it. But whenever I see the film, or even worse, actors on the stage performing the play version, I get a much stronger emotional impact. I feel like that part of my life is being pushed back right into my face. It could just be that cinema and stage are more direct mediums than the book, you don't have control over turning the page or setting it down, you just have to let what happens unspool, but I find it quite unsettling. After seeing it loads of times, I'm finally getting to the point where I'll just be able to look at it as a film without the emotional baggage."

Any films out there that Irvine would have liked to have been involved in.

Irvine: "I'd love to play a Bond villain. It would be a dream come true, to be able to give that mad world-domination speech, just before being topped in a grisly, unsuspecting way. I'd do it a cheesy as fuck, a total 'ah Mr. Bond, I've been expecting you...'"

Is there a message in the film / book, which has not been touched on yet?

Irvine: "The message is a fairly universal one, which is 'drugs are great fun, then they get crap and then they kill you'. I think a lot of anti-drugs propaganda of the 'just say no' variety messes up because they don't show the fun side of drugs, and therefore don't tally with people's experiences. I think another thing is the way we can lead each over a cliff like lemmings, basically because we're having fun and establishing loyalties. Sometimes we have to turn our back on the gang and be boring, if only for the sake of our own survival. Our laws on drugs are crazy, and so are our laws on public order. You can get into a row on a Friday night in a busy street at closing time, and basically spend the night in the cells and pay a fine. The same behavior near a football ground nowadays will land you in prison. It seems the laws are there primarily to protect multi-million pound industries (football and television) rather than members of the public."

I read in one interview, that the journalist said in his opening statement 'Entertaining Irvine Welsh is a nerving business'. So why does Irvine think reporters have a fear are cautious of him?

Irvine: "It's the old class system thing in Britain. You get some middle-class people who have led sheltered lives, even if they might have the conceit that they are 'down with the people' and some of them read the book and think I'm going to be some savage nut job who's going to attack or abuse them. The reverse is true, I was brought up to display good manners and I always try to be polite and respectful to journalists. Most of them are fair, but a few display fear and discomfort when they meet somebody who is working-class. Some of them admit to being nervous, which is stupid in my view, but fair enough, while others will sit there terrified and then, out of embarrassment, do the keyboard hard man thing, promoting themselves as cool, as you as an arsehole. It's always good fun to run into those guys. I had one guy who was so nervous he could barely speak or look me in the eye, but when you read back his copy, he'd written himself as this swashbuckling cross between James Bond and Oscar Wilde."

I read in the same article Irvine got drunk at an after an awards presentation and it was a messy one on a train, arrested and held for 5 hours, what was the story there, pal?

Irvine: "I was doing some filming with Jonathan Ross and afterwards we went to Soho House and had some champagne. Then I was getting the Paddington train down to the West Country. On the train, I met an old football mate from Hibs; he was dressed in a smart suit and had just got a big promotion in his job. So more champagne followed, and I can't drink champagne. I suppose I was a bit demob happy having just done all the publicity for my book Filth, and we started recounting old tales and got a bit too pumped up. Next thing I know is he was having it with some yokels at the bar and we had a police escort waiting for us at the next station. I was happy to take the rap for him; it would have possibly meant that he would have lost his job, while it was just some headlines in the Sun and a few more book sales for me. I woke up feeling shabby in the cells at Exeter police station. I was half-expecting a kicking, because police in a couple of forces had removed books from shop windows because it was regarded as offensive to them. Instead the coppers had copies of the book for me to sign. They are all fine, and took it in the proper spirit; I think it's only the big brass that is responsible for the corporate image of the force that takes offense. I learned for that incident, and a couple of others, that if you have any degree of fame or recognition, you have to behave yourself in public."

Being the intellectual Irvine has an interest in politics: With the way the 'house' is run, in the U.K, did Irvine agree comedians should be given a crack at running the show? My choice would be Monty Pythons crew, the hilarious Eddie Izzard, Trigger from only fools and horses maybe even The Scots very own Billy Connolly.

Irvine: "I thought comedians were running things already, and I was quite looking forward to us getting some competent and principled politicians in. When I was growing up, there were people like Tony Benn and Enoch Powell in mainstream politics, and whatever you thought about their views, they called it as they saw it and were genuinely guided by some ideological standpoint on the world. Now all politicians are guided by are focus groups, their numbers and the polls. It says it all for me that the candidate for change in the recent US elections was an African-American from a single-parent family, while our 'candidate for change' is a white, upper class, old Etonian and Oxbridge Tory. That just about sums up my disillusionment with the UK political scene."

Been there, done that. Survived and came out to tell a tale or two. Irvine was on 'H' for 3 years. Some people said he had only been on 'H' for 5 minutes, and what did Irvine know? So, did Irvine think he would've been a more credible 'H' spokesperson if he'd invested more time.

Irvine: "It's a crazy way to look at it. What I've never got with that way of thinking is: at what point do you become ideally qualified to write about it? Is somebody with 20 years addiction four times more credible than somebody with 5 years? Or are they just four times more stupid? All I know is that if I'd invested any more time in heroin, there would have been no book, and possibly no me! Doing loads of drugs won't make you a better writer. The top crime writers in the world have never committed grisly murders as far as I know. It's the old story; everybody has a book in them, but it's when you try to get it out onto paper that the real hard work begins and if you've a serious long-term habit, writing a book is probably one of the last things you'll be able to do or want to do. Shooting up heroin is a simple procedure, and the effects of it are generally the same. It isn't rocket science and I spent more than enough time on it for writing purposes, to the extent I wish I'd done a lot less, not more."

Irvine once said 'people should be able to express their culture without getting into that entire chauvinistic thing'. Does Irvine see this in any type of 'culture'?

Irvine: "I think I was getting at the fact that in Britain, we tend to be very partisan about our culture. It's the class thing again. British working-class culture isn't just about violence and drugs; it's also about dress, music, respect, pride and looking after each other."

It was said in one interview our young Scot liked to return to Scotland frequently for his fix of clubs and football. Also made a comment that 'his Edinburgh' past is an exhausted vein. Was the '80's and '90's his best years?

Irvine: "I think I'm like anybody else who enjoys life; you try and get the best out of every era you're in. I loved those times and wouldn't change anything about them, but I'd be hard pushed to say that they were better than what I have now. I've got the lifestyle I want, with the girl I want, so I don't think I'm hankering back for anything. I think that the 80's and 90's were astonishing times, because they were the last days of an indigenous British working-class culture, before globalization set in. Now it's a world market for music, clothes and language, and it's a bit more boring and naff as a result. I can't help it, but living so much in the States I just cringe when I go back home and hear the word 'awesome' in a UK accent. But I have to accept that a lot of my disinterest in what I see as the globalised, media-driven culture of today, might simply be because I'm too old, rather than because it's too bland. You always have to doubt yourself and it's quite possible that I've turned into what I despise; the moaning old git who goes about how things ain't what they used to be."

Now the luxury some of us have is a pal here and there, which can pull a few strings. You know V.I.P's on the list. Front of the line kind of deals even a handshakes from those that have golden pulling and pushing power. Our fellow mate, Irv' has his fair share of top names as mates. He was in Amsterdam with none other than Howard Marks, so were there any stories there?

Irvine: "There are always stories with Howard. He's a fantastic guy, full of life, fun and mischief. The last time, as I hazily recall, we were trying to get a prominent member of the British establishment to take an industrial strength line of 'Charlie'. I'd better not say who or they'll have me in the Tower the next time I'm in the UK. It's usually pretty riotous when we get together. He's one of these guys that you just get into that mad fun thing with, so we try and stay out of each other's way as much as possible! He's one of life's good people though, a real legend and a true gentleman."

Now I know a joke or two. An Englishman, an Irishman and a Scotsman. This is one fella, that I am sure could certainly have a mother of all comebacks. I think I will save those jokes for another time. Blinding fella, ol' Irv'. Glad he is a pal.

Garry Bushell

No family was complete without the age-old argument of what was considered 'real Music' and poison to another's ears. The generational gap was firmly coined within our house. All be it soul and reggae laid a concrete path of fundamental roots within us 3 brothers, there also existed and what was clear to see or hear was the need to compete with each other in music taste. This was accomplished by justifying each other's liking of our preferred music genre by attempting to out play each other by both volume and repetitiveness. This was key to what music would be classed as the better between us. Being the eldest allowed me an added bonus of winning most debates on what was 'in' and allowed to annoy both mum and our neighbours. To my younger brothers, the typical loss of what was played could only be overturned by none other than our in house jury and final word on the matter and that of course was mum.

My personal pet peeve was the watered down crap that main stream media would push on the younger crowd. I felt it was my responsibility, as an older brother, to dispel this drivel that would pollute the inner walls of our home. Slowly but surely the young heads would acknowledge the tones being emitted from my 1200's. Not that the young jury was a contributing factor in what was acceptable or not. It was nice to see they eventually made a step in the right direction and certainly away from mainstream to the ideals of an older brother (I wish it was that easy to get them off the chelski band wagon). On occasion I'd let one of them venture with me to one of my vinyl outlets. Whether it was Bluebirds, Red records, Black market or Peckings what mattered most was they were part of the experience I'd gained in listening to what I considered proper music. Which was hard to impress on them in the beginning, it was the importance of being able to discriminate between just your every day middle of the road pressings to record label owners, that had put in real effort and footwork into finding and promoting music that mattered. It was an endless task but to this day, I have great memories of both my brothers in my days and what music meant to me.

David Rodigan best represented the English reggae scene. At the 'OI!' helm and all that supported it had an ambassador of its own Garry Bushell. A man that had his finger on the, 'OI!', pulse from its very conception. Everyone agreed and accepted that no one described the terrace sound any better. If there was a person I could've wished to have been in the education needed in my early years of my musical relationship with my brothers than it would've been what Garry had kindly contributed. Not a single beat or insight is missed with the writing or knowledge shared. Like everyone, Garry was more than willing to help out in what preserved my memories with music and what it created between us.

Garry Bushell

'Oi' was hooligan rock, rebel music from the backstreets of urban England. Stripped down to basics, it was about being young, working class and not taking shit from anybody. It was anti-police, anti-authority but pro-Britain too. Oi's roots were in Punk, just as Punks roots were in the New York Dolls, but they weren't the same animal. For starters Oi was the reality of Punk and Sham mythology. Punk exploded between 1976 and 1979 because stadium rock had been disappearing up its own 'Jacksy' for years. The album charts were full of po-faced synthesizer twiddlers and pretentious singers belting out meaningless pseudo-poetic lyrics. Punk seemed different. It was raw, brutal and utterly down to earth. Punk sold itself as the voice of the tower blocks. Most of the forerunners were middle-class art students. Malcolm McLaren and Vivienne Westwood tried to intellectualise punk by dressing it up in half-arsed situational ideas, all the better to flog their over-priced schmutter to mug punters.

Sham 69, from Surrey, were the first band to capture the growing mood of disillusionment. Street punks were disgusted both by the proliferation of phony's and posers and the Kings Road conmen with their rip-off boutiques. But how much did Sham's Jimmy Pursey really know about borstals, football and dole queues, and how much was he feeding off the people around him? The Last Resorts Millwall Roi might have overstated the case but he summed up a common attitude when he wrote, "I wish it was the weekend everyday" But Jimmy Pursey didn't get his way. He liked to drink but he didn't like to fight. He didn't get his fucking homework right. The Oi polloi didn't need Punk's proletarian wrapping paper invented backgrounds, adopted attitudes, accents and aggression because they really were the cul-de-sac, council estate kids the first punk bands had largely only pretended to be.

The forerunners of Oi! were bands like Cock Sparrer, Menace, Slaughter & The Dogs and the UK Subs although none of these bands were as successful as Sham. Before he went potty, Jimmy Pursey gave the kiss of life to the two bands who defined the parameters and direction of original Oi, the Angelic Upstarts and the Cockney Rejects. Singer Tommy Mensi Mensforth and guitarist Ray Cowie, known as Mond, formed the Upstarts in the summer of '77 after getting blown away by the Clash's White Riot tour. Childhood mates, they had grown up together on the Brockley Whinns council estate in South Shields and attended Stanhope Road Secondary Modern School. Mensi worked as an apprentice miner after leaving school. Forming the band at 19 was his escape route from the pits. Mond worked as a shipyard electrician right up until their first hit. The Upstarts' original drummer and bassist quit after violent crowd reactions to their first gig in nearby Jarrow, to be replaced by bakery worker Stix and bricklayer Steve Forsten respectively. The band were also soon to recruit the services of Keith Bell, a self-confessed former gangster and one-time North Eastern Countries light-middleweight boxing champ, who as manager, bouncer and bodyguard was able to maintain order at early gigs on the basis of his reputation alone. The Upstarts soon attracted the attention of the North Umbria Police Force, who haunted the band's early career like a malignant poltergeist. Police interest stemmed from the Upstarts' championing of the cause of Birtley amateur boxer Liddle Towers who died from injuries received after a night in the police cells. The inquest called it "justifiable homicide." The Upstarts called it murder, and "The Murder of Liddle Towers" (b/w Police Oppression) was their debut single on their own Dead Records. Later re-pressed by Rough Trade, the song's brutal passion was well received even by music press pseuds, although not by the Old Bill who infiltrated gigs in plain clothes. Charges of incitement to violence were considered. Only the Upstarts' mounting press coverage dissuaded them. For their part the band was uncompromising. They appeared on the front cover of the Socialist Workers Party's youth magazine Rebel soon after and accused their area police of being largely National Front sympathisers. Official police action might have been dropped but unofficial harassment continued unabated. Mensi claimed he was constantly followed and frequently stopped, searched and abused by individual officers. The band blamed unofficial police pressure for getting them banned from virtually every gig in the North East of England, via the promise of raids, prosecution for petty rule breaking, opposing license renewals and so on. The Upstarts got the last laugh though when in April '79 they conned a Prison Chaplain into inviting them to play a gig at North Umbria's Acklington Prison (where ironically Keith Bell had finished his last sentence). 150 cons turned up to see a Union flag embellished with the words 'Upstarts Army', a clenched fist, the motto 'Smash Law And Order' and a pig in a helmet entitled 'PC Fuck Pig'. The band hadn't managed to smuggle in a real pig's head (they usually smashed one up on stage) but the cons reveled merrily in the wham-bam wallop of rebel anthems like 'Police Oppression', 'We Are The People' (about police corruption), and a specially amended version of 'Borstal Breakout' retitled 'Acklington Breakout'.

The Daily Mirror splashed with Punks Rock a Jailhouse (wrongly identifying me as the bands spokesman.) The Prison Governor and local Tories went ballistic, with Tynemouth MP, the aptly named Neville Trotter, condemning the gig as an incredibly stupid thing to allow. Socialist Worker printed a true record of the gig, quoting Mensi telling prisoners they'd be better off in nick if Thatcher got elected that summer, and urging punks to vote Labour as Thatcher's government will destroy the trade union movement. The bands salty populism and savage post-Sham punk attracted a massive following of working class kids in the North East, the self-styled Upstarts Army, while the power of their debut single convinced Jimmy Pursey to form his JP label with Polydor. The Upstarts were the labels first signing and also their first sacking after a jumped-up Polydor security guard tried to push the band about. He took on Mensi in a one against one fight and went down like the Belgrano. Polydor dropped the band. They never bothered to ask for Mensis side of the story. Soon after the Upstarts signed with Warner Brothers. Their second single, the Pursey produced I'm An Upstart, was released in April '79, charted, and was chased hard by the Teenage Warning single and album The Cockney Rejects were also the real deal, this time the sons of dockers from London's East End, but their music wasn't political. Thirty years of lame Labour local government had stripped them of any worldview except cynicism. Their songs were about East End life, boozers, battles, police harassment and football. I met them first in May '79. Two cocky urchins adorned in West Ham badges bowled into my boozer spieling slang and through their tatty demo tapes into my hand. Like them it was rough, ready and suffused with more spirit than Doris Stokes. I put them in touch with Pursey who produced their first demo tape. These songs re-emerged as the Small Wonder debut ep Flares & Slippers that included the essential guttersnipe anthem Police Car (I like punk and I like Sham I got nicked over West am). It sold surprising well and earned them the NME epithet of the brainstorming vanguard of the East End punk renewal. The kids were the Geggus brothers Mickey and Jeff, the latter soon known to the world as Stinky Turner. Both had been good boxers, neither of them had ever been put down in the ring, and Jeff had boxed for the England youth team. They had little trouble transferring their belt onto vinyl.

The Rejects story began in the summer of '77 when seventeen-year-old Mickey was first inspired to pick up a plectrum by the Pistols 'God Save The Queen'. Incubating in back garden performances in their native Canning Town as The Shitters, the Rejects only emerged as a real group after council painter Mickey recruited twenty-one-year Vince Riordan as bassist in 1979. Previously a Sham roadie, Vince (whose uncle was Jack The Hat McVitie the hood murdered by Reggie Kray) had marked time with loser band the Dead Flowers before he heard the Cockney call. Drummers were to come and go with the regularity of an all-curry diet until Stix transferred from the Upstarts in 1980. Live, the band hit like Tyson, with Mickey's sledgehammer guitar the cornerstone of their tough, tuneful onslaught. Schoolboy Stinky was a sight for sore eyes too, screwing up his boat-race into veritable orgies of ugliness, and straining his tonsils to holler vocals best likened to a right evil racket.

I was the Rejects first manager and I stayed with them until me and Pursey negotiated a £125,000 four-album EMI deal for them, before quitting to concentrate on his writing. Under their next manager Tony Gordon, the Rejects career soared briefly then crashed and burned. After getting evicted from Polydor's studios for running up a damages bill of £1,000, the band got stuck into serious recordings with Pursey at the production controls. Their second EMI single Bad Man was superb, like PiL on steroids, but it only made the fag end of the charts. Their next release, a piss-take of

Pursey called 'The Greatest Cockney Rip-Off did better, denting the Top 30. Their debut album 'Greatest Hits Vol 1' did the same, notching up over 60,000 sales. Unlike the Upstarts, the Rejects first following wasn't largely skinhead; in fact at first skins didn't like them. Stinky's school pals the Rubber Glove firm aside, The Rejects crew came from football and consisted largely of West Ham chaps attracted by Vince's involvement, and disillusioned Sham and Menace fans. I was first aware of the nature of their appeal when the band supported the Tickets at the Bridge House shortly after the release of their 'Flares & Slippers' debut EP. It wasn't just the RGF in their audience. There were older West Ham fans such as Johnny Butler, Gary Dickle and Carlton Leach - all notorious in their own right as the Britannia Disco Groovers. Grant Fleming was there too, through the Sham connection along with some of the old Secret Affair mob, like Hoxton Tom McCourt. Other West Ham faces included Gary Hodges, Wellsy, Binnsy and Steve 'H' Harmer. Then there was Barney Rubble, who was the poet laureate of West Ham, notorious terrace characters like Bernie Hoolihan, Ken and Frank, Doug with his perm, Danny Harrison, Mad Dickie and Mark Nelson, formerly of the Beacontree skins. Others included John O'Connor, who was Arsenal and a Menace fan, Danny Thompson, the boxer, Mutt and Jeff, the Dim brothers from Leytonstone, plus some of the other Brit Disco Groovers like Ted Lack.

There was a real range of youth cult styles in that audience as well, from soul-boys to suede-heads, as well as terrace geezers. If you'd looked closely you'd have seen ex-skinheads, Mods and Glory Boys with grown-out crops, tonic jackets, Sta-Prest, Levis and Harrington's. A real amalgamation. There were boys from North London, South London, Essex and Kent. They were mostly smart and as hard as fuck. It was the most awesome collection of street-fighters and head-cases that I'd ever seen gathered in any one place that wasn't a football ground. The band went down really well. The crowd called them back on for an encore. Stinky shrugged and said: "OK, punish ya'selves." There was a real buzz about the group all over London from that night on. The review in Sounds called them "the real Sham." Stinky recalls, "After the gig I remember sitting talking to this big geezer who turned out to be Hoxton Tom and I thought what a nice fella.

Tom and the other older blokes were telling us all about Sham days. They seemed to take to us because we were the real thing, East End boys. We weren't playing at it and dropping H's for effect. It was quite amazing. All these faces had turned up and it felt so right. We had met the people who were to become the hardcore Cockney Rejects firm." Later their ranks would be swelled by other notorious characters strongly associated with the ICF (Inter City Firm) such as Andy Swallow, Scully, Tony Barker and the Meakin brothers, Danny and Ricky; the ex-Glory Boys realising that here for the first time was a band exactly the same as them.

By as early as November 1979, the Hammers support for the band was so strong that mass terrace chants of "Cockney Rejects oh, oh" were clearly audible on televised soccer matches to the tune of Gary Glitter's "Hello Hello I'm Back Again." The first stand-alone Oi scene developed around the Rejects and their regular gig venue, the Bridge House in Canning Town, East London. It became the focus for an entire subculture. In 1980, this was the LIFE! None of these faces were 'Nazis'. Most of them weren't political at all, beyond the sense of voting Labour (if they bothered to vote at all) out of a sense of tradition. A tiny percentage was interested in the extremes of either right or left. As a breed they were natural conservatives. They believed in standing on their own two feet. They were patriotic, and proud of their class and their immediate culture. They looked good and dressed sharp. It was important not to look like a scruff or a student. Their heroes were boxers and footballers, not union leaders. Unlicensed boxing was a big draw, as were the dogs and stag comedians like Jimmy Jones and Jimmy Fagg, resident comic at the Imperial Crown at Bow. They liked to fight around football matches the West Ham ICF were fully represented at most local Rejects gigs. The young men oozed machismo, and some of the women were just as tough. But they weren't mugs. These were bright kids and a surprisingly large number of them have gone on to carve out successful businesses in fields as diverse as the music industry, pornography and clothing manufacture. They're the ones who didn't end up in jail of course. They related to the Cockney Rejects because at the time at least the Rejects mirrored their audience. Rarely in rock history have a band and their followers been so identical. The Rejects and the

Upstarts had plenty in common shared management, shared experiences of the Old Bill, shared class backgrounds and were soon identified (by me) in the music press as the start of something different, a new more class conscious punk variant, which was known at first as 'Real Punk' or 'New Punk' and which had little in common with 1970's self-styled punk rockers in their second-hand images and wally bondage pants. It was a pairing they obviously approved of with both bands frequently jamming together at each other's gigs. Unlike Sham, the Rejects had little Nazi trouble. They wrote off the threat from the British Movement (we called them the German Movement) in their first Sounds interview. "We can handle them," said Stinky. "If anyone comes to the gigs and wants to have a row, we'll have to row. Pursey couldn't do that. We're not gonna' take no bollocks." Strong words that they had to back up the first time they played outside of the East End, supporting the Upstarts at the Electric Ballroom in Camden. When a large mob of BM skins started harassing punks in the audience, the Rejects and their twelve-handed entourage (including two of the fledgling 4-Skins) took 'em on and battered them. Mickey Geggus commented: "our gigs are for enjoyment. No one's gonna' disrupt them or pick on our fans. Troublemakers will be thrown out by us if necessary."

They had another major run-in with the far right at Barking station the following February, and once again the master race contingent got bashed. Tom McCourt recalls: "That started the week before. Dick Barton, the BM's main man, was on leave from the Foreign Legion. Barton and his mob insulted an ex Becontree skin who was black. H jumped up and head-butted Barton to the ground. The BM backed off. All week they were making threats by phone. The following weekend, the Bridge House was packed. All the firms were there, hard-core to be honest, a few Glory Boys too, Dave Lawrence and Danny Harrison. The BM bottled it. One of them came in to deliver a message and Mickey Geggus knocked him out. Later we went outside their boozer, the Barge Aground, and they wouldn't come out. At the end of the night, we were at Barking station and just when we thought it was quiet and the night was over, a massive mob of BM turned up. There was only a small mob of us left. They were saying they were going to do to the Rejects what they'd done to Sham. They were older than us and thought we'd back down, but H just smacked Barton on the chin and knocked him sparko. We done them, after that they couldn't say or do fuck all again. Stinky Turner called it: "The greatest Nazi retreat since Stalingrad." Most of the Rejects' London gigs were trouble free, especially the ones at the Bridge House, which was to London Oi! what the Roxy had been to Punk. Managed by Terry Murphy and his tough boxer sons, the Bridge never had a serious punch-up or any sieg-heil saluting. No one dared step out of line against the Murphy's. The Angelic Upstarts also fought and won a couple of sharp battles against the far right. They played numerous 'Rock Against Racism' gigs too, including one at Leeds where the band sported SWP 'Disband The SPG' badges. Like the Rejects, their real agg' came from other areas principally their manager, Keith Bell. Sacked by the band when he started to knock them about, Bell and his henchmen set about trying to intimidate Upstart fans, even assaulting people buying their records, before threatening Mensi's mother, smashing the windows of her house and making threatening and abusive phone calls to her. Reprisal incidents included Mensi and one time Upstarts drummer Decca Wade smashing one of the Bell firm's car windows and a midnight visit to Bell's own home by Decca's dad, club comedian Derek Wade and Mensi's brother-in-law Billy Wardropper who blasted one of Bell's henchmen in the leg with a sawn-off shotgun. Hitting back, Bell threatened to kill Wade Senior. Three of his cronies set fire to a stable belonging to Mensi's sister causing almost £5K worth of damage. In ensuing court cases both Bell and Billy Wardropper were jailed while Decca's dad copped a year's suspended sentence. Presiding Judge Hall told the Upstarts team: "I accept that all of you suffered a severe amount of provocation, which was none of your seeking. But at the same time I have a duty to condemn the use of firearms, particularly a sawn-off shotgun." The Upstarts' recorded their opinion in 'Shotgun Solution': 'Shotgun blasts ring in my ears/Shoot some scum who live by fear/A lot of good men will do some time/For a fucking cunt without a spine'.

With the Rejects, football was the trouble. It was understandable because they had been fanatically pro-West Ham aggro from the word go. Even at their debut Bridge House gig they decked the stage out with a huge red banner displaying the Union Jack, the West Ham crossed hammers and the motif 'West Side' (which was that part of the West Ham ground then most favoured by the Irons' most violent fans). Their second hit was a version of the West Ham anthem 'Bubbles' which charted in the run-up to West Ham's Cup Final Victory in the early summer of 1980. On the b-side was the ICF-pleasing 'West Side Boys' which included lines like: 'We meet in the Boleyn every Saturday/Talk about the teams that we're gonna do today/Steel-capped Doctor Martens and iron bars/Smash the coaches and do 'em in the cars'. It was a red rag to testosterone-charged bulls all over the country. At North London's Electric Ballroom, 200 of West Ham's finest mob-charged less than fifty Arsenal and smacked them clean out of the venue.

But ultra-violence at a Birmingham gig really spelt their undoing. The audience at the Cedar Club (owned by Kevin Rowland of Dexy's) was swelled by mobs of Birmingham City and Aston Villa skinheads, these bitter rivals uniting to face the perceived Cockney foe. The mob terrace-chanted throughout the support set from the Kidz Next Door (featuring Grant Fleming, now a leftwing film maker, and Pursey's kid brother Robbie). By the time the Rejects came on stage there were 500 in the audience; 200 of them were hostile skins at the front hurling abuse. During the second number they started hurling plastic glasses. Then a real glass smashed on stage. Stinky Turner responded by saying: "If anyone wants to chuck glasses they can come outside and I'll knock seven shades of shit out of ya'. That was it; glasses and ashtrays came from all directions. One hit Vince and as a Brum' skinhead started shouting "Come on, Mickey dived into the crowd and put him on his back. Although outnumbered more than ten to one, the Rejects and their entourage drove the Midlands mob right across the hall, and finally out of it altogether. Under a hail of missiles Mickey Geggus sustained a head injury that needed nine stitches and left him with what looked like a Fred Perry design above his right eye. Grant Fleming, a veteran of such notorious riots as Sham at Hendon and Madness at Hatfield, described the night's violence as the worst he'd ever seen. Taken to the local hospital for treatment, Geggus had to bunk out of a twenty-foot high window when tooled-up mates of the injured Villa and City fans came looking for him.

Back at the gig, the Londoners emerged triumphant from the fighting only to discover all their gear had been ripped off; total value, two grand. The next morning, the Cockney contingent split into two vans. One went on to the next gig at Huddersfield, the other containing Mickey and Grant that went cruising round the city looking for any likely punters who might know the whereabouts of their stolen gear. Incidents that morning in Wolverhampton Road, Albury, involving Geggus, three locals and an iron bar, resulted in Mickey being charged with malicious wounding.

Eight months later, both he and Grant had the luck of the devil to walk away with suspended sentences. Maybe as insurance, in the summer of 1980, the Rejects played two Bridge House benefit gigs for the Prisoners Rights Organisation, PROP, arranged by Hoxton Tom and me with the help of Terry Murphy. Tom's aunt was involved with London PROP because his uncle, Steven Smeeth, had been jailed for his part in George Davis's doomed comeback caper. The gigs were two of the best I'd ever seen the band play. Brum' had meant the end of the Rejects as a touring band however. They had to pull a Liverpool gig when hundreds of tooled-up Scouse match boys came looking for confrontation. Road manager Kevin Wells was threatened at knifepoint. At first Mickey seemed to revel in it all, acting like he was living out some Cagney movie.

The band's second LP called, surprisingly enough, 'Greatest Hits Vol 2', reflected his apparent death wish with sleeve-notes boasting. From Scotland down to Cornwall, we dun the lot, we took 'em all. On the song 'Urban Guerrilla' he spoke these words: "Some folk call it anarchy, but I just call it fun. Don't give a fuck about the law, I wanna' kill someone." Me? I think he meant it. But in the long build up to the trial, a change came over Mickey. He swapped his little blue pills for ganja and started to mellow. Correspondingly, the Rejects' music began to move away from hooligan racket towards more mainstream rock. 1981's 'The Power & The Glory' sounded like The Professionals. 1982's 'The Wild One', produced by Pete Way, was more like UFO. And if 1984's 'Quiet Storm' had been any more laid back it could have been bottled and sold as Valium. 'The Wild Ones' remains a great rock album, with stand-out tracks such as

'City Of Lights'; but the old fans were actively hostile to their new sounds, while abysmal marketing meant potential new fans never got to hear them. Stalemate. The Angelic Upstarts lost their momentum in 1980 as well, being dropped by Warner's in the summer. And although they were snapped up by EMI, going on to release their finest studio album, 'Two Million Voices' in April '81, they barely played live and fans were getting frustrated.

During 1980, hooligan audiences, especially in South East London, found new live laughs in the shape of Peckham-based piss-artist pranksters Splodgenessabounds, whose brand of coarse comedy and punk energy scored three top thirty singles that year. Their debut single, 'Two Pints of Lager & A Packet of Crisps' was a Top Ten smash. Tongue firmly in cheek, I dubbed them 'punk pathetique' along with equally crazy bands like Brighton's Peter & The Test-Tube Babies and Geordie jesters The Toy Dolls. Singer Max Splodge insisted: "The pathetique bands are the other side of Oi! We're working class too only whereas some bands sing about prison and the dole, we sing about pilchards and bums. The audience is the same." Pathetique peaked in the autumn of 1980 with the Pathetique Convention at the Electric Ballroom.

West Ham's boot-boy poet Barney Rubble was Man of the Match. Elsewhere a second generation of hardcore Oi! bands had been spawned directly by the Upstarts and the Rejects. The Upstarts inspired Criminal Class from Coventry, and Infa-Riot from Plymouth via North London. The Cockney Rejects inspired the ferocious 4-Skins, and Sunderland's Red Alert. Edinburgh noise-terrorists the Exploited also cited the Rejects as their major influence. In London, a whole host of groups sprang up around the Rejects too including Barney & The Rubbles, Garry Johnson's Buzz Kids and Stinky's Postmen combo. A movement was evolving at the grass roots. I called it Oi! Oi! was and remains a Cockney street shout guaranteed to turn heads. Stinky Turner used to holler it at the start of each Rejects number, replacing the first punks' habitual '1,2,3,4'. Before him 'Oi! Oi!' had been Ian Dury's catch-phrase, although he'd probably nicked it from Cockney comic Jimmy Wheeler whose catchphrase had been 'Oi, Oi that's yer lot'. Entertainers Flanagan and Allen first used 'Oi!' as a catchphrase in their 1930s variety act. As I was compiling 'Oi! The Album' for EMI (released in November 1980), more like-minded combos sent demo tapes from all over the country. There was Blitz from New Mills, The Strike from Lanarkshire and Demob from Gloucester. But the first real challengers for the Rejects crown were the 4-Skins. They made their debut supporting the Damned at the Bridge House in '79 with Mickey Geggus on drums. The 4-Skins developed through various line-ups playing low-key London pub gigs sporadically before arriving at their definite line-up towards the end of 1980: Gary Hodges, vocals; Hoxton Tom, bass; Rockabilly Steven Pear, guitar; and John Jacobs, drums. There was a blessed with a driving dynamism. Their stand-out song was 'Chaos', a horror movie fantasy of urban chaos and skinhead takeover. But most of their three-minute blasts of fury concerned unemployment and police harassment ('ACAB', 'Wonderful World'), the horrors of war ('I Don't Wanna' Die'), thinking for yourself ('Clockwork Skinhead') self-pride ('Sorry') and class ('One Law For Them'). Both the 4-Skins and Infa-Riot were emphatic about the need to learn from the Rejects' mistakes and get away from football trouble. The 4-Skins favoured no one team (Hodges was West Ham, Hoxton, Spurs, Steve, Arsenal and Jacobs, Millwall) and no one political preference (Hoxton was a liberal; Steve was Labour Left; Jacobs apolitical; and Hodges was a reformed right-winger very pro anti-unemployment campaigns with a soft spot for Labour PM Jim Callaghan). Infa-Riot were the same, professing no football affiliations. Mensi wrote their first Sounds review, and he and Jock McDonald got them their first London gigs. Musically, they were a lot like a lither, wilder Upstarts. Like most Upstarts-influenced groups Infa-Riot played gigs for Rock Against Racism (an apparently noble campaign that was actually a front for the extreme Left SWP). Criminal Class played RAR gigs too, and a benefit for the highly suspect Troops Out Of Ireland movement (an organisation who had strong links with Sinn Fein and consequently the IRA.) The 4-skins refused to play RAR gigs, not wanting to be poster boys for Trotskyism. The Oi! bands converged to publicly thrash out their stance at the Oi debate held at Sounds in January 1981. Everyone agreed on the need for raw r 'n 'r, and the good sense of getting involved with benefit gigs, but there was a heated difference of opinion on politics.

Stinky Turner was violently against politics and politicians. Mensi argued that Labour still represented working class interests and claimed, "The Tories still represent the biggest threat to our kind of people." It was the same divide that had always separated the Rejects and the Upstarts. They managed to be agree about reclaiming Britain's Union flag for the people and, 'that was it. Although a few black and immigrant kids were into Oi, it was mostly a white working class phenomenon. The West Indian kids into Oi were cockney Blacks like the now famous Cass Pennant who'd rejected the pull of Rastafarianism and reggae. No Oi! band professed racialist or Nazi leanings (in fact, Demob had two mixed race boxers in the band) and the teething trouble that dogged early gigs was all to do with the football legacy bequeathed by the Rejects. As Punk Lives commentated later "Anyone who went to Oi! gigs could tell you didn't get sieg-heil salute at them." Ironically Madness and Bad Manners had most trouble with Nazi skins at the time. All Oi! went on about was class!

For the first half year of Oi the movement there were only two bad incidents of gig violence, both around Infa-Riot. The band headlined the first 'New Punk Convention' at the tail end of 1980 with the Upstarts and Criminal Class. It ended in disaster as Poplar Boys fans slugged it out with an Arsenal crew led by the then infamous Dave Smith who followed the Upstarts. In March 1981, Infa-Riot played the Acklam Hall in West London with Millwall skinhead band the Last Resort. Tooled-up local Queens Park Rangers supporting skins and straights besieged the venue looking for West Ham. At one stage they tried to smash their way in through the roof. Ironically, most Hammers Oi fans were safely in Upton Park at the time, watching their boys battle a Russian team. The model of the sort of gig the bands wanted came in February 1981 with the second New Punk Convention, this time held at the Bridge House with the 4-Skins headlining (and introduced by the king of rude reggae himself, Judge Dread). The pub venue was packed far over capacity with a motley crew of skins, working class punks and soccer rowdies drawn from the ranks of West Ham, Spurs, Millwall, QPR, Arsenal and Charlton. There wasn't one ruck all night. This gig set a precedent for peaceful co-existence that lasted even when Oi! shifted venues to Hackney's Deuragon Arms. It was living proof that Pursey's old dream of the Kids United could happen. But united for what? It was around this time that the leading bands and I entered into a conspiracy to pervert the course of youth cult history. We held a conference to plan the way the Oi! movement could develop in a positive, united manner. The idea was not only to arrange gigs and set up an Oi! record label, but also to plug away at the central theme of the folly of street kids fighting each other over football teams. We wanted to give Oi! a purpose by playing benefit gigs for working class causes. At the time I was living on the Ferrier estate in Kidbrooke, South East London, as was Frankie 'Boy' Flame (now of Superyob). In addition, bands frequently made the pilgrimage here to stay in our maisonette while they were playing London or just to shoot the breeze in the Watt Tyler pub. Some petty jealousies and band rivalry existed, but the Oi! scene was far more united than any other youth cult in British history. We tried to build on that.

The first Oi! conference was a small affair attended by reps from the Rejects, the 4-Skins, Splodge, Infa-Riot, the Business and the Last Resort, the latter two being the latest recruits to the burgeoning movement. The Business was then known as 'pop-oi' because of their tuneful anthems. They came from Lewisham, South London. They were fronted by Mickey Fitz, who like guitarist Steve Kent, had attended Colfe's Grammar School in Lee (as I had done) and had developed a terrace following which peacefully included West Ham, Chelsea and Millwall. Kent was a truly talented musician. The Business was managed by West Ham vet Laurie Pryor who was also known as Fatty Lol and Ronnie Rouman. The Last Resort were a skinhead band from South London via Herne Bay, Kent, based around the Last Resort shop in Petticoat Lane, East London and financed by the shop's owner Michael French. They too saw Oi as being bigger than skins. "Oi is uniting punks, skins and everyone," growler Millwall Roi told Sounds in their first interview. "Now we've just gotta' get away from football." Lee Wilson of Infa-Riot agreed. "Oi is the voice of street kids everywhere", he said. "That's why we're gonna' grow, that's why we're gonna win." And Oi was growing all the time.

By spring, as I was compiling the second 'Oi' compilation 'Strength Through Oi' for Decca (released May '81) over fifty bands had aligned with the movement, including the Oi/ ska squad the Buzz Kids whose singer, Garry Johnson's lyric writing far outshone his vocal ability. He had already had some lyrics published in a poetry collection by Babylon Books called 'Boys of the Empire'. I encouraged him to ditch the band and branch out as Oi's first entirely serious poet. Johnson's humour and his bitterly anti-establishment verses added yet more credence to Oi! as did the plethora of good fanzines that had sprung up around it; the best being Rising Free, Ready to Ruck (which became New Mania) and Phase One.

In June a second Oi! conference was held in the Conway Hall at Red Lion Square, attended by 57 interested parties including reps from bands all over the country. There was much concern voiced about the movement's violent image, which was felt to be unjust. The sublime Beki Bondage from the Oi-bolstered punk band Vice Squad complained that the aggressive skin on the front of 'Strength Through Oi!' made the movement look too skinhead orientated. Everyone agreed. And once again conference voted unanimously to back pro-working class campaigns. Ron Rouman was delegated to write to the Right To Work Campaign that week to set up gigs.

The main themes of the day were the need to unite working class kids, and stick together. Punk Lives called it 'a glimpse of the future Oi! could have had'. When the 4-Skins, the Last Resort and the Business played a gig at the Hamborough Tavern in Southall six days later, the riot that surrounded it and the acres of hysterical newsprint that ensued drowned out that possibility, and any chance of Oi getting a fair hearing, for good. WHEN THE shit hit the headlines during 1981's summer of discontent, I sincerely believed that the truth would be out. That the smears against the Oi bands would be laughed at in the same way that the slurs against the Sex Pistols and The Clash had been. The whole idea that the bands had gone into Middlesex to provoke a race riot was absurd. We'd been talking strike benefits, not NF marches. No Oi band had sported swastikas like the Sex Pistols had done. No Oi band had sung lyrics like "too many Jews for my Liking" as Siouxsie Banshee did. No Oi band had lifted their name from the SS like Joy Division had done. What contributed to Oi's undoing however was the movement's utter hostility to the middle classes in general and the trendy left in particular (see the Garry Johnson/ Business anthem 'Suburban Rebel's). So as well as incurring the wrath of the right-wing establishment, Oi also alienated the left-wing of the middle class media whose backing had seen the punk bands through their own particular backlash (and who were later to defend rap and hip-hop which were far more violent than Oi had ever been, and anti-Semitic to boot.)

Besides me, there was no one else in the media to defend the bands. Very few rock journalists had ventured into the East End to see the gigs. (Indeed the idea that the NME was ever THE punk paper is a complete myth. That paper rubbished 'Anarchy In The UK' and their first review of The Clash suggested they "should be returned to the garage, preferably with the motor running." Parsons and Burchill loved Joe Strummer and co for their politics alone.) The Oi! bands and their fans were guilty of that most terrible of crimes being white and working class with chips on their shoulders. Ironically, Alan Rusbridger in The Guardian was the only journalist to give the Oi bands a fair hearing the superficial evidence against Oi seemed strong, the Southall riot and 'Strength Through Oi'. The Oi! gig at Southall's Hamborough Tavern had been arranged by West London 4-Skins' fans fed up with having to travel to the East End to see the shows. The press painted sinister pictures of skinheads being 'bussed' into a predominantly Asian area. FACT: there were just two coaches hired by the Last Resort who hired coaches to transport their away-firm of fans whenever the band played anywhere outside of South London. TV and radio reports gave the impression of skinheads battling Asian youths and the Police. FACT: the Oi fans were all inside the Tavern enjoying the gig when the first Asian petrol bomb sailed through the window. The cops were protecting the Oi kids. The press said the peaceful Asian community had risen spontaneously to repulse right-wing invaders who had terrorised the town. FACT: there'd been just one incident involving young skinheads from Mottingham, Kent, in a chip shop earlier in the evening. "They probably asked the geezer how many rupees a packet of chips cost", Max Splodge later shrugged.

The sheer quantity of petrol bombs used by the Asians indicated they'd been stockpiling them for some days before. The young Asians were definitely on the offensive. Young white Oi fans were assaulted by Asian youths on buses going TO the gig, and a minibus containing Business fans from Lewisham and Garry Johnson was attacked by Muslim youth wielding swords without any provocation (see Johnson's book The Story of Oi for full details). In fact the apparently placid Asian community was to riot again within the week with no 'outsiders' to pin the blame on. The idea that the bands had gone to Southall to deliberately provoke a race riot just to be able to cash-in on the ensuing publicity is just daft. It goes completely against everything we'd been trying to achieve for the previous eight months. The 4-Skins manager Garry Hitchcock said "If we'd really wanted to go to Southall and smash it up, we'd have come with geezers and left all the birds and the kids behind." "People ask why the Oi bands played Southall?" commented Hoxton Tom, "but you've gotta' remember, in them days any gig was welcome. No one thought for a minute that there'd be trouble there. The Business had played Brixton before. The Last Resort had played Peckham, we'd played Hackney often and they're all areas with large black populations, and yet those gigs were always trouble free. Oi had to break out of the East End to have any chance of growing." To the mass media, the events of July 4th were manna from heaven: Yobs. Immigrants. Anarchy. The Thin Blue Line But the Oi crowd were reluctant participants. As soon as it was obvious real havoc was brewing, the Oi bands attempted to negotiate with the Southall Youth Movement through the police. They didn't want to talk. "We didn't want trouble", said Tom, "but that's all they had on their minds." Under attack, the Oi-polloi had no other option but to fight a defensive rear-guard action and retreat. The Hamborough Tavern was razed to the ground. And the press distortion began.

According to some reports right wing hate leaflets had been found in vans the following morning in the same vans that had been torched. Were the leaflets printed on asbestos? Hacks even descended on the Bridge House and tried to bribe kids into giving the sieg-heil sign for their cameras - £5 per salute. One was kicked out of the pub by Si Spanner who is Jewish. But who cared about the truth? Storm-trooping skins made shock-horror headlines. The fighting at Southall could have been worse. Scores more Oi! fans were turned back by the police before they had even got to the gig, including Indian workmate of Hoxton Tom's (the press never mentioned the few black, Asian and Greek kids inside the Tavern). Ironically, reports of a race riot on the radio induced mobs of West London bikers to rush to the scene eager to stand alongside their old enemies, the skins, against the Asians. The cops turned them back too.

I take full responsibility for 'Strength Through Oi'. I gave the album its title. But it was never knowingly a pun on the Nazi slogan Strength Through Joy. Let's be honest, who knew? How many people my age was that up on Third Reich sloganeering? The Skids had released an EP called 'Strength Through Joy' earlier that year, and that is what I based the pun on (asked later, Skids singer Richard Jobson said he had taken it from the Dirk Bogart's autobiography). It was either that or 'The Oi of Sex' which I had dismissed as too frivolous! 'D'oh! Southall' and 'Strength Through Oi' are examined in much more depth in my book Hoolies. Southall proved the catalyst for a spate of anti-government riots and there was no doubt where the Oi! bands stood on that issue, with the 4-Skins, Blitz and the Violators celebrating the popular uprisings with songs like 'One Law For Them', 'Nation On Fire' and 'Summer of '81'. Faced with a bucket-load of crap from the media, the Oi bands realised that simple facts were not enough to win the propaganda battle. They had to prove their protestations of innocence. Gary Hodges went on TV to say that the 4-Skins would play an anti-racist gig as long as it was organised by an independent body, although the band split before it occurred under the tremendous pressure and after just one more gig advertised as country band the Skans! - At a Mottingham pub. The Business declined to play RAR gigs for the old 'RAR as Trot front' reasons, but instead put together their own unwieldy named 'Oi Against Racism and Political Extremism. But Still Against The System tour' with Infa-Riot, Blitz and the Partisans. Infa-Riot played a Sheffield RAR gig and Blitz played at the Blackburn leg of the Right To Work March.

In late August 1981, I complied the third Oi! Album, 'Carry on Oi!', released by Secret Records in October 1981. Eager to stand by the bands, I reformed my own late 70s band The Gonads to contribute 'Tucker's Ruckers Ain't No Suckers' to the compilation. On first release, it sold 35,000 copies. Melody Maker's review stressed that Oi!'s intentions were not to divide but to unite the working classes'. The same month The Exploited smashed into the top forty with 'Dead Cities' (shame about that Top Of The Pops appearance), while The Business released their superb debut single Coupling 'Harry May' backed with 'National Insurance Blacklist' & an attack on the unofficial employers' blacklist operated against militant trade unionists in the building trade.

Paradoxically, the period from September '81 to the end of '82 saw the strongest ever Oi! releases thanks to Secret, and the excellent Malvern label No Future's series of twenty-two singles from the likes of Blitz, the Partisans, Red Alert, Peter & The Test-Tube Babies, and Derbyshire 'Clockwork Orange' band the Violators. Punk Lives mag calculated that Oi sold over two million records in the first four years. Recognising its 'cultural significance', left-wing playwright Trevor Griffiths wrote a play called Oi For England, which was broadcast, by the ITV in April 1982 as well as being taken round England on a tour. The play was more than a little far-fetched. It featured four unemployed skins in an Oi band approached to play a Nazi gig, and revolved around their arguments about it and the riot outside. What Griffiths seemed to be saying however was that in any group of skins, you would have one susceptible to the lure of race and nation, one drawn to class struggles, and two who couldn't give a toss about politics. Unfortunately, Oi's vinyl health during 1982 was not reflected on the streets. The 4-Skins split, and then reformed with drummer Jacobs on guitar, new boy Pete Abbott on drums, Hoxton Tom still on bass and roadie Panther (Tony Cummins) on vocals.

341

Later Millwall Roi sang with them. However, by then Tom was the only surviving original, and sales had slumped almost out of sight. They split for good in 1984. The Rejects were dropped by EMI in '81, disowned Oi for HM, and did not play again. The Upstarts soldiered on, playing the US punk circuit in '82 but musically they went down the khazi. Under pressure from EMI the Upstarts released a poor, synth pop-saturated sell-out LP 'Still From The Heart' that flopped miserably. (Infa-Riot tried a similarly doomed direction change, releasing an LP of unbelievably 'ordinary' rock in 1983 before finally breaking up the following year). The Upstarts were the subject of a Channel 4 documentary in 1984, but their chart success was long behind them. The Last Resort never ever got to the singles stage; they were not allowed a life independent of Michael French's boutique. What he wanted was a house band, a singing advert for his t-shirts.

Before Southall he opposed moves to send the bands on a US tour & he wanted the scene to stay at the small club level. The cynical claimed he did not want commercial competition for 'his' skinhead clothes market. Sadly, the Resort suffered when their London fans smashed up a pub in King's Lynn called the Stanley Arms. Virtually the same crowd was also involved in a BBC televised ruck with local skins at Benny's Club in Harlow. Both incidents happened in January '82, at a time when everyone else was trying to prove that Oi! meant more than rucking. The Last Resort split with French later in '82 to re-emerge as The Warriors, but they were never sufficiently motivated to build on their potential.

The Exploited meantime had shed their skin look, adopting a mutant Mohawk image and becoming the darlings of the Apocalypse Now punk revival. Singer Wattie went on to close down two thirds of Western Europe to other punk bands by smashing up dressing rooms. Back in '82, Blitz and The Business had clearly emerged as the new vanguard Oi desperately needed. Blitz specialised in belligerent boots 'n' braces brick-wall Oi - pure youth anthems like 'Fight To Live', 'Razors In The Night', and the haunting 'Warriors'. Their debut LP 'Voice Of A Generation' went top thirty and was the Oi LP of '82 but they were never that hot live. A disastrous gig at the Hammersmith Clarendon at the end of '82 was the beginning of the end. In '83 Blitz split in two, their former engineer Tim Harris taking over from the popular Mackie as bassist (Mackie later formed the short-lived Rose Of Victory with Blitz guitarist Nidge Miller) and pushing the band into trendier synthesizer sounds with scant public appeal. They did not last into '84. The Business split and got punkier. Guitarist Steve Whale (ex-Gonads) contributed greatly to their harder sound. They were haunted by politics - internal and external. To back-up their 'Blacklist' song, Business manager Ron Rouman and the Oi Organising Committee (an ad-hoc body set up after Southall) met with blacklisted building worker Brian Higgins and other trade union militants to organise a big pro-union benefit gig. The band bottled out and sacked Rouman, replacing him with bikers' pin-up Vermilion Sands.

Deprived of Rouman's drive and terrace connections, the band fell apart. The Business reformed in 1984 and was smart enough to realise you had to tour to survive (ironically, they signed to Rouman and Mark Brennan's Link Records). They have been playing ever since to growing audiences, especially in the USA. Back home, Oi as we first knew it died at the end of '82. It never had room to grow, and its vanguard fell apart ignominiously. It was like a stream, when it is moving it stays healthy, but when it is blocked up and stagnant all the shit rises to the top. The Oi stream was definitely blocked up. Also the poor quality of the new combos showcased on the fourth Oi LP 'Oi Oi That's Yer Lot' (produced by Mickey Geggus and released by Secret in October '82) confirmed it. The new bands were either too unoriginal, too weak, or, in the case of Skully's East End Badoes, too limited in their appeal to a square mile of Poplar, to mean anything. When great Oi-influenced bands did break through in '83 they all fell at early fences.

Croydon's Case were cracking they specialised in a ballsy brand of high-octane pop fresher than Max Miller chewing polos in a mountain stream and were fronted by the exceptionally expressive Matthew Newman. Case attracted acclaim from most quarters (including the Daily Mirror and Radio One) but fell apart when Matthew swapped the stage for domestic bliss with Splodge co-vocalist Christine Miller. Similarly, Taboo rose from the ashes of the Violators and specialised in non-wimpy pop. But the band split when wonderful, vivacious vocalist Helen decided to get pregnant and leave. Finally there was The Blood, one of the best Oi bands ever to come out of 'Old Blighty'. Emerging out of the wild excesses of Charlton's Coming Blood, The Blood's debut LP 'False Gestures For A Devious Public' was an invigorating blend of Stranglers, Motorhead and Alice Cooper influences that hit the UK Top Thirty and was voted one of the year's best by the Sounds staff. On stage they were awesome and OTT in equal measure. They filled blow-up dolls full of butchers' offal and cut them up with chainsaws. And their lyrics were a cut-above the usual, with lines like 'The Pope said to the atheist, "In God's name I do swear, you're searching blindly in the dark for something that isn't there"/The atheist said to the Pope: "There ain't no getting round it, you too were searching in the dark for nothing... but you found it."'

They asked me to manage them and I was happy to, but it was a frustrating experience largely because the bands were lazy bastards who never wanted to tour. The days when you could scam your way to chart success were long gone. Cock Sparrer reformed in 83 and recorded the LP they always should have made, 'Shock Troops' (Carrere), but they never had chart success in the UK again. Modesty forbids a detailed history of the Gonads, considered by many experts to be the finest Oi! band of them all, but you can read all about them at www.the-gonads.co.uk. At the fag end of '83, Syndicate Records launched a new series of Oi! Albums which lacked both the bite and the sales of the originals & 'Son of Oi' was nudging up to the 10,000 mark when Syndicate went bust the following year, that bankruptcy itself a reflection of Britain's shrinking Oi market.

The two best new bands were Burial and Prole, the latter a studio creation put together by Steve Kent and me from The Business. Scarborough's Burial cited Oi and 2-Tone as forebears and mixed the sounds of SKA and rowdy bootboy punk in their set. The only Oi! band to have any success were the Toy Dolls who scored a top ten-novelty hit with their version of 'Nellie The Elephant' at Xmas 1984. As British Punk degenerated after its

'81 boom, the skinhead scene became a political battleground and turned sour. The cream of the '81 generation went casual. A few even turned rockabilly. Meanwhile Nazi kids who had never been part of Oi started turning up at the gigs, obviously attracted by the media's 'reporting'. When they found the truth was different, they turned nasty: Garry Johnson was beaten up by Nazi skins in Peckham. I was attacked by a mob of fifteen Nazis (not skins) at an Upstarts gig at the 100 Club and had my home address published by the YNF magazine Bulldog that denounced me as 'a race traitor'. The same Nazi who had tried to stab Buster Bloodvessel in Camden stabbed Si Spanner. Attila the Stockbroker, the good-natured left-wing Oi poet / Wally, was whacked on stage in North London. Infa-Riot were attacked at the 100 Club by Nazis. You get the picture.

In East London, it was a different story - the British Movement was taken out of the frame by the Inter City Firm. In early 1982, Skully and other Oi regulars had organised a march protesting about the jailing of their fellow ICF member Cass Pennant. The BM threatened individuals, putting pressure on them to cancel this "march for a nigger." The following Monday the ICF had been planning to take on Tottenham fans (as West Ham were playing Spurs that night). Instead they confronted and smashed the East London neo-Nazis who were drinking in the Boleyn Arms. They were never a significant presence on the West Ham terraces again, but they remained a problem elsewhere. When they could not find Oi bands to toe the master race line, the neo-Nazis created their own nationalist skinhead bands around the Blood & Honour banner. Skrewdriver, the veteran punk band first featured on Janet Street-Porter's punk TV documentary in 1976, came back as skinheads and were the cornerstone of the new hate-punk sound. Opposing them was a raft of equally extreme if more musical Trotskyist bands like the Redskins and the Newtown Neurotics, and poets such as Attila and Seething Wells. Quietly, and apart from all the polemics, a small, smartly dressed alternative skinhead scene developed underground. Hard As Nails fanzine reflected this growing trend. Two young kids ran it from Canvey, Essex, both Labour Party members. Nevertheless, they insisted the mag was about style, not politics. They had some cross-over with the scooter boy scene and attracted the few remaining suede-heads to their orbit. Oi never ever became respectable, but the movement that NME once said I had 'invented' still reverberates around the world. Mega bands like Rancid, the Dropkick Murphy's, Good Charlotte and Green Day cite the UK Oi bands as influences, and superb Oi bands such as Stomper 98, Perkele and Evil Conduct flourish in Europe. Two great CDs, called the Worldwide Tribute To The Real Oi released in the Noughties included tracks by the Murphy's and hardcore heroes Agnostic Front.

Lars Frederiksen from Rancid recently formed his own Oi band, the Old Firm Casuals. And most of the original Oi bands have reformed, playing to thousands all over the globe. The message is still the same as it always was. Oi's self-definition of 'having a laugh and having a say' got it right on the button. The laughs were ten a penny for Jack the Lads knocking back pints and pills and pulling at the pubs, rampaging at the football grounds and reveling in rebel rock 'n' roll at the gigs. Oi reflected that, but it also cried out against the injustices weighed up against the young working class. In that sense Oi was a real voice from the backstreets, a megaphone for dead-end yobs. At its best, it went beyond protest, and dreamed of a better life: social change; the kids united.

Everyone talks about 1969 as the birth year of Britain's skinhead phenomenon. But the cult actually evolved much earlier and can be traced directly to the 'suits', a Spartan branch of mod first spotted on the London club scene around 1965. They were very much a smart, working class alternative to the dubious lure of psychedelia and West Indian culture exerted a major influence on the evolution of skinhead style. SKA, from which skinhead reggae sprouted, was a Jamaican development of American R&B embellished with jazz touches like the omnipresent horn section. Wailers guitarist Ernest Ranglin said that the word Ska was cooked up to describe the 'Skat! Skat! Skat!' scratching guitar strum that goes behind. Emerging as a recognised form in 1956, by 1963 Ska dominated the Jamaican music scene and reflected the optimism of the people who have been granted Independence under a Jamaican Labour Party government. Ska arrived in Britain in the early '60s via West Indian immigrants and was accepted as a credible alternative to American soul on the hard mod scene.

In Britain, it was called 'blue-beat' because it was Melodisc's Bluebeat label that released the bulk of this new music by groups like Laurel Aitken and the Carib Beats, Basil Gabbidon's Mellow Larks and Desmond Dekker and the Aces.

The first British bluebeat hit was Millie Small's bouncy bundle of joy 'My Boy Lollipop' (with Rod 'the Mod' Stewart on mouth organ). Ska was the music of the first generation British blacks and the teenage immigrants who also adopted their own look and a name - the Rude Boys. Rude Boys was the name assumed by Jamaica's tough and volatile young ghetto hooligans who were noted for their savage gang wars and lawlessness. Ska records often aimed at persuading the Rudies to cool it, but perversely the Wailers' first single 'Simmer Down' and later songs like 'Rude Boy' and 'Jail House' only helped to glorify the cult. The Rude Boy rig-out sported by West Indian youths in South London was a direct ancestor of skinhead style: crombie-type coats, trousers worn higher than the norm to emphasise white socks and black shoes, and all topped off with pork pie hats and wrap-around shades. Razor hair-partings also originated with the young blacks, and it is highly likely that the skinhead crop, although having roots in the mod crew cut, was accentuated as a means of imitating the Rude Boys' hairstyle. In the beginning these shaven-headed white kids were known by a variety of names (peanuts, crop heads, boiled eggs, no-heads and so on) but became identified as Skinheads as early as 1967.

In Jamie Mandelkau's 'Buttons: The Making Of a President', the biography of the Islington-born British Hell's angel leader Peter 'Buttons' Welsh, he talks of battling 'the Walthamstow Skinheads' in late '67. Of all the names, only skinhead really did justice to the new cult's tough, aggressive and passionately working class stance. By the summer of '68, the skinhead look had taken off as the working class youth look, spawning a new media demon: the boot-boy. Ian Writer claimed in New Society to have seen 4,000 skinheads running rampage at one soccer Match. 'They all wore bleached Levis, Dr Martens, a short scarf tied cravat style, cropped hair,' he wrote, adding, 'They looked like an army and after the game went into action like one'. By the following summer the cult had reached its peak, and Skinhead was 'the look' for young working class kids. Fighting, dancing, fashion & these were the skins' main preoccupations. Rucking was largely territorial and occurred mostly at or around football grounds, although the mass media was more interested in the shock-horror mileage to be had from stories of skinhead attacks on minorities, homosexuals, squaddies, long-hairs (from my own childhood I can recall 'hippy-types' getting off at the next stop on the train rather than risk a beating from the kids off the Ferrier Estate in South East London) and Pakistanis, although these attacks were more to do with cultural than racial differences. A fine distinction to be made after you had just been clobbered over the head with a half-brick to be sure, but an important one nonetheless. Pakistani teens, unlike the West Indian kids, were not cool, they did not mix, and in fact they were equally (if not more) disliked by West Indian skinheads or Afro Boys, as they became known.

A Rudie spin-off, the Afro Boys were plentiful in cities like London and Birmingham, and were equals in skinhead gangs, initially at least; although the skinhead kids from the Collinwood gang interviewed in The Paint House testify that tensions stirred up by sexual rivalry generated ill feeling. Battling at football matches; which neither began nor ended with skinheads resulted in the adoption of various weapons or 'tools', possibly the nastiest being home-made Kung Fu metal filed into star shapes to be chucked like darts (which were also popular) at your opponents. Millwall fans came up with the 'Millwall brick', a cosh made from a simple tabloid newspaper folded until it became lethally hard. The most popular 'helpers' however, were the simple metal comb and steel-capped Dr Marten work boots. It is unlikely that the good nineteenth century Bavarian, Doctor Marten, had the slightest idea of just how seminal his patented Air-Wear soles (resistant to fat, acid, oil, petrol, and alkali, and topped off handsome leather uppers) were to become for generations of British Hooligans. Martens, or DMs, were an essential ingredient of the early skinhead look. Then they were usually brown or cherry red, and just eight hole affairs as a rule. Girls never wore DMs, they favoured monkey boots.

The very best guide to the evolution of skinhead sartorial style over the golden age of '68 to '71 was written by Jim Ferguson and published in Nick Knight's Skinhead book (although his essay and Harry Hawke's handsome reggae discography are the only things worth buying the book for, as the rest consists of over-generalised, under-researched, pseudo-sociological claptrap about the late '70s skinhead resurgence). Simplifying, early workday/football wear would be boots, braces (to emphasis working class origins and loyalties), any unfashionable shirt, an army or RAF great coat, a Levi or Wrangler jacket, or a donkey jacket. For best, dances and such like, all skins aspired to possess a decent suit, preferably a mohair, 2-Tone or Prince of Wales check affair, worn with brogues, and later loafers. The all-time favourite skinhead coat was the sheepskin overcoat & 'crombies' did not really catch on until suede-head time. Hair was razor cropped, but heads were NEVER shaved bald. The razors were set to different lengths, 1-5, with the number one crop being the shortest. The favourite shirt was the Ben Sherman with button-down collars and back-pleats. Bens were usually checked (NEVER white) and worn with the top button undone and the sleeves turned up once. Brutus check shirts and later the humble Fred Perry were also acceptable. Smarter skins replaced Levi red-tag jeans with Sta Press trousers. Black and white skins mixed freely at dance halls. Reggae was 'the' skinhead music, but it was a markedly different reggae from the simple Ska the rudies had introduced Mods to earlier on in the decade.

Around 1966, Ska in Jamaica had developed into Rock Steady, which was faster and funkier than the original, in much the same way as US R&B had developed into Soul. Alton Ellis' definitive dance hit 'Rock Steady' was typical of the new genre which itself developed, until by 1969 it was producing massive British chart hits like Desmond Dekker's 'Israelites'. This 'reggae of the '69 kind' was a major chart factor for the following few years with some Jamaican artists quite shamelessly pandering to their English audience (the best example of overtly skinhead-orientated reggae was the Symarips 'Skinhead Moonstop'). In the earlier part of the decade, a bluebeat aficionado would have to go to Brixton (where Somerleyton Road and not Railton Road was then the front-line) and clubs like the Ram

Jam to hear the music, or South East London pubs like the Three Tuns. We would trek miles to Lewisham market where the latest imports were stocked. But as the music moved into pop's mainstream, so reggae nights became regular features of dance halls like the local Palais. US soul was still extremely popular too, and artists like Booker T had a large skinhead following, although inevitably the music lived more through DJs in the pubs and clubs than on stage.

No youth cult stands still however. The skinhead look became progressively smarter, with boots and braces dropped in favour of belts and loafers even during the day, evolving into the suede-head style. Suede-heads wore their hair longer & it was comb-able & and favoured the 'crombie coat (an Abercrombie overcoat, preferably with a velvet collar). Some suedes developed a 'city gent' look sporting bowlers and brollies, although the classic suede image was the Harrington jack named after Rodney Harrington who wore it in the TV show Peyton Place (like the city gent look, it was originally briefly fashionable with Mods) Sta-Prest trousers (white ones looked best) and ox-blood Royals.

By the end of '71, suede-head had developed into the 'smoothie' look with the hair even longer, Fair Isle yoke pullovers, polo necks and later tank tops, and shirts with hideous rounded collars. The favoured smoothie shoes were called Norwegians. They were lace-ups and had a basket weave design on the front. With the gargantuan growth of glam and glitter between '71 and '73, Skinhead was finished as a mass movement, although some die-hards dyed their Docs rather than ditch 'em. Now it was the turn of ex-Mods like Bowie and Bolan, and bands like Slade and Sweet to influence the teeny hordes. But Skinheads never died out completely. Small pockets of skins, and the odd few dedicated individuals, were untouched by the lure of fashion. The Shipley Skins in West Yorkshire, for example, claim to have kept the faith throughout the dark years of the early '70s while others were succumbing to the colourful pull of Rupert the Bear trousers, Fair Isle yoke pullovers or bright, crepe-soled shoes. In London too, a hardcore few stuck to their boots while all around them switched styles to suede-head, smoothies or glam. Garry Hitchcock, one-time manager of the infamous

4-Skins, recalls: "There were always skins somewhere. For instance, in the early seventies there was this geezer at Arsenal who had cropped hair; an inch crop so it laid down and wore a 'crombie while us young 'uns were wearing Budgie jackets or later going for the college boy look." Hitchcock was one of the first of the second generation of skinheads who had caught the tail end of the cult at school. He says: "We always said that if it ever came back we'd be skins again. Nothing else was really us."

In 1976, Hitchcock was wearing a Harrington jacket, DM boots and straight jeans & the only thing he lacked was a crop. Seeing other kids, his own age that had gone all the way was all the push he needed. The earliest '76 skins were from different parts of London, but once they had established contact with each other, they kept closely in touch. Garry Hitchcock and his mate, Tony 'Panther' Cummins (who went on to sing with the 4-Skins), were from Shepherds Bush in West London. Panther supported Chelsea and from football, he knew a kid from Camden called Graham McPherson (Hastings-born McPherson was later to find fame and fortune as Suggsy, the singer with Madness & see chapter five) and Terry Madden from Kilburn who had been a skinhead since his early teens. On the Clock End terraces, Garry Hitchcock befriended Arsenal Binnsy who came from Hampstead and had been a skin since school. This small group was the nucleus of the skinhead revival. The first skin to emerge at Upton Park was Steve Harmer, known as H, who went on to roadie for the Cockney Rejects and play guitar for the 4-Skins. Gary Hodges, who was to be the first singer with the 4-Skins, followed him quickly. Garry Hitchcock recalls: "Glen Bennett and Kevin Wells were others from that side of London who were Skins real early on, but West and North London was where the skinhead revival started." Wellsy became the Cockney Rejects road manager; Bennett became a Nazi. Terry Madden remembers how it was in the early days of the revival: "I used to have to go from Kilburn to Boreham Wood just to have a drink with other Skinheads", he says. "There were only a few of us but we all kept in touch." Hitchcock, "In those days whenever you saw a skinhead you didn't know you'd talk to him. There was a feeling of almost comradeship. There were very few of us about."

The return of the skinheads ran parallel to the birth and the growth of punk. It was not punk inspired, but punk boosted it in to a mass movement. "When we became Skins again", says Terry Madden, "You've got to understand that the only other things to be were soul boys, which was dull and mostly a black thing anyway, or Teds & Showaddywaddy. To us, they were a joke."

Hitchcock: "When punk came along we didn't relate to it at all. We didn't like punks, they were too untidy; and another thing, I'd always associated skinheads with the working class and despite all they said the punks I met were all middle class plastics." Although they did not appreciate punk style, the new skins grew in its shadow for the simple reason that back then, nightlife options were limited to discos or punk clubs and the discos would not let them in. The revivalists remained true to the first skins' sartorial standards. None of them was impressed with the D-I-Y scruffiness that surrounded them. Like their predecessors, they prided themselves on being smart and clean, searching out obscure shops to buy authentic Skinhead clothes: Ben Sherman shirts, Sta Press strides, narrow braces, DM boots or brogues, tonic suits for best, sheepskin coats, crombies or Navy coats. Hitchcock: "I remember Suggsy used to get his Sta Press from this little shop in Kilburn. Panther and I found a place in Earls Court, which had all the old gear left over from the first days. The bloke was dusting off boxes for us; he thought he had had a right result. We got Ben Sherman's for thirty bob (£1.50), tonic suits for £2.50, and DM boots for two quid. It was the bargain of the century. But of course when other people heard about the shop, he sussed on and his prices rocketed." The new Skinheads never shaved their heads bald like later boneheads did. They'd have number two crops, and wear Levi red-tags or jungle greens; smart ones that fitted, not the scruffy baggy ones which caught on in the '80s. This generation would look on in disgust when a few years down the line the Skinhead name became associated with bald punks with ludicrously high boots, torn jeans and face tattoos. Hitchcock adds, "And needless to say we never sniffed glue either. What a disgusting habit that was. The first people on the scene that I remember sniffing glue were the filthy punk squatters at Kings Cross. We used to batter 'em."

By 1977, this group of skinheads had emerged as the vanguard of the revival, meeting regularly in the top bar of the Vortex. They were not the only new Skin mob in town though. The Ladbroke Grove Skins, known as the LGS, had also been around their West London manor since 1976. Like Hitchcock's mob, they were largely London Irish, but they also included many West Indian teenagers in their ranks. The LGS were led by a character called Chrissie Harwood and were famously non-racist. The LGS pioneered the original 2-Tone badges: black and white buttons boasting the legend 'Skinhead Reggae', over two years before the actual 2-Tone explosion. Tom McCourt (a.k.a. Hoxton Tom), who became the bassist with the 4-Skins and is recognised as an authority on the cult, also recalls early skinhead gangs from Archway in North London who had a lot of black members too, as well as Toks and Chalky who was a roadie for Menace and Madness. Other early skin gangs emerged from Becontree in Essex and from Packington in North London.

The Packington were first spotted in 1976 and were noted for their look of crops, boots and Adidas t-shirts. Unlike the LGS, several of Garry Hitchcock's firm had far-Right sympathies Hitchcock included. "We were political, a few of us", he recalls. "But we never tried to bring our politics in to the scene, not at first anyway, because the rest were just into fashion, the look. I would not even have said we were troublemakers especially. We had fights because people started on us. We didn't use to go around smashing up gigs."

One historic ruck took place in the Angel pub in St Giles Street, near Tottenham Court Road in Central London. Early on in 1977, the skinheads chanced upon a group of older football nutters who supported Charlton Athletic (Charlton had quite a firm in the mid-Seventies.) It did not take long for things to kick off. "The Charlton mob got the hump because we were dressed like skinheads and they'd been skins the first time round", Hitchcock recalls. "And also, ironically, because one of our number was a black kid. There was a lot of eyeballing, things were said and before long they steamed into us and battered us. The following week there were only half of us left, but that was a good thing because the ones who stayed were hardcore." Six months later, there were still very few skinheads about. Hoxton Tom Recalls: "I was a punk in 1976 and it was quite a shock to me when in the autumn of 1977 I bumped into a bloke in full skin regalia: Sta Press, Ben Sherman, Crombie and Loafers. The last proper skins I remembered were my uncles and cousins in '69/ '70. Should I stay a punk or go skinhead? To me it was no contest. The Skin was different and sharper. At first being a skin was class. Everyone who got into it went looking for the right gear, visiting every old tailor and army surplus shop hoping to get Ben Sherman's in the 'wooden boxes'. Me and my mates in Hoxton preferred loafers and brogues to boots. They looked smarter and were just as hard. Hair was a Number 2 crop with a classic razor parting. I raided my uncle's old room for records and original Sherman's. He had the lot, Tighten Up Volume 2, Tamla and Stax." "At first it didn't matter where you were from. We met the Archway skins, Suggs and Toks, Joel McBride from Kilburn and the Becontree lot & Nelson and Lawrence. We met the Croydon, the East End skins & H and Hodges. Away from the grounds, football rivalries and political differences did not matter. We were Skins. It was us against the world and there weren't many of us." The thing that transformed the new Skinheads from a minor cult into a mass one was the band Sham 69, led by their gangly and engaging singer Jimmy Pursey. Pursey has told so many tall tales it's hard to know what to believe, but It's likely that the band derived their name either from old graffiti on a toilet wall in their Surrey home town of Hersham & 'Hersham '69' with the 'Her' eroded by wear, tear and time. Although it was widely believed in 1977 that they had taken their name from a notorious Skinhead riot in Kent: Skinheads at Margate, 1969. Either way they hailed from a tranquil village and Pursey who is usually viewed as either a loveable ham or a loud-mouthed buffoon was their spokesperson and soon to be self-appointed voice of a generation.

James Timothy Pursey was an immensely likeable and generous 'Jack the Lad' who would have sold his soul to have been born within the sound of the Bow bells (he missed by about twenty miles). He was never quite the innocent victim that he likes to be seen as, but he was generally well intentioned. Jimmy was born on a humble farm in Turners Lane,

Hersham, on February 9ᵗʰ 1955. His dad was in the army, his mum was a cinema usherette. He was a Skinhead at 14, the first time round, and was adopted by an older gang as a kind of mascot. They used to take him to their fights and leave him watching the action from their van. At 15, Pursey was expelled from Rydens comprehensive for organizing a pupils strike and blowing all the power in the school in the process, he got the other kids to wrap silver paper round every plug. After school, by day, he slugged through more than thirty dead-end jobs, everything from factory-hand to washer-upper in a Wimpy Bar. However, by night Jimmy came alive. His musical career began at his local disco, the Walton Hop in Walton-On-Thames. Here, aged seventeen, he led a bunch of mates on stage and, dressed in finest Bay City Roller tartan, drunkenly mimed his way through the Rolling Stones' 'Satisfaction'. They called themselves Jimmy & The Ferrets and their spot miming to all manner of chart records became an established facet of Hop bacchanalia. Encouraged by the Hop's homosexual proprietor, the Ferrets developed into a real band. They included bassist Albert 'Albie' Maskell, who lived on a local pig farm (Sham 69's first rehearsals were to be in Albie's dad's pigsty). The Ferrets were a fairly ordinary pub rock band to begin with, playing rock 'n' roll standards and setting a few of Jimmy's own early lyrics like 'Let's Rob A Bank' to basic twelve bar formats. The Sex Pistols made all the difference. Jimmy caught one of their earliest gigs at Weybridge Food College and was converted on the spot.

By the summer of '76, and newly christened Sham '69, the band played their first ever show as a punk band, supporting Albertos Y Lost Trios Paranoias at Brooklands Technical College. The resulting shower of eggs, spit, tomatoes, beer and metal bolts made half the band immediately question the change of musical direction, so Jim sacked them. In January 1977, he and Albie recruited local guitarist Dave Parsons, who was playing Beatles and Stones covers in a band of schoolmates called Excalibur. The last member was drummer Mark Cain (a.k.a. Doidie Cacker) who they met at the Hop and who auditioned for them in his Mum's kitchen. After a session of songwriting and pigsty rehearsals (wearing gloves, over-coats and balaclavas because there was no heating in the place), Sham 69 were ready to face the world again. Their first gig was at Guilford University. After that, there was no stopping them. They headed into London regularly, gatecrashing West End punk clubs like the Roxy, blagging gigs and building up a following. They recorded a demo tape and Jimmy put his motor-mouth to good use, dropping off a copy at Miles Copeland's office and telling all who'd listen that Sham were the best punk band around. Copeland was intrigued enough to give them a bottom of the bill slot at the Acklam Hall supporting Chelsea, the Lurkers and the Cortinas. Miles brought a friend along, John Cale of the Velvet Underground, who was so impressed by the band's influence and Jim's big gob that he talked Copeland into signing them for a one-off single.

That Step Forward three-track, released in July 1977, included 'Ulster Boy', 'Red London' and 'I Don't Wanna': raw bursts of brick-wall punk with a right-wing populist message. 'Red London' was specifically anti-socialist: 'London streets are turning Red, there's no democracy/I remember yesterday we were all free/Free yourself from this/Individuals rule'. This boisterous conservatism played well with Copeland whose dad worked for the CIA (Miles' brother Stewart played drums for the Police). Other numbers in Sham's set targeted exploitative punk boutiques like SEX and BOY: 'Tell the kids to get to grips/Don't wanna' buy or eat no more/From Kings Road shops that make us poor / and time is running out for us / It's just & a fake / Make no mistake / A rip-off for you / And a Rolls for them'. 'Hey Little Rich Boy' hit out at the middle classes ('I'll never believe you're better than me') while 'The Song Of The Streets' & which was given away as a free disc at gigs and better known as 'What Have We Got' – banged the anti-politicians drum ('I'd like to buy a shotgun/Shoot them in the knees/Conservatives and Communists / They're all the bleedin' same'). The band hit a nerve. Mark P of Sniffin' Glue called them "the first true punk band! with cleverly constructed working class anthems. Sham were the very essence of punk! the true successors to the Sex Pistols." Danny Baker and I were early fans. So were the new skinheads. According to Jimmy, he just happened to notice a mob of skins at an early Sham gig in West London and perchance remarked, 'Oh skinheads, I used to be a skin." Tony Cummins remembers it differently. 'Pursey used to wear jungle greens and have his hair cropped and go around saying 'Skinheads are back", he recalls. "That's why we used to follow Sham everywhere." "Sham 69 was the first band we followed", agrees Garry Hitchcock. "I can remember getting on stage with Pursey and he used to sing 'What have we got? We would all go 'FUCK ALL' because what did we have? Nothing!! We were working class kids out of school who no one gave a shit about. We really didn't have a future." Sham was in the right place at the right time. A focal point for the new skins, they also appealed to working class punk rockers disillusioned by the high dilettante and debutante count diluting and polluting the self-styled street movement. Many of these punks became skinheads, recognising the skin style as a genuine repository of proletarian values. Sham also seduced many football hooligans into adopting the cult, kids who at other times would have been content to confine their leisure time to tear-ups on the terraces. Crossing the raucous chants of the soccer crowds with the energy of punk, Sham rapidly built a massive street following. Although usually confused, Pursey's lyrics were always anti-pose, anti-middle class and anti-system. Their general message was clear: we may not have much but no one is better than we are. Pure populism. 'Borstal Breakout' summed up the mood of guttersnipe bravado perfectly. For Jim it was a song lyric, but a lot of his early audience had actually spent months of their teenage years sitting in cells! Sham's angry protest hit the spot. They went Top 40 with 'Borstal Breakout' (their first single on Polydor), penetrated the Top 20 with the follow-up 'Angels With Dirty Faces' and went on to have three Top Ten hits before 1979 was over: 'If The Kids Are United'. 'Hurry Up Harry' and 'Hersham Boys'. But as we shall see, the kids were not united and that was to prove Sham 69's un-doing.

Meeting and growing around punk clubs, the new skins became increasingly associated with Sham; but there were other bands around at the time who also appealed to skins and terrace regulars. Of these, Cock Sparrer was the most exciting. Forming at school in East Ham, by 1976 the band were gigging locally in East London, sprinkling their set of souped-up r 'n 'r with choice covers from the Small Faces, Humble Pie and T.Rex song books and generally kicking mic-stands about the stage a bit. Early reports about the Sex Pistols filtered through to them. To Sparrer they sounded like kindred spirits, so they contacted Malcolm McLaren about management. Malcy turned up at their rehearsal room above the Roding pub in East Ham and left a trail of merriment in his wake. He would come to the East End wearing spurs. The band ran through their set and Malcy was bowled over. They adjourned to the public bar where McLaren declared them "the next big thing." He made it clear that he wanted to manage them and offered them a support slot on the Pistols' next shows. Insanely, Sparrer turned him down, saying they would never support anyone. What happened next beggar's belief. Miserly Malcolm refused to buy a round. The band was so disgusted that they kicked him out and that was that. Drummer Steve Bruce later admitted: "It was the biggest mistake of our lives." Undeterred, Sparrer went on to build up a sizeable East End following, winning the particular attention and affection of a group of West Ham nutters known as the Poplar Boys, who had chanced upon the band at an early gig at the Roxy. They had a reputation for heaviness, but the Poplar Boys' presence at every subsequent gig put paid to crowd trouble. Favouring a skinhead and boot-boy image rather than a standard punk one, Cock Sparrer revived Doc Martens and Sta Press years before they became fashionable, and, as the video to their 'We Luv You' single shows, singer Colin McFaull also noticed Clockwork Orange imagery ahead of the herd. This single, and its scorching predecessor 'Running Riot' (both released by Decca), show just how fine a raw rock band Cock Sparrer were, and give you some idea why Jimmy Pursey once remarked that Sparrer were "too good to be a punk band." They should have been massive but managerial hassles put paid to the band's career. "We just signed a lot of dodgy contracts", bassist Steve Burgess explains. "And then we went to the States and no-one wanted to know. It all added up and we got disheartened. To top it off Decca offered us a two grand advance for a five-year deal, which worked out to about thruppence a day! and we just fizzled out really." This was in April 1978 just a year or so before bands like the Ruts, the UK Subs (who had been a Sparrer support band) and the Angelic Upstarts were hitting Top Of The Pops with a similar strand of street fire.

Bad timing was the story of Cock Sparrer's career. Menace were another bunch of could-have-been-contenders who broke up too early and reformed too late. Never quite as dynamic as Sparrer, this North London quartet got together in early '77 and was fronted by 'Mad' Morgan Webster. With their armory of brick-wall guttersnipe anthems, Menace was tailor-made for the job of Sham support band. They soon built up a solid following of their own, separate from the Sham crowd Hoxton Tom McCourt and Millwall Roy Pearce (a.k.a. Roi The Boi who went on to sing for the Last Resort) were both Menace roadies. The band proved their prowess on plastic with 1977's 'Screwed Up' (on Illegal) and '78's essential 'GLC' (Small Wonder). The music press was unwilling to accommodate a second Sham and in the face of constant press hostility, Menace petered out with more singles released after they disbanded than before.

Then there was Skrewdriver. Famed for their notoriety rather than their ability, the band formed in Blackpool, Lancashire, around vocalist Ian Stuart, real name Ian Stuart Donaldson, a factory manager's son from near-by Poulton-le-Flyde. Originally a Rolling Stones cover band called Tumblin' Dice they moved to London to become a punk band and were given the name Skrewdriver by their record label Chiswick. They were still punks when they appeared, performing abysmally, on Janet Street-Porter's LWT show 20th Century Box; and on the sleeve of their first single, the dismally Uninspiring 'You're So Dumb'. Their second single was better & a cover of the Stones' '19th Nervous Breakdown' coupled with their own good and anthemic 'Anti-Social': 'I'm anti-so-cial/ I hate the world'. They were not political at this point, other than being vaguely against society, but they had cropped their hair and adopted an unshaven skinhead look augmented strangely by a penchant for lumberjack jackets. No one took Skrewdriver seriously as a punk band, but Stuart was shrewd enough to realise that the skin revival was the next big thing and acted accordingly. "Ian Stuart approached us at a Sham gig at the Roxy", Garry Hitchcock remembers. "He told us about Skrewdriver and said that they weren't like Sham, that they were real skins." The word spread and come Skrewdriver Mark 2's gig at the Vortex there was a massive turnout of Skins, which surprised even Hitchcock. "We never knew there were so many around", he says. "And no-one there looked under twenty-five." Stuart told the skins that he would not slag off their violence like Sham had started to do.

Unfortunately, they took him at his word. After a disco warm-up of classic Trojan reggae, Skrewdriver hit the stage and the majority of the crowd went nuts, smashing up everything in sight. Skrewdriver were immediately banned from the Vortex, the Roxy and even the 100 Club. They also lost the support slot on the Travers tour that Chiswick had bought them onto. Unable to follow Sham into the charts, Skrewdriver eventually dropped the skinhead look and tried again as a punk band, once again failing to attract either interest or record sales. Pretty soon, Stuart was a skin again and the band had gone through more line-up changes than a death row inmates' football team. He began flirting with various far-Right groupings and winded up agreeing to play a National Front organised Rock Against Communism gig at London's Conway Hall in August 1979. At the death though, Stuart bottled out of the show and before long, he'd called it a day and disappeared back to Lancashire - unfortunately not for long. Returning to London in 1980, Stuart joined the Manor Park Royals (who never played a gig) with neo-Nazi Glen Bennett before reforming Skrewdriver again with himself as the only original member. Every other month or so he'd materialise in the offices of Sounds and Melody Maker telling anyone who'd listen that he was just a misunderstood patriot a stance he could keep up until about the sixth pint before breaking up the band once more. He reformed Skrewdriver for the final time in 1983, and after a brief attempt at being accepted as an "apolitical skinhead band", Stuart pinned his true colours to the mast and aligned the band to the rump of the decaying National Front declaring me the movement's natural enemy. Stuart produced leaflets saying 'Beat the ban, beat Bushell' as if I were responsible for them being banned from any self-respecting London venue. Flattering I suppose, although if I had had that power I would have used it against Soft Cell too. Back in 1977, as the skinhead cult grew, it became increasingly aggressive. Defensive violence was no longer enough. Inevitably, the Skins were drawn into the punk v Teds battles on the punk side; although earlier on, veteran Skins like Terry Madden and Arsenal Binnsy had hung about with rockabillies. With the street clashes escalating, such collaboration became impossible. Tensions had already been building up between skins and Teds down East London's Brick Lane, where the rival cults co-existed uneasily. The Teds had frequented the Black Raven pub and the Wimpy Bar there for years, while Skins drank in the Green Gate. Petticoat Lane was always a popular hang-out for Skins because of the clothes shops in the area (decent loafers and brogues could always be found in Blackman's in Brick Lane). It was only after they had beaten off the Teds that far-right activists followed the right wing skins into the area and pubs such as the Crown & Shuttle and The Bladebone became notorious neo-Nazi drinking dens. As street violence flared between the cults, the trouble spread to a punk stall in the market run by a long-time rag trade character called Mickey French and his missus Margaret. The Teds tried to trash it so the Skins defended it. The stall finally took up permanent residence as a punk boutique called the Last Resort in Goulston Street before switching to a largely Skin fashion emporium in 1978, which is the way it has remained to this day; although it has always sold punk schmutter too, and after the 1979 Mod revival, French started to sell Mod gear there as well for a while. Fashionable with later Skinheads, back in 1978 the shop was regarded as a bit of a joke. Garry Hitchcock says, "No serious Skinhead would buy anything at the Last Resort, except the braces." The Skins did not hate the Teds in particular; they just hated anyone who wasn't a Skin. Not even Punks were safe. Tom McCourt remembers Punks being moronically hit over the heads with hammers for their tickets outside the Roundhouse when Sham played with the Adverts in 1977; although they probably suffered less than other cults simply because many of the new Skins had been Punks and the two tribes still went to the same gigs and followed over-lapping bands. Skinhead gangs began to fight other Skinhead gangs too. The on-going war between the Packington and Hoxton mobs could be seen as the first example of internecine Skinhead rivalry this time round. The motivation was purely territorial however, with soul-boy mates fighting on both sides too. Elsewhere, football rivalry was the biggest source of skin-v-skin aggro. Inevitably, there was a lot of trouble with bikers & the Becontree mob rowed with local motorcycle gangs all the time. Skinheads in Wickford beheaded two Hell's Angels. The warnings were all there for Jimmy Pursey when Sham 69 played the Reading Festival in August 1978. Jimmy fled the stage in tears as his Sham Army steamed in to bikers, hippies and other festival-goers. The most serious aggravation however came from a group who were just as hard, just as working class and far more numerous than the Skins Soul-Boys. Tension between the two cults culminated in a small war around the Angel Islington from November 1977 onwards. For Tom McCourt this ended when he was jumped by a gang of 'soulies' on his way home from a Menace gig in '78 and severely stabbed. Similar territorial clashes erupted all over London. In Stepney, a right-wing Skin firm led by Ian Hettinger was turned over by a soul-boy crew led by Jay Williams in the Black Boy. Out in Becontree, the Skins encountered serious and sustained opposition from a mob of straights and soul-boys who called themselves the C.A. L. that stood for Chelsea Arsenal Liverpool. Yet ironically, the many brutal clashes between skins and soul-boys attracted far less attention in the media than other skinhead related violence. Certainly, it generated far less column inches than the trouble between Skins and Pakistanis in Brick Lane. "Hard as it may be to believe that really did start by accident", testifies Hoxton Tom. "In fact, ironically, one of the first skins down the Lane was Asian. I remember him appearing at the start of all the fighting with the Teds, and he was dead smart. He used to wear a crombie and a shirt and tie with a tie pin. Then one Sunday we went down there after the Teds and the Asians had put up a barricade. They were going mad. I suppose they did not like us fighting each other in what they saw as their area. However, when they got stroppy, it was like a red rag to a bull. "Garry Hitchcock concurs: "They got the hump", he says, "Because we were always down their ghetto." Although football rivalry was the biggest source of gig violence, politics occasionally entered the equation. For example, the violence at Sham's Kingston Poly gig was between right-wing skins and the Croydon Boys who were largely left wing. Sham 69 suffered from all sorts of grief, but how innocent was Jimmy Pursey? To this day, veteran far-Right skins insist that the Sham front man encouraged them. "Pursey used us", says Garry Hitchcock. "He dressed like us and encouraged us to come to his gigs, but as soon as he started getting famous he didn't want to know." In truth, it was only ever the right-wing skinheads who Pursey turned against. He says he never encouraged the racialist element. I first knew him as a fan, and a fanzine writer in late 1977, and he always argued against racialist ideas and the growing Nazi tendency. He aligned himself with the newly formed Anti-Nazi League and told me: "Every gig I do is a Rock against Racism." This infuriated the small but committed National Socialist element among his fans. Terry Madden then had the rare distinction of being both an Irish Republican and a neo-Nazi (single-handedly inspiring a News of the World report on the 'Nazi wing of the IRA'); although he is since shed the Nazi side of his politics. Madden pulled a blade on Pursey and demanded he agree to lead a National Front march. So how did these odious politics come in to a youth cult, which owed so much to black music and West Indian culture? Many commentators assumed not unreasonably that the far-Right groups consciously infiltrated the punk scene having been attracted by punk's confused political symbolism. This was not the case, not at first at any rate. True the National Front did make propaganda plays for white rock fans, with a whispering campaign spuriously claiming support from stars such as David Bowie and Rod Stewart. Later members of Spandau Ballet were the subject of equally unfounded whispers. But on the streets in 1976/7, the NF were viewed as the soft option, and the hardcore ultra-right minority among the early London skins were attracted to the less astute, but more extreme, British Movement. Crucially their Nazi elders did not approve. "The British Movement thought we were degenerate for going to gigs", recalls Hitchcock. "They considered the music business to be completely Jewish controlled. They thought the Jews were trying to corrupt white youth through punk. Their disapproval was the reason we brought politics in to it and started leafleting at gigs and steaming people. We wanted to prove to the BM that we weren't softening up and that we were there to spread their word." The Nazis, known colloquially as "the right-arm mob" or contemptuously as the German Movement were only ever a tiny minority of Skinheads. Nevertheless, just as a small cog can move a much larger one, so they were able to create an impact far in excess of their actual strength. In 1977, their numbers were swelled by the notorious bully boy Matty Morgan (a.k.a. 'Mad Matty') who was to become a leading element and whose brother, Steve Morgan, was already an established name on the West Ham terraces. These were the people later bands would have to face and defeat, but in '77 and '78 they were a significant disruptive force. Sham and the Lurkers suffered most from ultra-Right violence. As the BM skins cranked up the action, the older Nazis mellowed in their attitude to the cult. "The right-wing was courting the skins during the summer of '77", recalls Hoxton Tom, who was never a Nazi. "They would hang about in Brick Lane especially, buying drinks, trying to get people on side. Meanwhile the Left tended to ignore us." In fact, the left-wing skinhead tradition goes back just as far as Right, and countrywide the Left probably attracted more skin support (although the bulk of Skins were either apolitical or vaguely Labour by tradition). The LGS and the Archway with their black skins were there from 1976. Skins in Croydon and Oxford were renowned for their socialist sympathies. Sharon Spike, a skinhead, contributed to Rock against Racism's Temporary Hoarding magazine. And when Jimmy Pursey briefly visited the Brixton ANL Carnival in September 1978, it was heartening to see scores of Afro Boys come out of the woodwork - over a year before 2-Tone erupted and enticed thousands of black kids to resurrect the Rude Boy style. Revolutionary socialist band Crisis, from South London, had a skinhead following and a skinhead bassist in Tony Wakefield, who edited the Socialist Workers Party youth mag Rebel. And there was a short-lived Skins Against the Nazis group formed by four East End skins in Hackney in August 1978. A mention of the group's creation in Temporary Hoarding brought in more than sixty letters from Skins all over the country requesting membership forms, with Acton skins proving a hotbed of support. Both Pursey and Menace's Noel Martin gave the SAN their blessing. I interviewed founder member Laurence Newis, a young Clock End skin in Sounds, but after his photo appeared, he got so much stick from Nazis that he later claimed (falsely) to have been an NF mole all along just to save himself from hidings. Two years on, Joe McAvoy, a stoical ex-Stalinist skinhead from Chelsea, launched the League of Labour Skins. A mention in Sounds brought hundreds of positive letters flooding in, but the League was frustratingly inactive. Outside the capital, socialist skinheads could be found in abundance. Left-wing skins organised around political issues in Sheffield and Glasgow the Glasgow branch of the Sham Army was featured positively in the Trotskyist Socialist Worker and they contributed much muscle and manpower to 1978's summer Right to Work March. There was significant skinhead involvement in Rock against Racism around the country too. The far Right was stronger in the Midlands but they were not unopposed. In May 1978, a multi-racial group of West

Bromwich skinheads led an anti-Nazi demo against the NF. Some of the white ones infiltrated the NF meeting and heckled so enthusiastically that it had to be abandoned after just eleven minutes. It would be fair to surmise that whichever political side ruled the streets in any area also ruled the skins. From the very start, Sham 69's existence was marred by violence, most of it football-related rather than politically motivated. At first, Jimmy had been optimistic about his following. In 1977, he had told me, "See, skinheads are not acceptable because they represent violence, but you can channel that violence, that energy and excitement, into something good and show you can be a rebel with a cause." He was right; it was just unfortunate for Jimmy Sham and the innocent bystanders in his audience that he was not to be the person to achieve that noble aim. At the start, the bulk of Sham's London following came from Ladbroke Grove and Lewisham, but before long the hard-core were aggressively West Ham. They including such notorious claret & blue street-fighters as Binnsy, Gary Dickle, Johnny Butler and Vince Riordan who became a Sham roadie alongside Albie Maskell (Albie had been kicked out of the band in late 1977 and replaced on bass by the more competent Kermit, a.k.a. Dave Treganna.) Vince was later to play bass in the Cockney Rejects (see chapter six). By 1978, West Ham's Grant Fleming (who was to be the first of the new Mods at Upton Park) had become Jimmy Pursey's right-hand man, and the neatly turned out Dean of QPR was the only LGS regular left. Football clashes plagued innumerable Sham gigs. The bloodiest was the brutal Arsenal v West Ham battle at their Hendon College gig in January 1979. The violence at Hendon was awful. Jimmy was so horrified that he took an overdose of sleeping tablets. If it were not for the prompt action of his girlfriend's Mum, Jim would have died. The riot prompted Pursey to make the first of several "That's the last gig we'll ever play" proclamations. Unfortunately, he never stuck to them. Small wonder some observers began to see him as a Dr Frankenstein unable to control the lurching monster he had created. At first, he tried to soothe the savage beast through his lyrics. 'If The Kids Are United' was a powerful plea for youth unity over football rivalry: 'If the kids are united, they will never be divided'. The chorus was lifted and modified from the chants of the previous year's Grunwick picket line: 'The workers united will never be defeated', which made more sense, but no matter, the song, became Sham's first Top 5 hit. It didn't stop the violence though, so Jimmy tried another tack, directing Sham towards the sort of good-time rowdy pop that Slade had pioneered and turning out sing-along terrace gems like 'Hurry Up Harry' and 'Hersham Boys'. If he had stopped playing gigs and stuck to churning out hits, Sham would almost certainly have thrived and survived. As it was, it was Pursey's attempts to combat the far Right head on that sowed the seeds of his downfall. Again, at first, Jimmy had been optimistic about his chances. In 1977, he said, "It's not true that all Skins are Nazis, but I'd rather have an NF skinhead come to my gig so I can turn around and say 'I'm anti-Nazi, what do you think of that, than some robot who agrees with my every word." Good as his public statements, Pursey would argue for hours with racist fans. In 1978, he made personal appearances at both the massive Anti-Nazi League carnivals, memorably joining the Clash on stage at Victoria Park to Sing 'White Riot'. No doubt, he did reach and influence a hell of a lot of kids, but the tiny Nazi rump was significantly pissed off by his actions. They felt betrayed. Slogans like 'Sham are Red cunts' were sprayed on East London walls and, at the end of their 1978 tour, trouble flared at the Electric Ballroom gig in Camden when BM Skins turned on the rest of the audience. Reggae band the Cimarons, whose current single was 'Rock against Racism', were the tour support, but they had been mysteriously dropped from the Ballroom bill after an apparent altercation with the bouncers. Given the atmosphere at the gig it was probably just as well. It was evil. Poisonous gangs of BM skins prowled around picking on individuals asking them if they liked Sham. If they said yes, they were called "Red cunts" and occasionally belted. The BM skins could not get at the band because of the massed ranks of West Ham heavies (all wearing crossed hammers t-shirts) at the front of the stage, but the audience was terrified. The next night there was no trouble and a defiant Pursey changed the words of 'Song of the Streets' to include the lines: 'Conservatives and National Front/ They're all a shower of shit'. Throughout 1978 however, especially in London and the Midlands, supporting the NF, or saying you did at least, was becoming a natural side-bar to being a skinhead. It was a trend the national press went out of their way to encourage, rarely writing about Skins without linking them unthinkingly to the Front. Why was this? Part of the problem was lazy, irresponsible journalism but a greater part was the failure of the traditional working class parties to relate to white working class teenagers who felt rejected by society and ignored by politicians. It could have been a bumper period for the neo-Nazi British Movement, but the Master Race dumbly shot themselves in the foot by demanding that every member prove their loyalty by having a BM symbol tattooed on their arms. As a result, scores left the sect; one of them Garry Hitchcock who said that the tattoo decree coincided with his own personal realisation that Nazism was no good. For Jimmy Pursey the pressure was to prove too much. After surviving his post-Hendon suicide attempt Jimmy bounced back, launching his own JP label through Polydor and then shot off to France to record the 'Hersham Boys' single and album. Both were hits. This was the apex of Sham's commercial success and unexpectedly the chance of a lifetime, the chance to leave Sham and its troubled legacy behind for good, presented itself. Pursey was offered the chance to replace Johnny Rotten in the Sex Pistols. The new line-up was to be Jimmy (vox), Steve Jones (guitar), Paul Cook (drums) and Kermit on bass. Leaking half-truths to the press, jubilant Jim announced that Sham was over, killed by the uncontrollable element among their fans. A farewell gig was announced for 29th June 1979 at the Glasgow Apollo. None of us in the audience knew what was about to happen, but maybe we should have guessed when we spotted Virgin Records boss Richard Branson in the crowd. For the encore, Sham were joined by the pair of self-styled "working class tossers" Cook and Jones. Covers of 'Pretty Vacant', 'White Riot' and Sham's own 'If The Kids Are United' followed. It was a vision of a future that was not to be. After the show, the plan for the new Pistols was unveiled. In the party atmosphere that surrounded the whole affair, only two voices of sanity were heard and sadly ignored. John Lydon said the enterprise "smacked of desperation", while the deposed Dave Parsons observed "I don't think it's gonna last long because Jim always likes to be 100 per cent in control." Nostradamus, eat yer heart out. Overcome with emotion, Jimmy Pursey enthused about his future in the new Pistols and decided to play a farewell gig in London as well. "It would break my heart if we couldn't say goodbye to London", he said. Oh dear. The Rainbow was booked for July 18th 1979. It was the day Sham 69 died. From the minute

I stepped off the tube at Finsbury Park I just knew it was going to end in tears. The first thing I saw was a pint glass smashing into a teenage boy's face because he had a ticket and the gorilla with the glass had not. The British Movement had mobilised in force for the farewell show. They congregated in the George Robey pub opposite the venue, giving the sieg-heil salute at passers-by. Black and mixed race skinheads were attacked and passing immigrants subjected to sick, gory sing-songs about the "showers of Belsen."

The atmosphere was pure evil, but their intentions were crystal clear. Young Nazi London was united in one aim, united like a pack of animals under a whip: They were going to destroy Sham 69. I do not suppose there were more than forty actual BM members, but as always, the hardcore head-cases exerted an influence far greater than their numbers. The support bands, the Little Roosters and the Low Numbers, played to a barrage of abuse and hurled coins. In between sets, a gang of around two hundred skins ran amok through the unseated venue. Pursey had new personal security a scruffy mob of Road Rats and barrel-chested bikers from Surrey had replaced his West Ham minders. They kept well out of the way. When the safety curtain finally rose to the strains of '2001 & A Space Odyssey', Jimmy looked understandably brown around the trouser department. Fuelled by an instinct for self-preservation, the band stormed into 'Song of the Streets'. They sounded savage, vital, and harder than they had ever been before, but by the fourth number, 'Angels with Dirty Faces', all pretence of normality was over. One by one, hulking neo-Nazis and other embittered ex-fans invaded the stage. The safety curtain dropped and Sham retreated. The Nazi-led mob gave the Nazi salute in triumph. They were still a minority but with no organised force to confront them they were unbeatable. After about twenty minutes, the stage area was cleared. Insanely the band returned and smashed into 'Angels' again. The mood of the non-Nazi element of the crowd lifted. Could it be that now they'd had their protest the boneheads would let the band finish in style? Some hope. Seven stunning numbers followed. Then the second stage invasion started. Pursey finally cracked. He hurled the drum kit across the stage, grabbed a microphone and shouted: "I fucking loved you! I fuckin' did everything for you! And all you wanna do is fight!" A tear rolled down his cheek. It was all over. Robbi Millar wrote in Sounds: "Jimmy said goodbye to London, and London kicked him in the teeth." Celebrating their victory, the BM went on a beano. The next night, they hit a Jobs for Youth benefit gig organised by the Young Socialists in Brent's Gladstone Park with Misty and the Ruts playing. Just under a hundred Nazi-led Skins stormed the stage, tore down the Red flags and Nazi saluted their defiance at the helpless crowd. The gig was then abandoned. This summer was the zenith of neo-Nazi strength on the street. Paradoxically, it was also their undoing, as it rapidly became clear to the unconverted that all the BM stood for was the destruction of bands, gigs and therefore of skinhead culture. The Movement never grew any bigger and the new breed of skinhead-orientated bands never repeated Sham's many mistakes, or showed that kind of weakness in the face of far-Right aggression. These were the Oi bands spearheaded by the Cockney Rejects and the Angelic Upstarts. The BM's campaign of violence also led directly to the growth of a new, hard, street-level Trotskyist hit squad called Red Action, a 'workerist' spin-off from the Socialist Workers Party, who were determined to meet fire with fire and were arguably just as suspect. As for Jimmy Pursey, his bid to turn John Rotten into Johnny Forgotten petered out. By the end of August, the new Pistols had split without ever playing a proper gig. Dave Parsons was right, they just couldn't work together. Besides, who'd want to risk that kind of tour mayhem? In September, Jimmy reformed Sham but the band was never the same. Deeply fucked up by all he had been through Pursey seemed to have lost the knack of writing decent songs. The 'Hersham Boys' album went silver but it had as much bite as a toothless pensioner. It was not until the follow-up album, 'The Game', in May 1980 that Sham came anywhere near finding their old form and by then they'd been surpassed by the Cockney Rejects and the Angelic Upstarts. The rest of Sham's releases document the decline of a band that were once the ultimate in street-punk aggression. I last saw Jimmy Pursey on TV performing some kind of bizarre ballet dancing routine. He appeared to have gone nuts. It was a sad end for someone who had been a great performer, a decent man and a friend. Jimmy once told Danny Baker: "My attitude might seem thick to you cos I was brought up to be thick to keep rich cunts in money." I think it probably seemed thick because he was a bit. Jimmy was articulate, but the crux of what he said often made little or no sense at all. His words came straight from his heart and into his head without ever connecting with his brain. He was out of his depth and he paid a terrible price for it. But it's sadder still that scenes of that sorry riot at the Rainbow have been tattooed in to the public memory as the lasting image of the late '70s skinhead scene.

- This article is abridged from the book 'Hoolies' by Garry Bushell

Actors and homegrown productions

An actor or actress is a person who acts in a dramatic production and who works in film, television and theatre. Well that is what the books will tell ya'. For many of us it was some person that allowed us to live vicariously through them and the part they are playing, with the greats seen in early productions from the James Bond era, through to the new breed like Guy Ritchie and Gary Oldham. It is a refreshing view that the home grown producers and directors can still be spawned within our great shores. Popularity is by a different measure in the U.K when it comes to the success of films and productions. Though I would have to agree, that all actors would probably appreciate and like the status and fame of many of their international counterparts.

Film and the rewards can also bring much needed publicity and attention to ones craft. With the ever-growing speed and exposure of the internet, it is easy to see how Bill Gates and Bill Clinton can get more interest than Jesus can! (Google hits for October 24 2005) Film production in the UK had experienced a number of difficulties. Although many elements can be used to gauge the success of the industry, the number of British films produced each year gives an idea. What often allows a breath of much needed fresh air, are the smaller less known production companies. With private investing in the early '90's, allowed many homegrown companies to produce not only timeless pieces, but also some that would arguably put many larger production companies back to the drawing board. After all, there are only so many mass explosions and over budget films, we can tolerate; The Full Monty was rumored to have netted 10 times what it cost to make!

Ricci Harnett

For me, inspiration came from losing my youngest brother. -Jason Allday. December 2008.

To define a man's legacy, his life and equally important a mark in history, there is very few young actors in today's film industry that could have held their weight where it was needed for the role of Carlton Leach. Some may have pulled it off. Some would have been an insult to a man that wanted to leave his name etched in a film detailing 3 decades of his life. To show the caliber required to emulate what was needed in terms of quality, realism, and above all knowing the score, this is one clued up actor, and the end result shows, by far the best choice.

With a mix of a cockney rebel, the rawness of any football hooligan and the darkness needed, he played so well in the role of Carlton Leach, is it any wonder Ricci is so highly respected. The responsibility he accepted and maintained in portraying a highly respected man and detailing of his life is clearly captured on film. This is not my biased opinion. See the man in action. Speak to him, and realise the commitment he gave for the lead role. Equally the amount of respect that he got in return from those in 'the know'. Look past the role, the name he was carrying and portraying and accept Ricci was alongside some real 'heavy weights' from the British film industry and he still shone like a pedigree with a depth of knowledge and experience.

Ricci Harnett:

So, far from being a serial killer in the making or being raised on a daily dose of murder and mayhem, where did you get your start in the world of acting?

Ricci- "I've been acting for almost twenty-five years. My first professional job was Crime watch. I had to play a boy that had been murdered whilst out fishing. I suppose some child actors were happily doing the Pink windmill show around that time but there I was about ten years old standing on a doorstep dressed as the murdered boy with my mum who was my chaperon in silence waiting for the real mum and dad to open the door. My introduction in to the world of acting had started off in a very dark place."

When an edge was needed to carry one of the most respected names in terrace history and some of the most violent and darkest times in a person's life, you had a good start in terms of source material!

Ricci- "I suppose it was this fascination with the dark side of life that as lead me to play a lot of murderers, villains and rebels over the years. The one's that really challenge you as an actor are playing people that actually exist, parts like Neil Acourt in the Murder of Stephen Lawrence or more recently Carlton Leach in Rise of the foot soldier. A bit extra pressure comes with a job like that. Once you have finished celebrating getting the job. You do think to yourself "bloody hell hang on a minute am I gonna' be able to pull this off.""

In the case of Rise of the foot soldier, it would mean that I was going to have to put my body through lot. It has been said that it is not the size of the dog in the fight, but more the size of the fight in the dog. This could not be any further from the truth. Taking into account your smaller stature than Carlton, how did Carlton weigh you up for the part?

Ricci- "I remember the look on Carlton's face when he first saw me standing there, five foot seven and weighing about eleven and a bit stone with a flat cap and glasses. He must have thought that the director was taking the piss. I read all about how in the early nineties Carlton was sticking pins in his legs, arse and arms and pumping himself full of steroids. I had seen photos of him in his hay day weighing around sixteen stone. I knew I had couple of options. Either go all method and get on the gear myself or try to pile on the weight naturally. Now considering what I'd read about steroids and how they have a tendency to make you a little bit cross coupled with the fact that with me being the lead actor in the film, which would mean that, I'd be in every day for long hours. There might be a time where I might have a minor disagreement and the last thing I wanted was to have a 'roid rage attack and smash the whole fucking set up. My girlfriend had told me she'd leave me if I did anyway."

So, back to basics no pain, no gain. You had to put the work in!

Ricci- "Yeah it was hard graft. Being a low budget film meant that I was pretty much on my own. This was not some Bond film where Daniel Craig gets a top person trainer for six months. I went back to see an old mate of mine called Alan who worked as gym instructor on a council estate near Watford where I grew up called South Oxhey. He's only a little fella but blimey did he push me. I went from bench-pressing nothing to 100 kg by the time the filming started.

I was taking just about every legal supplement available from Bulgarian trebalis to Horny goat weed. I'm a vegetarian so steaks were off the menu so I'd be chucking 1500 calories of protein shakes down my neck every three hours. In the two months, I had managed to bulk up to a shade under 14 stone. OK I was still two and a half stone lighter than Carlton but I hoped that once the film was shown that the big screen would add the rest."

Months later, no 'roids, rules from the misses and above all the man himself was going to be about to see you carry him on the big screen. The responsibility you accepted and maintained in portraying a highly respected man and detailing of his life was about to be captured on film!

Ricci- "So that was half the battle the other half was getting to know Carlton and try to understand his world. I know this might sound silly but Carlton and I are both Pisces. It might have been clutching at straws but I knew we had some thing in common. I felt I owed it to Carlton to make sure that what came out my mouth was accurate. Every now and then, I might read a sentence line that sounded cool and I would ask myself if Carlton would really say that? The good thing with Carlton being a mate was I could ring him anytime and ask him."

Only fair, I am sure a lot of people would agree. Let us face it, Carlton's life is about to be made into a film. Not many people have that opportunity, and if you are going to get one chance, well, no time for messing about!

Ricci- "I remember one of the first hurdles we had to get over was when he asked me a simple enough question "What team do ya support?" Oh dear I thought. I am about to have to break the news to one of the most feared members of the ICF that the fella' that was about to play him in the film of he's life is in fact a Gooner and to be fair he actually took it pretty well.

He asked if I knew 'The Bear'? I did know Denton. He was lovely massive black fella and Arsenals top boy for years. In fact, Carlton said that the pair of them had gone one on one a few times. I had known Denton through the Pet shop boys. He used to look after them on tour. There was a time when Chris Low, Denton and me drove up to Manchester to see prince Naseem fight. I remember how Ian Wright came over and threw he's arm around Denton at ringside."

There is an acceptance of friendship with many of the lads, which was on the front line on football hooliganism back in the day. Like a lot of the lads from the '70's and '80's, when a general goes down, those that understand the reasoning and difference from a tear-up and a time of respect spoke well of Denton.

Ricci- "Everyone knew him even the old girls in the Little Chef who gave us free food on the way up there. We even ended up in a hotel room with Keith Flint. That was a messy weekend. Unfortunately, Denton died in a car crash in Russia a couple of years ago whilst looking after the Petshop boys. I remember getting a text on Saturday night from a good friend and ICF member Steve saying that the Bear was dead. I was mini cabbing at the time, and working through the night. As soon as the sun came up on

Sunday morning I drove over to Columbia road flower market, just as the blokes were setting up and brought twenty or so red and white roses and drove up to the emirates to lay them on the roundabout next to a solitary bunch of flowers and looked up at the new stadium and cried. Later in the day, you couldn't see the roundabout for flowers RIP, mate."

Hindsight is a wonder full thing! How many times have you thought "Maybe this way or should I have said less, more...?"

Ricci- "Looking back would I had done things different? No, I don't think so. I gave it my best shot. Carlton and his family are happy with it and that is all that matters to me at the end of the day."

The likes of Tim Roth, Gary Oldman and Ray Winstone all played what have been labeled as timepieces. They have all contributed to playing some roles that have stretched from one type of role to another. This allows them to be thought of as more versatile and I see a similar trend with you.

Ricci- "I've played some fairly dark people over the years that have done stuff that's a bit difficult to get my head around. I've had to kill a lot of people on screen. What interests me is the look on the killers face after they've done it. Some are in shock some are angry and some are even happy and relieved with what they have just done. I can end up shaking sometimes after doing stuff like that."

Some of the greats that have lead similar roles.

Some films out there have certainly made an impression and paved a way for young actors such as you. For the football lads Alan Clarke with 'The Firm' through such hard-hitting classics like 'Scum'.

Ricci- "My favorite actor's Gary Oldman, a London lad that as refused to be pigeon holed. I was in L.A a few years ago and most of them thought he was an American. He has also directed my favorite film "Nil by Mouth" A powerful piece of work. I also look up to Ray Winstone. He is a real survivor and a brave actor who has he is not frightened to take roles that most other actors would swerve, films like War Zone and Nil by mouth. I hope I get the chance to work with him that would be something."

Back in the world of the regular 'Tom', a pound note needs to be earned. Are you happy sitting back and watching 'bits and pieces' pass you by?

Ricci- "Like many of my mates who are actors, and get feed up waiting around for scripts to come through the letterbox, I have started writing. It will be good to get something made just to show the teachers that booted me out of school that I'm not so stupid after all. It's hard finding the time though. I spend about fifty hours a week working has a motorbike courier, which isn't easy given all the snow we've been having. I have a lot of respect for couriers they're tough fucking people. We've got blokes and girls that go out no matter how harsh the weathers. I like the sense of freedom and I go all over the country. It can get a bit hairy being blown about by the lorries on the motorways, but I rather do that than do some shit bit of telly just for the money. The good thing about a fella' is you can carry on acting until you're a hundred. There is a lot more roles out about for old blokes. I'd loved to have gone from Foot soldier on to big stuff straight away but there's no rush."

What have you got coming up?

Ricci- "I have just done a short film set in a prison called Stained written by ex prison officer Ronnie Thompson. Frank Harper and Craig Conway are also in it. It was great to finally work with Frank. He's been around the block and knows the game inside out. Ronnie is working with Colin Butts on the script for the feature. If things go well we should start shooting in the summe.

I've also got a horror film coming out in the summer called Psychosis that's directed by Reg Travis. It stars the American actress Charisma Carpenter. I play this groundsman from Yorkshire and I've got a massive fucking great big ginger beard and have to run about the woods bollock fucking naked. Then there's Breathe a really low budget film I did straight after Footsoldier that's coming out on DVD around February. It's an urban love story. I play a bloke who has to look after his teenage sister because the Dads a piss head and beats them up. It's very different to 'Footsoldier'; There's no nailing people to the floor, and waving shooters about, but I still had a laugh making it. It's a bit like it's up to you to pull it off."

With such pieces done to show the film industry and critics alike, actors like Ricci Harnett has proved he hasn't conformed to an industry standard nor swayed to 'pop films' to follow suit and simply follow the pound note trail. Ricci has tested the water and has already welcomed with open arms controversial roles that would typically be questioned in terms of the impression it could leave for an actor's career. With greats that already exist in the British film industry, Ricci is set to be amongst them.

Neil Maskell

It was inevitable that junior would follow Chelsea. This was the main team in terms of a fan base in west London. His pals were mainly all Chelsea and those that were not, Junior would still embrace within his circle of friends. Being one of my late brother's favorites along With the heavy theme of Chelsea carried in the story line, it was without question I had to include Football factory in my memory list. Football factory promoted classic one-liners and reenactments within our household. All too often, I would have to remind the Chelsea lemmings that it was simply entertainment. This did not sway their attempts at voicing the greatness of their team within our home. Like all siblings, there were favorite films that always promoted a laugh and without them, we would have had fewer conversations and fewer memories for those no longer with us.

One question I am asked regularly by people that are not into football (there are a few and that alone I have questioned!) is how can football be a part of people's lives so religiously? My opinion is a simple one. Football, like most sports, is one if the best forms of discipline in a persons' life. Without question and certainly in a child's life, the commitment and involvement as both a fan and those that play the sport, represents many of the qualities and necessities for a healthy life. Exercise, being one huge part of it and quite alarming, it has also been suggested in reports there is a decline of sports in many schools! Also, what should be considered, is What better way to understand your personal level of proficiency and strengths on the many levels of social skills that are necessary in your everyday Monday through Friday that are gained from a person's involvement in sports. I would say that sports are part of the essential building blocks in a young person's life. As much as the academic level of pen and paper is vital to education, so are sports.

One luxury and privilege I have is a circle of good people that are real friends. They are all levels from your everyday market trader, to those that provide a level of protection to some heavy weight players in the underworld. Not to make it a pissing contest, I'm simply grateful of their friendship. In conversation with a chap in the film industry, I was asked if there were any actors that might spark a good conversation, from any of the favorites that existed in our film collections. Neil Maskell, who played Rod, was in our biased opinion, one of the more likable characters in the shared lead role with Danny Dyer in football factory. So one Californian sunny breezy afternoon I am on the phone, for what I know would have been one conversation, my late Chelsea loving little brother, would have been in his absolute element about.

Neil Maskell

Youth and the very culture it feeds! The general population has a soft spot and love affair for modern day youths and the lives that are promoted within the mentioned genre. This very social order has held court with all levels of our society and the ornate characters it promotes. With the increase and success of 'real life' TV shows and the escalating social interest from those that would typically be alienated to such a world, a culture is born from this and it's these outsiders that are hot on the tails of the urban warriors.

When an actor chooses a part, their basic identity must remain intact. After all, he or she is playing a 'role'. The part the actors promote has to be a convincing one, and where the prolific image of the good person has much an identity and foothold, so does the love-able rogue in many successful films. Far from being new to the scene, Neil Maskell has been in listed and involved in respected productions pre days of super grassing and cricket bat-wielding mayhems. His start was in 1992 and has since flourished to the much liked and respected parts that hold notice, namely two characters; a like-able one, and one that questions the moral fabric of right and wrong. Who better than to play the role of Rod in 'The Football Factory', and Darren Nichols in 'The Rise of the Foot Soldier'?

It is true that those in pursuit of appreciation for their work would typically rely on their fans and followers. With the classic one liners in tune with the roles of 'there for your mate no matter what' and being the card that brought the house down, the role of Darren Nicholls has to be said a far stretch from the justifiable actions played out as Rod, but none less in terms of an impressionable one. Accepting the part of a person, that gains far from any respect from those of certain standing (the underworld) when Neil played the 'king of grasses'. An actor in many people's opinions should play parts that are unpredictable, thus showing both their acting and their potential. Only fair I say as nothing worse than the mundane. This certainly was a pivotal and moral questioning part ('fucking grass!' was my thought as a result at the convincing portrayal of Darren Nicholls). I could go on to say he's a classical example of versatility in an actor that has promise of exceptional growth and future to match. So let us have a chat with the penge minge loving lad that also played a part in the demise of one of Essex's most violent firms.

Your story, your start!

Neil- "I was born in Barts Hospital; London and grew up mainly in Bexleyheath. Staying loyal to my dad's team, Arsenal who are not a bad bunch, and that's worked out too bad I suppose (laughing). I always used to have a season ticket, for a long time in fact, but with the acting it's been difficult to keep up going and to spend out the money for something I've not had time for; although I do get over there as much as I can."

Your beginnings are solid, but yet unfolded to the masses. You have been a busy chap since '92!

Neil- "My acting if you like started in Islington on a Friday night at a place called The Anna Schers Theatre; where Phil Danials, Kathy Burke and also a lot of the cast and faces that you see in EastEnders and The Bill went to also. Well I started there, it would cost 50p a week, they had an agency attached, and if they liked what you did, you could get a bit of acting work. I mean that's how a good few London actors started. My routine was to go to school in South London then go to acting class on a

Friday night and a Saturday afternoon. You know, do a bit of acting a bit of improvisation and stuff. Then I got a part in the film about the murder of Stephen Lawrence that took place in Eltham. I played the role of one of the killers alongside Ricci Harnett. It was from there I was introduced to an agent that was more known for adult actors and I have worked consistently for the last 18 years."

A career in acting, I imagine can be a love hate relationship. Do you consider what you do as a job or something else?

Neil- "With acting I do feel that it's something that isn't just a job or a means to an end. I'll be honest. I am not really much cop at anything else (laughing). Over the years there has been times where I've had low times in acting and people have said to me if I've thought about giving it up, you know, and I've thought 'well, to do what?' I can't do mini cabbing for the rest of my life or go back to university and there's not a lot I'd wanna' do in life as I've really committed myself to it. I mean I have just written and directed my first short film, so I've branched out a little bit into doing other stuff, so I think it's true to say for me with acting. It's just part of the make-up of who you are."

Is there any Diverse acting roles or any that left an impression?

Neil- "I think to a certain extent I have been type cast due to the fact if you've got a London accent then you can end up doing a lot of gangster, and villain parts, as there is a certain amount of industry prejudice about working class London accents and what that represents. It's nowhere near as bad as what it's like for London black actors, as I have some mates that have played drug dealers as many as 8 times in 1 year. I think there's a terrible racial prejudice within the industry, and I feel you can experience a little bit of that as a Londoner too. For me I think the more diverse roles has actually come from the comedy roles; like when I played a part in an American film called Eight ball. Not the greatest film in the world but a very different type of gig, and it's that I feel is quite interesting. That as an actor is what you wanna' be doing; playing as many diverse roles as possible, in this game you want to be trying on as many pairs as shoes as you possibly can. I want to do as much as possible really, not just running around south London estates bashing people up, but saying that I've had some really interesting roles inside that genre, and worked with good directors, and other good actors. Much like with Football Factory, it was all good fun and we was all good mates, I've worked with Ricci (Harnett) a bunch of times, and we respect each other very much as actors, so there's plusses and minuses to both sides in terms of doing the same thing, but it is nice to do different things."

A cult classic; Gary Oldman, Ray Winston, Kathy Burke, displayed a story that brought 'home' to many inner city families a true reflection of the everyday struggles. With Nil by Mouth, I feel Gary displays life's battles, hardships and above all the fight within all of us. In my opinion this is reflected by the characters found within the cast that some can relate to.

Neil- "Well with that film involvement I was only 18, and was on set for only three days. I was overwhelmed to be honest, even fair to say intimidated by it all, the surroundings and all that was going on. Now the interesting thing was at the time, none of the cast including Ray (Winston) was considered a film star, but they was all people I admired and looked up to, as I was growing and coming up as a London actor. Ray was a hero of all of us, even as kids. He had been forgotten by the British film industry, partly due to the result of the prejudice that I was talking about earlier. Kathy Burke probably had the highest profile because of her part in Harry Enfield's work, but all of the actors knew that everyone was pretty special and important, so it was exciting for me from that point of view. The people that I was working alongside like Charlie Creed-Miles, who was a couple of years older than I was, and Steve Sweeney were people that I looked up to. Steve, well we worshiped him a bit, as he was such an interesting character. Everyone knew he was a loose cannon actor, and had this type of fierceness in terms of intensity about him, so it was very exciting to be working with them. Gary Oldman is the big Hollywood style you know, making a piece that was local to me really and to be honest, it was low on the pecking order for crew members, like runners and assistants would be saying things like "he (Gary), doesn't know what he's doing, his shooting style, he doesn't know what order it's gonna' go in, this film's gonna' be a fucking mess." I think it was about two years between shooting it and the release. We then went down to see the showing for the cast and crew, and since then I'd say it was definitely the best thing I've ever been involved in. I'm so glad to have my name in that cast list, and certainly amongst those other actors. I'd go as far to say it's probably the best film ever made about working class Londoners, It's the real deal. It's one of those films where you feel you've been in the same type of rooms with those types of geezers; it's so accurate. It's always moving, and you can identify with the struggles and the relationships with those inside the film. Kathy is a very sympathetic character, and where I know and have also spoken to some people that don't know of those struggles, or know of people that have lived in that world, have said it was like watching animals in a zoo. What I think Gary accomplished with that film is to at least evoke empathy in some people that do not know anything of that world, but no question, it is a very special piece of film."

Objectivity and honesty is not the same thing. A writer draws from not only their experiences, but also their opinions. Some could also say their view, so with this thought, were there any subtle differences with 'Nil by Mouth' and your screen debut in Football factory?

Neil- "The main difference that I noticed between a project like Nil by Mouth and Football Factory was firstly, it was a bigger budget amongst other aspects. It was the first time I would be a supporting lead in a film, I mean I'd done a bit on the TV though. Working with Nick, I found the dialogue was both recognisable and funny, and to be honest I found that aspect very easy; as all you had to do was, make sure you got those words out. I think it's a bit unfair that the some of the praises I got for my work in that film were a bit undeserved in some ways, as the writing was so good. I think it's not seen by people how often you're dealing with bad scripts and inauthentic dialogue, when you're working with something like the script I had on Football Factory. It makes your job so much easier. As much as anything it was a real laugh, I mean, I knew the entire main cast as they're mates from even before working on the film. I know Frank Harper, I have been mates with Danny Dyer since I was about 17, Roland Manookian and I worked before together, it was about five or six years previous, and got on blinding. Calum McNab who played Raff who I actually taught at college in Dartford. So there was a relationship there to. Tony Denham was actually Frank's mate, so we were all pals from going out drinking and for me it was a mix between working and being on a beano most of the time and having a laugh for six weeks. Even a lot of the extras that was in the film, were mates or mates of mates that was involved one way or another. So yeah, it was just like a lads jolly. It was just great."

Again you had some quality people around you, and Frank Harper was one.

Neil- "Frank is a very good mate. He's actually putting together a film called St. Georges Day and he's moving more into the producers' role. You know creating his own work, and what's good about Frank, is he's not in any way underappreciated. He can actually represent and produce things that may be ignored or under appreciated. I mean, there's a lot of plastic cockney characters and frank wants to get a bit under the skin of it, he certainly deserving of international roles and recognition. He wrote that script for St. Georges Day, so the script you know is going to be very accurate."

With the film being a much-liked one with the footy lads, is there a role that you would have liked to play other that Rod?

Neil- "No, I don't think so. I mean I think I had a plumb role; I had a good result getting that role (laughing). Thinking back, I do feel that was the right one for me. I certainly wasn't envious of anyone else's role on the crew, and again I was very happy with that part, it suited me, and Nick knew us all anyway so a lot of that was written with the actors in mind, it was tailor made to some extent."

To give merit to any part of the film that you felt was something special. Your stage, your scene?

Neil- "Yeah, the day we shot the scene in the restaurant with the girl and her parents, and I got all coked-up and then decide to go off and fight at Millwall, that was a special feeling. You do all your years of doing your episodes of The Bill, and things like that, and then knowing that you've got a big show piece in a film that you think this is gonna' be good, and then of course you're excited about. It was a couple of hours before the shoot, and I remember I was feeling as happy as I could be, and Nick asked me if I was nervous, and I said "no, I'm just really happy." Thinking about it now I've been very lucky with all the different things I've worked on since then, as at the time it was the biggest thing I'd done, and it was a real special day, my time to shine if you like. It felt like it was the pinnacle of my career. It had all been worth sticking at it and not going into East Enders or something as a regular routine. Hacking away and then to be given a scene like that makes it all worth it for me. It was a special day."

Favouring a beer with pals over a row with the lads?

Neil- "For me it's very different from my experience as a football lad as I've never been involved in football violence or involved with a group of lads that go for that. I mean, obviously I knew a lot of people growing up, and even now some lads to some extent that are involved in that side of things, but again that was never me. What I think the film does is quite interesting is. It doesn't demonise people to be psychotic, it shows that there are people that like who go out at the weekend to have a drink, have a fight and football can become a means of doing that. Then again, you can go into any pub in any town, and that stuff happens on a Friday or Saturday without the football. I think it was made in a way that wasn't condemnatory or judgmental in either way, nor can anyone sit down and say "oh that was cool." I think it has shown that there is a shallowness and emptiness especially in the older characters, which are still running about involved in that. I also think that it didn't send a message that it was all barrel of laughs or these people are cool. What I think it shows, is a little bit of the venerability in someone's character. I mean if you look at Frank Harper's role in the film, I think it shows something that is sometimes overlooked. That is how the low self-esteem of character and the only way they can feel or express their emotions or status is through violence. I thought it was an interesting look at that subject."

Much of modern filmmaking is geared towards drawing in the audience, it sounds cliché, but now it is simply about filling the seats in the movie theatre, and the box office numbers. If anything can be learned from British cinema, is that real success is measured by the length of time both the actor is remembered and the quality of writing found within a film. I mean, I honestly believe the 'industry' has a habit on cashing in on societies troubles or interests. This being the case, what film would you like to see made if football factory is a reflection on lad's passion across the country?

Neil- "I think with the film I've just directed; my first film. That I guess is what I'd like to see being made. It' about a young man coming apart at the seams, behaving badly and then dealing with certain demon qualities. I think you see it more in television than you do in film, and that is people who are explored in a very two-dimensional way. In any good film, making it should allow the audience to be ambiguous; nothing is simply black and white. Obviously, you need your Batman and whatever, so you can have your goodies and baddies, but when you're looking at your social realism and your groups of people in society I think it's important to show the shades of grey."

Rise of the Footsoldier-

For me, when I read 'Bloggs 19', it seemed as though Darren knew all along, what he was involved in and what would be the price of such an involvement. What was your view of Darren when you were researching the role?

Neil- "Well I knew about the film as I'm very good mates with Ricci who was preparing himself self for the role of Carlton Leach, and obviously to Ricci that involved a lot of physical preparation to bulk right up as Ricci was very thin. Then I got a phone call unexpectedly saying Julian Gilbey wanted to meet Frank Harper and me on the same day at some flat in

Soho and have a chat. He said straight away it's not a massive part but it is important to get it right. So I got on with the research, read Nicholls book; Bloggs 19, and a few other books on the subject, and through a mate of mine outside of the film industry, I managed to talk to a couple of people that actually knew Darren Nicholls and they shared their view of him. It was very different view than that he portrayed in Bloggs 19. In Bloggs 19, Darren portrays himself as a very innocent person caught out in a world he didn't understand, and I don't think that's necessarily true. What I did find interesting, and remembering film truth is very different to reality anyway, is that there is a lot of tough guy, hard man roles in the film. So what I thought would be best in terms of the character and the films interest was to try and diversify from that a little bit so there was a range of characters in the film, and there wouldn't be everyone rolling about throwing their weight about. I played Darren as a mixture of how he portrayed himself in Bloggs 19; as this naive not anyway knowing of the dangers involved, and the person he wanted to be. When I re-read Bloggs 19 just recently for another role, I also read a few others books on the subject, and not to be over critical I found a lot of them very badly written. They, as a rule were very episodic; this happened, then that happened. It was simply one thing happening after another. Now what I found interesting, was the writer; Tony Thompson, gave a lot more social context to what happened and gives a perspective on it, than those that say more in the thick of it and were involved themselves. I don't necessarily agree with the way that Darren Nicholls portrayed himself in that book, but in terms of that piece of writing it is a better, more intelligent book, than a lot of books on the subject.

One thing I learnt through people that actually knew him, was that he was a total piss head. For the scene in the hospital I tried to play a mixture of being a bit pissed and a bit of a melt. I didn't want to play him as though he was a particularly attractive character. I didn't want to give the character the innocence, naivety, and central figure that Darren paints himself to be. I saw him on the periphery of these people and slightly out of place almost as if he couldn't hold his own with that company, and not that he was necessarily an innocent."

Time for some reflection. Do you have any thoughts on the project now it is done and dusted?

Neil- "I'll be honest, I'm not often pleased with the choices I've made with certain things in film, you know, you can look at things after and say I should have thought about this, or done things that way, but when I looked back and saw the finished product I liked the choices and decisions I made. With Nicholls, I think and hope that I did get it right for the film. When, and if you do things as a lead, there's a different pressure that you have to deal with and that can ultimately make you play things differently."

You played the role and put time in. So what could have been missed by someone on the 'character' of Darren Nicholls?

Neil- "What also is a commonly missed point is when the likes of Darren Nicholls grass. It's not because they feel it's a genuine sense of social responsibility or to get violent criminals off the street. They do it to save their own skin. It's simply for selfish self-preservation. What's also worth noting is like a lot of street level villains, Darren was an electrician; married with a kid and often in 'gangster' films. When things are explored a little bit more thoroughly, it is these level that people aren't earning millions of pounds; be it them serving up a bit of puff, or as with some of the people in Rise of the Footsoldier, they was doing work around Tony Tuckers house, so this shows their real criminal involvement. We have this punitive system here where if you're caught dealing drugs, as this was the main business of all the villains in the Essex Boys, you'd get 10 years in the nick and most of the people I know of that have been involved in that level of business are actual grafters. They do a normal job, and to supplement their income or so that they can give their family a holiday every year, and I'm not an apologist for drug dealers, but in many cases its just to earn a little bit extra. I mean, I'm lucky in the respect I could get a phone call tomorrow to do a voice over for an advert that gets me enough to go on a little holiday, But most people in this country haven't got that opportunity. They graft all the time and just about pay their bills, and the reason why people get involved in certain aspects of crime is again to be able to go stay in a hotel with their partner, or take their kids to Butlins once a year and it's that detail that can be easily to be missed. Again, as I've already said, I don't necessarily have a very high opinion of Darren Nicholls, he had a normal family, he had a job and he was involved in that side of things because he wanted the things that wealthier people take for granted."

As an actor, you have played some impressionable roles; can you name some of your favorites?

Neil – "I'd have to say an American project I was involved in called paintball. Just because it was very different; again diversifying on in my acting. Looking back on Football Factory, as it were such a great laugh, your pals, and the whole essence of what being involved with the cast and simply enjoying all that went along with it. The work I did on another British production, Bonded by Blood had a great director in that film who allowed me a lot of room to make decisions and allow me the flexibility to do what I felt was necessary, to make the character work and come across. That's what you want more than anything I think. In general, as an actor, what you want to do is work with good people. People that are good practitioners, be they actors, directors, or whoever is involved in that production. There's nothing worse than feeling like you're just a piece of furniture doing your lines as quick as possible and then fuck off. You want someone that will give you the opportunity to express yourself, and maybe then help you with your choices and nudge you in the right direction. You also want them to be clear what it is they want you to do and you want to work on material that is different. It has a different look, a different feel, and that you learn something from it. so 'Nil by mouth' was a big one for that. Right now I'm working with a fella' from the States called Ben Wheatley, who is a brilliant writer. My thoughts are to do, as many different things as I possibly can, and even if the role is not different, than the project and who you're working also should be. I mean, I'm absolute murder, mate, I love being out and talking to different people. I simply enjoy people's company, chatting with people, telling stories, talking bollocks, and having a laugh. So film sets the perfect place for me really, there's lots of hanging about, there's always different people you're working with, to have a chat with, who have themselves had different experiences, from the make-up girls, to the sparks, to the stunt-men, other actors. I enjoy being around people and I can't be alone for any length of time. So it really is the perfect atmosphere for me, I just love being on a film set."

Being that you have played such diverse roles, do you have any thoughts on what you would like to be involved in long term, maybe continuing in film or TV?

Neil- "Well, I'll be honest, I'd never get myself in a situation where I'm in a regular soap or T.V series, that would be my worst nightmare really. I'd like to do a bit more theater, as I've not done any since 2002, and too long off the stage for any actor. I think for any actor it's good to do theatre once in a while, and to prove you can do two hours in one go. And to be fair, if I'm going to' do telly, than I want to do good stuff that's worth seeing, and not the factory mentality where you're just churning stuff out episode after episode. I want to do as many different roles as I can in film and meet as many different people as I possibly can. That's the whole game really, but as you know, it doesn't always pan out that way, but touch wood it's all going all right at the moment. However, I'm still working on my craft if you like, still maturing as an actor."

Your film: your budget, your actors, and your story.

Neil – "There's a fella' that's offering to do a feature off the back of my short. To write and direct one, but to be honest I haven't got a whole story or film certainly not that I'm convinced that's the right fitting for me to do. I seem to be asking myself that question a lot at the moment. As far as films concerned, in the last year there was a movie that was released called Fish Tank, written by Andrea Arnold. That's one of the best British films I've seen for years."

The international audience and market is looking for a mass product, do you think its more quantity than quality now-a-days?

Neil- "Well it's a business. The films that are made outside of the U.K, be it action or your romantic comedy's are what they are. I mean they serve a purpose. In terms of what I personally like or enjoy as an audience member, I am much more interested in European cinema than the big budget films. If I do go and see a film, I typically go to the British Film Institute on the South Bank. There you get to see more world cinema."

With Home grown films, what allows us, the U.K, to still be respected even though we do not have the budgets or the luxury that the Hollywood scripts get?

Neil- "I'd have to say the ideas and maybe even the writers and also the techies involved. You'll see a lot of Hollywood movies shot in England so that they can use British crews, as some of them are the best trained. Remembering you have to be creative when you don't have big budgets and also be able to produce something that's different and original."

With all you have accomplished and the greats you have worked alongside, what would be a role that would solidify Neil Maskell as both an actor and a person?

Neil- "I don't think there is just one, and most actors would probably give you the same answer. Some ones character isn't just one character in particular, as it goes back to being able to demonstrate ones versatility as an actor. You can only really solidify both yourself as an actor and your standing in the industry by playing a range of roles and by showing you can diversify yourself. It's only across a number of years, and a number of projects that you're given the opportunity to be able to do that, and I don't think one role in particular necessarily is going to have the effect you can hope for only a body or cannon of work is what will do that."

Leo Gregory

"Respect can transcend a man's differences."
- Jason Allday. May 2009.

The name and face is not a stranger to the English youths eyes or ears. Leo has been up against some formidable names and literally in some cases. He has rowed with Geoff Belle, shared the scene with some of the most feared hooligans in the country and in a shared opinion with many, he has been in two major hit films, carrying the style and the weight needed to portray the history and notoriety of the I.C.F.

Leo is one of four brothers. Raised in the great working class of the city we call home. He has the respect and admiration for his single parent mum who raised her youngsters on her own. Likes his football, no, he loves his football. Been behind the 'one's and two's' for a spell, and graced the streets of London with a sway and style that has even earned him an award or two. Like some of the greats within the British Film scene, Leo has made a great mark in the start of his career. Always looking to create an art form within his own field of acting, Leo boasts an energy and aura seen in some of his idols within the British film community. Gary Oldman and Ray Winstone again raise attention here, as like some before and after Leo, have the respect of the 'new bread' of actor coming through the ranks.

For my brothers and me, Leo created both a conversation and a buzz. He was a local lad, football supporter and was bang into his clobber and as a result of me, "West Ham 'til I die", was in two films giving credit to the Iron's supporters, namely the I.C.F.

Now call it coincidence, but Leo has many qualities seen in another other greats coming through the ranks of the homegrown actors. I am thinking if we have Ricci Harnett, Neil Maskell and Leo Gregory gracing the shores of our beloved country, we may have our very own De Niro's and Pacino's in the making! You be the Judge, but speak wisely, as the fella's have the respect of many' that know the 'Apple'.

One such memory was a phone call and a conversation with my brothers, on the film containing a hobbit and some known pals back in London. This was Green Street Hooligans. This was a film on the hooligan element of football, which had governed both the tabloids and conversations for the best part of thirty years, and of course not forgetting his part in Cass. Now for many lads this was nothing new. At face value, this was just an attempt at coining and capturing an element that sells anywhere in the world. I'm talking about violence. This was from a different angle though; this was backed with an American element and a German director. An added twist was that the imported director had some first hand knowledge of hooligans, having family members involved back in her homeland.

A subtle introduction was best suited for Leo Gregory. What question would best suit both this quiet and reserved actor? He has graced the screen with some real heavy weights in the English film industry, and yet he still maintains self-control. Not deviating from his self art form in acting, Leo is on the same lines as some of the greats that have already set a benchmark for the new breed coming through the ranks.

An ancient civilization used a method called 'augury', in which a person would sit in a particular spot and carefully observe everything that was happening there. This was how I interpreted Leo. He was a carefully thought out individual that chose not necessarily his work, as much how he chose the character to be portrayed. For a picture or presentation to be interpreted, Leo would take his acting formula, and play it out well for the desired result.

The first thought I had when given the opportunity to talk with Leo was his known passion and love for football. It would be an easy chat I guessed, only then discovering he was a Tottenham fan! Well, if there is a difference in two teams than it is here. Along with the passion, we both have for football. There is also another similar story, that both Leo and I share that is not a rare one and is a common story amongst many families.

With the absence of a fatherly figure, both Leo and I witnessed the efforts and commitment given by a single parent. For myself, I accepted many life learning, moral testing added responsibilities. This is a part of child hood that should warrant a sound, structured family environment and may be common place in some families, but was not a privilege some of us was granted. If anything, we shared some common ground in terms of background and life experiences. The fact remains that there has always been banter between teams, people of different areas and backgrounds. I personally believe a lad's passion can be seen when he gets to talk with the 'opposition'. Being that Leo was up for the cause and someone who is a fan of football on every level, I was guaranteed a quality conversation from start to finish regardless of the colour of his shirt. So who is Leo Gregory the actor, London chap and football fan?

Leo: "I'm just me, you know. Just a geezer, a little bit of talent, had a bit of luck along the way, ups and downs like anyone else, that's it really, just a regular fella'. I'm not the sort to suck my own knob on that one, just a regular fella."

We all have a varied past and all have a stories to tell. Source material was my excuse for a colour full past and some lessons learned. As a wise ol' mum once told me, "you've got to have some trips and falls, to be able to learn from your mistakes, but if anything we all try to have a laugh along the way." Leo demonstrated in his acting, that he has not always been the lad of the terraces or the rock and rolla. His time as a youth also was spent sending people back and forth. A bit of back and forth if you like, a little bit of up and down. No, I am not talking about anything other than some of his time behind the one's and two's. Of course, I mean the turntables. Leo did a bit of D.J'ing back in his teens. Therefore, what was all that about?

Leo: "When I was a lot younger, I was seeing this bird at the time (Jackie O), she was a lot older than me, we was living together and what not, and we started D.J 'ing. We used to do many clubs about town. At the time I wasn't even old enough to get in the gaffs (chuckles), anyway, we would D.J at various places and do parties, also around town.

Look at any of the film greats, and they have all had a break in their career at sometime. A varied past. Some breathing space if you will. Time spent away, can be thought of as time invested in thinking, cultivating your art and having a laugh. This was much the same story with Leo as he too had a break from his start in acting, returning in his late teens.

Leo: "I guess deep down, without knowing, I always wanted to do it, and I sort of stumbled into it. I was in school and I was no angel. Being in school stopped me doing it, then a certain way of life got me kicked out of school, when I was about 15. This was when I also got into D.J'ing, and when I come to around 18 or 19, I realised that wasn't necessarily the best lifestyle for me, as in a career in your life, so I got back into acting.

It was here that I realised that we're not all put on this planet or destined to have good or easy lives, and as much as it may have or not have helped people around you, and at the end of the day, it's only ever you that's gonna make a life for yourself. It's pretty easy to have a miserable enough time in your life without too much trouble; especially in London. For me it's one thing I've ever done that I've enjoyed. That's important as anything else, and it's also something that you could possibly make a livelihood from. When I first got into acting at 12, I was just a young kid; going to all these crazy places, do a little job here and there, it's all a bit mad really. So, when I did get back into it, I took it a lot more serious. I learned what it was all about. Learning, listening, making a craft from it. I learned when to listen and when to watch, and that's when I really fell in love with acting."

All within this time of 'learning', some have had a real hero within the family. Mine, was much the same as all my brothers and sisters had family members. How they all ever put up with the antics of us as children I will never know, but what all three brothers agreed, we could've never got through or over all the troubles we got into as lads, without their help.

Much like Leo, my brothers and I never had the luxury of a father to play the role. Luckily pals around us and some of our own family always backed the lads of west London whatever the troubles, whatever the aggro', true family always back their own. Our little angels as we were called. Members of our family were without question the backbone of our lives, who was a great influence to Leo growing up?

Leo: "First and foremost it was my mum. I have triplet brothers, shortly after they were born, my old man, 'done one'. My mum had a 5 year-old and 3 new born babies and she was on her own. None of us has done a stretch, and every one of us is working and doing it. Considering the times and what it is like in this day and age, I think she's done well with all of us. She was a single mum, and pulled a blinder. Then there's my granddad as well, god bless him. Obviously, without my old man being around, my granddad got me into football, and all that kind of stuff."

What were the interests you had growing up?

Leo: "Well as a youngster, growing up in the '80's, films played a small role. Your Rocky's, Rambo's, all the '80's films, again like 'Running Man', 'Terminator', much the same as most boys around that time. Then as I got into music, as a nipper I was into certain types of music, but as I got older, house music, hardcore at one stage, but thankfully I grew out of that pretty quickly, a bit of drum and bass. Then of course football played a role, Tottenham, their players at the time, Hoddle, Waddle, Gazza' and Lineker."

In the next part of the conversation, Leo tells me he is the eldest of three younger brothers. Being that Leo has turned out an all right fella, done a bit of this and that and ended up in some pretty good films it only just we ask about the young-uns, any different to big bruv'. Football lad's maybe, possibly another actor in the midst?

Leo: "Well, I'm the eldest and they're good lads, I mean one is a fellow Yid. The other two are Gooners; like mum. It made it all the more fun, growing up in the same house" (laughing).

There has been more than a pretty penny spent on understanding why fans support teams away from their cultural upbringing. For me, growing up in West London, the 'natural' choice should have been Chelsea (Nah, not my style!), Tottenham (no way!) or Arsenal (Not a bad team, but again, not for me!). So like it's been said, you follow your roots. Mine is East London and West Ham is my reason, my team and colours! So with a whisper that Leo had some youth ties to South London, only fair then we ask why the lads from White Hart Lane! How did that come about?

Leo: "Well being young, and not knowing what my knob or football was for that age, it was in fact my granddad was a Tottering fan, so it all started there, really. As you know, once you have your team, that's it."

All movies displays a message, information or a way of live we relate to or understand. With the ever-growing call for action, violence and cultural movies, it was inevitable that football and all that can be seen in terms the package deal would come into our lives. For my brothers and me Leo's name started with Green Street Hooligans, the ever so passionate member of the firm, detailing loyalty and a hard-hitting role. He played a West Ham fan. As funny, as it sounds he is actually a Tottenham fan (with your passion in the west end.). Now, credit where credit is due, Leo played for the other firm with convincing commitment.

Leo: "To be honest, there's two ways of looking at it. On one hand, as an actor, you want to make it as real as possible, and you want to believe everything you're doing as much as possible. So on that hand, you're doing it, you're an actor. I mean if you ever have to play a murderer or a terrorist, it's something you can't afford to do is think 'well, what does Leo think about this', because then you're not playing the character, It's just Leo pretending to be the character. That is not a problem, and when you step back and think about it, all you have to do is look around, and you've got Frodo standing on the other side of the room, that puts you into a certain perspective and you know it's not reality, and you're doing a job. At the end of the day, I've done two West Ham films now, and they paid for my season tickets both times. And I could never get too wound up about it,

I was getting it off, and we had a lot of the I.C.F down on the set, and then on Cass we're at it, obviously there's a bit of banter there, but I'm still getting my season ticket paid for."

Ultimately, Leo's point is not to place absolute trust in one particular role or model, whether it is a rational or relevant, here or there, but in staying in tune with his principle belief in his acting style. This is not an influence from pals, family or even other actors, but instead something that he has found along the way. As we all know, it is all too easy for an actor to fall into the trap of 'my agent feels...' or 'I think this same role again is where I'm best suited', Leo has remained true to his thoughts and feelings on his chosen gamble. His career in acting is one that can dictate not only if and when there's work but also can all too often an actor can be 'set' in his style of work and perception if he simply follows the pound note.

I am sure since the finishing of Green Street Leo has had plenty of time to reflect on the film and the part he played in it. The laughs he had on set and in production, but what, if anything, would he, as a lad of London, and having insight in the world that surrounds football hooligans, would he change in terms of the content in Green Street?

Leo; "Well, if it was my film, there would be a few things I would have changed. If I wrote it, if I was directing it if I was staring in it, obviously I would make a different film. I mean, I'm an actor, and when I'm offered a job I take that role, it's then my job to take those words of that particular piece of paper that are relevant to you and make them into something real. So that's what you do as an actor, but if it was my film it wouldn't be about 'b' West Ham, 'b' it wouldn't have an American fella coming over and I mean I could go C, D, E. I could go through the whole alphabet but at the same time, it was an American film and the film was out of L.A.

Duggie Brimson was one of the writers, the producers were based out of L.A, Elijah was based out L.A, the geezer with the dodgy accent was based out of L.A, so it was an American film and all the deals were done in dollars, blah, blah. So again, on one hand if it was my film, it would be completely different, on the other hand, you've got to say, for what was primarily an American film, they didn't do a bad job considering they're sitting in the sunshine in Melrose place. It was one of them ones, you know; we knew what it was about. We grew up knowing what the world of football smells like, tastes like so for them to be sitting over there, they did a half an all right job."

How many times have you heard an actor, producer or writer say after the release of their efforts, say 'What I think I'd like to have done'. What would our friendly London lad of the big screen have to say in terms of what if. Would Leo have had anything taken out or added?

Leo: "Well again, they did a good job. I'm not going to say it was all bad. But if I were going to change anything, it wouldn't be what some would consider obvious changes. A small cast change, maybe here and there. But you know, hindsight is a wonderful thing, with hindsight, I would've picked last weeks' lottery numbers, you know."

With other films and experience under your belt, what did Leo get in terms of experience from working on Green Street that was new or different to the other roles he had played?

Leo: "Well, it was a laugh, I had some pals on it, it's a world I know a lot better than say some other worlds or films I've been involved in, so that was all nice. At the end of the day, it was another film. Cass was a similar thing. Films are similar in as much as there's a bunch of actors, a crew, and whoever else. Half may be some you've never met before, if you're lucky there's a few you've met before, and you're all in this weird little family, and however long it is, maybe 3 or 4 months, and then you're off to the next one. It was more banter I suppose than a period drama, with a bunch of 'Tarquin's' but then that's because you're all similar lads, equally good times has been had on other films and what not."

It has been suggested that banter and all that goes along with it can be perceived by the place you are from or the team you support. This could not be truer with West Ham and Tottenham. Leo, can discriminate his job as an actor with what and where his loyalty is. So, with the history of all London clubs, I was curious if his 'team' had any more or less to say to their fellow terrace star. With Cass, West Ham, being carried on Leo's shoulders once again, was this a burden for the White Hart lane follower?

Leo: "A bit, you know. Even when you get West Ham up this end, you get the 'Oi, Oi'. 'Who do you want to win?' and a bit of the other, but it is all fun and banter from the boys. I never get any real aggro' or unnecessary trouble. It's always a bit of friendly banter, some of my lot call me I.C.F, which is quite funny, as when I've been on other films, I've shouted out 'YID' on set. At the end of the day, they know where I stand and where my loyalties are, so there are no worries there."

Stepping into other roles, on other films, productions and the like, has this given you any indication of what type of work/ roles you enjoy more (in terms of type of film etc.)? This was a question I am sure a lot of actors are asked. Leo, calm and collective, not basking in the glory of his success as an actor, gave a measured and controlled response, showing he is of mature standing and has accepted the role of a seasoned young actor.

Leo: "Yeah, I suppose. The ones that I like are the interesting ones. You get some films that just want you to turn up, smile look pretty and say the words. That really isn't 'my cup of tea'. Whether they're the good boy, the bad boy, whatever the role, if they're an interesting character, then it's going to' be fun and ultimately a more interesting performance."

Leo has played his roles very well (he again is a passionate Tottenham lad, played West Ham pretty well I might add!). Did he immerse himself in his characters too much, or any more or less depending on the role/ job in hand? Some actors, in their early years of success, are easily drawn into the ego that is easily inflated from playing a role that allows them early popularity. I'm hoping that our Lad from the smoke isn't being drawn into the ways of the dark side, although there is a lot to be said for the actor that researches his or her role. The complexity and essence is often needed when trying to capture and convince the audience.

Leo: "To be honest, yeah, I do and I have done, but increasingly people don't want to let you do that. The days of Martin Scorsese and Robert De Niro sitting down and going 'bosh', I mean I'm not a drama school graduate or similar, I do what I have to do, to get into a character, or feel like the character, or be a character."

For many of us mere street folk, there is maybe a chance of being in the presence of some of the greats, some from the telly, maybe a local hero. Young Leo has had the opportunity to work with some real heavy weights, Geoff Belle being one. What was it like working with some greats?

Leo: "Yeah, Geoff's a good man. We've done Green Street, Daylight Robbery. He's good stuff, Geoff. I've worked with some strong actors. James Franco, Paddy Considine, David Morrissey, Ben Wishaw. They're all strong actors."

I will keep it simple. Leo showed composure and maturity in his response. Acknowledging the greats before him, Leo shows his contrast as both a great actor and his respect for those before him. Stepping back into the football hooligan role... (-Cass) was this anymore aggro from his pals back at White Hart Lane? What was nice to see, is that Leo had not sat back in the 'been there, done that before' seat of contentment. Playing a key role, he gave a performance that again carried the weight needed for a character needed in a timepiece. But in a world of pals and on the terrace, what was being said?

Leo: "Yeah, same again. For me it's a way to pay for my season ticket. I get a bit here and there, week in week out. But there's never any question of where my loyalties lie. Where I stand at the ground, with a few chaps, and it's not like West Ham are waving at me from the family enclosure end. I stand where I stand. Everyone knows where I am, again it's at most a friendly bit of banter, but I've been there that long, everyone knows. If there's someone new or never seen me there before, I might get a bit of friendly 'aren't you...?', but I also think everyone around me must get a bit bored with it all now, you know what I mean!"

What was different from the two movies that held conversations and memories with my brothers and me (Cass and Green Street)? OK, I can hear them now. Yes, Mr. 'enough hooligan movies, please stop' is back. I was down the battle cruiser the other night and I was wearing my chosen, and best team and firm in the land football shirt, when a little fella (I say this because of the size of his brain, what could be obviously measured by the level of intelligence and the words that came out of his mouth), said to me that one hooligan movie was more than enough! Well, this is not the first time I have had a 'chat' with some one of this 'intelligence'. Here's a thought, to ignore one level of society or act in a way to show no understanding, is surely a form of ignorance. If you are to simply dismiss actions as though they don't exist, with no thought as to why, or even go as far as to simply give a simple negative quotation, than you are as ignorant as the world you live in. He left scratching his baldhead with his hairy palm. Wanker!

Leo: "Well, for me Cass was a man's life story, he was on set, it was a more intelligent film, it was trying to be a real film, as opposed to Green Street. Green Street was a bit more contrived, a geezer coming from Harvard, and all that. That's a Hollywood story. For me, Cass was about a geezer, who grew up in London, did what he did, and there's his story bosh! More real, a lot more personal, he's reliving his memories, we stood in the same room, there's a lot more respect involved, and I think it was ultimately a more intelligent film."

Fashion... the clothes we all love. It was said it one publication, that us lads spend a third of our salary on our gear. It is a shame the hard earned money spent on the mentioned merchandise (most of the time) does not last as long as the memory of owning the gear. Equally, a key figure in both... both a West Ham element, again, great to wear the clobber that is part of the 'parcel'.

Leo: "It was nice to see the old Diadora Gold, you Gazelles, your Lois cords, Tacchini and all that. Your Lyle and Scotts and a few other bits are still on your terraces."

He played the roles well. He has done a bit before and a bit after. If Leo was to be offered another hooligan role... what would he do different?

Leo: "To be honest, I don't think I'd do another one. It would have to be something more. It would have to prove to me it wants to be better than a firm. I've done two now. Obviously, there was a connection from Green Street to Cass. I'm not here to name any other actors, but I don't want to be like a rent a cop."

Being that Leo has shown he is artistically ready for many a role, I would like to see this young fella grace the screens in some more pieces that would also hold merit and he could have any budget what movie theme, would he like to produce or write?

Leo: "That's hard to say, I mean there's so many good stories out there. If you talk about a film that would mean something to me, in my eyes, it couldn't be touched any way, I'm talking about films like Nil by Mouth. You could take something like that, but then know one could touch that. A film that means something as opposed to some lovely tits and a few explosions, a couple of fast cars, a sunset you know, a film that means something to people. I'd like to be involved in a lot of films, that's what an actor is all about. Obviously you want to be involved in an ionic film, but again being involved in a film that means something is the bottom line."

There is a lot to be said about being typecast. Leo has played two great roles in the named films. The pro of being typecast of course you are known for that specific 'role'. Having the experience could prove a success in terms of guaranteed work, but the flipside to this situation of course, is that is all you are associated with, and so a question is born. If Leo was to be typecast for a role, what would it be, action, footy or thriller?

Leo: "I would never want that to be honest. I'd never want to be typecast. I've done a lot of different types of work, period, middle class roles, vampires and the like. I've done all sorts. I'm known for doing Cass and

Green Street, and they have their audience and quite rightly so. I'd never want to be the gangster, or the action hero or the football hooligan".

When in the midst of social change, we sometimes lose our sights and perspective of what was once a clear and unchallenged goal. We (the English) have lost some greats to the depths of the ever growing and ever so hard to resist mainstream audience. What was once a cult figure has now become a 'celebrity'. Noticing such an edge with Leo's on screen acting, where did our terrace lad like to think he would be in 10 years. Highlighting the U.K scene or Hollywood action?

Leo: "It all depends where the work is, you know. If it works out the best films at the time are coming out if the U.K, then that's brilliant. If they're coming out of the States, OK, you know. I really want to start making some interesting films".

Closing the conversation with Leo was one as I did with Jason Mariner. It was like a couple of regular lads. We had chatted about a bit of footy, a few birds that might have caught or mince pies, and how the week ahead looked. Leo has no delusions of self-grandeur nor was there a self-made pedal stool or platform for himself as a person or as an actor. Life is enough with the contradictory bollocks it throws your way daily. Often these hurdles are made into ammunition for a laugh with pals, and dismissed as just more countless rounds within a persons' life.

Call me philosophical, but I thought about the grace and style Leo shows in not only his acting, but also when we had our chat. If I was asked of my interpretation of Leo as a person, it would be simple. I took what Leo said as to realise an actor's potential, you have to simply be yourself and learn from all those around you, good or bad. To realise an actor's true limits is only set by your own standard of limitations and lack of vision. In addition, risk, scary and a terrifying word for some, but if used as a motivation and not as a barrier, you will be in a better place as not only a person but also in your everyday life.

Women

Human nature and the way we act are two things we often speak of yet truly have no way to illustrate. Each time one of us has a row, falls in love, grumbles about the every changing society we live in, we are basically, operating as a human with our own individual identity.

When we see a cat chasing a mouse or a dog chasing a car, we all have a laugh. The dog gains nothing other than a mouth full of dust and an agenda to simply chase another car, and with as much eagerness and sport, we demand for the cat to catch and claim its prize. With the dog, the question remains then of what purpose was there in chasing the car to begin with? Does the dog have any real interest in the car? Probably not, just that there was fun in the 'chase' or maybe just to confirm his vitality. With the cat, more often than not, the instinct played the role in the catch and later the prize to be displayed for all to see.

Who is better than us lads to exemplify this 'nature' and 'way'! The dogs that we are have been chasing women for centuries. With reference to cats, we all have had dreams and goals at some stage of a trophy piece for our pals to see.

Our perception of the opposite sex has changed considerably too. What was accepted as a low key, gritty behind the sink role and routine, has made way for more of a leading role. Clearly seen in politics, the extra earner in a household, and many a man's lust and dream, a girl getting all down and dirty in film and TV (Angelina Jolie couldn't look any better when she's in action).

Tracey Elvik- Rice

Why? Why not!

Cor blimey! Look at those numbers, are those real? Page 3, all looked at 'em, and loved most of them. The routine was an easy one, back page sports and the telly pages for what is on tonight. Then of course page three! If there was some extra time, maybe we would read the other rubbish enclosed. Typically, all doom and gloom, so we will flick back to our lovely ladies on page 3, and look at those pair of lovely's! Offering more than the daily 'news', the papers would give you an insight of the beautiful girls found within the shores of England. Much a tradition, the page 3 girls were with me when I got on the underground, to when I returned home that night. Sometimes I would have a pop at the cross word, but I can only assume the fella's that made those bloody things all too often forgot that I'd left my crayons at home. So, the fixture for the lads of London would be to marvel at our future wives. Well, that is how we would see it.

The start of the all topless deal was started in 1970, when it's reported that as a result of the top less acts, the newspapers, that did the right and honorable thing and allow such a bevy of loosely clad girls bare all for us lads across the country, gained almost double in sales of the daily rag. There is certain criticism associated with the institution that is 'Page 3', in that the Page 3 girls were considered to be demeaning to the female race. Well, the naked girls' is nothing new and two simple facts come to mind when I hear such objection. If we did not have an interest in the opposite sex, then where the bloody hell would we be, as two million years ago, we'd be rubbing up against a tree! There is not much chance for the human race there, Sherlock! Secondly, there have been artifacts dug up in mainland Europe dating back at least 35,000 years of naked figurines! All I can say is thank god for women!

A picture speaks a thousand words. Many of those pictures would numb you into submission and the beauty found within this daily publication allowed us to see hordes of distinctive 'girls next-door types' (I think I need to move then!) to marvel over. No amount of story or technical mumbo-jumbo surrounding these goddesses would alter your gaze or wish. You simply had to commit to opening the page and there they were, all for you. No extra charge, your very own Page 3 stunner and our very own Tracey, can certainly bring truth to that.

Many people I speak with on a regular basis gave praise to the idea behind the book in memory of my brother and several asked if amongst the lessons from all those that contributed, if any were going to be of the female variety? A couple of the lads that actually contributed mentioned a chapter 'for the lads' and one that Junior would have marveled at and said it would be a good idea. A few phone calls and a few suggestions were given for a couple of suitable options. General opinion was obviously playing a role in this chapter, so a bit of thought was needed in terms of who best would fit the bill. Numbers do not lie, so if anything was to be gained from that comment alone, then why not go with someone that's been at the forefront of beauty and splendor scene. The biggest selling tabloid in the U.K is of course the Sun. Page 3 is without question the largest viewed topless bunch of girls seen over the years of all the daily rags. One such lady that has all that would be welcomed by anyone to see (OI OI!) was more than happy to take part (and off) for the lads. Without question there is a lesson that I gained from my time spent talking to Tracey, and only fair that it be shared. A little meet just outside of West London was set up. A great deal of phone calls were also invested from Tracey to me, and I know what was 'shown' is something that along with my late brother is there for all football loving, god fearing and casual clobber-wearing lads to enjoy.

Tracey Elvik

I fell into Page 3 almost by accident.

It was my ex boyfriend who first showed me the paper and suggested that I'd make a good P3 model... I said he was off his head and thought nothing of it. The first time in my life that I'd ever even seen The Sun newspaper was when I met him in July of 1985. Sheltered life you see.

For my Christmas present in '85 he got me a photo session in London with a mate of his who is a photographer called Nick Daley. The crazy thing is that I was so naïve that when we drove down from our hometown of Warrington in Cheshire, I was sure that all was involved was a few beauty snaps and wasn't even phased by the lingerie shots I was to do, as most normal girls would be. I was never what you would term as a 'normal' girl, all I knew is that I hated work, hated being bossed around and had a real problem with authority: so I had to try something different and modeling seemed a way out.

We arrived in Farringdon on a rainy cold January evening, and Jan and I made our way up rickety stairs to a rather fabulously seedy loft studio. I like a typical wide eyed Northerner and thought it all terribly glamorous.

My face was painted, my short hair slicked back and the session began. It was surprisingly easy and like everything in my life, I just threw myself into it. I did the usual shots of head, lingerie, dress and swimwear. I remember them going nuts about my body and thinking, "Wow, are these cool artistic people talking about me?" I was always such a dreamer and just did things without questioning unless they were completely against my moral character.

On the last shot that the photographer dropped in the photographer said, "Tracey, turn your swim suit the other way round. The shot would be so much better topless." I nearly died on the spot and looked at Jan for support. The makeup artist pulled me to the side of the studio and said, "Honestly love, it's nothing seedy. You'd make a great Glamour Model. You've got the face of a Vogue girl but you just haven't got the height." "What's a glamour model?" I asked. I wanted to be on Vogue for god's sake. I was getting a bit upset from what I remember, so Ian the photographer gently led me to a table and set out a load of Model Agency books and together we scanned through them.

These books were amazing to me, and were full of glamorous and artistic pictures of beautiful girls in various states of dress and not one of them was doing anything rude! It opened my eyes in an instant. There was no cajoling in it. The whole crew was brilliant, taking an interest in showing me how NOT seedy the industry was and telling me it was my call. It literally took me ten minutes to make my decision. The swimsuit was turned backwards and I was thrusting my boobs out with pride. I took my first glamour shot dreaming of making it big in this exciting new industry, a surreal experience to say the least and was another instance of me taking life well and truly by the balls. Fuck the consequences and I just had to go for it.

My first Page 3 picture appeared in The Mirror of all papers, back in the day when they had a Page 3, but the girls only showed cleavage. I sent my pictures to Robert Maxwell himself and soon received the call to come to London. So off I trotted on the 5.55am, Warrington to London, National Express and ended up appearing on Grand National day of '86 in full racing regalia.

Beverley Goodway was the next photographer to show interest in me and called me to test for The Sun. It was all moving so fast and I did the shoot, and the following week I appeared as a Page 3 girl for real and stayed there for a total of 10 years. I am still one of the longest running Page 3 girls in its 30-year history.

It was that simple. The rest was just kind of history I guess. Things tended to fall into my lap. In fact, they still do – my mates used to call me Golden Bollocks and that was before Beckham!

I was with Samantha Bond Management for my entire career. I absolutely loved her and still do. I gave her so many headaches over the years, especially in the first three. On one hand I got every casting, I ever went to and on the other hand, I was a total flake and ruled by a nasty controlling boyfriend who called himself my manager. Poor Sam was always trying to advise me against letting Jan call in at 6pm to see what jobs I had or trying to negotiate my rates when the person had no clue what he was talking about. He was the typical Svengali type and the kind of person that latches onto a naïve girl and takes over, tells her what to wear, what to say and doesn't let her out etc. I was so controlled. I lived a double life back then, the hideous home life of meanness and fights, and the glamorous London life where I was free and ran around the East of London with my portfolio feeling ever so grown up. I was only 17-20 but fame came quickly and I did harden up quite fast at least in my career, if not at home. I'd advise girls never to involve their boyfriends in their modeling career. It's just not their place... it's your job, end of. Would they have you in their meetings? No, man up if you're in this position. I did eventually to the relief of my family, mates and agent.

My fame went from strength to strength. I became a calendar girl, doing at least 10 trips to far off places a year. I did shoots for the likes of Lambs Navy Rum, Mintex, GKN chep, Forodo, Hausen Algraphy, Marlboro, to name but a few and became Warrington's own 'Vladivar Vodka' girl. 'Fiona Vladivar super spy', and was shot wearing a million quid's worth of Cartier Jewelry at Harrods at the launch of Vladivar 'Gold." My head was spinning and after the first year, I was signed off for three months with exhaustion.

By 1989, my relationship with Jan was well and truly over and one night I was out with a model mate of mine, Donna Fletcher at Strings, when this Sauvé guy sauntered up to me, asked me to dance and I left Jan for him shortly after. The roar of Press coverage and my first centre page 'kiss and tell' spread was sold by my ex. Jan and he told the press that I was a sex maniac who did it everywhere and loved outdoor games! Well who doesn't? My life started with Phil, the father of my son. We split five tumultuous years later but the wonderful Cameron was born. As they say, every cloud has a silver lining.

Meeting Phil, Cameron's dad changed my career for the best. I moved to London and became one of the beautiful people I suppose. I was going out clubbing to places like Browns, which was 'THE' place to be back in the day and this was patronized by the likes of George Michael and Prince and everyone who was anyone. I was also invited to celebrity parties and film premiers. I was 'papped' coming out of every club I went to and always managed to give a huge grin no matter how leathered I was. Getting in and out of cars was always a problem, as I am a trained dancer so you would think I'd be very graceful. However, I tended to fall out of cars like a right lump through fear of showing myself up. The pictures that appeared in the 'People' sections were often priceless but all fun and I managed to keep my bits covered in most cases!

I was on the Mintex calendar shoot with Byron Newman one year in Portugal. Trips (that's what we called them) were always a riot. You bonded quickly while thrown together in a villa with a crew of 10 strangers when there's so much naked flesh around. To make sure the girls didn't have tan lines you tend to sunbathe naked. One boozy night after dinner we'd all drunk a little too much and were lounging around the living area, I was sitting at the knee of the stylist at the time. During dinner, we'd all had a game of truth or dare, like you do. The stylist was asked whether she'd ever slept with a woman and admitted it to huge applause. So back to the living room: I was sitting at her knee on the floor and I could see Byron the photographer glaring at her. Everyone was chatting and having a laugh so I ignored it. Bryon's glare got more urgent and on turning around, I saw our stylist with her knickers pulled to the side playing with herself while twiddling my hair! She was pissed out of her head. At bedtime, she asked me to join her for 'a little fun'…

Kiss and tells are always something to be wary of if you want to be in the Glamour Industry and I've had two and they were corkers.

The second one was by a disgruntled boyfriend who sold a story to The People for a reportedly HUGE sum of money. The headline read: Page Three Tracey Elvik in four in the bed Cocaine fuelled lesbian romp! That Christmas I had to go to a family party. You can imagine how I felt while walking into the room full of the posh and very conservative Hambleton's. Mum just said, "Hold your head up dear." It was excruciatingly embarrassing, but 'if you can't take the time, don't do the crime!' as they say.

Most photographers are good people in general – not what you'd expect at all. They are professional and really don't see boobs or bums as anything other than appendages at the front and back of their work colleagues, appendages that need to be perky and well lit – but just appendages. Hard to imagine, but it's true. Practically every snapper I ever worked with was a gentleman through and through. Mel Grundy, Byron Newman, Chris Thompson, Harry Ormesher and Beverley Goodway to just scratch the surface, all top glamour photographers' and not a one of them ever said anything inappropriate or sleazy to me.

There was one who I didn't really see eye to eye with though. Although by the end of my career, we became fairly good mates and because of this I'll omit his name. Let's just call him G. G was a scream. I'd go to his studio in Back St, Farringdon every few weeks to shoot for The Star and he had this really brash way of dealing with his girl's. He was constantly screaming and bitching at us. No one was left out. He had no favorites. He took no shit and spent a lot of time slagging us off and brow beating us into ditching boyfriend's by saying that, "all men will shag around," and "he's only trying to hold you back".... Yes – I know! He actually had a point, but his delivery was so misogynistic he drove me NUT'S every time I worked with him. I would leave feeling totally bullied and jaded.

He booked me with a huge group of other top-flight Glamour models of the day, Gaynor Goodman, Helen Labdon, Sarah Hollet etc. to go to Cabo San Lucas, Mexico for three weeks of shooting 'stock' shots. We knew it would be hard work as stock shooting is relentless. A million shots a day in a thousand changes and G would squeeze every ounce of blood out of us to get his money's worth and be a total bastard to boot.

He lived up to his word and was his usual bullish self, interspersed with moments of inspired photography and a great laugh. He'd been having a go at one of the other model's all day and getting right up my nose as I hate to see timid people picked on so I called him a knob. He lost it and gave me a telling off, calmed down then sloped off to sort out the next shot. A little later, he walked down the beach towards me, growled, "Your next!", and threw a pair of water skis towards my feet. "I'm not going in there G, there's a fucking anti-cyclone going on!" I retorted.

All that day the swell of the sea was so huge, we'd all been battered and bruised doing shots crouching and kneeling in the surf. "You'll do it or you don't get paid," he shouted over his shoulder climbing into a tiny speedboat just off shore. I marched up to the boat and a row ensued with lots of threats of non-payment of fee etc. and he finally agreed, after my suggestion, that he would water ski first to show me that I'm being a wimp, and if he faired ok then I'd do it.

I climbed into the boat and we pulled him up and headed out to sea. The swell was so bad that he couldn't keep his skis together as one was at the top of a humungous wave while the other was in a trough. I was cracking up as he fought to stay up and not take a nosedive. By this time I'd told the boat driver what the score was plus he'd witnessed the ruck we just had so after a few wide circles of G struggling and wobbling the driver grinned and said, "Watch this." Pulling the wheel hard down he swung the boat into a sharp turn and G went flying into the ocean spluttering and swearing. It was priceless. We pulled him into the boat. The funny thing was – he'd been dropped into a shoal of tiny little jellyfish and his arm was covered in them and he was howling in pain! I nearly pissed myself.

I had to honour my side of the bargain and proceeded to have a cool ride, looking glam with some fabulous shots taken and didn't even get wet as I skied to the shore once I'd finished. I stood there with my hands on my hips and he hopped off the boat and came towards me smarmily saying, "See? That wasn't so bad was it?" I told him to fuck off slapped his face, and stormed off the beach. The other girls were gob-smacked. What no one had realised was it was the hardest ski I'd ever had and it nearly killed me trying to stay on, look good and fuck him off at the same time. Although I covered it up well, I was bloody furious and kind of in shock by the time, I'd finished. I thought I'd die out there.

In 1992, I was arrested for taking part in 5 Million pounds worth of Mortgage Fraud... The Sun and all the other papers covered the sensational story with relish. I became anathema and the papers wouldn't use me in case I was a future felon. My career ground to a halt while the papers that I thought loved me tore me to shreds. 18 months later after a court case at Isleworth Crown Court, 12 jury members acquitted me on 4 counts of 'gaining monies by deception'. My full gallery of supporters went wild. An ex-boyfriend witnessed for the prosecution against me, hand-writing experts had proved my part in this drama – I was going down for a minimum of 9 years and had my bag packed. After two weeks of examination and cross-examination, I was cleared of all counts and at the words 'not guilty', I fainted.

The Sun called me up immediately to shoot for them. I said, "No thank you. I'm hanging up my G- String!"

I carried on modeling for a further 4 years, working in TV and bringing up baby. Appearing in papers topless and doing my calendars. Pictures of me still appear on random calendar's today, which is odd. It's all like a dream to me now, and I miss it a little. But when I look back, I look back with pride and not an inch of regret. My son's nearly 17, a real gentleman and an aspiring DJ with a lot of talent and I know live in Cairo; Egypt with my wonderful husband Will Righton. I've also returned to my first love of writing. I now write Ancient British Tribal History and am soon to be published. For a ditzy northerner I did well.

My career spanned for 10 years in total, I partied with Film stars, TV personalities, boxers, pop stars, and gangsters. I shot for Playboy, Lui

Magazine and even did the Diet coke advert. My career was immense and I feel blessed. I'd lived the high life – and then some. But in 96' I gave up modeling for good. With a career in pictures to look back on and a thousand memories and stories to 'NOT' tell my grandkids, I definitely feel it was a job well done.

The moral of my story is don't let lovers take control. Stay clear of drugs. Work hard. Keep your head down. Don't do anything you will later regret (you're mum will see it!), and always, always have fun. Tracey Elvik. xxxxx

Photographer-Byron Newman

Photographer-Mike Crawley

Photographer-Mike Crawley

Photographer-Mike Crawley

Photographer-Mike Crawley

Photographer-Mike Crawley

Stand tall and stand strong.

Phil Dalby

O nce in a while a person will come along that has a genuine life story that you can relate to. When one of the older lads at West Ham heard of my brothers passing, he told me of his own struggles and fights. Phil's life holds an uncanny resemblance to my late brother. I have often wondered what Junior would have been like and how he would have faired in life, if his own life, had it not been cut short. Phil is someone that was exposed to the same cruelty and harshness that society can unfairly deal to a young lad. The only difference between Junior and Phil of course, is that Phil succeeded. He fought the same demons and learned how to take down the obstacles that not only questioned his right to a happy childhood but ensure the same bullies would think twice before picking their next victim.

With the right people around you, most situations can be dealt with. Those very same situations tested Phil and many more like him regularly. Not once, did the education or experience Phil receive growing up in and around East London ever let him down. Like it's been said, certain people carry a code that can't be bartered or bought. Never a truer word said than with Phil. If you get that middle-classed tweed jacket Saturday afternoon shopping done by your lesser croquet player feeling, and you honestly believe you are in a position to question the violence that some feel is not a way of everyday life. I'd ask you to put down your prawn sandwich, try and not spill your Perrier water and ask you, 'Sir, is it more of a crime to do nothing when the same violence is questioning your well being or those you care for?' The same violence can be morally unsparing. Until certain political figures accept there is a broken Britain that is untouched by promises and pennies, the likes of Phil and a fair few of the older and wiser lads will always hold more weight and merit in young men's lives like my own.

The illusionary world that initially offered me comfort was nothing more than a mass media of confused individuals that were only too willing in giving criticism to my mass of pain. It is more of an excuse than reason reprise, certainly none of these 'professionals' were anyone I could relate to. To give material gifts is easy, it means nothing and that in fact comes from monetary privilege, but to give of ourselves is truly unselfish. I needed answers and reasoning for the death of my baby brother. Phil had lived, experienced and found a path of survival that Junior never did. With all the time and effort, every one gave in this book those personally invested life experiences, brought an understanding and rationalism to the much-needed closure to my personal ordeal.

Over several months, Phil shared his opinion and view on the reasons he faced and dealt with bullies, both in and out of uniform. The same bullies that my brother was more than willing to and did stand up to. There is not a year or a month that went by where Junior was not standing up to or against certain authoritative figures and as a result he received equally as many arrests and injuries. This did not make Junior, Phil, I or even anyone else I know anti-authority, it simply meant we all knew the difference between right and wrong.

Phil Dalby

I was born on the 9th of November 1959 on a British army base. The location was Berengaria in Polymedia, Cyprus. I was named Phil Dalby and was son of Sgt. Douglas John Dalby who was a Sapper in the Royal Engineers with 22 years full service. My Mother is Evangelia Dalby, a Greek lady who was born on the island of Samos. This was about the same time as when the Germans launched the invasion of Greece and it's Islands during the war, a time when the kids were barefooted and starving. I remember hearing how the German troops would throw bread out in the square and the children would scramble to get the bread, only to be in the sights of the German rifles, which would shoot indiscriminately at the kids as they tried to collect the bread from the dusty floors that were tainted with blood. My mum received three bullet wounds. One through her neck and two through her legs, she survived but many never! After recovering from this cowardly attack, she eventually got the strength and the courage at the age of six to stow away on a ship with her brother Dimitri, which was guarded by the German troops and both headed to Athens to earn money to send back to her mother and their three brothers and two sisters. They lived in a room no bigger than 5ft by 5ft and had a curtain separating the room where they had one single mattress between them. Together they would go onto the streets of Athens and polish people's shoes. This is where she met my father years later while he was on duty in Athens. She gave birth to five sons and I was the fourth to be born.

My story begins here in England. My first memory was being flown from Akrotiri air force base in Cypress to Reading on a rickety R.A.F jet and landing at Reading air force base. The cold was the first memory I had. My mum was fed up of being dragged around army bases with 4 sons in tow. My youngest brother Paul was born soon after we moved into The Reading Barracks. She decided to move us all into my Aunt Chrisa's house in Mawney rd.; Romford while my dad served the rest of his time with the Army. We never stayed at my aunts long as my mum was offered a council house in Cranham. She just wanted a home to call her own, not that it was ever going to be her own. We were just another family of misfits that will fill the groggy battle ship grey terraced housing estate, which was filled from the over spill of east London. These brand new council estate homes were to be the start of a new life for me, and many others.

I was 6 years old when we moved to Roseberry Gardens, the same age that my mum was gunned down by the German Troops. This estate was not even a square mile big, but was to be the start of many stories and characters of which West ham was the combined making of many kids and new friends my age. Little did I know that these new friends I were about to meet would be my friends for life, even though I got off to a bad start of being teased and bullied because my mum was Greek and I had her dark looks, I soon overcome this by fighting back.

My first week on this Estate was a nightmare. I would wander off by myself and get abuse thrown at me because of my dark tan colour. This continued throughout my growing up on the estate, even some of the elderly people would taunt me, but I chose to ignore them they were old and narrow-minded. I soon learned how to fight and in my first few days of walking round the back alleys of Roseberry, I had my first fight with the neighbour across the road to me, his name was Phil also and he was a twin. I punched Phil so hard I broke his nose and blood just spurted from it. He ran in to his mum crying. Directly after this fight I noticed a blonde lad smiling at me who watched it all. He had piercing blue eyes. I said to him "What are you smiling for?" His reply was "It's about time someone done that to him!" He continued, "You're the new kid across the street yea?" I said, "Yes!" He introduced himself as Paul. At this point, a tall lad came out of a back gate from about eight houses down and walked toward me asking what's going on, so Paul told him. He said "Hi, I'm Tel and I live just up the road." Paul Tyler and Terry Marley were the start of my new friendships in this town that I'd already began to loath. Roseberry gardens were full of mostly poor families and this road was the start of many stories and the making of Roseberry gardens and Cranham boys.

We all went school together but never fitted in. We were caned and physically punched by some teachers and it was here we said enough was enough. We rebelled by hitting teachers back and one day I was dragged by my hair and punched by Mr. Metcalf in front of all the class. I was maybe 11 or 12. I punched him back and then ran out of school to my mates house Nicky Groat, who lived across the road and waited for him to come home. When he did, I told him to get his telescopic .22 rifle out at which point I returned to the school, and opened fire taking out every window and light bulb. The boys joined in but the next day we were arrested. Our parents had to pay for all the damage and I felt gutted because my mum never had much money back then. As a result of this, we met all the other misfits of Cranham who loved what we done and wanted to befriend us because we were willing to fight back. Ray Searl, Ray Evans, Ginger Ralf, Steve El, Chimp, Froggit, Squidley Didley, Jon Mathews, even the twins Phil and Stuart Ridley, Gary King, Mart Troy, Mickey

Martin, Billy Williams, Tony Green, Phil Thomas, Neil Amos and the list goes on. The firm was growing in numbers and strength. We graffitied the school with West Ham and on school open evenings, we would go to the school and let the teachers tires down. This is how much we hated the system. The 'army style' order in school, the rules, standing in lines, being screamed and shouted at might be ok for some kids, but not for the council estate kids. Our mind set was very much different. Our kind of fun was to get 2 scrappy motors and put them in 'Lingies field'. Terry at one end of the field revving the engine, Paul Tiggy at the other end in the other car and sit as many of us we can on each roof and head down at full speed-a-head and see who can stay on the roof the longest. It was our way of an initiation and was a great way to toughen us up, even though it hurt sometimes.

Our first encounter with the Hornchurch lads was when we were about thirteen. We were all at Upminster station heading to Upton Park, and we could hear the noise and the abuse being given out by some of them. As they came down the stairs, you could see a sea of boots and braces, Ben Sherman shirts and the close-cropped hair. Then all of a sudden, the attention focused on us as if we had something they wanted. That something was our West Ham scarf's. I wont say the names, they know who they are, but they came face to face and said, "Give us your scarf cunt!" I looked at them and laughed. My boys were right beside me in an instant, all of them, no questions, no hesitation. Suddenly I threw out my hands and grabbed little shit by the collar of his green bomber jacket, lifted him off the floor and turned him parallel with the railway lines directly below him. Then I calmly asked him, "Do you want my scarf or do you want me to drop you in front of the next train to Barking?" His face was glowing red and I could see both the fear in his eyes and the silence from his friends. This told me one thing and that was that they never expected it. All of a sudden, the platform to Barking was extremely quiet. I gently lifted him back on the platform and from that day on, the Hornchurch and Cranham learnt to respect each other and became good friends and allies and some of them became very close friends.

By 1975, the Cranham and Hornchurch lads were now well established. Two proper firms that were getting more and more respected and feared by those who wanted to try to have a pop at us! One night we were down the Robert Beard, youth club and we'd heard a firm of very naughty Elm park boys were on their way to take us. Now when I say naughty, I mean very naughty knife merchants and well known for it. There were seven of us, and thirty of the Elm Park. Incidentally the people running the club were affiliated with the Hells Angels and grown men. We were sitting down sipping our soft drink when all of a sudden Dave Stoddard walked in; he was one of the Elm Park lot. He walked over to us and said "Oi, Dalby, Keith's got a firm outside what are you going to do?" Cool as a cucumber I said "Dave, tell 'em we will be out when we finished our drinks. Oh, and Dave are you his runaround. Why don't he come in himself and ask me? Oh! I forgot Dave you're scared of him ever since he stuck that carving knife through your face!" Dave was scared of him and we knew it. He was shocked and in disbelief when I told him, we will come outside. He frantically scarpered off to pass on the message. The doorman said, "are you guys crazy?" Well the only reply I could give was "Yes!" They said to the boys and me "We will be behind you" My thought was how's that forty year old Hells angels behind us, fifteen year old kids! I knew if we pulled this one off this would be the talk of Essex for years to come and both me and Tel' knew if we failed, everyone would want a go at us.

It was shit or bust. There was the alternative that we could have run out the back door of the youth club, but this was not a program that was installed in our brains! We would have to live with the thought of us doing a runner haunting us and not just me, but Tel, Tiggy, Bonesy, Johnny M, Jim Nev and Steve El for the rest of our lives. We only moved one way and that's forward, there was no other option than finish our drinks and go through the front doors of the Beard. I knew in my head what I was going to do before I even walked out the door. I had to take the Top man out Keith. This is a young man who installed fear into not just his friends, but everyone in the London Borough of Havering. He would give the orders, he was a controller and he would drain the energy out of people through the fear of him, and if they didn't do what he told them they would be hurt. I had to drain his energy now.

As we walked to the door I shot out like a bullet from a gun, I could hear him edging his boys on, but by the time he said come on lads do him, my fist was at his face. One of his boys ran behind me and tried to have a go at Jimmy Nev' who was the smallest build out of all of us, but he was soon pounded to the ground by Tel' and Honesy who went to work on him. Keith fell to the floor and I ripped my shirt open, "come on you mug stab me!" I shouted. Every time he tried to get up, I knocked him down. Again I screamed "come on stab me and if you can't finish me off, your boys can have a go and if they don't kill us then we will come back with a firm so big and hunt you mugs all down."

All this time Mick, Tiggy and Steve El' stood beside me watching and were ready for anything that came, while Tel and Bonesy were still having fun pummeling the guy who ran behind me. I had drained his energy and I knew it. Not just his energy though, I had sapped all the energy out of his firm and they could only but look and see this man that they all feared laying on the floor and been given the chance to fight me one on one, but he never had the asshole or the bollocks even with the advantage of a knife. We had mugged them all off and we felt like glorious nutters. The doormen of the club were shaking their heads in disbelief, that we had overcome this infamous firm and rattled them from their heads to their toes. The news spread fast and our firm was rising in the ranks. Even some of the Elm Park boys who were there that night wanted to join us; people like Wolfie, Paul Coombes, Mickey Beale, Chillo, hairy Ben became good friends after that evening. Strange how things turn around!

People forget that Cranham may have well been a small council estate, but everyone on the estate was well up for it and were loyal West Ham boys. We grew up with Pikeys in the field next door to Lingies field. The reason we called it Lingies field was that a mum and dad put a stable at the back of the field for their daughter, whose name was Sue. It was never their field at all, it was our playground and the field next door to Lingies was

430

jam packed with over fifty caravans. This was our battleground with the Pikey's and us, and used to be our field before the Pikey's moved in. We were always rumbling with them. The biggest rumble was when we were around thirteen or fourteen years of age. One of the top Pikey's ordered both myself, and the Rosebury boys out of the field. I told him that it was our field before they moved in, so he could fuck right off. He then picked up a long stemmed axe and ran at me, at which point I ran into him and as he tried to strike a blow down on my head, I blocked the stem of the axe with my forearm and connected with a perfect right hook. At this point, a few more Pikey's came running at me. Lucky for me my mates Tel, Tiggy, Mickey and El got the catapults out, and fuck me they were good shots and pushed the Pikey's back behind the caravans. So, we had plenty of practice in these fields, which would lead us onto the Terraces, and was a good toughening up process.

Manchester United vs. West Ham 1975

It was the big day 1975 West Ham –Manchester United at home. We'd heard rumours thousands were coming down for us. We were ready at Upminster station. The platform was heaving with the Cranham and Hornchurch firms. A sea of claret and blue all buzzing all prepared for the battle that was about to happen. The train pulled in and we were rammed in, no room to turn or move it was that packed. The sound of 'I'm forever blowing bubbles' ringing in your ears as we stopped at the next station, Upminster Bridge to cram even more people in. We were like cans of sardines. When we got to Upton Park we joined the thousands more heading to the ground, though we weren't heading straight for the ground, we were hunting the Manchester United firm, the Red army. We arrived at the ground buzzing with the sound of Bubbles. We met up with Ray Searl, Dave Rayon and Ray Evans (It was Ray Searl that introduced us to Carlton Leach and the Mile End boys and that was the start of another friendship.) The nerves were kicking in, we were all waiting for this day, it was the day the new boys who joined our firm wanted to prove themselves, wanting to show everyone that they were part of this machine. They may only be a small-cog at this moment in time but it's those small cogs keep the wheel turning. This was going to be one part of the city thrown into terror, a day that for the so called 'Red army' everything will go horrifically wrong, but the battle on the outskirts of this town was just the beginning, there can only be one winner, our sole objective to track down and attack the Manchester United firm.

Today we were about to send a message to the world in no uncertain terms, that West Ham is the top firm. This was the bloodiest battle that London had ever witnessed. It was coming up to midday when was this going to happen. We had a few false alarms, running down the road in and out of the moving traffic, but then it happened. At least three coach loads of Manchester United fans, all game and calling it on. We were well outnumbered but upon seeing them, our pace fastened up to a sprint, all racing forward all giving each other confidence and guidance into the ensuing battle. Then the shout "Come on West ham lets have it!" We charged at full sprint, now heart pounding, a sort of nervousness but also a fucking big rush. People were running out the way of us and the Man United's hooligans were throwing whatever they could at us, to try to halt the stampede of the frenzy. Probably hoping that in some way, we would stop, but we never stopped. We kept running at them until fists met with fists, the pounding sounds of Dr. Martin boots kicking and jumping on bodies that were curled up into a ball. There was no holding back; they were not expecting this onslaught by our boys. Many of them were now franticly running backwards trying to pick up their injured soldiers from the floor. While this was going on the young cogs in the machine were smashing up the coaches of the rival fans, leaving the shattered carriages strewn by the side of the road, this resembled something more like a war scene. The sound of sirens were coming on thick through the battled haze, the meat wagons were screeching almost on two wheels to try and quell this violent disturbance in the mid afternoon sun, more sirens and yet more sirens it was time to retreat.

Those of us that managed to escape the Old Bill regrouped outside the entrance to the south bank. Cranham were the hardest hit that day for number of arrests! Sixteen of our boys were nicked during the violence and a few Hornchurch. We were now in the South bank section. Carlton, Ray Searl, Dave Rayon, Al Robinson, Tiggy, Mickey Martin, Steve El, Glen Gowler, Mathew Thomas, Bomber, Noster, Jimmy Neal, Arthur Collinson and Neil Amos; all the rest were in police cells facing violent disorder Charges. I remember seeing Chimp and Froggit being loaded into the back of the meat wagon, but had no idea 'till the next morning that they were all nicked. We were to make world headlines, hunted down like animals in the East End; those were the exact words that the press used which were very fitting. So here, we were again in the south bank, a police line dividing us from the Manchester United fans rejoicing over the triumphant battle that took place earlier only to be heading into another battle in the Southbank. After being spat at by the northern shits, we stormed the thin line of police who ran everywhere and nowhere. The thin blue line had collapsed, its ranks had folded to this new West Ham and the new warriors of football were now deep in the Manchester United section. It was carnage, they were falling everywhere and they were experiencing a new surge of West Ham terror that was hailing down upon them. Punch after punch; kick after kick and West Ham kept going forward. I remember them all trying to get onto the pitch, but the fighting was still going on at the top of the South bank. We were pushing them further and further back, they called it on but once we ran at them they lost all heart for the fight. They were getting battered and there was nothing any one could do about it. The match was stopped while the Old Bill tried to regain order. The job had been done! West Ham showed to the world that we are the Hammers. The new West Ham had been born and was unstoppable.

After this day, Carlton L was coming more and more regular to the Bridge House pub with us, and he was always there for us when we had the gang fights with different firms from around Essex. We were going to away games and always somehow managed to get in the rival teams end ready to unleash on them. Tottenham, Arsenal, Millwall and Chelsea were amongst our main rivals. On one occasion, we were all in the Tottenham park lane end, all waiting for the rest of the firm to show. Carlton L, Dave Rayon, Duke, Mickey Martin, Pigeon, little pigeon, Jimmy Neal, Keith Morley,

Steve El, and Ray Searl. Tiggy, Glen Gowler and Jim Nev' we were all standing downstairs waiting by the bar rest of the Hornchurch to show when Jimmy Neville decided to pull his colours out. The result was mental, there was us waiting, taking our time so we had a bigger firm and Jim went and called it on early. We had to start the fight there and then. One person ran up to Carlton and from out of a football magazine pulled out a blade. No sooner had he pulled it, and then I knocked him out bang cold with one punch. We ran at them and they were coming down the stairs in there were dozens of them, but we all just went full advance mode but because there were so many of them, they were falling over by the stairs. Now we had them on the retreat, we were proud of the younger firm, Duke and pigeon and little pigeon as well, Nut held their own with us. I recall Froggit who was a big lad, twenty plus stone at the time having a go at two Tottenham lads, and had one under each of his armpits and he was running their heads into the wall. You can only describe Froggit as a bit like friar Tuck, a monster of a man.

The world was calling us thugs and hooligans. Let's get this into the right context, we were fighting for our Manor and our turf, and those that come down wanted to fight us, wanted to take our Manor. We were not attacking innocent men woman and children we were fighting the hard core of other firms. Describe a Thug! A thug in our eyes are bullies and cowards that would attack innocent people, rob them or mug them and even worse burgle old people's homes using violence and in many cases murdering innocent people for what, a bit of cash a little bit of jewelry? These are the lowest of the low, the snakes, and the scum that had no recognition in our world. These are the people that don't belong in society, so let's not get confused between them and us. Our only love was fighting, we send thousands of troops to war but they are called heroes, and for what someone else's land and someone else's oil which every government wants a slice of. Forget the poor souls that give their lives for that slice of oil?

1975 had gone and 1976 was here the hottest summer Britain had ever witnessed, I had arranged to meet some of the boys at East Ham then make our way to the Ground. Tiggy had bought his Girlfriend along Sue.

A smiley girl of Irish decent, a lovely quiet girl, and Mickey was there along with Chillo and Paul Coombes. Unbeknown to me this day in East Ham there was a march by the National Front, I never thought a lot of it at that moment. We all went into a little corner shop to buy some drinks, to cool us down from the early afternoon heat and as we walked out the shop the demonstration was upon us. The N.F were shouting abuse to some of the locals, objects were being thrown and it was starting to turn into a battle zone, when all of a sudden two men which I can only describe as monsters and about forty-five years of age and hard looking ran at me and said without warning "Get this little fucker!" I had heard rumours about the N.F that were scary. Oh fuck, they grabbed me by my left arm and started dragging me away and my mates looked on, not knowing what to do. My only thought was I'm going to end up dead down some back alley way if I don't do something. My only conclusion at the time was that these men were N.F and because I only have to look at a holiday brochure to catch a tan these guys must have thought I was of Pakistani origin. What do I do? They were dragging me by my left arm but my right arm was free with half a bottle of red top milk that I had bought from the corner shop. I felt my body twist round as I swung my right arm as fast and as hard as I could with the glass milk bottle and connected right on the top of the first blokes head. Blood poured from his wound and as he let go of his grip the one in front turned around. He must of been 18 to 20 stone and just jumped on me pinning me to the ground, my mates were lost in the heavy crowd and I was alone. They both picked me up and now had both my arms behind my back I knew this hold! They marched me off and as we turned the corner, I could see the steps of East Ham police station. "You have had it!" they kept saying to me. They were not N.F at all; they were under cover Old Bill. At this moment my only thought was 'for fuck sake, Phil you just done a copper'. My mum and dad are going to' go ape shit, I have to escape.

They marched me all the while punching me in the sides, repeating "You're gonna' get it you little cunt, no one does coppers on our manor." Up the stairs we went, how was I going to escape with them both gripping me? At the top of the stairs, which had no side railing there was a set of solid wooden double doors with glass segments and wire in the glass. As they went to open the doors I felt their grip loosen and this was my chance. I swung round and threw them both down the stairs and I legged it like I'd never legged it before. The crowd outside the station was cheering me and then I noticed my friends were there at the bottom of the stairs, but I had no time to stop and chat. Little did I know that when I threw the Old Bill down the stairs, that I broke one of their ankles.

I kept running and there were hundreds cheering me who were all on their way to the game that I was supposed to be heading to. I was a man with one objective and that was to get away. I kept running and running but I could hear the sirens, loads of them all coming for me. My chest was tightening, I'd run so fast and the afternoon heat never helped at all. The sirens were getting closer not two not three but four meat wagons were sent to get me. They didn't want this one to get away that was for sure. The two meat wagons raced in front of me and blocked my road ahead, and one turned into the road next to me, while the other screeched right beside me. I was fucked, out of breath and I'm not one for giving in, but I felt I done the best I could. Some burly Old Bill jumped out the wagon but they never put me in the wagon they lifted me off the floor with my arms behind my back, and let me tell you it hurt and they carried me all the way down the road that I had ran down. As we got to the police station, my mates were outside and watched me being carried in. As the two Old Bill got to the doors this time, they entered with a different approach. They tilted my body at a forty-five degree angle, and used my head to open the doors not just the front doors but also another two sets inside the station. They then threw me into a cell and shouted 'Strip down to your pants you little fucker!'

My dad was a staunch soldier, a Sergeant in the Royal Engineers with plenty of medals and he was always a firm believer that if you've been nicked son, then you have done something wrong. He was out of the army now, many times I told him when we were growing up that the Police in Cranham had it in for me. Always trying to stop and search me, which my reply to them was fuck-off! If I had done something wrong then yes, but not day in and day out, especially by PC Easter and PC John Hill who was a black belt Judo champion. One day when John Hill, who was new to our estate, had been warned about me, he decided to pay us all a visit bringing with him two car loads of Old Bill and pulled up at the junction of Avon Rd and Front lane, Cranham. This was the first time I'd set eyes on John Hill. PC Edwards, who I respected, warned me that the new copper on the beat was a bulldog and that they'd send him first into riots. When he saw me, he got out the panda car, I was with the Roseberry firm and he come bowling over to me. I laughed as the only thing that was missing was some fruit to go with his bowl. He came face to face with me, then with his size nine steel toe cap Dr. Martin boot he stamped his foot down on mine and started pressing really hard down onto my foot, and said "Dalby, this is my manor now!" and then pressed even harder down. It was hurting but I would not show it, I said to him "You're not hurting me, you fat cunt" at which point he pressed harder. My answer was still the same, "You're not hurting me you fat cunt". He said, "Come on, hit me Dalby," and I replied in front of his two car loads of Old Bill, "Take off your uniform you fat cunt, and me and you will take a walk behind this back alley that runs parallel with Avon Rd, and I will beat the shit out of you. Take your uniform off and your boys will watch me kick your fat ass." He still had his boot on my foot, but I never buckled to his intimidation. His arsehole went and I said, "I'm not stupid enough to hit you with your uniform on, but if you take it off we will see who the man is." He released his foot, as he was not expecting me to give him the offer of walking round the back alley. Any of the coppers looking in on that scene can only take it, that big boy Judo expert riot queller John Hill, lost his bottle.

Anyway, back to the point I was making. My father never believed that these things ever happened, until one day many years later. My dad and I were on holiday in Athens with John Kastenada, Alias John Thong do dat ding. We were just taking a pleasant walk through Athens, when all of a sudden two police bikes and a police car raced up to us, jumped out the car with machine guns and bundled me and John to the floor and handcuffed us. We were held for hours, and then I was told it was a case of mistaken identity! John was an Australian, whose family ran The Hotel

Athina on Koz Island. He was an affiliated Cranham and was a West Ham boy who was always coming over from Koz to Cranham to be with the boys for some action when the holiday season was over.

So I'm sitting in the cell almost stark bollock naked with just my underpants on, thinking about my old man and his old ways of thinking, he is never going to believe me. 'You been nicked son, then you done something wrong' kept going round and round in my head, but I had done nothing wrong. He will never accept my version, even though I had witnesses to what happened. I can't see my old man believing me, my thoughts were disturbed when I heard the key turn in the cell door and the door was then suddenly thrown open and the charge of ten massive police men running at me shouting "You little cunt, no one does that to any of ours!" not on this manor. I tried to get up, and throw a punch at the 1st one who came at me, but they were too strong and overpowering. They slammed me down face first on to the wooden bench, and then it was blow after blow to my body. One of them was grabbing my head by my hair, and was slamming my head down to the face of the cold wooden bench time after time. Punches and kicks rained down on me, while I was held down flat on the bench and they pounded and pounded into me and I just kept shouting at them, "Cunts, you're all cunts. You're cunts, you're cunts."

Then I heard the cell door open and they all left me laying in a battered and bruised heap on the bench. My head was bleeding and I could feel my face had swollen right up. I felt like Galen out of planet of the apes. I jumped up and started screaming is that the best you can do you fat cunts. I was punching the cell door repeatedly and shouting "come on you mugs you're all a bunch of wankers, you have not even hurt me you fat bunch of faggots. Yes that's what you are a fat bunch of faggots. You fucking mugs, you fucking mugs I've had gnat bites that hurt me more than you mugs." I was not stopping, and my abuse kept on and on. I had completely forgotten about the thoughts of my old man and what he would think and at this moment in time, I did not give a shit about what my old man would think or what he would say. I couldn't give a fuck I was not going to let any of these mugs break my spirit and my abuse kept coming and coming. Then I calmed down and sat on the bench that had been the scene of police brutality and realised that I will be missing the Mighty Hammers game. An hour went buy then I heard the lock in the cell again I jumped up ready but this time it was a policewoman with my clothes, she looked at my face and I could see she was disgusted by the what had happened. She asked me to get dressed and then she left the room. I put my clothes back on and waited, for what I was not sure, as I hadn't been charged yet.

Another hour went by and I was laying on the bench in a sort of half sleep when I heard the key in the lock again. This time two policemen walked in I jumped up with my fists ready and they said "Calm down, we have to take you to Plaistow police station. What the fuck do they want to take me to Plaistow police station for? They then said, "We will have to handcuff you ok lad!" So I held my hands out and was handcuffed, it was then they took my name and address and shoved me into the back of the meat wagon heading for Plaistow. By this time, my face had swelled right out and looked like I had a good beating. I could not work out why they were taking me to Plaistow for the life of me. I sat in a cell at Plaistow until early evening, and then I was told I was going back to East Ham.

Now what the fuck is going on, I thought. I never had a clue. Once back at East Ham they put me in a cell again. Soon after I heard the rustle of the keys in the door, a policeman came in and said "You have to come downstairs with me, your fathers here and you will be charged". I was charged, then sent to a room where my dad was sitting with the head of East Ham police drinking coffee! I walked in and said "Dad, look what they done to me, I want to press charges. The first thing out of my dad's lips were "Son you must of done something wrong" I knew it, I fucking knew it. The head of police at East Ham sweet-talked my dad into talking me into not pressing charges against the police. I shouted "Bollocks dad! You're sitting there drinking coffee with them, letting them convince you that they are a bunch of Angels. I'm not going with it dad, sorry they are all a bunch of bullyboys and are trying to pull the wool over your eyes." They released me that evening, court date pending on two counts of GBH against the Old Bill.

Day of the court I had my witnesses present. I had the photos of my face, my mum was there also there and even Tiggy's girlfriend came to court, who has no criminal record and you know just by looking at her that when she talks it will be the truth, a very staunch catholic girl and very religious also. The Judge was a lady, the police stood up and said what they had to say but adding a few lies in between, telling the Judge that they showed their I.D's when they grabbed hold of me at East Ham and that was when I got Violent. My witnesses including Sue, told the truth and said that they had just grabbed me with no I.D or proof at all that they were policemen and that it was rather scary for Sue, who also thought that they were N.F. Then the Judge asked the police a crucial question regarding my injuries, because according to the police report my injuries were sustained when I tried to escape when they were moving me from East Ham to Plaistow. I apparently escaped and was rugby tackled to the floor and that's why they moved me! It all makes sense now, my friends were outside the police station when they carried me back from when I first escaped, they saw and testified even Sue, that when I was carried back after I threw them down the stairs, that there was not a mark on my face! So the Judge asked then questioned "How full were the cells at the time Dalby was taken to Plaistow? The policemen replied, "Pretty empty really, only 1 or 2 other inmates." So she then said, "So why was he moved to Plaistow if the cells were empty?" The copper stuttered and was lost for words saying something like "Well it was a West Ham match that day and with the N.F march in East Ham, we may have needed the cells." The Judge jumped straight on him again and then said, "Then why did you not take the other inmates also?" She never believed their story and she let them know it, but I was still charged for the offenses and she gave me a two year suspended sentence, which in my eyes was better than jail.

It was 1977, the year Gary Gilmore was executed in the state of Utah, the first execution since 1967, it was the year that Elvis, Mark Bolan, Bing Crosby, and Charlie Chaplin also passed away, and it was in that year that I nearly joined them. It was the Queens silver jubilee party, celebrated all over Britain and the commonwealth countries. The Queen embarked on a large-scale tour of Britain, having decided she would like to meet as many of her people that were possible; no other sovereign had visited so much of Britain in the course of 3 months. In London alone, in early June there were over 4000 street parties, an estimated 500 million people watched it on television as the procession returned down the mall.

The boys and I were invited to one of these street parties in Deyncourt Gardens, Cranham; this was the plush side of town. Cranham is divided by one road, Front lane and if you drive down Front lane from the Arterial end the A127, the council estate is on the left hand side. This is the plush estate where people like Jimmy Greaves, and Bobby Ferguson the West Ham Goal keeper lived. We were set on the right hand side of Front lane, and it was a stone's throw between those who had nothing to those who had it all. We had all been drinking and celebrating this day on our side of front lane, then after we headed down to Deyncourt Gardens. Johnny Mathews was staggering in front and me, Tiggy, Mickey Martin, Ginger Ralf and Steve Greenhill were behind him and Al Robinson was lagging behind. We approached one street party at the bend of Deyncourt Gardens, but we were going to the next street party at the top end. It was at this moment in a drunken state that Johnny Mathews picked up one of the sand buckets that were put evenly across the road to stop any traffic passing through and threw it up into the air, we were behind him about 20 feet. We carried on walking and within one minute two, men whose ages were around 45 and well built came running out at us with a golf club each in their hands. The exact words one of them said to us was "Fuck off back to your council estate" This enraged me, I flipped and replied "Who the fuck do you think you are coming up to us with golf clubs in your hands? Put the clubs down and I will have it with the both of you, you're a pair of mugs." I started walking toward them and they hesitantly started walking backwards. "I'm calling the police," he said "Call the fucking police" I replied "You mugs, I will sit here and wait for them if you do" They ran indoors and this was witnessed by over one hundred people that were at that street party. I sat on their front wall, the alcohol never helped, but the abuse from me continued until a woman came out to talk to me. She was very polite and pleasant and very calming. I asked her if the guy was her husband she said he was. I said "I'm not being funny they come out with golf clubs using foul language and telling us to fuck off back to our council estate, who do they think they are? He may think he owns the street but he don't own me", at which her reply was "We don't want no trouble will you please leave?" I shook her hand and said, "Being that you've very polite to me, I will leave right now but I think your husband and his friend are tossers". At this point, I turned around and started to walk away from the lady.

I heard nothing the sound of the revelers at the party and the music drowned out any clue of the spineless gutless piece of scum that was charging at me from behind with the golf club in full swing. The first blow to the back of my skull, fractured my skull and sent me to my knees in execution style. I was at his mercy, on my knees, and blood was pouring out of the first strike, but he had no mercy. It was as if I was waiting for the second bullet to penetrate and the second blow hit me to the left side of my head. This was the blow that put me on my back. In medical terms, it was a depressed fracture of the skull, but in my language, it shattered my head inwards, just as if an egg had been hit with a tablespoon. I could feel my life being sapped out from me, but I refused to shut my eyes. A third blow came down hard on my chest, but still I refused to close my eyes. I could hear woman screaming at him "Stop your killing him, your killing him." The sky was spinning furiously, it was as if I was free falling out of a plane but the difference was I was on my back and the sky was free falling down on me. Then another blow to my chest and still I refused to shut my eyes because I knew if I did I would die. That was my inner strength telling me to not give up.

At this point, which all happened in less than ten to fifteen seconds, I could see out of my eyes from in front of this coward my friend Steve Greenhill charge in with a perfect Karate kick to his chest. It gave me time to stop the sky from spinning and gave me time to live again, but as the kick connected in his chest a mighty blow from the golf club hit Steve bang on the top of his chest. I had to get up but the spinning was still there but not as manic as it was before. I knew if I never got up, he would come back at me. This is why you have friends. Mickey, Tiggy, Ginger

Ralf, Lou Burridges and Al went storming in with a barrage of kicks to send the man running backwards. I jumped up onto my feet not knowing the damage to my head was severe and the coward ran behind his solid wooden front door.

I kicked and kicked, but the door would not budge and out of nowhere the Old Bill came running at me and tried to arrest me as someone must have called them! I threw the first police man to the floor, and then I saw his face. There was a look of terror as he was looking at my head as my sudden movements had made the blood pump round my body fast and my head was like a fountain. The jets of blood streaming out were unstoppable, the second wound to my head left a hole inverted inwards of four inches by two inches, the bones had gone in so deep and the wound was open and clearly penetrated into my brain. The police jumped on me and handcuffed me to a lamp post. No, they were not arresting me, they were trying to keep me still to try to prevent me from losing too much blood before the ambulance arrived. Without the intervention of my friends that night, I would definitely be dead, but this nightmare had just begun!

My friends gathered round me and the police had a towel over my head to try to stop the blood from coming out. I could hear the ambulance coming, the party was stopped and the sand bollards at the other end of the road removed to allow the ambulance in. Mickey said to me "I'm going round your house to let your mum know Phil" We never had mobiles in them days. I said, "Mick don't, she will only worry mate." My only thought was that they would just stitch me up and let me go home, how wrong I was. Mick agreed not to say anything to my mum, but he was just saying that to stop me from stressing. They could all see the hole in my head and that it there was far more than just a few stitches required! I arrived at Harold Wood Hospital, and when the nurses said they'd have to keep me in for observation I knew something was not right. The police came for a statement but the nurses ushered them away and told them I was in no fit state at that moment to make any kind of statement. They stitched me up and put me onto a ward, I felt ok to be honest but I did what I was told. During the night, things were starting to go horribly wrong. When I woke up in the morning, the whole right side of my body was lifeless, and my speech had gone. I couldn't even talk not a single word. The nurses came and asked if I wanted a cuppa' and they knew then that I had received severe brain damage. I was rushed to Oldchurch Hospital in Romford, where they had a neurological unit. I was rapidly slipping away and this hospital was well renowned for the Neurological ward, which was one of the best in the world at that time. It broke my poor mum's heart to see me in that state, so much so that she had a nervous breakdown. I went into a coma and was jump-started a couple of times, with enough volts put through my body to light up Southend pier. I needed an Emergency operation that would take at least seven hours due to the delicacy and nature of the operation and the human brain. The brain surgeon Dr. Fairburn told my family that there was very little chance of me surviving, and if I did survive that I would more likely be in a vegetative state for the rest of my life. He, of course, had to cover himself and let my family prepare for the worse.

The strange thing was while I was in the coma I could hear the Dr. talking to my family and friends, while they were sat around my bed in the I.C.U unit in Oldchurch.

I was trying to respond to them, to let them know I was not going to die but had no way of getting the message across. I could hear everything, every single conversation, but my body would not let me transpose it. I remember waking up, can't remember how many days or hours or maybe even weeks after the operation and the first thing I heard on the radio was the Commodores, 'I'm easy like Sunday morning'. I felt the tears run down my face. They were not tears of sadness but tears of joy that I was alive. I still couldn't talk, but my speech would return with in time and with a lot of therapy.

After much therapy for my speech and physiotherapy for the loss of feeling to the right side of my body, I was released from hospital in late August. I was very frail, and still very weak and ahead of me was a never-ending journey to the neurologist unit in Oldchurch Hospital, there making me ready for the next operation, so that when I get stronger they could rebuild my skull with a Titanium skullcap. This would be placed over the top of my skull and would be screwed into the bones that were not damaged, very much like Robocop but hidden under my skin.

In my first week of leaving hospital, Tiggy, Sue and Mickey wanted to take me out for a curry in Upminster to help me get back into the swing of things slowly but surely. I could not drink because of the medication I was prescribed and because I had lost so much weight, I felt vulnerable. On the way home, we waited at the bus stop and my head was still shaven and bandaged. Lo and behold, PC Easter and two panda cars pulled up by us. They jumped out the car, said I was nicked for drunk and disorderly, and started dragging me toward Upminster police station. No matter what my friends told them that I had not touched a drop of drink they took no notice. PC Easter was getting me back for all the times when I was younger and stronger. I just ignored him and told him to fuck off every time he tried to stop and search me. All the Old Bill in my manor knew I never carried a weapon, but this was his moment of glory, his only moment in my weakest state and just when he knew I'd just come out of Brain surgery to get one up on me.

Both PC Easter and another PC threw me over the chain link fencing that was outside the Station, ripping my jeans and cutting my leg. They sat me on a chair in front of PC Hill and John Hill asked, "What's the charge?" "Drunk and disorderly" replied Easter. I looked up at PC Easter and just said to him "You're a cunt Easter, a cunt" From out of nowhere he punched me on the left hand side of my head knocking me off the chair. I jumped up and managed to get my hands around his throat, screaming at him "you're fucking dead" but I was too weak to stop the intervention of the other officers who pulled me off him and ran me into the cell. I never stopped shouting out my threats to the weasel and I wanted to kill him. He knew how I would react. No one hits me and gets away with it, I played right into his hands and for that the drunk and disorderly charge was dropped and I was charged with threatening to kill a police officer.

Money was scarce in them days and to hire a solicitor to defend me would have cost a fortune, and even if I did who would believe me against the statements of three policemen? I had to attend Romford Magistrate Court, and either plead guilty to the charge there and then, or otherwise if I pleaded not guilty, I would have to attend Chelmsford Crown court and if found guilty face three years or more in jail. So, I pleaded guilty even though I kicked up a stink in the court about the weasel of a policeman and why he was not here on that day but sends another policeman in his place to speak for him who was not even there that evening and I did kick up a stink. The press from the Romford Recorder I will never forget as they were laughing at the abuse I was throwing at Easter. But, I pleaded guilty and was dealt with there and then with a heavy fine. Also the Judge knew I just came out of a Traumatic time in hospital, so I think he was a bit lenient toward me, but this won't help toward the court case that I was to attend at Chelmsford for the attack that happened to me and I knew it. I had to get fit and strong again for myself and for the second operation on my head, which happened to be around two months before the case at Chelmsford court. The man who hit me with the golf club (from behind) was charged with attempted murder, GBH and assault, but I found it strange that the police who were pressing these charges against him, never had any other witnesses from the street party that night, only my friends. The guy ran his own haulage firm and owned a Rolls Royce and soon after I was in Oldchurch Hospital, sold up and moved out of Cranham. Money talks, eh?

I had to give the love of my life up, West Ham for the next 2 years while I waited for the second operation. It gutted me, but my head was weak and the left hand side felt like a paper lantern. It was just skin and there was no protection between that and my brain, but I trained and trained hard mixing weights with the punch bag. I was getting fit and strong again, and from that moment on, I swore that I would never turn my back on any one ever again. That was the first time I did and look at the result. My attitude was I didn't give a fuck what they have in their hands. I would rather die going into them and go face on to any weapon, rather than turn my back, most people after an incident like this would probably not come out of their front door ever again, not me this made me stronger in will, and in mind.

It was 1979 and time to have my head rebuilt. I was fighting fit and it was only to be a couple weeks in Neurology. At least this time I had all my marbles with me. The operation was a success and my head felt strong after. It turned out it was stronger and much tougher than ever before. The court case at Chelmsford was looming round the corner, but I knew deep down that a man with the money and resources that he had, could get anything he wants including a top lawyer, and my thoughts turned to reality when it came to the week of the court case at Chelmsford.

Judge Greenwood was heading the courtroom that week. We had the brain surgeon Dr. Fairburn on our bench giving evidence and explaining that the strikes that hit me round the head would have killed any normal person, and that the attacker Brian McFayden was trying to kill me that night. However, his lawyer had done his homework and looked into my record, which I knew would be the case. It was as if I was on trial again, but the Judge was on our side all the way. He told the jury that despite what I had done earlier in my life against the police, this man had no right to go round the streets attacking sixteen-year-old boys with golf clubs, but his lawyer had planted the seed, and the seed was growing. After listening to all the evidence the jury returned a verdict of not guilty to attempted murder, not guilty to GBH, but found him guilty of common assault. Judge Greenwood was disgusted in the verdict, and made it clear to the jury that this was not a common assault and said if he had his way, he would have kept him on an attempted murder charge and put him in jail for the maximum term. But, since they came to this verdict the only thing he could do was fine him and give him a 2 year suspended sentence. The Judge then told the defendant that he was an evil bully and that he was ashamed of the jury's verdict.

I later heard a rumour that PC Easter played at the same golf course as McFayden. It was all timed perfectly, my arrest before the court case would insure a good result for him, maybe it was all pre planned, but it was too late for if's and buts. My hatred for the police and the system grew deep inside of me and kept festering. Very much like a day not long after the court case, when 2 off-duty police officers from Hornchurch picked on my mates Gary King, Miley, Lou and Jimmy Burridge outside the Chinese in Upminster.

As I walked out with my takeaway asking what's happening, one of the PC's punched me in the face and told me he is Old Bill, now fuck off! That was it; next minute I was smashing his head against the gate at the funeral directors next door to the Chinese. No one hits me, off duty or on duty. He was on the floor getting pummeled by me, when a police car pulled up and two young Old Bill jumped out that knew me. They pulled me aside and asked what's going on. I explained that this guy had started on me so I retaliated. While we were talking his colleague, who'd done sweet fuck all when he was watching his pal being smashed against the fence, then decided to punch me in front of the uniformed officers. I looked at the officers and said, "Did you see that!" They chose to turn a blind eye, so I just steamed into him punching him straight to the floor. The uniformed officers put me in the car and said "Phil, we hate these two, they go around off duty giving it large." My friends stood and watched as they drove me off. While we were driving, they told me that they are quite sure that these two guys would not press charges out of embarrassment, and the fact that they thought they were hard. When they come to Hornchurch nick, they would never live this down, but we are going back now, and if they do decide to press charges then we will have to nick you. I thought that was fine at least they warned me what may be and what can't be! We went back and must have only driven for a couple minutes and the two young officers in uniform asked the assaulting off duty cops if they wanted to press charges against me? Exactly as the uniformed officers predicted, the off duty officers said no, they just wanted to forget it. What a result!! I just battered two Old Bill, and walked free from it.

It was now 1980 and my head was super strong, and so was I. It was my first football match since my head was rebuilt, WEST HAM v ARSENAL at Wembley. I had a ticket as well, which I was well impressed with. We all went up by train and were drinking in the Greyhound pub; well in fact outside of the pub. The atmosphere was buzzing, everyone had consumed loads of booze but the police presence was making it volatile, and they were looking for anyone to nick for any reason. We were singing in the direction of the Old Bill 'who ate all the pies, who ate all the pies, you fat bastard, you fat bastard you ate all the pies' when they just charged at us. I saw Martin Troy get jumped on by the Old Bill and I was not going to sit there and watch my mate get nicked. I was carrying the Cranham Banner and I just tore in and just let loose with the banner smashing them over the heads, while Martin was punching at them like a man possessed. I could see bottles and glasses coming down over my head, raining down on the Old Bill as it was turning into a riot. There was too many police on us; even with the missiles flying, and they had more police to back them up. Yes, I was nicked again, and thrown into the van along with Martin.

Typical I thought to myself, I have a ticket for the final and now going to spend the day at Wembley Nick, along with Froggits younger brother, Martin. We were kept in all day until late evening. I remember the Wembley Old Bill saying to me "What is it with you and us, you have a terrible record of violence against us, and now you have another?" We were charged with threatening behaviour, breach of the peace, and assaulting police officers with a banner. When we appeared in Harrow court, they let Martin go in first. He came out and said he received an 80 quid fine and a two-year suspended sentence. Then they called my name and asked me to go to another court up the Hallway. Martin laughed and said, "You're going down mate, and I thought I was also. The Judge slammed me and said, "Your record is disgraceful, your war against the police ends here and now, this is your last chance. I'm fining you and giving you another two year suspended sentence, and if you commit any crime at football or where ever, then you will be going to jail." It was the last chance saloon even though I had a two-year suspended; it was not going to stop me from going to the mighty hammers. The final score was West Ham 1, Arsenal 0, goal scored by Trevor brooking, I had the ticket and the tea shirt but missed the match.

'The man that goes into a just battle for a just cause although to others feels unjust, will always stand by his men and fight to the end.' Top words by Jason Patrick Baker. This applied to myself, Terry, Tiggy, Mickey Martin, Ray Searl, and Steve Heron the night of the party up at Argyle gardens in Upminster; one evening when Tel' just got out of jail.

We pulled up on the curb outside the party, and noticed my younger brother Paul and his mate Percy outside talking to an older man. We had been invited to this party, and thought nothing of it. As we all got out the car and slammed the doors shut, a monster of a man ran out the front door and headed straight for my little brother and knocked him clean out with one punch, then said to my brother and Percy "Now fuck off you mugs."

That was the start of a night of violence, which left 18 people in hospital and some in a very critical state. I tore into the man as he walked back into the party, and by the time, I had finished with him he was crawling on the floor trying to get in, but I kept on punching him down stamping on him. No one does that to my younger brother, I showed no mercy, and I was fuming and kept pummeling him until he was not moving. Claret was coming out of every part of his face, then I turned around to the boys and said "Don't look like we are going to this party, we better fuck off." At that moment Tel' said, "Watch out Phil!" I quickly turned around, and a firm of more than twenty handed from Wickford started running out at me through the front door with baseball bats, lumps of wood and shovels. We tore into them and I was smashing them down as fast as they ran out the door, avoiding every blow that was aimed at my head. It was better than a scene out of the Warriors film. This was real and full on, one guy even tried to wrap a fifteen ft. length of wood over my head, but by the time he came through the front door lifted it back to get a swing at me, he was out cold. Every one of us was fighting back to back, the bodies on the floor were mounting up and as this was happening the young Cranham in the party realised it was us. People like Lenny, Duke, Dish, Tony.T, Jim Cox, the Dobsons, Leso and Rusty all came running out from within the party and made a full attack on this firm from behind. We never even knew who was inside the party. I saw big Tel' fighting with another bloke when out of nowhere a huge lump with a shovel in his hand ran up behind Tel' and smashed him so hard round the back of his head, that the power of it knocked Tel' and the bloke he was fighting straight to the floor. I felt it, and the first thing I thought of was what happened to me. The bloke with the shovel then shouted, "Who else fucking wants it, you mugs!" All the young Cranham ran backward this was not good and with Terry down, then he said "I'm gonna' take his fucking head off you cunts!" and started turning the shovel into the position to cut his head off. His arms were just about level with his chest and he was raising the shovel to bring it down on his neck and I shouted out "I will have it with you, you mug." I ran at him like a steam train and I knew I had to get above that shovel out of his hand. As I ran at him, I jumped into the air but was still moving forward. I knew the punch that was going to come down on him from above, had to count. It had to connect spot on and if I missed then he would have definitely have the upper hand. I did not miss, the precision was perfect and one of the most powerful punches I have ever thrown in my life. It floored him to the ground instantly, and then I unleashed so many blows to his limp body that I broke his ribs and jaw. No one does that to my mates or me, and you have to kill me to stop me. I picked Terry up and the young Cranham were just jumping on the mass of bodies that were lying in the front garden, jumping on their chests and kicking them in the head. The grass was not green any more it was claret. We could hear the sirens and it was time for us all to leave.

We all went back to my house. I had just moved into my own house and that was the first house that I bought, the first house that I owned. 35 Peterborough Ave, Cranham, was the new place to be. In the garden, I had a gym that was 50ft. long by 20 ft. wide with all the equipment in it. Kids from all over Cranham, Hornchurch and Havering would come down and train.

This night we all came back and like lads do, we talked about what had just happened and praising each other. Tel' and Ray left a little later, Mickey, Tiggy, and Steve decided to crash at mine for the evening. Early that morning the police came through my doors. It was John Hill with a lot of police behind him. He was smirking all over his face, his first words were "Dalby, you are going down for a long time, we've got yours and Terry's name written in blood on the walls. Attempted murder, GBH, you won't be out for a long, long time," He then told us they had to get a fleet of ambulances backward and forward to the hospitals, and that some were in a serious condition. I looked him straight into the eye and said "John, before you arrest us, I think you need to get your facts right. Firstly, we were outnumbered four to one and secondly John each and every one of them come at us with baseball bats, lumps of wood and shovels. You know damn well I have had serious brain injury from an incident, and there is no way I am going to stand there and let anyone put anything over my head ever again. Yes, we did hurt them John, but you know, and I know, that in any court of law you have not got a hope in hells chance of making these charges stand, because it was simply self-defence. So if you would like to arrest us, feel free. But firstly, I would advise you to contact your boss and go question people at the party, and you will find out that we are telling the truth that we were outnumbered and just used our fists while they had weapons." Mickey, Tiggy, and Steve backed my story up to the Old Bill, and they walked out of my front door with all of their heads down and confused. Just as if they'd received a good spanking off the headmaster with the cane and were waiting for mummy and daddy to come and tell them off. It was at this moment I wished I had a camera. Watching two meat wagons of Havering's finest Old Bill drive off with their tail between their legs and being told to go and do their homework. We heard nothing else of it since.

Because of this incident and another in Cranham, John Hill was desperate to have me arrested. There was an incident involving a nutter with an axe outside the Cranham Tandoori, which I also sorted. I disarmed the man and left him in the road by the bus stop, unconscious waiting for the ambulance to pick him up. I hid the axe and if it was not for the Indians who ran the restaurant, and the customers inside who told the police the truth they would have arrested me. John Hill asked me for the axe. I asked, "If I give it to you, will arrest me?" He said, "No, we will put it in the amnesty bin." He was starting to respect me and had a slight admiration for the way I do things. Scotland Yard categorized me 'extremely dangerous'. Why do I fight people and act in a way I do, it's because I fight the people the police want to fight, but within the law they can't, but will still show prejudice against the man that will? Who is right and who is wrong?

League cup final replay 1981, Liverpool vs. West Ham.

The Cranham boys had hired a coach, but some went by train, Duke, Pigeon, Percy and Peter Harvey decided to take the train journey up to Villa Park. I had my face painted claret and blue, my brothers' wife Jackie done it for me early that morning just like the band Kiss, but West Ham colours, with stars around the eyes blue and the rest of my face claret. When we got to Villa Park; me, Froggit, Mickey, Tiggy, Steve El, Peter Palace and Martin Troy were in a completely different section of the ground. Bonesy, Tommy Williams, Kingy and all the other Cranham lads had tickets for another part of the ground and we were all segregated. We had settled in then we saw some of the younger lads Duke, Pigeon, Percy and Pete. Duke had been battered on the train up over a game of cards with the ICF. My initial thought was that they had been jumped by the scousers, but when they told us we were shocked that West Ham would do this to West Ham, it just broke all the rules and the codes. We said to the boys don't worry we will go down stairs at half time see if we can find them. Duke said "Phil you will never find them in this crowd." "We can try," I said. I could see the boys were nervous and told them to just point them out if you see them. Halftime came, so we went on our search. We walked down the stairs at Villa Park, where there was a bar at the bottom. Duke and pigeon were there, and pointed towards the bar. How's that we found them in less than a minute! It turned out to be Mad Jock and a huge firm all round the bar. Duke pointed out jock as the one who started it, so I approached Jock and said "Why did you jump my mates on the train, we are all West Ham here you don't do them things?" He turned around on his stall in front of his firm and pulled out a wad of money and said "See this you mug, I will have you shot!" then gently put it back in his jacket pocket. I said "Funny that, I take it you've not bought your gun with you then you mug?" at which point I hit him with four or five punches in a split second, knocking him off the stall straight to the floor. His mates, who were laughing at me when he pulled out the Wonga, were not laughing now. I immediately turned round to them and said "Any of you mugs want it as well, now's your chance" I grabbed one of his mates by the throat and said, "Do you want it?" there was nothing but silence. It was as if someone had sown their lips together. I then said "You're all fucking mugs" and we left the bar. We went back upstairs to where my mates were, and Dukes was telling everyone there "You should have seen it, guy flashed money to have Phil shot and bang! Bang! Bang! Phil sparked him and offered 'em all out". The young boys were excited. Young Duke at that time was a British boxing champion, his father ran Elm Park boxing club. Duke was good, but not used to being jumped on by a big firm of his own supporters. I don't think anyone expected to find them, but it was not over, round two was about to start, just as the second half of the match was about to kick off. Jock's pride was hurt and so was his jaw, but instead of giving in he got more of his boys and tried to launch a full attack on us from behind by running down the terrace at me. They could only recognise me because my face was painted, and obviously Duke, pigeon, Percy and Pete because they hammered them on the train. The second half whistle had just blown and the players started playing, when all of a sudden I heard "Watch out Phil!" I turned fast and saw loads of jocks boys running down at me. I had the advantage, they were running down at me and I ran up at them, it was as if I had a guardian angel watching over me. Not one of his boys touched me, but my fists were doing overtime smashing them to the ground one after the other. My mates were jumping on them and kicking them. That part of the ground became a battlefield, and they were falling like flies. Peter Palace, or 'Worm' as we nicknamed him, bit a chunk out of one of Jocks mates' ears. They had gone into a battle and they were getting the hiding of their lives. At this point, Jock stood right back and came screaming down shouting "I will do the mug." I'll take my hat off to him, he just sent twenty men at us and not one of them got close to me. Jock, hit me with some lovely punches that rocked me, but I was stronger and losing is not built into my mind set. As he ran down the terrace, a couple of his punches stunned me, but his biggest mistake was to bend down and try to run into my stomach with his head. I grabbed his head and slammed it down repeatedly on my knee. I could feel his bones breaking with the power of every thrust of my knee to his jaw and nose and I could see his teeth falling out with every strike. I refused to stop until he was pulverized and just a heap on the floor. I let go of him, and let him slump to the floor. At this point the guy I grabbed by the throat at the bar came running over with the Hornchurch, It was Reg' Brown and I heard Reg' say "No, not Phil Dalby", I said to Reg' "You don't know these mugs, Reg do you?" Well obviously, he did, I grabbed the guy by the throat again, and said, "You had your chance, now take my advice and fuck off, or I will seriously hurt you." The guy took my advice, Reg then said "Phil, be careful, I hear they got a big firm waiting for you outside and they wanna' do you Phil." Top Man Reg was. I always had time for him ever since, he got on top of the registry office in Hornchurch, when the police were chasing him and started throwing slate tiles down on their heads. I told Reg' "I don't give a fuck how many are outside I will go out and face them with my boys, I don't run Reg, you know that." Reg said "Well you'd better run, Phil, the Old Bill are coming for you from behind" I could not afford to get nicked again, so I ducked down in between peoples legs and ran to the front. I had to lose my painted face, or I will definitely have been nicked. I managed to find two girls, who got all the gear out of their handbags. They did a superb job of getting rid of my face paint. I was now paint free, and thought I'd gave it a while until the police had given up looking for me, and make my way back to the boys. They were buzzing with the fight that we all had, but I let them know the news that Reg had told me. "We must all stand together, because outside lads, they are planning on jumping us again." Credit to my boys, even the young ones said, "Ok, let's do it!" I knew I could do what I done with the Elm Park, as we walked out of the ground Reg's words were true. Jock was standing there with his face completely fucked with shit loads of men standing with him. I ran at him and gave him another punch, knocking him to the floor. Then looked at his men and said "Whose gonna' be the first brave man? Come on you mugs" My boys stood in line, each side of me ready for it to kick off, but it never. I think they realised after knocking half of them out inside the ground, that they were no match for us and the only one who had a fight in him was Jock, and I totally respect the man, he can take a hiding, and you have to be able to take a hiding in order to give a hiding. We walked away untouched. The funniest thing was that Duke, Pigeon, Percy and Pete got on the train home and low and behold Jock and all his crew got on the same carriage as them. Duke said 'We were shitting ourselves Phil, they were looking at us, but strangely they never laid a finger on us, as if we were protected by some strange shield?"

A warrior is not tested in victory, but tested in adversity and defeat. I have seen so many men who knew only Victory and become fearful once defeated. I never give up, never stop fighting, whether it is physical or mental, to me that is the sign of the warrior, I was born with this in my blood it ran deep through my veins like a river to the ocean! That evening we went to Curlys wine bar in station road Upminster and the story was being told far and wide about the battle we had that afternoon at Villa Park. The boys, who were segregated from us, were gutted that they were in another section now, and I could see they wished they were there with us, but it was a day the Cranham will never forget. They all stood together and done what had to be done for the sake of friendship, and believe me it will never be forgotten. This story is still talked about now in the Plough and surrounding pubs all these years later.

1982, England were playing Greece in Thessaloniki. A few of us were supposed to go to this match, but as the time got closer slowly and surely enough they all backed out due to financial reasons etc. So I decided to go alone. I landed at Athens Glyfada airport as it was in them days, and took a three-hour coach journey from Athens to Salonika. I was covered with England and West Ham scarf's. It was great! People were stopping me in Athens by the coach station wanting their photo with me. The game was originally going to be held in Athens, but officials thought it would deter English fans from coming by moving the venue to Thessaloniki; and that it did. I sat on the coach and met two Greeks who were going to the game, who warned me that I should take my colours off when we get to the coach station, because apparently there would be Greek supporters waiting for the English to arrive. I laughed at them and politely told them I take my colours off for nobody. They looked at me as if I was crazy and asked if I had a hotel to which I said no, they then offered to come stay with them and they'd set me up with a hotel, which was good of them. We pulled into Salonika coach station and the boys were right. There was a mob of Greeks waiting for the English fans, but it was just my rucksack and me. As I stepped off the coach they started throwing anything they could find at me, I immediately dropped my ruck sack and done what I did best, I started running into them thinking fuck it lets have it, and as I ran at them they started running back, but not from me. From the corner of my eye I noticed a police car speed across the coach park and cut in front of me and stopped between me and them, two police men jumped out and basically told the mob to go and then came over to me and asked me to get my bag and get in the car.

They put me in the back of the car and both turned around to me and said "are you mad, do you want to die?" in English. I surprised them and spoke back to them in Greek, well broken Greek what little I learned off my mother growing up, but was enough to string sentences together and get by. I told them basically that when it's time for me to die I will know it, and today would not have been the day. They laughed at me and started asking me questions about how I can speak Greek? Mama mou einai Ellinica autn einai apo Samos. Translated I said "my mother's from Greece and she is from Samos." They instantly took a liking to me, and then asked, "Then why are you wearing England colours? To which I replied "I was raised in England and only know the English ways, not the Greek" So they started to sing me a famous Greek song about Samos, well it was famous to them but I had never heard of it, but since that day, I've had people singing it to me many times. I remember thinking how weird is this, I'm used to being nicked, not sang to by the Old Bill! They were really genuine, and I don't often say it but lovely policemen. They asked where my hotel was, and we'll take you to it. I fumbled through my pockets and found the piece of paper the boys had given me on the coach. "Ella re" I said to them. They looked at the piece of paper and said, "Ok we know this Hotel" They even took me up to the room and one of them carried my rucksack. The boys answered the door and looked happy that I came back to their room. The

457

police shook my hand and said, "Now please, no more trouble" I laughed at them and promised I would be a Kalo pevi (a good boy). The Lads said they are going out for a meal and would I like to go with them? But to be honest, I just wanted to be with my own fans. I just needed to meet some English, so I told them "No it's ok, I need to shower first, and that I may meet them down the restaurant after the shower. Which I had no intention of doing. I did not want to appear to be rude, so out of politeness I said I might meet them down the Taverna.

I showered and then decided to take a walk around the city. I can't be the only English supporter at this match, it's impossible. I was starting to think that I was as I walked down the mainstream of this town. As I walked past every bar and tavern, I kept my ears open for the sound of English fans singing, but still nothing. I really was alone I thought, when from behind me two scooters pulled up and I heard "Fuck sake, we found one of our own!" It was an accent I was very use to, two cockney lads no older than 18. "How you doing mate, are we the only English here?" They introduced themselves Jason and Joey and were West Ham through and through. They had nicked the scooters, which made me laugh and I suggested we should look about and see if we can find more of our fans, also telling them to ditch the bikes and we all go by foot. I also warned them that the Old Bill carry machine guns here, and if they caught you on them bikes they may just use them, so the bikes were quickly ditched.

We walked another half mile and from out of a small Tavern we could hear Engerland! Engerland! Engerland! Engerland! Engerland! Engerland! We had found some of our own. We opened the tavern door and from the back, the singing kept coming. We started to sing, all three of us in time with them. Their faces lit up when they saw us. There was only 6 of them, Richard Grey from Derby, John King from Chelsea, Jerry from Arsenal, Mick from Manchester, Steve Lewisham from Lewisham but a devote hammer's fan, and Greg from Tottenham. They had all met just that evening and all thought the same as me, that they were all alone, so now there were nine of us. We had a few beers in that Tavern while we all got to know each other, Richey from Derby said that it would be a good idea that we all come and stay their hotel as it was cheap and they had plenty of rooms spare. That way we could all leave for the match together the following day, which was fine by us. So with a plan in order we carried on knocking the beer and the Ouzo shots back and were getting well steamed up, at this point we all decided to go to another Tavern that was down the road. The next tavern was welcoming, the owner loved us singing all English songs, even though we were steaming he was giving us free shots, I went to the toilet, and when I came back I saw two Greek men standing over our little group, they were drunk also but I could see the atmosphere had changed. The two guys were doing gestures to the lads, the gestures of we are going to cut your throats, and I don't think the boys knew how to handle it but I did! I went face to face with them and told them to fuck off and called them a pair of Greek Poofs in Greek then pushed them both backward. The manager ran over and said, "Please no trouble no trouble!" I told him to get these mugs out of the Tavern and everything will be fine, which he did and he locked the door behind them. The lads could not believe how I handled the situation, and that I spoke Greek. I think it shocked them, but also was a relief to them that I could speak the lingo, because my foul language got us out of that scene. But, a new scene was about to raise its ugly head. Within twenty minutes, the two guys had brought back a firm of over 30 Greeks and they were outside banging on the windows and doing cut our throat gestures. I told the boys not to worry and if they want us that bad, they will come through the glass windows like we would at West Ham and said let's wind them right up. By this time, we were flying with the amount of booze we had consumed. "What we will do is all line up against the window and give them all a moon, I know that will wind them up." We did, and it and they start jumping up and down like monkeys going mad. Carrying on the torment, we then stood by the window and we were giving them cock-sucking gestures. By this time, the lads were all pissed and just laughing at how we retaliated, and that they never even had the bollocks to come through the plate glass window at us. Then we saw the police cars turn up, and not one but three It seemed strange that just a few policeman could just talk to the Greeks and they would all go, and they walked in the door it was the two same policeman that took me back to the hotel, with a few of their friends. "Not you again my friend!" was the opening remark from the Greek policeman. The manager told them "no, no it was not them who started it was the guys outside." The policeman sat and had a coffee with us and asked if we wanted an escort back to our hotel? I said I was ok and was now staying with the rest of the English guys, but all I needed to do was get my bag. Their courtesy was extended yet again, and they insisted that they would take me to collect my things and take me to a new hotel. Where else in the world would you get that kind of service? The other police took my newfound friends to their Hotel, and I was soon to join them.

It was the day of the match our heads a little precious from the night before, but we still decided to have breakfast in the Hotel. Nothing fancy, it was only a continental breakfast. No English fry up; that would've gone down a treat, but instead just a cup of coffee and a croissant. The nine of us got ready and by about 1 pm made our way to the ground, which was only few kilometers away. We jumped on a bus, and noticed there were thousands of cars and scooters overtaking the bus, all covered with Greek flags hanging out of the windows, even people sitting on top of the cars. It was November, but the weather was still hot, I remember the bus was crammed and very sweaty. When we got off the bus, we found another five English fans, so we all made the walk to the stadium together. There were only fourteen of us. That was all of the fans that had made the two and a half thousand-mile journey from England to Greece, so we had to stick together. We bought our tickets outside the ground from a tout and had to laugh as not one of us who took the time to fly from England to Greece had a ticket, but are willing to make that long journey. Now that's dedication for you. As we entered the ground the Atmosphere was mental, we had had no problem so far walking to the ground, but things were about to change as we walked up the stairs through a tunnel right smack bang into the Greek fans. Some tried jumping down on us from the tier above, only to get battered by us. Both the police, and television crews could see the disturbance in the stairwell coming up into the ground and all attention focused on us from the TV crews and the police. We all stood together and made a charge at the Greeks and at this point you could see the whole crowd open up as if a bomb was about to explode. From above us, they started throwing flares and fireworks down on us which went down some of the England boys jackets and burnt the skin off from their shoulders. The scene was now very volatile and police sent in an army of Old Bill with clubs to make a circle around us, but they too were being hit with flares and rockets and to be honest they looked scared. Now the whole world was focused on us with the TV crews zooming in on the scene, and we were now penned in but we were all giving it back to the Greeks shouting, "Come on you muppets!" which made the scene worse. The police did not know what to do and they were ducking and diving from the missiles that were being thrown down on us from every part of the above tier. All of a sudden, more police came and decided to get us out of this part of the ground and the only way to do it was across the pitch and into the seating area with Bobby Robson and the England Team. As we got on the pitch some Greeks jumped the barriers to come at me, the police took no prisoners that day, they drew there truncheons and beat the fucking granny out of the same Greek fans that ran on the pitch at us. You could see their teeth falling out with every blow and while they were being dragged away by the Old Bill, they continued to beat the shit out of them on live T.V for the whole world to see. I later found out my friends were watching it in the pub in Cranham and cheering us, and more to the point gutted that they were not there to join me. England went on to win the match 3-0, the police kept us in with Bobby Robson and the team, and after the match bundled us into wagons and took us all back to our Hotel.

As soon as the Old Bill left we all headed into town. Then it happened, a firm of Greek fans found out that we were in a bar, and as we walked out of one bar down the road to another, they came at us with chains and lumps of wood. The two young West Ham boys were up front and suddenly came running back shouting "Phil, there's fucking loads of them mate! We're gonna' get killed, they're all tooled up, mate" I told them to grab whatever they could, bottles whatever, and told them we don't run. John from Chelsea grabbed a wooden chair from outside a Kebab shop and smashed it down on the floor breaking it into bits. Rich from Derby, Steve Lewisham from West Ham, Jerry from Arsenal and John took a leg each. I never forget a tall Greek lad came running through swinging a chain. I ran straight at him and ducked as he swung the chain. I could feel the air from the motion of the chain as it just passed over my head, then I came up with all my body weight from my legs down and connected right under his jaw, he fell like a sack of shit. At this point, the two young West Ham lads jumped up and down on his body and head. Rich, John, Steve, Jerry, and Mick from Manchester flew past me and stormed in with the legs of the chair to the Greek mob that were coming at us. We just kept going forward; we had to, as there was no other option. It was a fucking great feeling that these guys on any other day in a league match in England, would be fighting with each other and myself, but today we fought side by side against another country, and that's what it was, two nations now, and we were not prepared to lose. The screaming from terrified people outside the ice cream shops and Kebab shops said it all. People were running in every direction to get away from the mayhem and violence, while we just carried on like it was another day at West Ham. Then out of nowhere, I heard the sound of a machine gun clicking, then another and another. The Old Bill surrounded us and their guns pushed into our heads, and in broken English heard "Now lay on the floor or we shoot!" We were handcuffed, seven of us arrested, and waiting for them to bring a police wagon to put us in. Jerry, Steve Lewisham, Richard Grey, John King, Mick from Manchester, Joey the young West ham lad, and I were all nicked. It just so happened while we were fighting four Old Bill had just finished their shifts and were having a coffee before they all went home, that's why we never heard no sirens, just the click of the machine guns.

On the day of the court appearance, the policemen who arrested us told the Judge, in their eyes, I was the leader of the English fans. But to my surprise the two policeman who came to my aid on two occasions the day before the match, stood up and gave the Judge a wicked character reference on my behalf, I was taken aback. Words actually failed me, they told the Judge that they had met me twice on the day before the match and on each time I was polite and courteous toward them and told the Judge that there was, no way I was the leader of the English hooligans. Steve Lewisham, Richard Grey, Jerry, Joey and I were acquitted. Unfortunately, they had to make an example of the English fans, it was sad to see John

King, and Mick from Manchester receive a two-year jail sentence in the Heptapyrgion prison in Thessaloniki. John's sentence was shortened after his sister was attacked in London, so he was let out after 13 months on compassionate grounds. When we got home to U.K, I kept in touch with the boys; my mates and me would often meet up with Richard Grey and the Derby firm before the England Matches. Our usual rendezvous was to meet at the Regents palace Hotel, Piccadilly Circus before all the home England Matches. We also met John King and Jerry there, when he got out of prison. I never ever saw the two young lads again, but Steve Lewisham invited me down to meet his mates, so I met him in the Boleyn a week after we got home. As we walked into the South bank and who did he introduce me to, only Mad Jock and his firm. I said "Steve we have already met mate", but Jock offered me a beer so I had a drink with them, funny how things go.

I got the England buzz after the Greece vs. England Match. Myself, some of the Hornchurch and Rainham boys, Paul Stubbs, Smut, big Richy Attewell and his brother Cliffy, along with Johnny Dowsing who was the first armed blagger to get arrested as a result of his teeth indents that were found on the plastic part of the key in the getaway car. He was so nervous he was chewing the key that hard just before he robbed the Securicor van, and ended up doing a long stretch in Prison because of that mistake. We would drive anywhere to see England play. We would take two vans along with our fishing gear, which was a great cover and go camping. Some of the Cranham boys, like my younger brother Paul, Si Reed, and Lou Burridge joined us on a few trips abroad also. It was the time the music changed from hairy bearded men playing guitar, to New Romance music, then the Acid house scene, which lead on to the Rave scene in the late '80's. We toured everywhere, Euro 92 Sweden, we camped on a site about 15 Kilometres outside Malmo. We met up with a load of scousers whose camper van broke down in Disneyland France, so they found an identical one and nicked it, and just swapped the number plates, and drove over to Sweden in it, and that's where we met them at Lomma Beach. Holland, Norway, Denmark, Poland, Germany we went everywhere and not forgetting France world cup 1998.

I recall it was the early nineties, when we got the phone call at my house in Peterborough Avenue that Terry had been shot, in the back alley at Roseberry, the same alley that I met him in all them years earlier. The same alley we would climb trees and play with our catapults, and build dens in the haystack directly behind Tel's house, only to have our back sides bitten by whisky the dog, that was guarding the stables every time we slid down the make shift slide we made out of the green tarpaulin sheet, that covered the hay barrels. I was numb my brother Paul phoned me and said "you better get up here, I think something bad has happened to Tel." Myself, Froggit, Mickey, and Tiggy had all been working out in the gym in my garden that early evening. Froggit drove us there he had a reputation of driving like a nutter, so we knew we would get to Roseberry in no time. Our hearts had sunk. We were all speechless like I say, just numb, and hoping that the news was not true. When we got to Roseberry Gardens, which took less than a minute with Froggits driving, the whole of Roseberry Gardens was mobbed with armed O.B and normal O.B. We pulled up outside my house where my mum had raised us, and still lived there. My brother Paul was already outside and the Old Bill were making their presence known, telling all our neighbours to go inside and shut the doors. No one did and all of our neighbours congregated on their front gardens, we all grew up together this was our street and everyone was concerned for Tel' and not took a blind bit of notice of the O.B.

Froggit walked up the steps of Tel's house to go and see how his mum and dad were, Terry was in the back alley with the paramedics, who were trying their best to keep him stable. Tel' was very much like me, his pain was my pain, we were brothers and very well respected, and well known for being able to have a good fight, always watched each other's backs in countless scenarios.

Froggit closed the front door behind him; we were standing by his wall. I remember Del Anderson, Barry, and Chris Wells all in tears saying "he is dead, Phil, he is dead" I refused to believe it, and my thoughts at the time was, was that the Old Bill had shot him and the reason I thought this, was something that Tel' had told me a few weeks earlier, after police raided his flat in Cranham but Tel was not there. But they left him a little present. Two bullets with a note saying these are for you, which is why my thoughts were going in that direction. At this precise moment, Paul Biggsy drove up in his works van with Terry's younger brother John. They had obviously been on the lash and John stumbled out the car to race over to his mum's front door. As he tried to pull the crime scene tape up over his shoulders, which the police put across a few cars outside of Tel's house to prevent people coming on this side of the road, two O.B tore into John with their Truncheons, hitting him everywhere. He only wanted to see his family and here my rage for Old Bill raised its ugly head again. I flew in, dragged John away and threw the two Old Bill around like rag dolls. All my neighbours witnessed it and I said to them quite calm as you like, "You want to hit someone you mugs, then hit me, I will take them truncheons off you and shove them up your back passage you pair of cunts. It's cunt like you that give the Old Bill a bad name." Everyone was shocked at the Old Bill and what I just done, and this was the only thing anyone could do in that situation. It only takes one blow to the head with them truncheons, and John could well have been joining Terry in intensive care. Just goes to show how evil they can be, his brother was laying half dead in the back alley, and they were trying their best to make sure his other brother joined him. I don't tolerate bullies, whether they are street bullies or bullies in uniform, they are all the same to me.

It was classic, the O.B could not arrest me for assaulting the two officers. Why? Because too many people witnessed the incident. If nobody had been there then, I'm sure the story would be much different. John Marley, Chris Wells, Biggsy and myself went up Oldchurch Hospital, Matt Thomas was already there, waiting for us. They had to get in two army surgeons, who for some reason were in the neurological ward, on some kind of training program. The Neurologists were not use to gunshot wounds in this unit, and it was just by luck, that the army surgeons were there that evening. Gunshot wounds and explosives was what the military were used to, and if they had not been at Oldchurch that evening the ending would be very much different.

We had heard that the O.B had arrested Froggit, and had taken him down to Gants Hill police station, and had taken all his clothes for forensic evidence. They Kept him in for two days, until a friend of ours who use to knock about with us as kids and goes West Ham with us but had now become O.B told them they had the wrong man, if it were not for Gary Cook, Froggit may of been kept much longer for questioning. Tel' recovered well, and when he thought he was O.K he discharged himself, that's Tel' all over. If he can walk, then he's ok to go home, no matter if the hospital say no Tel' always did his own thing. To this day the gunman has never been caught.

We made it a ritual every Friday night that we'd meet down the Berwick Manor. A local of ours located on the border of Upminster and Rainham, a nightclub which was the place to be at the time. One evening a firm came down from Avely, the management knew them, and told us that they are feared throughout that part of Essex. Bullies more like it. This evening in particular, they had attacked a young lad outside in the car park with a baseball bat then walked around bolshie. I saw them in the toilets picking on some young kids, I had a slash and looked at them both and they both looked at me. Scary looking men to some, but not me I don't scare easy. I zipped up my trousers, and walked back to the Gangsters bar. It was nicknamed that, because all the hoods drank in there. It was situated past the dance floor, and past the entrance to the club. I Told Terry and Mick what I just seen, and that's when Tel' told me that they had just batted a kid outside of the club with the bat.

As we were talking about this, the bar door was thrown open and they walked in bogging at me. "You fucking looking at me?" he said to my face, with Tel' and Mick behind me. My reply was "do you want to fuck about or fight?" At which moment, I let out a volley of blinding punches which flew him from the bar area to the floor across the room. As I was bending over him punching down on his face, his mates tried to have a go. Only to be swiftly put down by Tel' and then I remember Tel' saying to the man he put down "You're fucked now you twat" and left him on the floor like a pile of shit, they were both done badly and I remember the managements faces, which were in disbelief and horror.

We thought it was all over, three weeks had past and we had forgotten about the incident a few weeks earlier. Terry, Mick and I were in the same bar on this Friday evening, having a drink when the door to the Gangsters bar flew open again, but this time they were not alone. The two that we pasted three weeks previous had brought a firm up of eight other men, who all had the look of boxers about them. I had my back facing them and it was Terry that spotted them walk in, and promptly told me to stay calm. Silly bollocks is here again with a firm. Did they not have enough last time, was the thought running through my head? At this point, Steinfold walked away from the bar and came behind me pointing me out to his firm, I hate people walking behind me, but I knew Terry and Mick were watching my back as he walked back to the bar then Terry said to me, "watch my back, I bet the stupid twat follows me into the toilet." How right Terry was, because as soon as the toilet door shut, Steinfold followed him. At this point, I told Mick to move over to where the steps are that led to the toilets. At least that way I never had my back to them, and I could watch every movement and hear every sound from the toilet.

Tel' was having a slash as Steinfold walked up to him and said "you were with him that night tell me his name or you're gonna get it as well", Tel replied back, "are you threatening me?" "No I'm fucking telling you that you're gonna fucking get it!" was his reply. Tel' said, "Take a look at my face, because it's the last time you're gonna see it" At that moment I could hear the screams coming from the toilet and I knew it was not Tel!

Mick and I ran at his firm who were standing by the bar, who by this time knew that their mate or the man that hired them, was not coming out of that toilet smiling and we tore right into the ones who were nearest to us. As we did so, they all ran out the door faster than they came in and left their mate to get a hiding. That is something we would never consider as we fight together, no matter what. I could not believe it that so many hard looking men were running and leaving their mate behind, or maybe it was just that he did hire them and it was a bit out of there league. Who knows or cares, it was all forgotten about but their pride got in the way and they returned to the club to obviously hurt us. But when it came to bottle, they lost their bottle completely and it did not end there!

The daft twats had decided to put a price on Tells and my head, a contract. We heard this because the people they gave the contract to, knew us also and warned us. In fact, they asked a few boys, and every bit of information got back to us. So, we arranged a meet with Steinfold and his boys down the Thatched house in Cranham. We chose Cranham in case we were about to be set up. Tel was doing some business up North that day, so my crazy mate John Kastaneda, who was over from the beautiful Greek island of Koz wanted to come along with me. We also have been in many fights together, in Athens against some American Marines, and on Koz island with a firm there, that me and John wiped out one night and was talk of the island for years. Another bullyboy bites the dust.

I knew John was good back up for me as we walked into the pub, across the road, and down the lane directly behind the thatched house where the rest of the Roseberry boys were looking and were being prepared for anything. John and I walked in the pub and it was just Steinfold by himself, we sat down beside him. I said, "What you playing at, we know what you been trying to do, it all comes back to us, now we can resolve this and call a truce or how do you want to be?" He listened and I could see he was scared, more scared that we knew what his plan was for us. Now we had turned it around on him, that night and a truce was called the next day. He had two of his boys deliver £10,000 sterling to the Plough Pub in Cranham, which was payment for all the boys involved and some for those who were not involved. We shared it out between all of us, as that's what friends are for.

It was not long after these incidents down the Berwick Manor that the Berwick closed down. So we found somewhere else to go which was Hollywoods in Romford, which was run by Tony Tucker and his doormen. It was a regular venue for us and not far from Cranham and usually guaranteed a good night. It was 1995, and just before my birthday on 9th

November. We all went down to celebrate Froggits and my birthday, and every one was mangled. We seemed to attract two Chinese martial arts experts who began to get out of hand, they were from Zimbabwe, so they said and one of them was the Zimbabwe kickboxing champion. Obviously, they had snorted too much cocaine and were wired to fuck. They were just being a total fucking nuisances, pinching Dave Troys girlfriend's backside and kept trying to grab hold of her. One of them had a long trench coat on and a tall leather hat; this is the one who was giving it all the mouth about how hard his mate was. I told them to keep their hands to themselves and that the girl had a boyfriend. They started getting brave then asking who the hardest man was on our firm and that his friend will take us all on. It was our birthday, and we really didn't want no agg'. Tucker and his boys were looking on, and could see something was about to happen. They persisted in giving us plenty of gob but it was when one of them said to me that he will shoot me and my mother. That's when I got him in a bear hug and lifted him off the ground. At this point Tucker and his men came running over, and I told them to get this mug out of here and they took him out of my tight grip and threw him outside. At this point he stripped down to the waist and offered the doorman out. You could see he was good with his Karate kicks and he would not leave until he had a fight with someone. His friend with the hat was outside with him coaching him on. Tucker and his doorman came back up the steps and made it known to all of us that he had offered them all out as well! But now he is waiting downstairs for me, how could I refuse? Fuck it, it's my birthday and I'm fighting again. As I walked down the stairs I was followed by Lou Burridge who said, "Phil, I hope he's not got his nunchuck's with him!" That comment did make me laugh. Duke, Danny Sawyer, Froggit and Scott Bromley all followed me down. They all wanted to see this fight, and so did Tucker and his doormen. As we got to the bottom Tucker said to me, "Can you take it round the corner, it's all cameras outside?" I laughed and saw this Karate kid doing some practice kicks and said to Tucker "I will try."

If only the Karate kid knew what he was up against, one of the strongest heads in the world, full of Titanium metal, then I'm sure he would have thought twice. As I stepped out of the front door of Hollywoods, his mate with the hat was smiling and looking at me saying, "You're a dead man, you're fucking dead" I replied, "Am I? Listen, can we take it round the corner," and whack! His first kick came straight at my temple. I managed to get my left arm up to block the full power of the kick. There was no time to take it round the corner now, then another kick, but I was testing him, I had to feel his strength and find my first punch, the audiences were all outside watching this, along with my mates, Tucker and his doormen. I moved into him then came another three fast kicks to my head, but as he put his foot down on the third kick, I came back at him with a blinding left uppercut, which knocked him off his balance slightly. Then a few more from my right hand hurt him and he tried to jumped up and grab my head to slam down on his knee, but as his knee came up to my face, I blocked his knee with my right arm. This was my opportunity for my right fist was now level with his balls and the punch was short but powerful I felt him go limp as I pounded his balls. Then I grabbed his testicles and lifted him up off the floor and his feet never touched the ground. Everybody was cheering and his grip on my head loosened. I charged him into a car, and I could hear Tucker shouting, "No not my car!" as I slammed his limp body against it. From there, I let go of his testicles and came up with a punch that came nearly from the floor, and as it connected, it opened his head up like a can of baked beans, from his temple down to his jaw. It was as if someone had struck a blade down his face and he was gone. Then another from my left arm opened him up again and took him to the floor, he had called it on and he got the Dalby hammer, or 'One Punch' as Andy Swallow nicknamed me. It may have been the Haymaker as others call me, but I used them all and he was out of the game and bleeding heavily. His friend with the hat was now being held by Tuckers doormen and everybody was clapping, even Tuckers boys. I walked over to the mouthpiece and grabbed him by the throat, and I said to him, "See you, you cunt, you got a ten gallon hat on a two pint head. Where the fuck did you say you were from?" He was shaking now and his mouth was not so motorized, as if his batteries gone flat. In a nervous stutter, he replied "Zimbabwe." I threw him to the ground outside Hollywood's and said go and pick up your mate and fuck off back to Zimbabwe you pair of cunts, and every one clapped again.

The next week after the incident with the kick boxer, I had to go into Harold wood hospital. It was for an operation on my knee, which I had been waiting for a long time. It was an easy operation to go in for and I went in on the Tuesday afternoon, and back out on Wednesday. It all went well, but I was not able to walk properly for a couple weeks. I had the use of the walking stick, but I never wanted to take that out with me down Hollywood's the following Friday.

I was hopping about on one leg, which was fine by me as long as I could stay out of trouble. Cliffy, Attewell, Russell Chadwick more commonly known as Rusty, and Paul Lesley, Leso, and myself headed down to Hollywood's, All was good at first until later in the evening I noticed two of Tuckers muscle bound steroid freaks set upon a young lad, Stuart Cox, while he was walking onto the dance floor with his beer in his hand. It was a doorman we nick named Dolly mixture who was well known for bullying and using weapons around Basildon. It was an old friend of mine called Tony Green, who introduced me to dolly mixture. Tony was now living in Basildon and was well on the smack. Tony had brought him round to my house in Peterborough Avenue once, to show him my gym, I'll never forget the moment I met him, because me, Dish, Scags, Shane, and Brad were working out on the punch bag. At my house, I had a side gate so anyone could walk in, and just use the gym. Tony walked in with Wayne (Dolly mixture), while I was pounding the punch bag bare fisted, and from that moment on, I had an instant dislike to Tony's friend; especially after the stories they told us about what they get up to in Basildon. The drugs had changed him and he was going downhill fast. Tony was a lovely lad in his younger days, a six foot tall Italian Brit'. At the age of eleven at Hall Mead he was the only kid with hairs on his chest, a strapping lad and could have a good row as well, but the drugs were killing him, and not much later after the visit to my gym Tony had died with a smack overdose. I was on holiday when Tony died, but when I heard of his death, I lit a candle for him in a church up the mountains on the Greek island of Koz.

Tony would be turning in his grave if he knew what was about to happen at this moment in Hollywood's, between me, and his best friend Dolly mixture. The two doormen were steaming into Stuart Cox, I had clocked it and give the young lad credit they never put him down but continued to attack him because he walked onto the dance floor with his beer glass in his hand. I saw what happened, they punched relentlessly and the young lad made no gesture at all to hit back. He was just stunned as the blows kept raining down on him. I came up behind them and tapped dolly mixture on the shoulder at which point he stopped. My words to them were, "Don't you think he has had enough?" "Fuck off Dalby or Dilby, whatever your fucking name is as you will get it as well" That was a threat to me in my eyes, and no one threatens me! That was it, I unleashed a sequence of punches that in an instant both doormen were spark out cold on the floor in front of the bar area. I saw Tuckers face it was shock. There were only six doorman on the door that evening, I know because I always count, just for the reasons like now and so I know what I am up against. Tucker and the rest of his doormen ran over and dragged their unconscious bodies away. So now, there are only four. My mates, came over and asked what you done Phil? I said "They're are all a bunch of mugs and told them" They replied, "Shall we leave?" "No I'm not leaving for no one, there are only four of them left and who gives a fuck, cause I don't." Tucker saw me fight the week before with the Kick boxer, so I know they were worried about me, so worried that he called in more doormen from the surrounding clubs in Romford. Twenty minutes I waited by the bar with my mates, then they came back with another eight doormen, from the local clubs in the area. There were now fourteen of them.

I stood head on with them, and they made a full circle around me, Dolly mixture now had a baseball cap on his head obviously to hide the lumps that were swelling up more on his head with each minute. Cliffy, Rusty, and Leso were outside of the circle just waiting and watching. Tucker moved closer to me and said, "Can you leave by the back door?" "Fuck off you mugs," was my reply. I then added, "I will leave by the door I came in," and walked right through their ring of steel. As I did this, they all ran around me and circled me again, and asked the same question, "Can you leave by the back door?" That was it, there was no way I was getting out of this without a fight and to be honest I really didn't give a shit and I tore into the lot of them. As I was fighting Cliffy, Rusty, and Leso came tearing in with me, the exit doors were swung open and we were now fighting on the top of the staircase that ran to the left of the entrance door. They were trying to throw me over the top balcony, but I was too strong for them. Fists and feet were incoming at me, but I kept going at them. I saw the boys having a fucking good go as well. I went down the stairs, taking a few of them with me and still punching as we rolled down the metal staircase. I saw cliffy run down the stairs and kick the doorman who was on top of me in the head, but in the fall down the stairs my leg that had been operated on was giving me too much pain and I could not walk. It was not broken, but I was down and could not get up. It was Leso, Rusty and Cliff that dragged me away, and really gave everything that night to stand beside me. Top boys.

You can't win them all! Like I say you have to take a hiding to be able to give a hiding. My leg was ok the next day, I was still hobbling and the only injury I received was a small gash under my left eye, which still has a scar. For fourteen powerful men, they should of at least put one of us in hospital and we were all fine. It was just another punch up to us. To be honest, Mad Jock at Villa Park rocked me more than Tucker and all his boys did at the top of the stairwell. Most of them were running back from me every time I let loose with a fistful of punches. The rest is history, on December 6 1995, on a cold winter's morning just a couple weeks after our fight with them, Tony Tucker, Patrick Tate, and Craig Rolfe were found shot dead in a Range Rover down a small farm track in the village of Rettendon. Michael Steele and Jack Whomes were arrested for the murders purely based on the evidence of Darren Nichols one of their associates. To this day Michael Steele and Jack Whomes still proclaim that they are innocent.

The second of May two thousand and six was an evening that will always stick in my memory. I had sold my house in Peterborough Avenue and bought a house back in my old road, forty-six Roseberry Gardens. In fact, it was the exact house that Froggit and Martin Troy were born in many years before.

Directly across the road Terry lived with his family and next door to Tel' lived Chris Sol who was married to Angela Greenhill, Steves Greenhill's sister. It was good to be back home with the people I grew up with. Terry, Wolfie, and I were having a beer in my living room when Wolfie's phone rang. I watched his face turn colour and go very pasty, his mouth dropped and he said 'my sons been shot.' My stomach turned, we could not believe what Wolfie just told us. "Where is he?" asked Tel'. "Oldchurch Hospital" replied Wolfie, "come on, let's get down there," said Tel'. The drive to the hospital was very somber; I just could not think why anyone would want to shoot Rocky. He was a fantastic lad. Like us, he was a bit of a scallywag but a good heart and was always polite with everyone, and just like his father, he was a joker and would joke about everything and nothing was serious. Who would do a thing like this? When heard he had been shot, putting his Kids into the car, and that one of the bullets out of the three that were shot just missed the kids by centimeters made it even more sickening. On arrival at the hospital, Wolfie was informed that his son had passed away. Wolfie and Tel went in to see Rocky to formerly identify him, I waited outside it was something I did not feel comfortable doing. I was shaking with anger and sadness for Wolfie and his family. This had ripped him and his family apart. There was nothing that anyone could do to take the pain and anguish away. I was to be married in less than a month, but this cowardly attack had cast a dark shadow over our wedding plans. How could I be happy when my good mate and family are so sad, it was hard to digest. I was Married June 4 2006, Tiggy and Micky Martin were my bestmen. Terry said he would not get up and do a speech, no way, so he was my usher instead of being best man, solely for that reason. He never had to stand up and do a speech, just look after me for the day and make sure I got to the wedding on time. Wolfie and Candy were there also and they hid the pain that they were going through, just so, they could be with us on this day. Nicky and I had a honeymoon in the Maldives, but soon after we got back, things went wrong and we split up just after the honeymoon. It must have been the shortest marriage in history. I was cut up. But I had to keep my mind occupied or I would fall apart. So I decided along with Tony Tarrington to do a charity fund raising day for the Dawson family. Their whole world had collapsed, Wolfie was struggling to get to work and to be honest that was probably the last thing on his mind and the debts were building up. The gym that Rocky use to train in sent them a final demand for what Rocky owed for the year for him and his girlfriend Sue. This was eating away at Candy, worrying about paying that, and all the other bills along with all the trauma they were going through, was about to send the pair of them into a nervous breakdown. Therefore, I took control of that. I took a bunch of flowers to the gym and gave them to the manageress and asked her to quash the bill, she told me it was not down to her and that it has to come from someone above her, so I met her also and told them to have a heart, which also cost me another bunch of flowers, but my hard work paid off and Candy got the phone call the next morning saying the bill was quashed.

Now we went on the mission to raise money and prizes to be raffled and auctioned off in the Plough pub in Cranham. Tony and I spent over a couple of weeks walking into every shop in Cranham, Upminster, Hornchurch and Guidea Park begging for gifts. Whether it was cuddly toys, computers, bicycles, even Chinese, Indian, Italian and Greek restaurants, we persuaded to donate. They had all read the papers saw the news and gave willingly. Meals for two, meals for six, we had every prize you can imagine. My nephew Richard and his girlfriend who at the time was Emma Louise were DJ's for the evening; Pete Booker and Sarah L Davey were the live music for the evening. We had Frank Harper from Lock, stock and two smoking barrels and another actor from that film but his name evades me now. But were there to have photos done with all the punters, which Terry and Big John organised. In the garden was a bouncy castle and other events paid for by Cliffy and Carol Attewell. Everyone had pulled together from the borough of Havering, right across East and South London and people came from everywhere and brought gifts with them to raffle. This day, we achieved much more than we set out to achieve, and it turned out a real success for the Dawson family.

We raised around thirteen thousand pounds for Wolfie and his family which was enough to pay off his debts and give the family a break that they all needed. Two men were arrested for Rocky's murder, and it was apparently a case of mistaken identity, maybe the muppets should have gone to SpecSavers and it would have avoided a lot of heartache. Still to this very day, the family cannot rest or settle.

Day in, day out the only question is why? All they need to know is who it was that gave the orders, and who paid the money, and they would be able to put the lid on it. What a waste of a young man's life, by a bunch of cowards who can pull a trigger easy enough, but probably can't punch their way out of a paper bag. GUNS ARE FOR PLUMS, you get no better respect than using your fists, to all you young lads that are out there and ever get a chance to read this, stay away from that road as it leaves nothing but heartache and anguish for those left behind!

After the fund raising event I was at loose ends, my wife had gone and I was thinking too much. Driving to work every morning I would see her walking to Upminster station. She was living back round her mother's in Upminster and it was cracking me up. Terry took my wedding ring off me and asked me "Why are you still wearing it?" Maybe I was just hoping that we could have resolved our differences, but I let Tel take it off me because deep down I knew it was over and I had to get away.

I had a brother in Cyprus, Alex, who married a Cypriot lady and I had not seen him for at least twenty five years. It would be a great chance to see the country I was born in, after all the years I had been stuck in Essex, and never spent a thought about my birthplace. What does it look like? It was in my head and I had to get away, I had to find myself again!

I landed at Pathos airport at the end of November 2006. My brother Alex picked me up, it was good to see him and his family that I had never met. I'd only spoke to them on the phone, not often probably only once a year, and now I had met his wife Maria and his daughter Fortini. They only had a small bungalow, but Alex had introduced me to his mate Andy. We called him Cornish, because he was from that part of the world Cornwall, an ex RAF man who served his time in the Iraq war and had seen plenty of action. I decided to move in with Andy, until I found my own place to rent. We lived in Ypsonas, which apparently was the rough end of Cyprus. Ypsonas, Kollosi, and Trachoni were Cyprus Mafia controlled areas, but to me it was paradise. Sunshine, sea, and a top pub run by Flob, whose real name Sean Skippy Knight, who was also ex-military. He'd served in the 2nd battalion Royal regiment of fusiliers, part of the N.I.T.A.T in Northern Ireland in the seventies, and ended up as Royal protection squad, close quarters for Princess Ann. His bar was the place to be, and it was Flob who gave me my new nick name 'BISH BOSH', after a couple incidents outside his bar. One incident involving a lady from Manchester, Alison Pilkington who was attacked by some Cypriot's while leaving the bar. They were all hassling her so she told them to get lost, which is when they got violent. We had heard her scream so I ran out, and in Flobs words, I bished them and I boshed them and then I nutted them and then it was all over. Cyprus is full of ex pats and especially military and I seemed to be settling in quite fine. Terry popped over for two weeks with his girlfriend Andre to see me, and then it was a steady flow of my mates from Essex. It was great! Who needed to be in Cranham, when Cranham was coming to me? Steve El, Martin Troy, Scaggsy, James Casewell, Tiggy and Sue, Tel's younger brother Charlie Marley, Tommy Tucker or Williams as he is known, Keith O Neil, Ginger Ralf and Tracy, Glen Gowler and Jens, Cliffy Attewell and Carol, Charlie Lawrence, it was like Hotel Paradiso, or Dalby Towers.

June 2008, Andy and I had moved into a three-bedroom house in Ypsonas, an area full of Bulgarians, Romanians, and Sri Lankans. It's full of little back streets and alleyways with traditional stone village houses plotted everywhere with tiny little court yards. Steve Trotter, a good friend of mine from Upminster, who was dealt a bad card in life, came to stay with us. He was paraplegic after he tested a motor bike out in Camden town, and was knocked down by a car that drove off. To make it worse, which I do laugh about, after he was hit by the car, a tramp came up to him while he was lying in the road and stole his boots off his feet! Steve laughs about it also. Anyhow, Steve was here and I promised his mum I would take good care of him. One evening, he went down to a little seedy bar, just down the road from us, and he upset some Russians with his tongue. Steve was very much like that, very blunt to the point of being rude. I have told him, in fact, every one told him but he never gave a toss. You can match him to the guy out of the TV program Phoenix nights a spitting and he is an image in everything he does. This evening he went out by himself and rolled himself down to the bar. He loved a drink Stevie boy, but then I do as well, I must of been asleep when he dodged out, but the noise he made coming back in woke up the neighbourhood, he fell out of his wheelchair drunk, and was screaming out my name to wake me and the neighbours. "Phil, Phil, Phil" he was shouting. It was like looking after a five year old, no matter what you told him he would do the opposite just to get his way. I told him to stay away from them seedy clubs! They are always trouble, but Steve didn't listen. Anyway, I woke up at 3 in the morning to his screams, run downstairs and he is flat out on the floor pissed with a black eye. I asked him "what the fuck happened?" He then told me some Russians just gave him a hiding. Fuck, that's all I needed this time of morning. So I put Steve in the car and drove down to the bar, thankfully only a minute away. I got Steve out of the car and rolled him into the bar. I know he can be a nuisance, but I don't care what anyone says you don't hit a man in a wheelchair. I was fuming and pissed off because I had been woken up. It was one of these bars you buy the girls a drink and they flirt all over you, and the more tips you give them the more erotic they got. I can only imagine that Steve had blown every penny he had on them, and had all the girls round him and that's probably why the Russians got the hump. This mixed in with and with Steve's 'I don't give a fuck attitude' probably told them to take a shit and eat it, and that is why he got clumped. So I walked in and Steve pointed them out. With this, they started shouting at Steve. That was it, I walked in front of his wheelchair, now I was smiling at the guys as I walked up to them. They were all standing by the bar and I gently moved the girls away from them and with a smile. I knocked two of them out straight away, the other one went to pick up a chair, but after seeing his mates knocked out cold decided to put it back down again, and held his hands up, in the gesture of no thanks mate you win. I turned around to Steve and said mate I think it is time for us to leave. In and out that's what I like.

After this night at the bar I made it a habit that when I went to bed at night I would dismantle Steve's wheelchair and take the wheels upstairs to bed with me, just so Steve could not go out and get himself into trouble. It's different if Andy or me were with him but Steve liked the nightlife. So we made it a rule, only weekends. But still, we hid Steve's wheels away from to avoid any temptation.

It was early June 2008, and we got a message from Johny Tango via Facebook, funny enough. I grew up with Johnny, he was a biker I had known him from the age of twelve. As a kid he was a loner, some say he was disturbed, but he was older than I was. He had an instant respect for me, and likewise, he was a warrior, a man with a rage and not a bullie's rage, but one of a rage to be tested as a man. He was the man who organised all the Tango and Rapture raves. He was the man who introduced me to all the biker gangs at Harwood Hall in Upminster, where all the biker gangs would meet once a year. It was through John that I met a notorious outlawed biker gang, with whom I got very friendly. In fact, when Rusty came out of jail we organised his coming home party at Carlton's Club in Brentwood. It was a full house and all the boys were there, and it was this night that Carlton asked me if I knew of this gang? "Yes, mate" I replied "why?" "Because my mate has upset them and now they have a contract out on him" "Don't worry I will speak to them" I told him. I spoke to Toby who had a lot of respect for me, and within a couple days, I phoned up Carlton and let him know that his mate had received a reprieve. This was all down to John really. John would ride his motorbike across Europe; he was welcome in the clubhouses in Holland, Finland, Russia, and Lithuania. When you are invited into the clubhouses in Russia and sit at the top table with the president that speaks volumes. John was this man. John rode his motorbike over to see us, driving through Austria, Bulgaria, and in through Turkey and hopped on a ferry from Turkey that landed him in Kyrinea which is in the North side of Cyprus, the Turkish occupied area.

It was 20th July 1974 that the Turkish armed forces invaded the North side, Code name operation Atilla, in response to the 1974 Cypriot Coup d'état, which had been ordered by the military Junta in Greece, and staged by the Cypriot National guard in conjunction with EOKA-B. It deposed the Cypriot president Archbishop Makarios and installed Nikos Sampson a leader in favour of ENOSIS the union of Cyprus and Greece. In July 1974, the Turk forces invaded and captured 3% of the island before a ceasefire was declared; the Greek military Junta collapsed and was replaced by a democratic government. In August 1974, a further Turkish invasion resulted in the capture of 40% of the island, the ceasefire line from August 1974, become known as the United Nations Buffer Zone in Cyprus, and was referred to as the Green line. John rode right over that green line and pulled up on our doorstep, with the motorbike that he had built himself and it resembled something like a scene from out of a Mad Max film.

It was June 12 2008 and John had settled in nicely. That evening around half seven we lit the charcoal for the BBQ. "No vodka?" John asked, "No worries John, I will pop down the shop and pick some up," I replied. The shop was a stone throw away from our house, set in amongst all the intricate alleyways that spur off and all lead up into the main square of Ypsonas alleyways that homed Eastern European families and many Sri Lankans who come to Cyprus looking for work. For some reason I left my phone on the table outside where we were all sat. I never leave my phone anywhere, it always goes with me no matter what, but this evening I did, and it was to be a blessing in disguise. For it was this evening that a gang of notorious racists called the G1 gang had planned an attack on Ypsonas. The ruthless gang thirty strong men all armed with clubs and metal bars were about to enter these alleyways and side streets, and set about any one from Romania, Bulgaria, Poland and Sri Lanka just because they are foreign.

I took a casual stroll up to the shop stopping and speaking to most of my neighbours on the way, as you do when you not got a worry in the world. I was just taking in the ambience of it all, the sunshine, the neighbours who always went out of their way to talk to us, and inviting us round for Zivaneer. The fact that you can go bed at night and leave your front doors wide open and nothing will get nicked, leave your car keys in the car, a far cry from Essex. At the end of Leontiou Street, which is the road that we lived in, I had to swing right to get to the shop. This was a small family run shop, but was well stocked up with everything you can think of and always had a great selection of vodka. The family who ran it are superb people. A Cypriot family that always made you welcome and if you were short of cash would say 'don't worry.' Nothing was an issue or as they'd say "no problemo" in broken English. The shop was busy this evening, so I grabbed my Vodka and waited in the queue. As I was paying, I heard a woman scream, a frightful scream, a scream of terror and then I heard a young boy crying out loud. I paid for my vodka and everyone in the shop ran out, even the shop owners. I ran out and was directly in front of the crowd that had emptied out from the shop. I could not believe what I was witnessing. A large gang was running in and out of the small village stone built houses that were situated in this maze of alleyways. The sound of a glass tables being smashed drew my attention to the house across the road where the screams were coming from. In and out of the alleyways, I could see the gang running into different courtyards. A scooter pulled up with two Sri Lankan men sitting on it, they stopped to see what was happening. The gang turned and tore into them. The people from the shop and those inside the shop advised me not to get involved. "It's dangerous," they said. They just turned their backs as if nothing was happening. I'm used to this kind of action, from my childhood all through to West Ham. We may have been called hooligans, but I know one thing, me or none of my friends from West Ham would sit and watch innocent men woman and children being attacked in their own homes. It's the lowest of the low. I had seen enough, I ran over to where the woman's house was who was screaming. Her husband was on the floor, being smashed to bits by the gang and her son was hysterical and so was she. I found out later, that the sound of the glass table breaking came when the table was thrown at her as she tried to run into her front door. The two Sri Lankans on the scooter were still under attack! "Malakas!" I shouted out to the gang, "You Malakas, what's your fucking problem?" Malaka in Greek means wankers. Unbeknown to me John had asked Andy to send me a text to get him some tobacco, but Steve was sitting outside when my phone went off and let them know that my phone was on the table. I now was two feet away from the gang. "Leave them alone you mugs" "Fuck you!" was their reply. "No fuck!" you was my reply. It worked, as all the attention was on me now. They had left the

Bulgarian who they were battering and the Sri Lankans who sharply drove away on the scooter as luckily they were both wearing crash helmets, or I don't think they would have survived. Now it was me and them and the one with the mouth who told me to fuck off was now face to face with me holding a reinforced steel bar in his hand. "You fuck with me?" he said. "Yes fuck you," I told him again. All the gang had now noticed that here is someone who wants to fight back. They all came running out of the courtyards where they made several other attacks on innocent people with families and children. I felt like Clint Eastwood in 'a Fistful of dollars' but the only difference was I never had a mule, just a bottle of Vodka. I looked them in the eyes, and waited for them to make a move. The mouthpiece with the ponytail made the first move. I saw his right arm come up to hit me round the head with the steel bar, but I was faster. My bottle of vodka smashed straight on his skull sending him crashing to his knees, he was fucked blood gashing out the wound that I had just made. I grabbed his ponytail and I did not give a fuck what happened to me. I was not going to let go until I had done him severely. I bent down, and I was smashing down onto his jaw and his nose. I was pounding and pounding him. I could feel the metal bars and clubs coming down on my shoulders but I was not letting go of mouthpiece until I truly fucked him. Every other second I was using the arm that I was punching him with to block the blows with the clubs and the bars. Now I was to finish him off. I heard his nose and jaw break, and left him on the floor like a pile of shit that he was. Now it was the other mugs turn. I ran into them blocking the bars and the clubs the best I could, but some were running behind me trying to smash the back of my knees away so that they could get me down, but I was not going down. I now had hold of another one and was smashing his head down on my knee several times, until I heard his nose go then a bar hit me to the left hand side of my head opened me up. This was only two inches away from where the golf club hit me all of them years ago, but I never let go of the prick whose head I was slamming down on my knee until he was hurt. I wanted to show them pain, and out of all the people to fight, they had to pick me. A man whose pain barriers are limitless, my only problem was there were so many of them I was running out of breath. Blocking many of the blows that were raining down on me and trying to fight at the same time was tiring me. This and getting smashed from every direction, on the chest, around the knees and head, I was not sure how long I could last. Which one of these blows would be the fatal blow? My hands were now fucked from blocking the metal bars and clubs. My thumb had a two-inch gash to the inside of it. My head had the same a similar gash. How much longer could I last until I was killed? I was not sure, but then to my relief I heard the cavalry. Where I had left my phone on the table John, Andy and Trotter decided to come up the shops to get the tobacco. "Oi you cunts, you want it?" The sound I heard was John. They told Steve to wait where he was as he was in his wheelchair. While John and Andy started sprinting toward my aid, the gang froze then out of panic, they started throwing some metal bars and clubs at John and Andy. What a big mistake. John and Andy now picked up a metal bar each, and one for me. I never felt so happy in all my life. John was first in striking out fast and hard just so he could get to me, then Andy came crashing in. They were getting it back from all directions now, and as a result, they started to split up. John smashed the granny out of the guys that were on me, enough for him to get to me and hand me a reinforced steel bar. The same ones they use in buildings when they pour the concrete. John shouted to me "Come on Phil, let's do these fucking mugs" I was smiling now. At this point, one of the gang ran at me with a club, but my reaction was so fast again that the reinforcing bar hit him on the head and bent around his head. I did not give a fuck if I had killed him. As he went down, I pulled the bar back and smashed his knees and I kept smashing his knees. His gang ran back, I shouted, "You want to see pain you mugs?" and I kept smashing the bar down on his knees. This scared them; I could see it scared them. Now it was our turn. John, Andy and I charged into them. They were going down like flies. We chased them all up the Ypsonas High Road leaving a trail of bodies behind us. They had started an attack on innocent people, and we were finishing it off on a bunch of scumbags that had no bottle. Like I always say, "Don't give it unless you are prepared to get it back".

The ambulances turned up, but never took us because we could walk, they said we have to take the Cypriots who are on the floor and I told the ambulance man I wouldn't piss on them if they were on fire, they are scum.

The ambulances took seven of the gang to hospital that evening and we went in my car. I needed stitches in my head, and my hands. Andy needed stitches also to the head also, but John was ok. The woman's husband and child were also up the hospital. She was still crying and injured. Her husband had to be kept in hospital, as his injuries were more serious. Some other Eastern European people were there also who had been attacked. The hospital staffs were looking at us like scum because we put these Cypriots in hospital. I said to John, "It seems to me that the staff of the hospital think we started all this mate." I could understand what they were saying. Now I'm thinking we going to get nicked here. Three Brits in a foreign country, they are not going to believe us and we did go to town on them. It was not until the police arrived, and the Bulgarian woman had calmed down, and started talking to the police that she pointed to us, and kept pointing to us. The police never came over to us they obviously were going around the hospital getting witnesses stories. After we were stitched up we simply up'd and left. As we came out of the hospital, we noticed dozens of armed police all round the entrance, "You have to come with us," they said. John asked, "Can't it wait till morning officer, I'm fucked and tired and need my sleep? It is half two in the morning." The officers reply was not what any of us wanted to hear. "No sir, sorry you all have to come to Limassol central now with us." That was it we thought, we were being nicked. We arrived at Limassol central twenty minutes later, and there was the woman and child, but this time she was calm and walked over to me and said, "I must thank you" I said to her it's not a problem. She carried on "No, you don't understand we are Bulgarians. Here in Cyprus no one helps us." Again I assured her that it was no problem and not to worry about it. At that moment, I felt good inside. Good for the reason that she had thanked me, and also good for the reason that she must have told the O.B the full story. So, there is no way we were going to get nicked. The police asked us this one simple question. "Were any of the gang in the hospital this evening?" I laughed and said "quite a few, yes" He then asked "Was it you guys that did this to them?" We had to reply yes. I then asked, "Are we being charged for anything?" "No not at all" the officer replied. "We have been looking for this gang for a while now. They have made several attacks in the Limassol area, but no one will say anything against them. But this attack is by far the worse" he said "and now that we have them in hospital thanks to you, it won't be long before we round up the whole gang." They were not wrong within a week they had arrested 27 of the gang. We had become National heroes and were even on TV three times a day every day for over a week. We had the mayor on our doorstep and press from Cyprus, Bulgaria, and Romania as well as Reuter's and the Greek Television. People were even asking for our autographs on the beach every time we went for a swim, so all in all, it was not a bad nights work from the three West Ham boys.

This was the first race riot ever to happen in Cyprus since the war ended in 1974. Government minister Stephanos Stephanou released a statement saying the Council of Minister's expressed the need for a concerted action against racism in Cyprus, and that a new law would be passed so that it could be taught in schools. Maybe they will call it DALBY'S LAW.

Am I dangerous? I will let you be the Judge of that, but let me leave you with one last simple phrase and that is dynamite comes in small packages!

Phil Dalby

"Battered Brit blasts Ypsonas race thugs"

WITH seven people now in custody in connection with Sunday's vicious racist rampage in Ypsonas, shocking details of the incident yesterday begin to emerge, including the fact that more people had been attacked than initially thought.

Philip Dalby was one of the four victims who reported being attacked: "I think they were cowards," he told the Cyprus Mail yesterday. "They were attacking people who could not fight back with sticks and bars. They were smashing people's cars and houses. When I fought back they all ran away," the 48-year-old Briton said.

"These things don't scare me, but I hate seeing people getting bullied like that. Cypriots living in the area were watching the incident and did nothing. There were people looking through garden walls and fences who did nothing to stop it. I had to do something," he said.

Dalby was targeted by the gang of approximately 30 youths, after he intervened to stop them as they were attacking two Sri Lankan men passing through the street. "As I went into a shop I saw a group of young people attacking a car. First I thought they were playing with a friend. As I came out I saw the same group attacking two Sri Lankan men on a scooter. They were hitting them with sticks and metal bars on the head and calling them names. They surrounded the scooter and wouldn't let them pass through.

"I told them to stop and they started calling me names. They asked where I'm from and I said Polemidia, which is where I grew up. They started punching me and hitting me with metal bars. There were about 30 of them. Two of my friends came to help me, and they started hitting my friends with the metal bars."

According to eye-witness descriptions of the gang, their ages ranged from

14 to 28. The two Sri Lankan men Dalby saw getting attacked managed to flee, but did not report their assault to police.

As Dalby and his friends fought back, the gang fled to his house, where they caused considerable damage to his car, parked outside. "We fought back and managed to chase them off, but there were a lot of them so I got very hurt. I have injuries to the legs, arms, chest and head. They then went to my house and started throwing bricks at the house and at my car, which caused considerable damage to my car," he explained.

Dalby has been living in Ypsonas for the last 18 months, and confirmed that he has never before felt targeted or unwanted. "I have never seen anything like this in Ypsonas before. It was the first time. People here are lovely, nice people. There are different nationalities living here: Bulgarians, Romanians. My neighbours are Cypriot and they are fantastic and friendly."

Government Spokesman Stephanos Stephanou yesterday released a statement saying the Council of Ministers expressed the need for concerted action against racism in Cyprus.

"The government expresses its unreserved and strong condemnation of the racist attack at Ypsonas. Such phenomena and behaviour are dangerous and are a stigma and shame for our country and society. Let's not forget that we are living in a multicultural country, which over the last years has developed from an immigration exit point to an immigration entry point and thousands of foreigners live and work here," the statement read.

Stephanou said the Council of Ministers has authorised the Ministry of Education to strengthen the promotion of a culture of respect, social acceptance and humanism through education.'

Taken from the Cyprus Mail dated 12 June 2008 with the kind permission of Jean Christou – Editor

http://archives.cyprus-mail.com/2008/06/12/battered-brit-blasts-ypsonas-race-thugs/

Phil's life has led him to pastures on a different part of the globe. The life he once led is one of the past but the memories and hard-earned experiences he shared along with some sound advice has stuck with me. It was not any more or less, than the advice I hade been given to me over the years, by my pals mentioned in this book. However, it was an important final piece of the jigsaw. As Phil says, "There for our own, Jase." So what does all this mean? For me, I interpret things in a way that I see conclusions and answers.

I see a way of getting my pals, family and heavy-duty people for a cause that can promote and save a life. I am far from the top boy, but if anything is to be gained from all the villains, hooligans and scoundrels it's one simple thing. I go with what I know.

R.I.P Junior Palmer

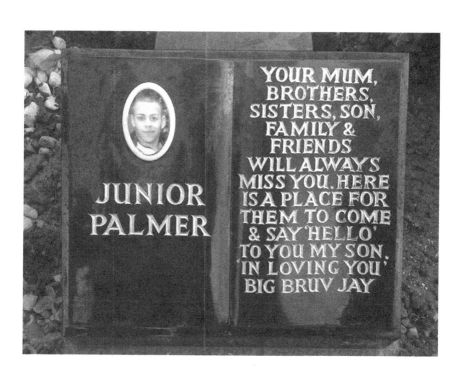